CULTURAL STUDIES

Theory and Practice

Chris Barker

with a Foreword by Paul Willis

Sage Publications
London • Thousand Oaks • New Delhi

© Chris Barker 2000

First published 2000

Reprinted 2001

SAGE Publications Ltd
6 Bonhill Street
London EC2A 4PU

SAGE Publications Inc.
2455 Teller Road
Thousand Oaks, California 91320

SAGE Publications India Pvt Ltd
32, M-Block Market
Greater Kailash – I
New Delhi 110 048

British Library Cataloguing in Publication data
A catalogue record for this book is available
from the British Library

ISBN 0 7619 5774 X
ISBN 0 7619 5775 8 (pbk)

Library of Congress catalog record available

Typeset by Mayhew Typesetting, Rhayader, Powys
Printed in Great Britain by The Alden Press, Oxford

As always,
For Julie
A path with heart

Kate, Emma and Edward
To all of you my love

In memory of Victoria Ward
Your commitment to Cultural Studies and your
capacity to inspire love and friendship
October 1999

Contents

Notes
for
community
Diversity

M

Foreword

Paul Willis

'Culture' is a strange and capacious category. It's one of those concepts, perhaps the best example, that we simply cannot do without – it is used everywhere – but which is also very unsatisfactory and cries out for betterment. No one can define it exactly, say what it 'really' means. That's partly why it's so useful of course, because we can always say later we meant something slightly different whilst getting on for now saying something nearly right of great importance. So many things are contained in the word.

At an everyday and human level, cultural interests, pursuits and identities have never been more important. This has to be broadly considered, of course, as individuals and groups bearing a felt responsibility for and wanting a hand in the making of the self as something more than a passive or unconscious acceptance of a historically/socially prescribed identity (simply *being* working class, black or white, young or old, etc.). Everyone wants to have, or make, or be considered as possessing cultural *significance*. No one knows what the social maps are any more, so it is more important not be left out, overlooked or misrepresented. Everyone wants a stake in the action, though no one is quite sure where the party is.

At the same time and in a connected way, 'culture' has become an important and much used theoretical and substantive category of connection and relation. Both in academic and popular writing and commentary we see countless references to 'cultures of . . . schools, organizations, pubs, regions, sexual orientations, ethnicities, etc.'. You name it and you can add, 'culture of . . .'. All those evoked domains of 'culture' are seen as containing a multiplicity of human forms and relations: from micro-interpersonal interactions to group norms processes and values to communicative forms, provided texts and images; wider out to institutional forms and constraints, to social representations and social imagery; wider out still to economic, political, ideological determinations. All can be traced back for their cultural effects and meanings, all traced for their mutual interactions from the point of view of how the meanings of a particular 'culture' are formed and held to operate.

Small wonder, then, that the mode of academic inquiry that seeks to comprehend some of this, 'cultural studies', should be a field of at times intractable complexity and perhaps the first great academic experiment in the attempted formation of a 'non-disciplinary' discipline. No one approach can hope to comprehend the above in one sweep; no one sweep producing some partial understanding can fail to notice what other sweeps might produce. We are condemned to a kind of eclecticism because of the very eclecticism and indissoluble combinations of the dissimilar in the increasingly complex 'real' world around us.

Whatever its complexity and disputed origins, cultural studies is now coming, perhaps, to a kind of maturity, a special kind of maturity, of course, in light of the above: the coming to majority of the first of the 'non-disciplinary' disciplines! Clearly we need new measures of maturity. The fullest test of maturity will be whether cultural studies is to be without discipline (bad), or capable of avoiding the pitfalls and really exploiting the advantages of 'post-disciplinarity' (good) to produce genuinely new and 'connected-up' knowledge. Previous cultural studies textbooks have made worthy and illuminating attempts to give a history of the subject, to plot its growth through successive waves of new thought and critique. But that kind of narration cannot give the essence of the nature of cultural studies' ambition to found a new disciplinarity of the disciplines. For in this endeavour even a notion of 'multi-disciplinarity', of the tracing of multiple linear paths, will not really do. What is needed is openness to and choice from strands (both past and present) within and between inherited fields of method, inquiry and theory. Their ability to illuminate complex empirical subjects of study, rather than their conformity to the particular tests and procedures of founding academic traditions, should govern these choices. Though welcome, it is hardly surprising that the early 'textbook' attempts to chart 'a cultural studies discipline' through a historical route should have engendered their own towers of Babel combusting with fierce debate and bad-tempered rivalries over true ownership and alternative myths of origin.

Chris Barker has pioneered a new and promising course. Clearly and coherently expressed, it is likely to be an exceptionally useful one for those confronting the undoubted difficulties

of teaching cultural studies and cultural studies approaches.
Rather than attempting to show another version of the proven-
ance of cultural studies, he has plumped for breadth and the
collecting together of relevant theoretical and empirical strands,
from wherever they might come. He presents a whole cluster of
modern perspectives judged for their usefulness to the understanding of contemporary cultural forms. In doing this, Chris
Barker certainly draws from theorists and writers who would not
necessarily situate themselves in cultural studies, thereby providing a whole range of theoretical resources, methodological
options and empirical connections which are useful for the understanding of any particular focus and which far outstrip those
available in any one traditional discipline. This leads him to
grapple with deeper and more serious concerns than would a
conventional 'introduction to . . .'. In reverse direction, it might be
noted that the variable and contested importation of cultural
studies perspectives into other disciplines and domains shows
their own struggle, from their own positions and histories, to
achieve greater adequacy and purchase in comprehending multi-
faceted and ruptural cultural change. There is, of course, no
guarantee that cultural studies will indeed be the privileged site
for the emergence of a discipline of the disciplines, or even that,
though necessary, the latter is even possible. There are and
certainly will be other contenders.

However, Chris Barker has made a bold thrust to grab the prize.
I was particularly impressed by the sections on contemporary
issues and problematics – 'World Disorder', 'Sex and Subjectivity',
'Space', 'Cultural Policy', as well as the more well-trodden ones of
'Identity', 'Youth Culture', 'Television', 'Ethnicity and Race' –
which reveal some concrete grounds of a complex and rapidly
changing 'real' world within which all approaches must now
situate themselves if they hope to contend with the contradictory
currents of contemporary change. At the same time, though, these
connected 'sites' are presented in selected theoretical contexts of
what has gone before and in the light of a constellation of theoretical insights, 'cultural studies' or not, which help to illuminate,
connect and place them.

One of the crucial issues in trying to produce a textbook for
a (first-stage) mature cultural studies is to find and argue for a
supra-disciplinary base, a loose coherence of connecting tissue or
metaphor, which is capable of anchoring a principled eclecticism
(rather than a theoretical anarchism) whilst still retaining a wide
empirical grasp. Here I have an uncertainty or perhaps lack of
competence in judging Chris Barker's path. Although a colleague

and a friend, certainly honoured in the asking, I was in some ways a strange choice to be invited to provide this Foreword. I have been (rightly) generally associated with an ethnographic/qualitative approach and (misleadingly) associated with a 'culturalist' formation within cultural studies, both of which are granted important but only finally subordinate status within this book. Like Chris Barker, I am not fussed about disciplinary boundaries, less fussed than he is actually about the privileged status of cultural studies, but I would seek to ground the complex, unwieldy and weighty category of 'culture' ultimately upon notions of 'experience' and 'practice', sensuously understood and (ethnographically) studied.* Contrastingly, Chris Barker proposes a 'language-game' account of the 'discursive formation' of cultural studies, seeing all cultural forms as structured like language, and ends, tellingly, with a Rortian emphasis on pragmatism within cultural studies as that which can influence 'reality', 'learning how best to cope with the world', but in no way 'reflecting' it. I have doubts about a model derived from language for understanding sensuous aspects of experience and lived practice, and cannot wean myself from a notion that in order to change reality, something of its actual music must first somehow be recorded and appreciated (ethnographically) in its own terms, even as, learning from Chris Barker, 'fractured subjects' and 'anti-essentialism' must hold some sway in how this is understood and presented.

Chris Barker wants his book to engender debate. It's worked already! I have learned a great deal from this book and respect its breadth and fairness, as well as finding points of difference and new departure for my own thinking. There is much here to help me develop more adequacy and elegance in my own work, continuous with and by no means contradicting that of Chris Barker. There is an excellent basis and framework here to help teachers lead students to an understanding of the necessary ambition of the cultural studies project and to make their own *informed and knowledgeable* decisions about how to approach and understand the importance, fullness, variety and pace of contemporary cultural change.

* See my *Life as Art* (Oxford: Polity, forthcoming) and issues of the new Sage journal *Ethnography*, edited by myself and Mats Trondman.

Acknowledgements

I would like to thank Chris Rojek and Jim McGuigan for their continued support and constructive comments during the writing of this book. I would also like to express my gratitude to Paul Willis for writing the Foreword. Paul and I would like to thank Helen Wood for reading the manuscript and giving advice based on her experience as a practising and effective cultural studies lecturer in a large teaching department.

Figures

Part One

1

An Introduction to Cultural Studies

Given the title of this book – *Cultural Studies: Theory and Practice* – it would be reasonable to expect a comprehensive account of cultural studies, including summaries and discussions of its main arguments and substantive sites of intellectual inquiry. Indeed, this is what has been attempted. However, I want to open this account of cultural studies with a kind of 'health warning' regarding the scope of the book.

CONCERNING THIS BOOK
Selectivity

Any book about cultural studies is necessarily selective and likely to engender debate, argumentation and even conflict. To offer a truly comprehensive account of cultural studies would be to reproduce, or at least to summarize, every single text ever written within the parameters of cultural studies. Not only would this be too mammoth a task for any writer, but the problem would remain of deciding which texts warranted the nomination. Consequently, this book, like all others, is implicated in constructing a *particular version* of cultural studies.

Though I do offer, under the rubric of the *foundations* of cultural studies, some (selective) history, most of the later chapters, the *sites* of cultural studies, draw on more contemporary theory. Indeed, in order to make the book as useful as possible in as many different geographical places as possible, there is a stress on theory over context-specific empirical work (though theory is also context-specific, and the text does try to link theory with empirical work). In doing so, I deploy a good number of theorists who would not describe themselves as working within cultural studies but who have something to say which has informed it. Thus, writers like Tony Bennett, Paul Gilroy, Lawrence Grossberg, Stuart Hall, Meaghan Morris and Paul Willis would probably accept a description of their work as 'cultural studies'. However, though extremely influential, neither Foucault nor Barthes would have described himself in this way, just as Rorty, Giddens and Derrida do not currently adopt this self-nomination.

This book is a selective account because it stresses a certain type of cultural studies, particularly that which places language at its heart. The kind of cultural studies influenced by post-structuralist theories of language, representation and subjectivity is given greater attention than a cultural studies more concerned with the ethnography of lived experience or with cultural policy, though they do receive attention and I am personally supportive of both. Cultural studies does not speak with one voice, it cannot be spoken with one voice, and I do not have one voice with which to represent it.

The title of this book is somewhat over-ambitious in its claims. Not only is this a selective account of cultural studies, it is one which draws very largely from work developed in Britain, the United States, Continental Europe (most notably France) and Australia. I draw very little from a growing body of work in Africa, Asia and Latin America and, as such, it would be more accurate to call this text western cultural studies. I simply do not feel qualified to say how much cultural studies, as I understand it, is pertinent to the social and cultural conditions of Africa.

The language-game of cultural studies

Further, this book tends to gloss over differences within western cultural studies, despite doubts about whether theory developed in one context (e.g. Britain) can be workable in another (e.g. Australia) (Ang and Statton, 1996; Turner, 1992). Nevertheless, I want to justify this degree of generalization about cultural studies. I maintain that the term 'cultural studies' has no referent to which we can point. Rather, cultural studies is constituted by the **language-game** of cultural studies. The theoretical terms developed and deployed by persons calling their work cultural studies is what cultural studies 'is'. I stress the language of cultural studies as constitutive of cultural studies and **highlight*** in each chapter what I take to be important terms, each of which can be referred to in the Glossary.

These are concepts which have been deployed in the various geographical sites of cultural studies. For, as Grossberg et al. have argued, though cultural studies has stressed conjunctural

---

* I have **emboldened** key concepts in each chapter on one occasion only at moments where I felt it to be useful or appropriate. I could find no systematic rule to govern when I should do this and rely on my judgement.

analysis, 'which is embedded, descriptive, and historically and contextually specific', there are some concepts in cultural studies across the globe which form 'a history of real achievements that is now part of the cultural studies tradition', and to do without which would be 'to willingly accept real incapacitation' (Grossberg et al., 1992: 8). Concepts are tools for acting in the world and their meaning is their usage. But for its unfortunate gender-coding, I might have called this book *A Tool-Kit for Cultural Studies*.

> The notion of theory as a toolkit means: (i) The theory to be constructed is not a system but an instrument, a logic of the specificity of power relations and the struggles around them; (ii) That this investigation can only be carried out step by step on the basis of reflection (which will necessarily be historical in some of its aspects) on the given situation. (Foucault, 1980, cited Best, 1997: 26)

Cultural studies as politics

It remains difficult to pin down the boundaries of cultural studies as a coherent, unified, academic discipline with clear-cut substantive topics, concepts and methods which differentiate it from other disciplines. Cultural studies is, and always has been, a multi- or post-disciplinary field of inquiry which blurs the boundaries between itself and other 'subjects'. Yet cultural studies cannot be said to be anything. It is not physics, it is not sociology and it is not linguistics, though it draws upon these subject areas. Indeed, there must be, as Hall (1992a) argues, something at stake in cultural studies which differentiates itself from other subject areas.

For Hall, what is at stake is cultural studies' connections to matters of power and **politics**, to the need for change and to representations of and 'for' marginalized social groups, particularly those of class, gender and race (but also of age, disability, nationality, etc.). Hence, cultural studies is a body of theory generated by thinkers who regard the production of theoretical knowledge as a political practice. Here, knowledge is never a neutral or objective phenomenon but a matter of **positionality**, of the place from which one speaks, to whom, and for what purposes.

THE PARAMETERS OF CULTURAL STUDIES

In defining cultural studies as a language-game, it follows that there is a difference between the study of culture and institutionally located cultural studies. Though the study of culture has taken place in a variety of academic disciplines – sociology,

anthropology, English literature, etc. – and in a range of geographical and institutional spaces, this is not cultural studies.
While the study of culture has no origins, and to locate one is to
exclude other possible starting points, this does not mean that
cultural studies cannot be named. As such, Handel Wright's
(1996) argument that we can see the origins of cultural studies in
Africa rather than Europe is provocative and polemically useful,
but mistaken.

Cultural studies is a **discursive formation**, that is, 'a cluster
(or formation) of ideas, images and practices, which provide ways
of talking about, forms of knowledge and conduct associated with,
a particular topic, social activity or institutional site in society'
(Hall, 1997a: 6). Cultural studies is constituted by a *regulated* way
of speaking about objects (which it brings into view) and coheres
around key concepts, ideas and concerns. Further, cultural
studies had a moment at which it named itself, even though
that naming marks only a cut or snapshot of an ever-evolving
intellectual project.

The Centre for Contemporary Cultural Studies

Though cultural studies has been reluctant to accept institutional
legitimation, the formation of the Centre for Contemporary Cultural Studies at Birmingham University (UK) in the 1960s was a
decisive organizational instance. Since that time, cultural studies
has extended its intellectual base and geographic scope. There are
self-defined cultural studies practitioners in the USA, Australia,
Africa, Asia, Latin America and Europe, with each 'formation' of
cultural studies working in different ways.

While I am not privileging British cultural studies *per se*, I am
pointing to the formation of cultural studies at Birmingham as an
institutionally significant moment. Further, though cultural
studies

> has tended to see itself as part of an intellectual guerrilla movement
> waging war on the borders of official academia. This romantic and
> heroic conception of cultural studies is now decidedly *passé*, not least
> because of the sheer success, in spite of obstructions to it, of cultural
> studies educationally and, indeed, in terms of research. (McGuigan,
> 1997a: 1)

Cultural studies has acquired a multitude of institutional bases,
courses, textbooks and students as it has become something to be
taught. As McGuigan (1997a) comments, it is difficult to see how
it could be otherwise, despite the concern that professionalized

and institutionalized cultural studies may 'formalize out of existence the critical questions of power, history and politics' (Hall, 1992a: 286). When McRobbie (1992) argues that cultural studies is a contested domain which cannot afford to lose disciplinary looseness, one senses romantic nostalgia. Cultural studies' main location has always been institutions of higher education and the bookshop. Consequently, one way of 'defining' cultural studies is to look at what university courses offer to students. This necessarily involves 'disciplining' cultural studies.

Disciplining cultural studies

Many cultural studies practitioners oppose forging disciplinary boundaries for the field. However, it is hard to see how this can be resisted if cultural studies wants to survive by attracting degree students and funding (as opposed to being only a postgraduate research activity) in the higher education systems of the West. In that context, Bennett (1998) offers his 'element of a definition' of cultural studies:

- Cultural studies is an interdisciplinary field in which perspectives from different disciplines can be selectively drawn on to examine the relations of culture and power.
- 'Cultural studies is concerned with all those practices, institutions and systems of classification through which there are inculcated in a population particular values, beliefs, competencies, routines of life and habitual forms of conduct' (Bennett, 1998: 28).
- The forms of power that cultural studies explores are diverse and include gender, race, class, colonialism, etc. Cultural studies seeks to explore the connections between these forms of power and to develop ways of thinking about culture and power that can be utilized by agents in the pursuit of change.
- The prime institutional sites for cultural studies are those of higher education, and as such cultural studies is like other academic disciplines. Nevertheless, it tries to forge connections outside of the academy with social and political movements, workers in cultural institutions, and cultural management.

With this in mind, we may consider the kinds of concepts and concerns which regulate cultural studies as a discursive formation or language-game. While some of these concepts are introduced now (though others do not appear until later), each is developed at greater length throughout the book and can also be referred to in the Glossary.

KEY CONCEPTS IN CULTURAL STUDIES
Culture and signifying practices

Cultural studies would not warrant its name without a focus on **culture** (Chapter 2). As Hall puts it, 'By culture, here, I mean the actual grounded terrain of practices, representations, languages and customs of any specific society. I also mean the contradictory forms of common sense which have taken root in and helped to shape popular life' (Hall, 1996c: 439). Culture is concerned with questions of shared *social* meanings, that is, the various ways we make sense of the world. However, meanings are not simply floating 'out-there'; rather, they are generated through signs, most notably those of language.

Cultural studies has argued that language is not a neutral medium for the formation of meanings and knowledge about an independent object world 'existing' outside of language, but is constitutive of those very meanings and that very knowledge. That is, language gives meaning to material objects and social practices which are brought into view by language and made intelligible to us in terms which language delimits. These processes of meaning production are **signifying practices**, and to understand culture is to explore how meaning is produced symbolically in language as a 'signifying system' (Chapter 3).

Representation

A good deal of cultural studies is centred on questions of **representation**, that is, on how the world is socially constructed and represented to and by us. Indeed, the central strand of cultural studies can be understood as the study of culture as the signifying practices of representation. This requires us to explore the textual generation of meaning. It also demands investigation of the modes by which meaning is produced in a variety of contexts. Cultural representations and meanings have a certain materiality, they are embedded in sounds, inscriptions, objects, images, books, magazines and television programmes. They are produced, enacted, used and understood in specific social contexts.

Materialism and non-reductionism

Cultural studies has, for the most part, been concerned with modern industrialized economies and media cultures organized along capitalist lines in which representations are produced by corporations driven by the profit motive. In this context, cultural studies has developed a form of **cultural materialism** which is concerned to explore how and why meanings are inscribed at the moment of production. That is, as well as being centred on signifying practices, cultural studies tries to connect them with **political economy**, a discipline concerned with power and the distribution of economic and social resources. Consequently, cultural studies has been concerned with who owns and controls cultural production, its distribution mechanisms, and the consequences of those patterns of ownership and control for contours of the cultural landscape.

Having said that, one of the central tenets of cultural studies is its *non*-**reductionism**. Culture is seen as having its own specific meanings, rules and practices which are not reducible to, or explainable solely in terms of, another category or level of a **social formation**. In particular, cultural studies has waged a battle against economic reductionism, that is, the attempt to explain what a cultural text means by reference to its place in the production process. For cultural studies, the processes of political economy do not determine the meanings of texts or their appropriation by audiences. Rather, political economy, social relationships and culture must be understood in terms of their own specific logics and modes of development which are 'articulated' or related together in context-specific ways.

The non-reductionism of cultural studies insists that questions of class, gender, sexuality, race, ethnicity, nation and age have their own particularities which cannot be reduced either to political economy or to each other. For example, issues of race should not be explained solely in terms of class. Equally, each *is* implicated in the other, so that to explore the question of nationality, for example, is to understand how it has been gendered. Nations are commonly spoken of as female and the notion of 'race' connected to the idea of the ascent of 'Man'.

Articulation

To theorize the relationships between components of a social formation, cultural studies has deployed the concept of **articulation**. This idea refers to the formation of a temporary unity between elements that do not have to go together. Articulation suggests both expressing/representing and a 'putting-together'. Thus, representations of gender may be 'put-together' with representations of race, as in the case of gendered nationality above, in context-specific and contingent ways which cannot be predicted before the fact. The concept of articulation is also deployed to discuss the relationship between culture and political economy. Thus culture is said to be 'articulated' with moments of production but not determined in any 'necessary' way by that moment, and vice versa. Consequently, we might explore how the moment of production is inscribed in texts but also how the 'economic' is cultural, that is, a meaningful set of practices.

Power

If there is one thing that cultural studies writers could agree on it is the centrality of the concept of **power**, which is regarded as pervading every level of social relationships. Power is not simply the glue that holds the social together, or the coercive force which subordinates one set of people to another, though it certainly is this, but the processes that generate and enable any form of social action, relationship or order. In this sense, power, while certainly constraining, is also enabling. Having said that, cultural studies has shown a specific concern with subordinated groups, at first with class, and later with races, genders, nations, age groups, etc.

Popular culture

Subordination is a matter not just of coercion but also of consent. **Popular culture**, with which cultural studies has been especially concerned, is said to be the ground on which consent is won or lost. As a way of grasping the interplay of power and consent, two related concepts were repeatedly deployed in cultural studies' earlier texts, though they are less prevalent these days, namely **ideology** and **hegemony**.

By ideology is meant maps of meaning which, while they purport to be universal truths, are historically specific understandings which obscure and maintain power. For example, television news produces understandings of the world which continually explain it in terms of nations, perceived as 'naturally' occurring objects, obscuring both the class divisions of social formations and the constructed character of nationality. Representations of gender in advertising, which depict women as housewives or sexy bodies alone, reduce them to those categories, denying them their place as full human beings and citizens. The process of making, maintaining and reproducing ascendant meanings and practices has been called hegemony. Hegemony implies a situation where a 'historical bloc' of powerful groups exercises social authority and leadership over subordinate groups through the winning of consent.

Texts and readers

The production of consent implies popular identification with the cultural meanings generated by the signifying practices of hegemonic texts. The concept of **text** suggests not simply the written word, though this is one of its senses, but all practices which signify. This includes the generation of meaning through images, sounds, objects (such as clothes) and activities (like dance and sport). Since images, sounds, objects and practices are sign systems, which signify with the same mechanism as a language, we may refer to them as cultural texts.

However, the meanings that critics read into cultural texts are not necessarily the same as those produced by **active audiences** or *readers*. Indeed, readers will not necessarily share all the same meanings with each other. Critics, in other words, are simply a particular breed of reader. Further, texts, as forms of representation, are **polysemic**. That is, they contain the possibility of a number of different meanings which have to be realized by actual readers who give life to words and images. Though we can examine the ways in which texts work, we cannot simply 'read-off' audiences' meaning production from textual analysis. At the very least, meaning is produced in the interplay between text and reader so that the moment of consumption is also a moment of meaningful production.

Subjectivity and identity

The moment of consumption marks one of the processes by which we are formed as persons. What it is to be a person, **subjectivity**, and how we describe ourselves to each other, **identity**, became central areas of concern in cultural studies during the 1990s. In other words, cultural studies explores how we come to be the kinds of people we are, how we are produced as subjects, and how we identify with (or emotionally invest in) descriptions of ourselves as male or female, black or white, young or old.

The argument, known as **anti-essentialism**, is that identities are not things which exist; they have no essential or universal qualities. Rather, they are discursive constructions, the product of **discourses** or regulated ways of speaking about the world. In other words, identities are constituted, made rather than found, by representations, notably language.

Language-game, politics, positionality, discursive formation, culture, the social, signifying practices, representation, cultural

materialism, political economy, non-reductionism, social formation, articulation, power, popular culture, ideology, hegemony,
texts, active audiences, polysemic, subjectivity, identity, anti-
essentialism and discourse are *amongst* the theoretical concepts by
which contemporary cultural studies has sought to explore and
intervene in our social worlds. At this stage I have not attributed
specific concepts to particular writers, though later chapters do,
because, in a sense, they are the collective 'property' of cultural
studies. Needless to say, cultural studies writers differ about how
to deploy these concepts and about which are the most significant,
for cultural studies is a space for healthy (and sometimes hostile,
noisy and rude) debate and argument.

THE INTELLECTUAL STRANDS OF CULTURAL STUDIES

The concepts we have explored are drawn from a range of theoretical and methodological paradigms. The remainder of this
chapter outlines the core ideas associated with those which have
been most influential within cultural studies, namely, Marxism,
culturalism, structuralism, poststructuralism, psychoanalysis and
the politics of difference (under which heading, for the sake of
convenience, I include feminism, theories of race, ethnicity and
postcolonialism). The purpose of sketching the basic tenets of these
theoretical domains is to provide a *signpost* to thinking in the field.
However, each is developed in more detail throughout the text and
there is no one place in the book to look for theory. Theory
permeates all levels of cultural studies and needs to be connected
to specific issues and debates rather than be explored solely in the
abstract.

Marxism and the centrality of class

Marxism is, above all, a form of historical materialism. It stresses
the historical specificity of human affairs and the changeable
character of social formations whose core features are located in
the material conditions of existence. Marx (1961) argued that the
first priority of human beings is the production of their means of
subsistence through labour. As humans produce food, clothes and
all manner of tools with which to shape their environment, so they
also create themselves. Thus labour, and the forms of social
organization that material production takes, a mode of production, are central categories of Marxism.

The organization of a mode of production is not simply a matter
of co-ordinating objects; rather, it is inherently tied up with

relations between people which, while social, that is, co-operative and co-ordinated, are also matters of power and conflict. Social antagonisms, which are an intrinsic part of a mode of production, are regarded by Marxists as the motor of historical change. Further, given the priority accorded to production, other aspects of human relations – consciousness, culture and politics – are said to be structured by economic relations (see Chapter 2).

For Marxism, history is not a smooth evolutionary process but is marked by significant breaks and discontinuities of modes of production. Thus, Marx discusses the transformations from an ancient mode of production to a feudal mode of production and thence to the capitalist mode of production. Each mode of production is characterized by different forms of material organization and different social relations. Each is superseded by another mode of production as internal contradictions, particularly those of class conflict, lead to its transformation and replacement.

CAPITALISM

The centrepiece of Marx's work was an analysis of the dynamics of **capitalism**, a mode of production premised on the private ownership of the means of production (in his day, factories, mills, workshops; and in more contemporary vein, multinational corporations). The fundamental **class** division of capitalism is between those who own the means of production, the bourgeoisie, and those who, being a propertyless proletariat, must sell their labour to survive.

While the legal framework and common-sense thinking of capitalist societies declare that the worker is a free agent and the sale of labour a free and fair contract, this, argues Marx, covers over a fundamental exploitation at work. Capitalism aims to make a profit and does so by extracting surplus value from workers. That is, the value of the labour taken to produce a product, which becomes the property of the bourgeoisie, is less than the worker receives for it.

The realization of surplus value in monetary form is achieved by the selling of goods (which have both 'use value' and 'exchange value') as commodities. A commodity is something available to be sold in the marketplace and **commodification** the process associated with capitalism by which objects, qualities and signs are turned into commodities. The surface appearance of goods sold in the marketplace obscures the origins of those commodities in an exploitative relationship which Marx calls commodity fetishism. Further, the fact that workers are faced with the products of their own labour now separated from them constitutes alienation.

Since the proletariat are alienated from labour, the core of human activity, they are, as consequence, alienated from themselves.

Capitalism is a dynamic system whose profit-driven mechanisms lead to the continual revolutionizing of the means of production and the forging of new markets. For Marx, this was its great merit in relation to feudalism, for it heralded a massive expansion in the productive capacities of European societies. It dragged them into the modern world of railways, mass production, cities and a formally equitable and free set of human relations in which people were not, in a legal sense, the property of others (as were serfs in feudal societies).

However, the mechanisms of capitalism also lead to perennial crises and will ultimately lead, or so Marx argued, to its superseding by socialism. Problems for capitalism include a falling rate of profit, cycles of boom and bust, increasing monopoly and, most decisively, the creation of a proletariat which is set to become the system's grave-digger. Marx hoped that capitalism would be rent asunder by class conflict, with the proletariat's organizations of defence, trade unions and political parties, overthrowing and replacing it with a mode of production based on communal ownership, equitable distribution and ultimately the end of class division.

MARXISM AND CULTURAL STUDIES

Cultural studies writers have had a long, ambiguous, but productive relationship with Marxism. Cultural studies is not a Marxist domain, but has drawn succour from it while subjecting it to vigorous critique. There is little doubt that we live in social formations organized along capitalist lines with deep class divisions manifested in work, wages, housing, education and health. Further, cultural practices are commodified by large corporate culture industries. Cultural studies has been partisan in taking up the cause of change.

However, Marxism has been critiqued for its apparent teleology. That is, the positing of an inevitable point to which history is moving, namely the demise of capitalism and the arrival of a classless society. This is a problem on theoretical grounds, for a determinist reading of Marxism robs human beings of **agency**, the outcomes of human action being predetermined by metaphysical laws (ironically posing as objective science) which drive history from outside of human action. It is also a problem on empirical grounds, namely the failure of significant numbers of proletarian revolutions to materialize, along with the oppressive totalitarian outcomes of those which made claims to be such revolutions.

In its engagement with Marxism, cultural studies has been particularly concerned with issues of structure, praxis, economic determinism and ideology. On the one hand, Marxism suggests that there are regularities or structures to human existence which lie outside of any given individual. Cultural studies, along with other disciplines like sociology, has sought to explore the characteristics of those structures. On the other hand, Marxism and cultural studies have a commitment to change through human agency achieved by a combination of theory and action (praxis).

Cultural studies has resisted the economic determinism inherent in some readings of Marxism and has asserted the specificity of culture. Cultural studies has also been concerned with the apparent success of capitalism, not merely its survival but its transformation and expansion, attributed in part to its winning of consent on the level of culture. Hence the interest in questions of culture, ideology and hegemony (see Chapter 2) which were commonly pursued through perspectives dubbed culturalism and structuralism (see Hall, 1992a).

Culturalism and structuralism

In the collective mythology of cultural studies, Richard Hoggart (1957), Raymond Williams (1965, 1979, 1981, 1983) and Edward Thompson (1963) are held to be early figureheads representing the moment of 'culturalism', which is later contrasted with 'structuralism'. Indeed, culturalism is a *post hoc* term which owes its sense precisely to a contrast with structuralism and has little currency outside of that debate.

CULTURE IS ORDINARY

Culturalism stresses the 'ordinariness' of culture and the active, creative, capacity of people to construct shared meaningful practices. Empirical work, which is emphasized within the culturalist tradition, explores the way that active human beings create cultural meanings. There is a focus on lived experience and the adoption of a broadly anthropological definition of culture which describes it as an everyday lived process not confined to 'high' art.

Culturalism, particularly for Williams and Thompson, is a form of historical cultural materialism which traces the unfolding of meaning over time, exploring culture in the context of its material conditions of production and reception. There is an explicit partisanship in exploring the class basis of culture which aims to give 'voice' to the subordinated and to examine the place of culture in class power. However, this form of 'left culturalism' is also somewhat nationalistic, or at least nation-centred, in its approach, and there is little sense of either the globalizing character of contemporary culture or the place of race within English national and class culture.

STRUCTURALISM

If culturalism takes meaning to be its central category and casts it as the product of active human agents, **structuralism** speaks instead of signifying practices which generate meaning as an outcome of **structures** or predictable regularities which lie outside of any given person. Structuralism is anti-humanist in its decentring of human agents from the heart of inquiry, favouring a form of analysis in which phenomena have meaning only in relation to other phenomena within a systematic structure of which no particular person is the source. A structuralist understanding of culture is concerned with the 'systems of relations' of an underlying structure (usually language) and the grammar which makes meaning possible.

Structuralism can be traced back at least to the sociologist Durkheim (1952, 1982), who searched for the constraining patterns of culture and social life which lie outside of any given individual. Durkheim rejected the empiricist view that knowledge is to be derived from direct experience, in favour of seeking out what he calls 'social facts' which are socially constructed, culturally variable and *sui generis* of particular consciousness. That is, they exist beyond individuals. For example, the beliefs, values and norms of religions, specifically the contrast between Catholicism and Protestantism, are said to account for variable patterns of suicide. In other words, the most individual act possible, suicide, is accounted for by normative social structures of belief.

DEEP STRUCTURES OF LANGUAGE

Since Durkheim did not emphasize the place of signifying systems, he is not a structuralist of the kind popularized within cultural studies. Structuralism in this sense takes **signification** or meaning production to be the effect of deep structures of language which are manifested in specific cultural phenomena or human speakers but which are not the outcome of the intentions of actors *per se*. Thus, structuralism is concerned with how cultural meaning is generated, understanding culture to be analogous to (or structured like) a language (Chapter 3).

The work of Saussure (1960) was critical in the development of structuralism. He argued that meaning is generated through a system of structured differences in language. That is, significance is the outcome of the rules and conventions which organize language (*langue*) rather than the specific uses and utterances which individuals deploy in everyday life (*parole*).

According to Saussure, meaning is produced through a process of selection and combination of **signs** along two axes, the syntagmatic (linear – e.g. a sentence) and paradigmatic (a field of signs – e.g. synonyms), organized into a signifying system. Signs, constituted by **signifiers** (medium) and **signifieds** (meaning), do not make sense by virtue of reference to entities in the 'real world'; rather, they generate meaning by reference to each other. Meaning is a social convention organized through the relations between signs.

In short, Saussure, and structuralism in general, is concerned more with the structures of language which allow linguistic performance to be possible than with actual performance in its infinite variations. It is noteworthy that Saussure talked of a science of signs, called **semiotics**, implying that objective, certain and scientific knowledge of signs was possible. We should also note a tendency in structuralism towards analysis through binaries, for example the contrast between *langue* and *parole* or between pairs of signs so that 'black' only has meaning in relation to 'white' and vice versa.

CULTURE AS LIKE A LANGUAGE

Structuralism extends its reach from 'words' to the language of cultural signs in general so that human relations, material objects and images are all analysed through the structures of signs. In Lévi-Strauss (see Leach, 1974), we find structuralist principles at work when he describes kinship systems as 'like a language'. That is, family relations are held to be structured by the internal organization of binaries. For example, kinship patterns are structured around the incest taboo which divides people into the marriageable and the prohibited.

Typical of Lévi-Strauss's structuralism is his approach to food, which, he declares, is not so much good to eat, as good to think with. That is, food is a signifier of **symbolic** meanings. Cultural conventions tell us what constitutes food and what does not, the circumstances of their eating and the meanings attached to them. Lévi-Strauss tends towards the structuralist trope of binaries: the raw and the cooked, the edible and the inedible, nature and culture, each of which has meaning only in relation to its opposite. Cooking transforms nature into culture and the raw into the cooked.

The edible and the inedible are marked not by questions of nutrition but by cultural meanings, for example the Jewish prohibition against pork and the necessity to prepare food in culturally specific ways (kosher food). Here, binary oppositions of the edible–inedible mark another binary, insiders and outsiders, and hence the boundaries of the culture or social order. Later, Barthes (see Chapter 3) was to extend the structuralist account of culture to the practices of popular culture and their naturalized meanings or **myths**. Barthes was to argue that the meanings of texts are to be grasped not in terms of the intentions of specific human beings but as a set of signifying practices.

In sum, where culturalism focused on meaning production by human actors in an historical context, structuralism pointed to culture as an expression of deep structures of language which lie outside of the intentions of actors and constrain them. Where culturalism stresses history, structuralism is synchronic in approach, analysing the structures of relations in a snapshot of a particular moment. In this, structuralism is also asserting the specificity of culture and its irreducibility to any other phenomena. It does not therefore subscribe to the notion that culture is determined by the material conditions of production.

Finally, where culturalism focuses on interpretation as a way of understanding meaning, structuralism has asserted the possibility of a science of signs, of objective knowledge. Indeed, structuralism is best approached as a method of analysis rather than an all-embracing philosophy. However, the notion of stability of meaning, upon which the binaries of structuralism and its pretensions to surety of knowledge are based, is the subject of attack by poststructuralism. That is, poststructuralism deconstructs the very notion of the stable structures of language.

Poststructuralism (and postmodernism)

The term **poststructuralism** implies 'after structuralism', embodying notions of both critique and absorption. That is, poststructuralism absorbs aspects of structural linguistics while subjecting it to a critique which, it is claimed, surpasses structuralism. In short, poststructuralism rejects the idea of an underlying stable structure which founds meaning through fixed binary pairs (black–white; good–bad). Rather, meaning is unstable, being always deferred and in process. Meaning cannot be confined to single words, sentences or particular texts but is the outcome of relationships between texts, that is, **intertextuality**. Like its predecessor, poststructuralism is anti-humanist in its decentring of the unified, coherent human subject as the origin of stable meanings.

DERRIDA: THE INSTABILITY OF LANGUAGE

The primary philosophical sources of poststructuralism are Derrida (1976) and Foucault (1984d) (see Chapter 3). Since they give rise to different emphases, poststructuralism cannot be regarded as a unified body of work. Derrida's focus is on language and the deconstruction of an immediacy, or identity, between words and meanings.

Derrida accepts Saussure's argument that meaning is generated by relations of difference between signifiers rather than by reference to an independent object world. However, for Derrida, the consequence of this play of signifiers is that meaning can never be fixed. Words carry many meanings, including the echoes or traces of other meanings from other related words in other contexts. For example, if we look up the meaning of a word in a dictionary we are referred to other words in an infinite process of deferral. Meaning slides down a chain of signifiers abolishing a stable signified. Thus, Derrida introduces the notion of *différance*, 'difference and deferral', so that the production of meaning in the process of signification is continually deferred and supplemented in the play of more-than-one.

Given this instability of meaning, Derrida proceeds to deconstruct the 'stable' binaries upon which structuralism, and indeed western philosophy in general, relies. He argues for the 'undecidability' of binary oppositions. In particular, deconstruction involves the dismantling of hierarchical conceptual oppositions such as speech/writing, reality/appearance, nature/culture, reason/madness, etc., which exclude and devalue the 'inferior' part of the binary.

For Derrida, 'we think only in signs'. There is no original meaning circulating outside of 'representation' so that writing is crucial to the generation of meaning. Derrida's argument is that writing is always already present in speech. There is no primary source of meaning and no self-present transparent meaning which can fix the relation between signifiers and signifieds. It is in this sense that there is nothing outside of texts or nothing but texts (by which is *not* meant that there is no external material world), so that texts are constitutive of practices.

FOUCAULT AND DISCURSIVE PRACTICES

Like Derrida, Foucault (1972) argues against structuralist theories of language which conceive of it as an autonomous rule-governed system. He also opposes interpretative or hermeneutic methods which seek to disclose the hidden meanings of language. Foucault is thus concerned with the description and analysis of the surfaces of discourse and their effects under determinate material and historical conditions. For Foucault, discourse concerns both language and practice and refers to the regulated production of knowledge through language which gives meaning to both material objects and social practices.

Discourse constructs, defines and produces the objects of knowledge in an intelligible way while at the same time excluding other ways of reasoning as unintelligible. Foucault attempts to identify the historical conditions and determining rules of formation of regulated ways of speaking about objects, that is, discursive practices and discursive formations. He explores the circumstances under which statements are combined and regulated to form and define a distinct field of knowledge/objects requiring a particular set of concepts and delimiting a specific 'regime of truth' (i.e. what counts as truth).

For Foucault, discourse regulates not only what can be said under determinate social and cultural conditions but who can speak, when and where. Consequently, much of his work is concerned with the historical investigation of power and the production of subjects through that power. Foucault does not formulate power as a centralized constraining force; rather, dispersed through all levels of a social formation, power is generative, that is, productive of social relations and identities.

Foucault conceives of the subject as radically historized, that is, persons are wholly and only the product of history. He explores the **genealogy** of the body as a site of disciplinary practices which bring subjects into being. Such practices are the consequences of specific historical discourses of crime, punishment, medicine, science and sexuality. Thus, Foucault (1973) analyses statements about madness which give us knowledge about it, the rules which prescribe what is 'sayable' or 'thinkable' about madness, subjects who personify madness and the practices within institutions which deal with madness (see Chapter 3).

ANTI-ESSENTIALISM

Perhaps the most significant influence of poststructuralism within cultural studies is its anti-essentialism. **Essentialism** assumes that words have stable referents and social categories reflect an essential underlying identity. By this token there would be stable truths to be found and an essence of, for example, femininity or black identity. However, for poststructuralism there can be no truths, subjects or identities outside of language, a language which does not have stable referents and is therefore unable to represent fixed truths or identities. In this sense, femininity or black identity are not fixed universal things but descriptions in language which through social convention come to be 'what counts as truth' (i.e. the temporary stabilization of meaning).

For poststructuralism, a person or subject is not a stable universal entity but an effect of language which constructs an 'I' in grammar. The speaking subject is dependent on the prior existence of discursive **subject positions**, empty spaces or functions in discourse from which to comprehend the world. Living persons are required to 'take up' subject positions in discourse in order to make sense of the world and to appear coherent to others.

Anti-essentialism does not mean that we cannot speak of truth or identity. Rather, it points to them as being not universals of nature but productions of culture in specific times and places. The speaking subject is dependent on the prior existence of discursive positions. Truth is not so much found as made and identities are discursive constructions. Instead of the scientific certainty of structuralism, poststructuralism offers us **irony**, an awareness of the contingent, constructed character of our beliefs and understandings which lack firm universal foundations.

POSTMODERNISM

While there is no straightforward equation of poststructuralism with **postmodernism**, and the sharing of the prefix 'post' can lead to unwarranted conflation of the two, they do share a common approach to epistemology, namely the rejection of truth as a fixed eternal object. Derrida's assertion of the instability of meaning and Foucault's awareness of the historically contingent character of truth are echoed in Lyotard's postmodern 'incredulity towards metanarratives'. Lyotard (1984) rejects the idea of grand narratives or stories that can give us certain knowledge of the direction, meaning and moral path of human 'development'. Lyotard has in mind the teleology of Marxism, the certainty of science and the morality of Christianity.

Postmodern writers like Lyotard (1984) or Rorty (1989) share with Foucault the idea that knowledge is not metaphysical, transcendental or universal but specific to particular times and spaces. For postmodernism, knowledge is perspectival in character and there can be no one totalizing knowledge which is able to grasp the 'objective' character of the world. Rather, we have and require multiple viewpoints or truths by which to interpret a complex, heterogeneous human existence. Thus, postmodernism, in its understanding that knowledge is specific to language-games, embraces local, plural and diverse knowledges.

While one strand of postmodernism is concerned with these questions of epistemology, that is, questions of truth and knowledge, an equally significant body of work is centred on important cultural changes in contemporary life. A sense of the fragmentary, ambiguous and uncertain quality of the world marked by high levels of reflexivity is said to be a characteristic of postmodern culture. This goes hand in hand with a stress on contingency, irony and the blurring of cultural boundaries. Texts are typified by self-consciousness, bricolage and intertextuality. For some thinkers, postmodern culture heralds the collapse of the modern distinction between the real and simulations (see Chapter 5 for a fuller discussion).

Poststructuralism and postmodernism are anti-essentialist approachs which stress the constitutive role of an unstable language. They argue that subjectivity is an effect of language or discourse and that subjects are fractured – we can take up multiple subject positions offered to us in discourse. However, rather than rely on an account which stresses 'subjection' by external discourses, some writers have looked to psychoanalysis, and particularly Lacan's poststructuralist reading of Freud, for ways to think about the 'internal' constitution of subjects.

Psychoanalysis and subjectivity

Psychoanalysis is a controversial body of thought. For its supporters (Chodorow, 1978, 1989; Mitchell, 1974) its great strength lies in its rejection of the fixed nature of subjects and sexuality. That is, psychoanalysis concentrates on the construction and formation of subjectivity. Not what a subject is but on how s/he comes into being. Psychoanalysis, it is argued, shows how psychic processes institute the humanization of infants, constituting the always gendered subject in the symbolic domain of language and culture.

THE FREUDIAN SELF

According to Freud (1977), the self is constituted in terms of an ego, or conscious rational mind, a superego, or social conscience, and the unconscious, the source and repository of the symbolic workings of the mind which functions with a different logic from reason. This structuring of the human subject is not something we are born with; rather, it is something we acquire through our relationships with our immediate 'carers'. Since the self is by definition fractured into the ego, superego and unconscious, the unified narrative of the self is something we attain over time through entry into the symbolic order of language and culture. Through processes of **identification** with others and with social discourses we create an identity which embodies an illusion of wholeness.

Within Freudian theory, the libido or sexual drive does not have any pre-given fixed aim or object. Rather, through fantasy, any object, which includes persons or parts of bodies, can be the target of desire. Consequently, an almost infinite number of sexual objects and practices are within the domain of human sexuality. However, Freud's work is concerned to document and explain the regulation and repression of this 'polymorphous perversity' through the resolution (or not) of the Oedipus complex into 'normal' heterosexual gendered relationships.

THE OEDIPUS COMPLEX

In classical Freudian thought, the Oedipus complex marks the formation of the ego and of gendered subjectivity. Prior to the Oedipal moment we are unable to distinguish clearly between ourselves and other objects, nor do we have a sense of ourselves as male or female. Pre-Oedipal infants experience the world in terms of sensory exploration and auto-eroticism. They seek physical satisfaction with a primary focus on the mother as a source of warmth, comfort and food. Consequently, an infant's first love-object is its mother, whom it both identifies with and desires. That is, the child wants both to 'be' the mother and to 'possess' the mother. The resolution of the Oedipus complex involves the repudiation of the mother as a love-object and the separation of the subject from the mother.

For boys, the incest taboo, symbolized by the power of the father as Phallus, means that desire for the mother is untenable and threatened by punishment in the form of castration. As a consequence, boys shift their identification from the mother to the father and take on masculinity and heterosexuality as the desirable subject form. For girls, the separation from the mother is more complex and arguably never completed. Girls do not entirely repudiate mother identification nor do they take on father identification. However, they do recognize the power of the Phallus as something which they do not have (penis envy) but which the father does. Since they do not have a penis (or symbolic Phallus), they cannot ever be it, they cannot identify with it. However, they can set out to possess it, which they do by seeking to have a child by the father or, more accurately, other men who stand in for the father as Phallus.

In so far as psychoanalysis is an ahistorical universal account of subjectivity marking the psychic processes of humankind across history, and, furthermore, one which is inherently patriarchal and phallocentric, it has proved to be unacceptable within cultural studies. However, sympathetic critics have suggested that psycho-analysis can be reworked as an historically contingent account of subject formation. That is, one which describes it only under specific historical circumstances. Changes in the cultural and symbolic order are said to lead to changes in subject formation, and vice versa. The subversiveness of psychoanalysis then lies in its disruption of the social order, including gendered relations, by trying to bring new kinds of thinking and subjectivities into being. Thus, psychoanalysis could, it is argued, be stripped of its **phallocentrism** and be made appropriate to the political project of feminism (Chapter 8).

The politics of difference: feminism, race and postcolonial theory

A theme of structuralism and poststructuralism is the idea that meaning is generated through the play of difference down a chain of signifiers. Subjects are formed through difference so that what we are is constituted in part by what we are not. In this context, there has been a growing emphasis on **difference** in the social field, and in particular on questions of gender, race and ethnicity.

FEMINISM
Feminism (Chapter 8) is a field of theory and politics which contains competing perspectives and prescriptions for action. However, in general terms, we may locate feminism as asserting that **sex** is a fundamental and irreducible axis of social organ-ization which, to date, has subordinated women to men. Thus, feminism is centrally concerned with sex as an organizing prin-ciple of social life where **gender** relations are thoroughly satur-ated with power relations. The subordination of women is evident across a range of social institutions and practices, that is, male power and female subordination are structural. This has led feminists to adopt the concept of **patriarchy**, with its derivative meanings of the male-headed family, 'mastery' and superiority.

Feminism is constituted by a range of analyses and strategies of action which have been called liberal feminism, difference or radical feminism, socialist or Marxist feminism, postmodern/poststructuralist feminism and black feminism. Liberal feminism stresses equality of opportunity for women, regarding this as achievable within the broad structures of the existing legal and economic frameworks. In contrast, socialist feminists point to the interconnections between class and gender, including the fundamental place of gender inequalities and the dual roles (domestic work and paid work) of women in the reproduction of capitalism. Instead of liberal and socialist feminism's stress on equality and sameness, difference or radical feminism asserts essential differences between men and women which are celebrated as representing the creative difference of women and the superiority of 'feminine' values.

Problems with patriarchy

A criticism of the concept of patriarchy is its treatment of the category of woman as undifferentiated. That is, all women are taken to share something fundamental in common in contrast to all men. This is an assumption continually challenged by black feminists, who have argued that the movement has defined women as white and overlooked the differences between black and white women's experiences. This stress on difference is shared by poststructuralist and postmodern feminists who argue that sex and gender are social and cultural constructions which are neither to be explained in terms of biology nor reduced to functions of capitalism. This is an anti-essentialist stance which argues that femininity and masculinity are not essential universal categories but discursive constructions. As such, poststructuralist feminism is concerned with the cultural construction of subjectivity *per se* and with a range of possible masculinities and femininities.

RACE, ETHNICITY AND HYBRIDITY

Another 'politics of difference' which has received increasing attention within cultural studies is that of **race** and ethnicity in postcolonial times (see Chapters 7 and 12). **Ethnicity** is a cultural concept centred on norms, values, beliefs, cultural symbols and practices which mark a process of cultural boundary formation. The idea of 'racialization' has been deployed to illustrate the argument that race is a social construction and not a universal or essential category of either biology or culture. Races do not exist outside of representation but are formed in and by it in a process of social and political power struggle.

There are two key concerns which have emerged in and through **postcolonial** theory (Williams and Chrisman, 1993), those of domination–subordination and **hybridity**–creolization. Questions of domination and subordination surface most directly through colonial military control and the structured subordination of racialized groups. In more cultural terms, questions arise about the denigration and subordination of 'native' culture by colonial and imperial powers and the relationship between **place** and **diaspora** identities.

The question of hybridity or creolization points to the fact that neither the colonial nor colonized cultures and languages can be presented in 'pure' form. Inseparable from each other, they give rise to forms of hybridity. In metropolitan cultures like America and Britain, this concept is reworked to include the hybrid cultures produced by, for example, Latino-Americans and British Asians.

QUESTIONS OF METHODOLOGY

Cultural studies has not devoted itself to questions of research methods and methodology, so that texts by Alasuutari (1995) and McGuigan (1997b) are exceptions to the rule. Indeed, my own concern here is not with the technicalities of method but with the philosophical approaches which underpin them, that is, methodology. Since this book is centred on the theoretical and substantive claims of cultural studies, I have opted to reproduce the same sin as cultural studies in general. That is, I offer only a very brief indicative discussion of methodology as a distinct set of concerns.

Epistemology

The most significant debate centred on **epistemology**, that is, questions about the status of knowledge and **truth**, has been between representationalist (realist) and anti-representationalist (poststructuralism, postmodernism and pragmatism) views. Since this concerns the character of language and representation, the subjects of Chapters 3 (on language) and 5 (on postmodernism), I offer only a brief summary here.

Those who maintain a realist line, often in its quasi-Marxist guise, argue that a degree of certain knowledge about an independent object world (a real world) is possible even though methodological vigilance and reflexivity need to be maintained. In contrast, poststructuralist/postmodern epistemology adopts Nietzsche's (1967) characterization of truth as a 'mobile army of metaphors and metonyms'. That is, sentences are the only things that can be true or false. Knowledge is a question not of true discovery but of the construction of interpretations about the world which are taken to be true. In so far as the idea of truth has an historical purchase, it is the consequence of power, that is, of whose interpretations are to count as truth.

Modern realist truth claims exhibit contradictory tendencies. On the one hand, they are universalizing and assert their truths for all people in all places. On the other hand, they embody the methodological principle of doubt by which knowledge is subject to chronic and continual revision (Giddens, 1990). The poststructuralist and postmodern emphasis is on the production of truths within the language-games in which such truths are founded. Poststructuralism and postmodernism accept the legitimacy of a range of truth claims, discourses and representations of 'reality'. This 'postmodern' understanding of knowledge is on the ascendancy within cultural studies but remains disputed. There are critics who feel that a more certain basis of knowledge is required for the political project of cultural studies to be maintained.

Key methodologies in cultural studies

Despite disputes about the status of knowledge, it is reasonably clear as to which methods are most widely deployed within cultural studies, though researchers disagree about their relative merits. We may start with the standard methodological distinction between quantitative and qualitative research methods, that is, between, respectively, methods which centre on numbers and the counting of things (e.g. statistics and surveys) and those which concentrate on the meanings generated by actors gathered through participant observation: interviews, focus groups and textual analysis. On the whole, cultural studies has favoured qualitative methods with their focus on cultural meaning.

Work in cultural studies has centred on three kinds of approach:

- *ethnography*, which has often been linked with culturalist approaches and a stress on 'lived experience';
- a range of *textual* approaches, which have tended to draw from semiotics, poststructuralism and Derridean deconstruction;
- a series of *reception* studies, which are eclectic in their theoretical roots.

ETHNOGRAPHY

Ethnography is an empirical and theoretical approach inherited from anthropology which seeks detailed holistic description and analysis of cultures based on intensive fieldwork. In classical conceptions, 'the Ethnographer participates in people's lives for an extended period of time, watching what happens, listening to what is said, asking questions' (Hammersley and Atkinson, 1983: 2).

The objective is to produce what Geertz (1973) famously described as 'thick descriptions' of 'the multiplicity of complex conceptual structures', including unspoken and taken-for-granted assumptions about cultural life. Ethnography concentrates on the details of local life while connecting them to wider social processes.

Ethnographic cultural studies has been centred on the qualitative exploration of values and meanings in the context of a 'whole way of life', that is, with questions of cultures, life-worlds and identities. As Morley remarks, 'qualitative research strategies such as ethnography are principally designed to gain access to "naturalized domains" and their characteristic activities' (Morley, 1992: 186). However, in the context of media-oriented cultural studies, ethnography has become a code-word for a range of qualitative methods, including participant observation, in-depth interviews and focus groups. Here, it is the 'spirit' of ethnography (i.e. qualitative understanding of cultural activity in context) which is invoked polemically against the tradition of quantitative communications research.

The problem of representation

Not withstanding qualifications about **reflexivity**, ethnography has tried to 'represent the subjective meanings, feelings and cultures of others' (Willis, 1980: 91). In this way, ethnography relied on an implicitly realist epistemology. The idea that it is possible to represent in a naturalistic way the 'real' experience of people has been the subject of considerable critique.

First, it is argued that the data presented by ethnographers are always already an interpretation made through that person's eyes, that is, they are positional. However, this is an argument that can be directed at all forms of research. Here it simply gives rise to 'interpretative ethnography'. Second, and more tellingly, there has been a brand of postmodern critique which, in addition to pointing to the problems of realist epistemology, argues more specifically that ethnography is a genre of writing which deploys rhetorical devices, often obscured, to maintain its realist claims (Clifford and Marcus, 1986). In other words, the products of ethnography are always texts. Clifford poses the issue thus:

> If ethnography produces interpretations through intense research experiences, how is unruly experience transformed into an authoritative written account? How, precisely, is garrulous, overdetermined cross-cultural encounter shot through with power relations and personal cross-purposes circumscribed as an adequate version of a more or less discrete 'other world' composed by an individual author? (Clifford, 1988: 25)

This argument leads to the examination of ethnographic texts for their rhetorical devices, along with a more reflexive and dialogical approach to ethnography which demands that writers elaborate on their own assumptions, views and positions. Further, consultation with the 'subjects' of ethnography is required so that ethnography becomes less an expedition in search of 'the facts' and more a conversation between participants in a research process.

The critique of the epistemological claims of ethnography does not mean that it is of no value or that it should be abandoned. There is no fundamental epistemological distinction between ethnography and a multi-layered novel whose purposes do not lie in the production of a 'true' picture of the world but in the production of empathy and the widening of the circle of human solidarity (Rorty, 1989). Thus, ethnography has personal, poetic and political, rather than epistemological, justifications.

In this view, ethnographic data can be seen as giving poetic expression to voices from other cultures or from the 'margins' of our own cultures. Writing about such voices is to be regarded no longer as a 'scientific' report but as a poetic exposition and narration which brings new voices into what Rorty calls the 'cosmopolitan conversation of humankind'. Thus, ethnographic data can be the route by which our own culture is made strange to us, allowing new descriptions of the world to be generated.

The continued redescription of our world which ethnographic research can achieve is a desirable thing to do because it offers the possibility of an improvement of the human condition achieved through comparison between different representations of social practices. Different practices and descriptions of the world can be played off against each other, compared and juxtaposed, in order to generate yet more new descriptions in the ongoing conversation of humanity in search of improvements to the human condition. For example, ethnographic research may help us to learn from other cultures, to supply those 'toeholds for new initiatives' and 'tensions which make people listen to unfamiliar ideas' which combat ethnocentrism and help enrich our own culture with new ideas (Rorty, 1989).

None of this means that we can abandon all methodological rigour. Firstly, evidence and poetic style are pragmatically useful warrants for truth and action epistemologically equivalent to the procedural agreements of the physical sciences. That is, scientific 'objectivity' is to be read as social solidarity and truth signals maximum social agreement (Rorty, 1991a). Secondly, the language of observation and evidence are among the conventions which divide the genre of ethnography from the novel.

Thirdly, the rejection of a universal objective truth is based on the impossibility of word–world correspondence and therefore of accurate or adequate representation. This does not mean that we have to abandon word–word translation. That is, we can achieve 'good enough' reporting of the speech or action of others without making claims to universal truth. It is better to use a tape recorder to document the utterances of research subjects rather than make it up because (a) we will be better able to translate and understand the words of others for practical purposes and (b) we will be better able to predict the actions of others.

The problems of ethnography are problems of translation and justification not universal or objective truth. We can consider languages (and thus culture and knowledge) to be constituted not by untranslatable and incompatible rules but as learnable *skills*. According to Davidson (1984) there can be no such thing as an unlearnable language for this would mean we were unable to recognize the 'other' as a language user at all. Ethnography now becomes about *dialogue* and the attempt to reach pragmatic agreements about meaning between participants in a research process. There is no *a priori* reason why this should succeed, agreement may never be reached, but there is no *a priori* reason why it should fail either (Rorty, 1991a).

I have discussed ethnography at greater length than I am about to devote to textual and reception studies, for two reasons. First, ethnography raises crucial epistemological issues which are relevant and, to a degree, generalizable to other methods. That is, questions about realism, interpretation and representation are also applicable to textual and reception methodology. Second, the vast majority of 'evidence' provided in this book comes from textual, reception or theoretical work. It thus seemed reasonable to devote more space to the somewhat neglected strand of ethnographic cultural studies.

TEXTUAL APPROACHES

Although textual work comes in many guises, including 'literary criticism', the three outstanding modes of analysis in cultural studies draw from:

- semiotics;
- narrative theory;
- deconstructionism.

Texts as signs

Semiotics explores how the meanings generated by texts have been achieved through a particular arrangement of signs and the deployment of cultural **codes** (Chapter 3). Such analysis draws attention to the ideologies or myths of texts. For example, semiotic analysis illustrates the case that television news is a constructed representation and not a mirror of reality (Chapter 9). The media's selective and value-laden representations are not 'accurate' pictures of the world but the site of struggles over what counts as meaning and truth. Television may appear to be 'realistic' because of its use of seamless editing and the 'invisible' cut, but such **realism** is constituted by a set of aesthetic *conventions* rather than being a reflection of the 'real world'.

Texts as narratives

Texts tell stories, whether that be Einstein's theory of relativity, Hall's theory of identity or the latest episode of *The Simpsons*. Consequently, **narrative** theory plays a part in cultural studies. A narrative is an ordered sequential account which makes claims to be a record of events. Narratives are the structured form in which stories advance explanations for the ways of the world. Narratives offer us frameworks of understanding and rules of reference about the way the social order is constructed and in doing so supply answers to the question: how shall we live?

Though stories take different forms, utilizing a variety of characters, subject matters and narrative structures (or ways of telling a story), structuralist theory has concerned itself with the common features of story formation. According to Todorov (1977), narrative minimally concerns the disruption of an equilibrium and the tracing of the consequences of said disruption until a new equilibrium is achieved. For example, an established soap opera couple are shown in loving embrace as a prelude to the later revelation that one of them is having an affair. The question is posed: will this spell the end of the relationship? A good deal of talk, emotion and explanation takes place before the characters are either reconciled or go their separate ways. Soap opera is the name of a **genre**. Genres structure the narrative process and contain it; they regulate it in particular ways using specific elements and combinations of elements to produce coherence and credibility. Genre thus represents systemizations and repetitions of problems and solutions in narratives (Neale, 1980).

Deconstruction

Deconstructionism is associated with Derrida's 'undoing' of the binaries of western philosophy and its extension into the fields of literature (e.g. De Man) and postcolonial theory (e.g. Spivak). To deconstruct is to take apart, to undo, in order to seek out and display the assumptions of a text. In particular, deconstruction involves the dismantling of hierarchical conceptual oppositions such as man/women, black/white, reality/appearance, nature/culture, reason/madness, etc., which serve to guarantee truth by excluding and devaluing the 'inferior' part of the binary. Thus, speech is privileged over writing, reality over appearance, men over women.

The purpose of deconstruction is not simply to reverse the order of binaries but to show that they are implicated in each other. Deconstruction seeks to expose the blind-spots of texts, the unacknowledged assumptions upon which they operate. This includes the places where a text's rhetorical strategies work against the logic of a text's arguments, that is, the tension between what a text means to say and what it is constrained to mean.

One of the central problems of deconstruction is that it must use the very conceptual language it seeks to undo. For example, to deconstruct western philosophy is to use the very language of western philosophy. To mark this tension, Derrida places his concepts **under erasure**. To place a word under erasure is to first write the word and then to cross it out, leaving both the word and its crossed-out version. As Spivak explains: 'Since the word is inaccurate, it is crossed out. Since it is necessary, it remains legible' (Spivak, 1976: xiv). The use 'under erasure' of accustomed and known concepts is intended to destabilize the familiar, marking it as useful, necessary, inaccurate and mistaken. Thus does Derrida seek to illuminate the undecidablity of meaning.

RECEPTION STUDIES

Exponents of reception or consumption studies argue that whatever analysis of textual meanings a critic may undertake, it is far from certain which of the identified meanings, if any, will be activated by actual readers/audiences/consumers. By this is meant that audiences are active creators of meaning in relation to texts. They bring previously acquired cultural competencies to bear on texts so that differently constituted audiences will work with different meanings.

On the theoretical front two fields of study have proved to be particularly influential: Hall's (1981) 'encoding–decoding' model and literary reception studies. Hall argues that the production of meaning does not ensure consumption of that meaning as the encoders might have intended because (television) messages, constructed as a sign system with multi-accentuated components, are polysemic that is, they have more than one potential set of meanings. To the degree that audiences participate in cultural frameworks with producers, then audience decodings and textual encodings will be similar. However, where audience members are situated in different social positions (e.g. of class and gender) from encoders with divergent cultural resources available to them, they will be able to decode programmes in alternative ways.

Work within the tradition of hermeneutics and literary reception studies (Gadamer, 1976; Iser, 1978) argues that understanding is always from the position and point of view of the person who understands, involving not merely reproduction of textual meaning but the *production* of meaning by the readers. The text may structure aspects of meaning by guiding the reader, but it cannot fix the meaning, which is the outcome of the oscillations between the text and the imagination of the reader (Chapter 9).

THE PLACE OF THEORY

A significant strand of work in cultural studies is not empirical but theoretical. **Theory** can be understood as narratives which seek to distinguish and account for general features which describe, define and explain persistently perceived occurrences. However, theory does not picture the world more or less accurately; rather, it is a tool, instrument or *logic for intervening* in the world through the mechanisms of description, definition, prediction and control. Theory construction is a self-reflexive discursive endeavour which seeks to interpret and intercede in the world.

Theory construction involves the thinking through of concepts and arguments, often redefining and critiquing prior work, with the objective of offering new tools by which to think about our world. This has maintained a high-profile position within cultural studies. Theoretical work can be thought of as a crafting of the cultural signposts and maps by which we are guided. Cultural studies has rejected the empiricist claim that knowledge is simply a matter of collecting facts from which theory can be deduced or tested against. Rather, theory is always already implicit in empirical research through the very choice of topic, the focus the research takes and the concepts through which it is discussed and interpreted. That is, 'facts' are not neutral and no amount of stacking up of 'facts' produces a story about our lives without theory. Indeed, theory is precisely a story about humanity with implications for action and judgements about consequences.

Cultural studies seeks to play a de-mystifying role, to point to the constructed character of cultural texts and to the myths and ideologies which are embedded in them in the hope of producing subject positions, and real subjects, who are enabled to oppose subordination. As a political theory, cultural studies has hoped to organize disparate opposition groups into an alliance of **cultural politics**. However, Bennett (1992, 1998) has argued that the textual politics which much cultural studies produces (a) is not connected to many living persons and (b) ignores the institutional dimensions of cultural power. Consequently, he urges cultural studies to adopt a more pragmatic approach and to work with cultural producers in the construction and implementation of **cultural policy** (Chapter 12).

SUMMARY

Cultural studies is a plural field of contesting perspectives which through the production of theory has sought to intervene in cultural politics. Cultural studies explores culture as signifying practices in the context of social power. In doing so it has drawn on a variety of theories, including Marxism, structuralism, poststructuralism and feminism. Eclectic in its methods, cultural studies asserts the positionality of all knowledge, including its own, which coheres around the key ideas of culture, signifying practices, representation, discourse, power, articulation, texts, readers and consumption.

Cultural studies is an interdisciplinary or post-disciplinary field of inquiry which explores the production and inculcation of maps of meaning. It can be described as a language-game or discursive formation concerned with issues of power in the signifying practices of human life. Cultural studies is an exciting and fluid project which tells us stories about our changing world in the hope that we can improve it.

2

Questions of Culture and Ideology

The concept of **culture** is by definition central to cultural studies, yet there is no 'correct' or definitive meaning attached to it. In describing it as 'one of the two or three most complicated words in the English language', Williams (1983) indicates the contested character of culture and cultural studies. Culture is not 'out there' waiting to be correctly described by theorists who keep getting it wrong. Rather, the concept of culture is a tool which is of more or less usefulness to us as a life form. Consequently, its usage and meanings continue to change as thinkers have hoped to 'do' different things with it. We should ask not what culture 'is', but how the language of culture is used and for what purposes.

The study of culture within sociology, anthropology, literature, etc., pre-dates cultural studies as a stream of thought with particular themes and theoretical leanings. While the study of culture has no origins, **cultural studies** as an institutionalized **discursive formation** does have a particular history, albeit one that takes on the status of myth. This means that British cultural studies, as exemplified by Hoggart, Williams and Hall, can be regarded as a crucial moment in the trajectory of what we now call cultural studies. In tracing the ways in which the concept of culture has been defined and deployed by them, we are in effect exploring the changing concerns of cultural studies.

CULTURE WITH A CAPITAL C: THE GREAT AND THE GOOD IN THE LITERARY TRADITION

According to Williams (1981, 1983), the word 'culture' began as a noun of process connected to growing crops, that is, cultivation. Subsequently, the idea of cultivation was broadened to encompass the human mind or 'spirit', giving rise to the idea of the cultivated or cultured person. However, during the nineteenth century a more anthropological definition emerged designating culture as 'a whole and distinctive way of life' with an emphasis on 'lived experience'. It is within these definitional tensions that British cultural studies has its discursive and mythological origins.

The nineteenth century English writer Matthew Arnold has taken on iconic status within the **narrative** of cultural studies. He famously described culture as 'the best that has been thought and said in the world' (Arnold, 1960: 6), with 'reading, observing and thinking' the means toward moral perfection and social good. Culture as the form of human 'civilization' is to be counterpoised to the 'anarchy' of the 'raw and uncultivated masses'. As such, Arnold's aesthetic and political arguments are a justification for what we commonly call 'high culture'.

Leavisism

The work of Arnold was influential upon the other icons of culture with a capital C, F.R. and Q.D. Leavis, whose work opens in the 1930s and spans four decades. Leavisism shares with Arnold the notion that culture is the high point of civilization and the concern of an educated minority. F.R. Leavis argued that, prior to the industrial revolution, England had an authentic common culture of the people and a minority culture of the educated elite. For Leavis, this was a golden age of an 'organic community' with a 'lived culture' of 'Folk-songs and Folk-dance' (Leavis and Thompson, 1933: 1) which has now been lost to the 'standardization and levelling down' (3) of industrialized mass culture. The purpose of high or minority culture, now reduced to a literary tradition, is to keep alive, nurture and disseminate the ability to discriminate between the best and the worst of culture. For Leavisism, the task is to define and defend the best of culture, the canon of good works, while criticizing advertising, films and popular fiction, the worst of mass culture with its 'addictions' and 'distractions'.

It was against such definitions of culture that cultural studies struggled and through which it defined itself. That, in Britain, Arnold and F.R. Leavis were the critical figures is part of the cultural studies narrative, but similar arguments were embodied by other writers in other countries and continue to be repeated today. While with hindsight it is not difficult to criticize the arbitrary and elitist character of Arnold and Leavis's work, they can also be said to have opened up the terrain of popular culture for study by bringing to bear on it the tools and concepts of 'art and literature'.

CULTURE IS ORDINARY

In contrast to an aesthetic and elitist conception of culture, Raymond Williams developed an understanding which stresses the everyday lived character of culture as 'a whole way of life'. Williams was particularly concerned with working-**class** experience and their active construction of culture. As such, his view of culture is no less political than Arnold's, but is, crucially, a different kind of **politics** which stresses democracy, education and 'the long revolution' (Williams, 1965), that is, the march of the working class through institutions of contemporary life and the democratization of culture and politics. For Williams:

> A culture has two aspects: the known meanings and directions, which its members are trained to; the new observations and meanings, which are offered and tested. These are the ordinary processes of human societies and human minds, and we see through them the nature of culture: that it is always both traditional and creative; that it is both the most ordinary common meanings and the finest individual meanings. We use the word culture in these two senses: to mean a whole way of life – the common meanings; to mean the arts and learning – the special processes of discovery and creative effort. Some writers reserve the word for one or other of these senses; I insist on both, and on the significance of their conjunction. The questions I ask about our culture are questions about our general and common purposes, yet also questions about deep and personal meanings. Culture is ordinary, in every society and in every mind. (Williams, 1989: 4)

Culture is both the 'arts' and the values, norms and symbolic goods of everyday life. While culture is concerned with tradition and social reproduction, it is also a matter of creativity and change.

The anthropological approach to culture

Williams' concept of culture is 'anthropological' in so far as it centres on everyday meanings: values (abstract ideals), norms (definite principles or rules) and material/symbolic goods. Meanings are generated not by individuals but by collectives, so that the idea of culture refers to *shared meanings*.

> To say that two people belong to the same culture is to say that they interpret the world in roughly the same ways and can express themselves, their thoughts and feelings about the world, in ways which will be understood by each other. Thus culture depends on its participants interpreting meaningfully what is happening around them, and 'making sense' of the world, in broadly similar ways. (Hall, 1997a: 2)

As McGuigan (1992) has noted, the adoption of an anthropological version of culture would be something of a banality were it not being applied to the lives and social organization of modern western industrialized cultures rather than to the cultures of colonized peoples. Further, within the context of English literary criticism, an anthropological definition of culture offered a critical and democratic edge. Comprehending culture as a 'whole way of life' had the pragmatic consequence of splitting off the concept from the 'arts', legitimizing popular culture and opening up television, newspapers, dancing, football and other everyday artefacts and practices to critical but sympathetic analysis.

Culturalism: Hoggart, Thompson, Williams

Within the retrospective narrative of cultural studies, Richard Hoggart, Edward Thompson and Raymond Williams have been credited with forging an anthropological and historically informed understanding of culture in modern contexts. This has been dubbed 'culturalism' (Hall, 1992a). Though there are significant differences between Hoggart, Thompson and Williams, what they have in common is a stress on the 'ordinariness' of culture and the active, creative, capacity of common people to construct shared meaningful practices. Further, all three are particularly interested in questions of class culture, democracy and socialism in the context of the history of the English working class. In the case of Williams and Thompson, there is also an engagement with Marxism and the notion that 'men [sic] make their own history, but they do not make it just as they please; they do not make it under circumstances chosen by themselves, but under circumstances directly encountered, given and transmitted from the past' (Marx, 1961: 53).

RICHARD HOGGART: THE USES OF LITERACY

Hoggart's (1957) *The Uses of Literacy* explores the character of English working-class culture as it developed and changed from the 1930s through to the 1950s. The division of the book into two parts – 'An "Older" Order' and 'Yielding Place to New' – indicates the historical and comparative approach which Hoggart brings to bear. In the first part, based on memories of his own upbringing, Hoggart gives a sympathetic, humanist and detailed account of the lived culture of the working class, including a day at the seaside and the creative appropriation and uses of popular song. To the ears of those of us bought up with commercial culture and pop music, Hoggart's view of working-class culture sounds tinged with nostalgia for the lost **authenticity** of a culture created from below, for, in Part Two, he gives a rather acid account of the development of 'commercial culture' figured by the 'jukebox boy', the 'American slouch' and loud music. Nevertheless, Hoggarts's important legacy is the legitimacy accorded to the detailed study of working-class culture; the meanings and practices of ordinary people as they seek to live their lives and make their own history.

EDWARD THOMPSON: *THE MAKING OF THE ENGLISH WORKING CLASS*

'History from below' is the central theme of Thompson's (1963) *The Making of the English Working Class*, which concerns the lives, experiences, beliefs, attitudes and practices of working people. Thompson, along with Williams, conceives of culture as lived and ordinary, though he is also concerned with that which he sees as not cultural but socio-economic. For Thompson, class is an historical phenomenon forged and created by people; it is not a 'thing', but a set of social relations and experiences.

> Class happens when some men [*sic*], as a result of common experiences (inherited or shared), feel and articulate the identity of their interests as between themselves, and as against other men whose interests are different from (and usually opposed to) theirs. (Thompson, 1963: 8–9)

Thompson stresses the active and creative role of the English working class in bringing themselves into being (though not under conditions of their own making) and seeks to secure working-class experience in historical understanding. As he famously remarked, 'I am seeking to rescue the poor stockinger, the Luddite cropper, the "obsolete" hand-loom weaver, the "utopian" artisan, and even the deluded follower of Joanna Southcott, from the enormous condescension of posterity' (Thompson, 1963: 12).

RAYMOND WILLIAMS AND CULTURAL MATERIALISM

Though Hoggart and Thompson have been influential figures in the development of cultural studies, the legacy of Raymond Williams has been the more enduring. For Williams, culture as everyday meanings and values is part of an expressive totality of social relations. Thus, 'the theory of culture' is defined as 'the study of relationships between elements in a whole way of life' (Williams, 1965: 63).

> We need to distinguish three levels of culture, even in its most general definition. There is the lived culture of a particular time and place, only fully accessible to those living in that time and place. There is the recorded culture, of every kind, from art to the most everyday facts: the culture of the period. There is also, as the factor connecting lived culture and period cultures, the culture of the selective tradition. (Williams, 1965: 66)

For Williams, the purpose of cultural analysis is to explore and analyse the recorded culture of a given time and place in order to reconstitute its 'structure of feeling', or shared values and outlooks, while always being aware that such records are part of a selectively preserved and interpreted 'tradition'. Further, Williams insists that culture be understood through the representations and practices of daily life in the context of the material conditions of their production. This Williams calls **cultural materialism**, which involves 'the analysis of all forms of **signification** . . . within the actual means and conditions of their production' (Williams, 1981: 64–5). Thus, Williams (1981) suggests that we explore culture in terms of:

- *institutions* of artistic and cultural production, e.g. artisanal or market forms;
- *formations* or schools, movements and factions of cultural production;
- *modes of production*, including the relations between the material means of cultural production and the cultural forms which are made manifest;
- *identifications* and *forms* of culture, including the specificity of cultural products, their aesthetic purpose and the particular forms that generate and express meaning;
- the *reproduction*, in time and space, of a selective tradition of meanings and practices involving both social order and social change;
- the *organization* of the 'selective tradition' in terms of a 'realized signifying system'.

Such a strategy might be applied to contemporary music and its associated images and practices, so that Rap, Hip-Hop or Rave are understood as formations of popular music produced within the institutions of record companies and advertising agencies. The mode of production of popular music would include the technical means of studio recording and the capitalist social relations within which such practices are embedded. Clearly Hip-Hop or Rave are musical forms which involve the specific organization of sounds, words and images with which particular social groups form identifications. Hence one could analyse the specific organization of sounds and **signs** as a signifying system and the way in which Hip-Hop, for example, reproduces and changes aspects of African-American musical forms and the values of its historically developed lived culture, that is, what Hip-Hop means to young African-Americans.

Culture as lived experience

In sum, culture for Williams is constituted by the meanings and practices of ordinary men and women. Culture is lived experience:

the **text**s, practices and meanings of all people as they conduct their lives. Such meanings and practices are enacted on terrain not of our making even as we struggle to creatively shape our lives. Culture does not float free of the material conditions of life; on the contrary, for Williams, 'whatever purposes cultural practice may serve, its means of production are always unarguably material' (Williams, 1981: 87). Thus, the meanings of lived culture are to be explored within the context of their conditions of production, thus forming culture as 'a whole way of life'.

HIGH CULTURE/LOW CULTURE: AESTHETICS AND THE COLLAPSE OF BOUNDARIES

Leavis and Arnold's demarcation between the good and the bad, the high and low, centres on questions of aesthetic quality; that is, judgements about beauty, goodness and value. Historically, the policing of the boundaries of a canon of 'good works' has led to the exclusion of popular culture for judgements of quality have derived from an institutionalized and class-based hierarchy of cultural taste. Such a hierarchy, formed within particular social and historical contexts, is employed by its apologists as representative of a universal set of aesthetic criteria. However, judgements about aesthetic quality are always open to contestation and, with the passing of time and the increased interest in popular culture, a new set of theorists argued that there were no legitimate grounds for drawing the line between the worthy and the unworthy. Evaluation was not a sustainable task for the critic; rather, the obligation was to describe and analyse the production of meaning. This had the great merit of opening up a whole new array of texts for legitimate discussion, for example the soap opera (Brunsdon, 1990).

A question of quality

'Until recently', argues Allen, 'the aesthetic discourse on soap operas has been marked by near unanimous disdain of the form' (Allen, 1985: 11). For mainstream criticism, the romantic idea of the 'artistic object', produced by the 'artistic soul', is allied to a sense of the complexity and authenticity of the work of art and the necessary skill and work required by the readers to access a genuine aesthetic experience. From within this paradigm the soap opera, as an expression of mass culture, was seen as superficial and unsatisfying. However, neither the form of art nor its context can secure universal meaning. The concepts of beauty, harmony, form and quality can be applied as much to a steam train as to a novel or a painting.

Concepts of beauty, form and quality are culturally relative. Beauty in western thought may not be the same as that to be found in other cultures. Art can be understood as a socially created category which has attached itself to certain external and internal signals by which art is recognized. Hence the 'art gallery' and the theatre. Art as aesthetic quality is that which has been so labelled by western cultural and class elites. To see art as 'a uniquely different kind of work, with a unique, indeed transcendent, product is a mistaken notion, wrongly generalized and taken to be essential to the value of art' (Wolff, 1980: 17).

Popular cultural forms such as the television soap opera have been by-passed for social as much as 'creative' reasons. Further, we may note not just differences but similarities between high art and popular forms. Neither the *Mona Lisa* nor *Dallas* is the outcome of the mystical practices of geniuses; rather, each is the product of work, a human transformation of the material environment through labour. Art is an industry with its owners, managers and workers operating according to the law of profit every much as is popular culture and popular television. Thus, there is little justifiable ground for excluding the soap opera from the artistic domain on the grounds that art, i.e. aesthetic quality, is a different kind of activity.

Form and content

Many critics have argued that the quality work is that which is formally subtle, complex and the most adequate in its formal expression of content. However, the form–content division upon which this argument relies is hard to sustain for they are indistinguishable aspects of the same object. Alternatively, one might argue that the quality work is that which is most adequate and expressive in relation to its referent. That is, good art is superior to bad art in its illumination of the real world. However, many writers would have difficulty in supporting the **epistemology of realism** which underpins the argument. Art is not a copy of the world but a specific socially constructed representation.

Ideological analysis

The attempt to produce criteria for aesthetic judgements which apply in all times and places inevitably falls foul of relativism, that is, the argument that alternative criteria apply in different times and places. Consequently, rather than chase after universal aesthetic standards, cultural studies has developed arguments which revolve around the social and political consequences of constructing and disseminating specific discursive constructions of the world. Cultural studies has developed evaluative criteria based on political values and ideological analysis (rather than aesthetics) so that the role of criticism becomes the development of a more profound understanding of our cultural and symbolic processes and the way in which they are connected to social, political and economic **power** (Eagleton, 1984). From this perspective, it makes little sense to discuss whether culture is formally and aesthetically 'good' or 'bad'; rather, we need to consider, from an inevitably value-laden position, its ideological construction and potential consequences.

For example, Cantor (1991) argues that domestic drama on American television is primarily a morality play about how we should live; in particular about how to bring up children and what constitutes appropriate love relationships. What gets on air, she argues, are representations of mainstream norms. While there have been changes in the representation of families and an increase in the range of types of families, the ideal remains the married couple/nuclear family. Even with the development of 'off-beat' families in the American sitcom, problems are always resolved in terms of the values of caring, togetherness, love and peace. The consequences of television's discourse of the family may be to demonize the majority of us who do not live in nuclear families, to support the main institution of the patriarchal oppression of women and to suggest that we seek solutions to social problems within the family by making it responsible for 'crime' or 'social care'.

The problem of judgement

The relativity of 'value' within cultural studies leads discussion into a dilemma. On the one hand, there is a desire to legitimize popular and non-western culture as valuable in the face of a traditional western high cultural aesthetic discourse. On the other hand, there is a reluctance to sanction a position in which we are disbarred from making judgements, because it would mean that whatever was produced by corporations of the culture industries would be acceptable because popular. Hence the argument that discourses of power and their social and political consequences are the target for criticism. While we must still make value judgements about what are desirable consequences, these are political rather than aesthetic judgements. Moral and political judgements are ones which we cannot escape, nor should we seek to do so for human life is centrally concerned with decision-making based on our values.

The argument that a universal distinction between high culture and low culture is unsustainable, combined with the rise in visibility and status of popular culture, has led critics to suggest that 'High culture becomes just one more sub-culture, one more opinion, in our midst' (Chambers, 1986: 194). However, though cultural analysts may question the universal validity of high–low cultural boundaries, this does not mean that such distinctions are not actively utilized to maintain social power. As Pierre Bourdieu (1984) has argued, questions of taste and cultural judgement remain resources in the lines of class distinction and social power marking out class boundaries, cultural competencies and cultural capital.

Mass culture: popular culture

A variant of the high–low cultural boundary, and one which reproduces the 'inferiority' of the popular, is that which decries commodity-based culture as inauthentic, manipulative and unsatisfying. The argument is that commodified capitalist 'mass culture' is inauthentic because not produced by 'the people', manipulative because its primary purpose is to be purchased, and unsatisfying because, being easy to consume, it requires little work and fails to enrich its consumers. These views are held both by conservative critics like Leavis and by the Marxist-inspired Frankfurt School. Thus, Adorno and Horkheimer coined the phrase 'the Culture Industry' to suggest that culture is now totally interlocked with **political economy** and the production of culture by capitalist corporations. In this context, the authors seek to explore the meanings of mass-produced culture and the kinds of people and social order which, they claim, such a culture is implicated in.

CULTURE AS MASS DECEPTION

Adorno and Horkheimer's attitude towards mass culture is stated clearly and boldly in the title of their essay 'The Culture Industry – Enlightenment as Mass Deception' (Adorno and Horkheimer, 1979). They argue that cultural products are commodities produced by the Culture Industry, which, while purporting to be democratic, individualistic and diversified, is in actuality authoritarian, conformist and highly standardized. Thus 'Culture impresses the same stamp on everything. Films, radio and magazines make up a system which is uniform as a whole in every part' (Adorno and Horkheimer, 1979: 120). The apparent diversity of the products of the culture industries is an illusion for 'something is provided for all so none may escape' (Adorno and Horkheimer, 1979: 123).

Adorno (1941) regarded popular music, and jazz in particular, as stylized, lacking in originality and requiring little effort by its audience. For Adorno, the aim of standardized music is standardized reactions and the affirmation of life as it is. This is a matter not just of overt meanings, but of the structuring of the human psyche into conformist ways. Adorno displaces notions of ideology (as ideas) with those of Freudian psychology to argue that the Culture Industries, in tandem with the family, produce 'ego weakness' and the 'Authoritarian Personality'.

In contrast, critical art for Adorno is that which is not oriented to the market and challenges the standards of intelligibility of a reified society. For Adorno, an example would be the atonal music of Schoenberg, which, he argues, forces us to consider new ways of looking at the world. We may note that critique here is largely a question of form rather than content, specifically of non-realism and the 'alien' nature of art which inspires through its 'utopian negativity'.

CRITICISMS OF THE FRANKFURT SCHOOL

The Frankfurt School analysis is pessimistic, it holds to an overly monolithic view of the Culture Industries and denies the effectivity of popular **cultural politics**. Popular culture is regarded as inferior and contaminated both aesthetically and politically. The Frankfurt School share with Leavis, from whom they are otherwise quite different, a reliance on textual analysis. This they call 'immanent criticism', that is, the critique of the 'internal' meanings of cultural products. In doing so, the Frankfurt School make the assumption that meanings so identified are taken up by audiences in an unproblematic fashion. They are thus subject to the criticism that they overemphasize aesthetics and the internal construction of cultural products, *assuming* audience reaction from immanent criticism. This is a position challenged by later cultural studies research in the **active audience** paradigm. Indeed, the arguments which surround the Frankfurt School analysis are indicative of a wider debate between those who locate the generation of meaning at the level of production/text and those who perceive it at the moment of consumption.

CREATIVE CONSUMPTION

Consumption-oriented cultural studies argues that while the production of popular music, film, television and fashion is in the hands of transnational capitalist corporations, meanings are produced, altered and managed at the level of consumption by people who are active producers of meaning. This is particularly significant in an environment of 'semiotic excess' in which the widespread circulation of **polysemic** signs makes it harder for any dominant meaning to stick.

Writers like Chambers (1987, 1990), Fiske (1989a, 1989b) and Hebdidge (1988) have discussed creative meaning-producing activities of consumers who become bricoleurs, selecting and arranging elements of material commodities and meaningful signs. Likewise, Willis (1990) argues that, rather than being inherent in the commodity, meaning and value are constructed through actual usage. In general, it is argued that people range across a series of terrains and sites of meaning, which, though not of their own making, are ones within which they can actively produce sense.

> To a rationalized, expansionist and at the same time centralized, clamorous and spectacular production corresponds another production, called 'consumption'. The latter is devious, it is dispersed, but it insinuates itself everywhere, silently and almost invisibly, because it does not manifest itself through its own products, but rather through its ways of using the products imposed by a dominant economic order. (de Certeau, 1984: xii–xiii)

Following de Certeau, Fiske argues that popular culture is constituted by the meanings that people make with it rather than those identifiable within texts. While he is clear that popular culture is very largely produced by capitalist corporations, he 'focuses rather upon the popular tactics by which these forces are coped with, are evaded or are resisted' (Fiske, 1989a: 8). Fiske finds 'popular vitality and creativity' leading to 'the possibility of social change and the motivation to drive it' (Fiske, 1989a: 8). Further, he argues that 'between 80 and 90 per cent of new products fail despite extensive advertising'. His point is that the Culture Industries have to work hard to get us to consume mass culture. Consumers are not passive dopes but discriminating active producers of meaning. It is worth noting that while critics who stress production talk of 'mass culture', writers who stress consumption prefer to call it 'popular culture'. The very terms 'mass culture' and 'popular culture' are evaluative with regard to the worth of commodities and the capacities of consumers.

POPULAR CULTURE

There are a number of ways in which the term **popular culture** has been used (see Storey, 1993). For example, it may refer to that which is 'left over' after the canon of high culture has been decided upon or to the mass-produced culture of the Culture Industries. These perspectives chime with the work of Leavis and Adorno in regarding popular culture as inferior to its partner in the binary division. In taking popular culture seriously, cultural studies works against the grain of these elitist definitions.

An understanding of popular culture embraced by critics who dislike commodity culture but don't want to decry the popular completely is to contrast mass culture with an authentic folk culture produced by the people. Such a view haunts the search for a golden age exhibited by both conservative cultural theorists and left-learning critics of the **commodification** of culture. However, as Fiske argues, 'in capitalist societies there is no so-called authentic folk culture against which to measure the "inauthenticity" of mass culture, so bemoaning the loss of the authentic is a fruitless exercise in romantic nostalgia' (Fiske, 1989a: 27).

Popular culture is primarily a commercially produced one and there is no reason to think that this is likely to change in the foreseeable future. However, it is argued that popular audiences make their own meanings with the texts of popular culture and bring to bear their own cultural competencies and discursive resources. Popular culture is regarded as the meanings and practices produced by popular audiences at the moment of consumption and the study of popular culture becomes centred on the uses to which it is put. These arguments represent a reversal of the traditional question of how the culture industry turns people into commodities that serve its interests in favour of exploring how people turn the products of industry into their popular culture serving their interests.

THE POPULAR IS POLITICAL

Cultural studies works with a positive conception of popular culture which is both valued and critically analysed. Cultural studies rejects elitist notions of high–low culture or the critiques of mass culture. As McGuigan has argued, cultural studies has a populist bent where 'cultural populism is the intellectual assumption, made by some students of popular culture, that the symbolic experiences and practices of ordinary people are more important analytically and politically than culture with a capital C' (McGuigan, 1992: 4).

Popular culture is constituted through the production of popular meaning located at the moment of consumption. Such meanings are the site of contestation over cultural and political values. As Hall (1977, 1981, 1996c) has argued, popular culture is an arena of consent and resistance in the struggle over cultural meanings. It is the site where cultural hegemony is secured or challenged.

Hall returns us to a political conception of popular culture as a site for the struggle over meaning. Judgements about popular culture are concerned with questions not of cultural or aesthetic value (good or bad culture) but of power and the place of popular culture within the wider social formation. The concept of the popular challenges not only the distinctions between high and low culture but the very act of cultural classification by and through power (Hall, 1996e).

CULTURE AND THE SOCIAL FORMATION

The political conception of culture that cultural studies employs has its roots in debates about the place of culture in **social formation** and its relationship to other practices, notably economics and politics. This debate developed historically in the context of cultural studies' Marxist legacy.

Marxism and the metaphor of base and superstructure

Marxism, or historical materialism, is a philosophy which attempts to relate the production and reproduction of culture to the organization of the material conditions of life (Chapter 1). Culture is a corporeal force tied into the socially organized production of the material conditions of existence and refers to the forms assumed by social existence under determinate historical conditions. The idea that culture is determined by the production and organization of material existence has been articulated in Marxism through the metaphor of the base and the superstructure, which is drawn from the following passage.

> In the social production which men [sic] carry on they enter into definite relations that are indispensable and independent of their will; these relations of production correspond to a definite stage of development of their material powers of production. The totality of these relations of production constitute the economic structure of society – the real foundation, on which legal and political superstructures arise and to which definite forms of social consciousness correspond. The mode of production of material life determines the general character of the social, political and spiritual processes of life. It is not the consciousness of men that determines their being, but, on the contrary, their social being determines their consciousness. (Marx, 1961: 67)

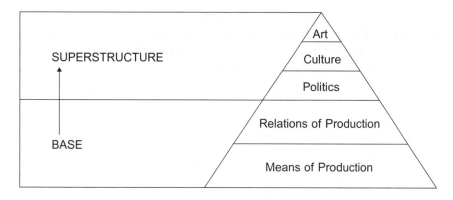

Note: Arrow indicates relations of determination.

Figure 2.1   *Base and superstructure in Marxist theory*

THE FOUNDATIONS OF CULTURE

A mode of production is constituted by the organization of the means of production (factories, machinery, etc.) and the specific social relations of reproduction (e.g. class) which arise from the organization of those productive forces. It is noteworthy that this mode of production is held to be 'the real foundation', of legal and political superstructures and that it '*determines*' the social, political and spiritual. Thus, the economic mode of production shapes the cultural superstructure (see Figure 2.1).

Culture, the consequence of a historically specific mode of production, is not a neutral terrain because 'the existing relations of production between individuals must necessarily express themselves also as political and legal relations' (Marx, 1961: 92). Culture is political because it is expressive of relations of power so that 'the ideas of the ruling class are, in every age, the ruling ideas, i.e., the class which is the dominant material force in society is at the same time its dominant intellectual force' (Marx, 1961: 93).

Further, the taken-for-granted nature of capitalist social relations in the sphere of the market obscures its exploitative base in the realm of production. The use of 'free' labour obscures economic exploitation, while apparent market sovereignty and equality (we are all consumers) obscures the 'real' foundations of inequality on the level of production. What is a historically specific set of social relations between people appears as a natural, universal set of relations between things, that is, contingent social relations are reified (naturalized as fixed things).

CULTURE AS CLASS POWER

In short, culture is political because it is expressive of social relations of class power in a way which naturalizes the social order as an inevitable 'fact', so obscuring the underlying relations of exploitation. As such, culture is ideological. By ideology is meant maps of meaning which, while they purport to be universal truths, are historically specific understandings which obscure and maintain power. Or, put more crudely, the ruling ideas are the ideas of the ruling class.

Expressed in this way, the relationship between the economic base and the cultural superstructure is a mechanical and economically deterministic one. By economic determinism is meant the idea that the profit motive and class relations *directly* determine the form and meaning of cultural products. Economic determinism would mean that because a television company is driven by the need to make a profit, all the programmes made within that company will be pro-capitalist. The influence of such a mechanistic and deterministic model has long waned in cultural studies. Rather, the narrative of cultural studies involves a moving away from economic **reductionism** towards an analysis of the autonomous logics of language, culture, representation and consumption. This has been the subject of much debate within cultural studies.

THE SPECIFICITY OF CULTURE

Most thinkers in cultural studies have rejected economic reductionism as simplistic in failing to grant cultural practices any specificity of their own. While the analysis of economic determinants may be necessary to any understanding of culture, it is not, and cannot be, self-sufficient. We need to examine cultural phenomena in terms of their own rules, logics, development and effectivity. This points to the desirability of a multidimensional and multiperspectival approach to the understanding of culture which would seek to grasp the connections between economic, political, social and cultural dimensions without reducing social phenomena to any one level. Here, the work of Raymond Williams (1965, 1979, 1981, 1989) again proved to be an influential in developing a non-reductionist understanding of the relationship between the material/economic and the cultural.

Williams: totality and the variable distances of practices

For Williams (1981), culture is both constitutive of and expressive of a social totality of human relations and practices. He discusses the relations between the economic and the cultural in terms of 'setting limits'. By this he means that the economic sets limits to what can be done or expressed in culture but does not determine in a direct one-to-one relationship the meaning of cultural practices. Williams speaks of 'the variable distance of practices', by which he means that the social relationships embedded in the wage labour process and the ownership of the means of production are the critical and dominant set of social relations. Other relations and practices are set at 'variable distances' from this central set of practices allowing for degrees of determination, autonomy and specificity. In short, the closer a cultural practice is to the central economic relations, the more it will be directly determined by them. The further cultural practices are away from the core capitalist production process, the more they can operate with their own autonomous logic. By this reasoning, individually produced art is more autonomous than mass-produced television.

Williams' arguments are suggestive and represent a move away from crude economic reductionism. However, while the production of television may be more embedded in capitalist production than painting, it is by no means certain that painting is any the less ideological or political. Nor does 'setting limits' tell us much about the form that television takes and why it is different from painting. Williams understood this and devoted much time to analysing the specificity of cultural forms. However, he did not adequately resolve or conceptualize the relationship between culture and economics.

Within Williams' schema, a crude base–superstructure model has been displaced in favour of a conception of society as an 'expressive totality' in which all practices – political, economic, ideological – interact, mediate and affect each other. As Hall (1992a) has remarked, the phase of theoretical development within cultural studies which followed Williams' culturalism can be identified with influences which interrupted this search for underlying totalities. This is the moment of **structuralism** (Chapters 1 and 3) in cultural studies and, in particular, of Althusser's structuralist Marxism.

Relative autonomy and the specificity of cultural practices

Structuralism describes social formations as constituted by complex **structure**s or regularities. These are analysed in terms of the various elements that make up structures and the way in which they are articulated or linked together. Rather than dissolve culture back into the economic (as in a base–superstructure model), the emphasis is on the irreducible character of the cultural as a set of distinct practices with their own internal organization or structuration. Structuralism is concerned with how cultural meaning is produced, regarding culture as analogous to (or structured like) a language.

ALTHUSSER AND THE SOCIAL FORMATION

Althusser (1969, 1971) conceived of a social formation not as a totality of which culture is an expression, but as a complex structure of different instances (levels or practices) which are 'structured in dominance'. That is, the different instances of politics, economics and ideology are articulated together to form a unity which is the result not of a single one-way base–superstructure determination, but of determinations emanating from different levels so that a social formation is the outcome of 'over-determination'. By this is meant the idea that any given practice or instant is the outcome of many different determinations. These distinct determinations are levels or types of practice with their own logic and specificity which cannot be reduced to, or explained by, other levels or practices.

This formulation was hailed by Hall (1972) as a 'seminal advance' because it allows us to examine a cultural phenomenon as a separate signifying system with its own effects and determinations irreducible to the economic. Indeed, the cultural and ideological can be seen as constitutive of our understandings of what the economic is.

RELATIVE AUTONOMY

Despite the specificity granted to different levels or practices, Althusser does not grant each instance total autonomy but gives to the economic level determination in the 'last instance'. Culture is then 'relatively autonomous' from the economic (a rather vague and problematic formulation which was once the subject of considerable debate). Althusser gives an example of what is meant when he explains that in the context of feudal societies it was politics, and not economics, which was the dominant and determining instance, but that this was itself a result of economic determination 'in the last instance'. That is, it was the very mode of economic organization of feudal society, its mode of production, which determined that politics became the dominant practice.

Though the intricacies of the Althusserian debate no longer command much attention within cultural studies, the attempt to get away from economic reductionism by conceiving of social formations in terms of relatively autonomous practices articulated

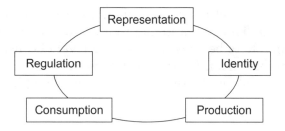

Figure 2.2   *The circuit of culture (modified from Du Gay et al., 1997)*

together in complex and unevenly determining ways has been of lasting significance. For example, it is the basis of Hall's formulation that: 'We must "think" a society or social formation as ever and always constituted by a set of complex practices; each with its own specificity, its own modes of articulation; standing in an "uneven development" to other related practices' (Hall, 1977: 237). By **articulation** is meant a temporary unity of discursive elements which do not have to 'go together'. An articulation is the form of the connection that *can* make a unity of two different elements, under certain conditions. Articulation suggests both expressing/representing and a joining together. Here, that unity thought of as 'society' is considered to be the unique historically specific temporary stabilization of the relations and meanings of different levels of a social formation (Chapters 3 and 12).

ARTICULATION AND THE CIRCUIT OF CULTURE

In a recent formulation of the issues, Hall and his colleagues (Du Gay et al., 1997) discuss the 'circuit of culture' and the articulation of production and consumption. In this model, cultural meaning is produced and embedded at each level of the circuit whose meaningful work is necessary, but not sufficient for or determining of, the next moment in the circuit. Each moment – production, representation, identity, consumption and regulation – involves the production of meaning which is articulated, linked with, the next moment without determining what meanings will be taken up or produced at that level (see Figure 2.2).

For example, the Sony Walkman is analysed in terms of the meanings embedded at the level of design and production, which are modified by the creation of new meanings as the Walkman is represented in advertising. In turn, the meanings produced through representation connect with, and help constitute, the meaningful identities of Walkman users. Meanings embedded at the moments of production and representation may or may not be taken up at the level of consumption, where new meanings are again produced. Thus, meanings produced at the level of production are available to be worked on at the level of consumption but do not determine them. Further, representation and consumption shape the level of production through, for example, design and marketing.

TWO ECONOMIES

While Hall maintains the need to understand the articulation of the different moments of the cultural circuit, other writers wishing to maintain a non-reductionist stance have separated the realms of the economic and cultural/ideological altogether. For example, Fiske (1987, 1989a, 1989b) describes two separate economies: a financial economy of production and a cultural economy of consumption. The former is primarily concerned with money and the exchange value of commodities while the later is the site of cultural meanings, pleasures and social identities. While the financial economy 'needs to be taken into account' in any investigation of the cultural, it does not determine it nor invalidate the power audiences have as producers of meaning at the level of consumption. Indeed, popular culture is seen as a site of semiotic warfare and of popular tactics deployed to evade or resist the meanings produced and inscribed in commodities by producers.

Throughout this debate the concept of **ideology** played a crucial mediating role between the economic and the cultural. As Turner (1990) has commented, ideology was perhaps the most important concept in the foundation of British cultural studies, which for a while could be seen as 'ideological studies'.

THE QUESTION OF IDEOLOGY

The Marxist concern with the concept of ideology was rooted in the failure of proletarian revolutions to materialize and the inadequacy of historical materialism in relation to questions of **subjectivity**, meaning and cultural politics. Put simply, the concern with ideology began as an exploration into why **capitalism**, which was held to be an exploitative system of economic and social relations, was not being overthrown by working-class revolution. Was the failure of proletarian revolution therefore a failure of the proletariat to correctly understand the world they lived in? Did the working class suffer from 'false consciousness', that is, a mistakenly bourgeois world view which served the interest of the capitalist class?

Marxism and false consciousness

There are two aspects of Marx's writing which might be grounds for pursuing a line of thought which stresses 'false consciousness'. First, Marx (1961; Marx and Engels, 1970) argues that the dominant ideas in any society are the ideas of the ruling class. Second, he suggests that what we perceive to be the true character of social relations within capitalism are in actuality the mystifications of the market. That is, we accept the idea that we are free to sell our labour, and that we get a fair price for it, since this is the way the social world appears to us. However, Marx argues that capitalism involves exploitation at the level of production through the extraction of surplus value from the proletariat. Consequently, the appearance of market relations of equality obscures the deep structures of exploitation.

We have two versions of ideology here both functioning to legitimate the sectional interests of powerful classes, namely:

- ideas as coherent statements about the world and the dominance of bourgeois or capitalist ideas;
- world views which are the systematic outcome of the structures of capitalism which lead us to inadequate understandings of the social world.

For Marxism, ideas are not independent of the material and historical circumstances of their production. On the contrary, people's attitudes and beliefs are held to be systematically and structurally related to the material conditions of existence. However, this broad conception of ideas and material circumstances leaves crucial questions unanswered.

- Just how are ideas related to the material conditions of existence?
- If a base–superstructure model is inadequate, as most thinkers within cultural studies would say, then what kind of relationship do ideas have to material conditions?
- To what extent is it the case that ideology is 'false'?
- Can we all be said to be living false lives? How would we know?
- Who has the ability to perceive the 'truth' and separate it from ideology? How would that be possible?
- If the problem of ideology is not so much truth *per se*, but adequacy, that is to say, ideology is not so much false but partial, from what vantage point would an adequate explanation be forthcoming?

These are the kinds of questions which the concept of ideology poses for us as it was developed by the influential thinkers Althusser and Gramcsi.

Althusser and ideology

For Althusser, ideology is one of the three primary instances or levels of a social formation. As such, ideology is relatively autonomous from other levels (e.g. the economic), though determined by it 'in the last instance'. Here ideology, 'a system (with its own logic and rigour) of representations (images, myths, ideas or concepts)' (Althusser, 1969: 231), is conceived as a practice which is lived and transforms the material world. There are four aspects of Althusser's work which are core to his view of ideology:

- Ideology has the general function of constituting subjects.
- Ideology as lived experience is not false.
- Ideology as misrecognition of the real conditions of existence is false.
- Ideology is involved in the reproduction of social formations and their relations of power.

IDEOLOGICAL STATE APPARATUSES

For Althusser, our entry into the **symbolic** order (of languages), and thus our constitution as subjects (persons), is the work of ideology. In his essay 'Ideology and the Ideological State Apparatuses' (Althusser, 1971), he argues that 'ideology hails or interpellates concrete individuals as concrete subjects'. Ideology 'has the function of constituting concrete individuals as subjects'. This argument is an aspect of Althusser's anti-humanism whereby the subject is seen not as a self-constituting agent but as the 'effect' of structures. In this case, it is the work of ideology to bring a subject into being because 'there is no practice except by and in ideology'. In short, ideological discourse constructs **subject positions** or places for the subject from which the world makes sense.

Subjects are the effects of **discourse** because subjectivity is constituted by the positions which discourse obliges us (because we are constituted in and by discourse) to take up. Discourse refers to production of knowledge through language which gives meaning to both material objects and social practices (Chapter 3). Since discourse constructs, defines and produces objects of knowledge in an intelligible way, while at the same time excluding other ways of reasoning as unintelligible, it is ideological because partial. Further, the incomplete ways of understanding the world into which subjects are constituted serves to reproduce the social order and the interests of powerful classes.

FRAGMENTED SUBJECTS

Within the Althusserian paradigm, subjects formed in ideology are not unitary wholes but fragmented subjects who take up plural subject positions. For example, class is not an objective economic fact but a discursively formed collective subject position. Consequently, class consciousness is neither an inevitability nor a unified phenomenon. Classes, while sharing certain common conditions of existence, do not automatically form a core unified class consciousness but are cross-cut by conflicting interests as they are formed and unformed in the course of actual historical development. Class consciousness is likely to be cross-cut by questions of gender, race and age, at the very least.

THE DOUBLE CHARACTER OF IDEOLOGY

Ideology is double-edged for Althusser. On the one hand, it constitutes the real conditions of people's lives, it constitutes the world views by which people live and experience the world. In that sense, ideology is not false for it forms the very categories and systems of representation by which social groups render the world intelligible. Ideology is lived experience. On the other hand, ideology is also conceived of as a more elaborate set of meanings which make sense of the world (an ideological discourse) in ways which misrecognize and misrepresent power and class relations. Ideology is said to represent the imaginary relationship of individuals to their real conditions of existence. Thus, if I mistake the class relations of exploitation within capitalism for the free and equal relations of humans to each other, then I am subject to and subjected by the illusions and delusions of ideology.

For Althusser, ideology exists in an apparatus and its associated practices; consequently, he goes on to designate a series of institutions, primarily the family, the education system, the church and the mass media, as 'ideological state apparatuses' (ISAs). While he regards the church as the dominant pre-capitalist ISA, he argues that within the context of capitalism it has been replaced by the educational system, which is implicated in the ideological (and physical) reproduction of labour power and the social relations of production. Ideology, he argues, is a far more effective means for the maintenance of class power than physical force.

For Althusser, education not only transmits a general ruling-class ideology which justifies and legitimates capitalism, it also reproduces the attitudes and behaviour required by major class groups within the division of labour. Ideology teaches workers to accept and submit to their own exploitation while teaching managers and administrators to practise the craft of ruling on behalf of the dominant class. According to Althusser, each class is practically provided with the ideology required to fulfil its role class society. Further, ideology performs the function of what Poulantzas (1976) called 'separation and uniting': it masks the 'real' exploitative foundations of production by displacing the emphasis of thought from production to exchange, stressing the character of people as individuals thereby fragmenting a vision of class. It then welds individuals back together again in an imaginary coherence as a passive community of consumers or behind the concept of nation.

ALTHUSSER AND CULTURAL STUDIES

The influence of Althusserms work was significant in elevating the debate about ideology to the forefront of thinking within cultural studies. Further, the legacy of Althusserian thinking about social formations as a complex structure of related but relatively autonomous instances can be seen in the work of Stuart Hall, Ernesto Laclau and Chantal Mouffe, amongst others (below and Chapter 12). However, much of Althusser's thinking about ideology is now regarded as problematic.

- Althusser's view of the operation of ISAs is too functionalist in orientation. Ideology appears to function behind people's backs in terms of the 'needs' of an agentless system. The Althusserian formulation of the question of ideology is also too coherent (despite the fragmented character of the subject) since the educational system, for example, is the site of contradictory ideologies and of ideological *conflict* rather than a place for the unproblematic and homogeneous reproduction of capitalist ideology.
- Althusser's formulation of the place of ideology within a social formation, that is, as relatively autonomous but determined in the last instance, is imprecise and threatens to return analysis to the very economic reductionism that it hoped to escape.
- Althusser's work is dogged by an important epistemological problem, that is, a problem of truth and knowledge. If we are all formed in ideology, how can a non-ideological view be generated which would allow us to deconstruct ideology or even recognize it as such? Althusser's answer, that the rigours of science (and of his science in particular) can expose ideology, is both elitist and untenable (see Chapter 3).

Though the work of Gramsci was written prior to Althusser's, its influence within cultural studies post-dates the former's enterprise (itself indebted to Gramsci). Indeed, the popularity of Gramsci within cultural studies was in partial response to the problems of Althusserian theory. In particular, Gramsci appeared to offer a more flexible, sophisticated and practical account of the character and workings of ideology.

Gramsci, ideology and hegemony

Culture is constructed in terms of a multiplicity of streams of meaning and encompasses a range of ideologies and cultural forms. However, it is argued (Williams, 1973, 1979, 1981; Hall, 1977, 1981) that there is a strand of meanings which can be called dominant or ascendant. The process of making, maintaining and reproducing these authoritative set of meanings and practices has, after Gramsci (1968), been called **hegemony**.

CULTURAL AND IDEOLOGICAL HEGEMONY

For Gramsci, hegemony implies a situation where a 'historical bloc' of ruling-class factions exercise social authority and leadership over the subordinate classes through a combination of force and, more importantly, consent (see also Chapter 12). Thus,

> the normal exercise of hegemony on the classical terrain of the parliamentary regime is characterized by the combination of force and consent, which balance each other reciprocally without force predominating excessively over consent. Indeed, the attempt is always to ensure that force would appear to be based on the consent of the majority expressed by the so-called organs of public opinion – newspapers and associations. (Gramsci, 1971: 80)

Within Gramscian analysis, ideology is understood in terms of ideas, meanings and practices which, while they purport to be universal truths, are maps of meaning which support the power of particular social groups. Above all, ideology is not separate from the practical activities of life but is a material phenomenon rooted in day-to-day conditions. Ideologies provide people with rules of practical conduct and moral behaviour equivalent 'to a religion understood in the secular sense of a unity of faith between a conception of the world and a corresponding norm of conduct' (Gramsci, 1971: 349). The representation of the formal education system as a meritocracy which offers all an equal chance in a fair society and the representation of people of colour as by 'nature' inferior and less capable than white people could both be described as ideological.

A hegemonic bloc never consists of a single socio-economic category but is formed through a series of alliances in which one group takes on a position of leadership. Ideology plays a crucial part in allowing this alliance of groups (originally conceived in class terms) to overcome narrow economic–corporate interest in favour of 'national–popular' dominance. Thus, 'a cultural–social unity' is achieved 'through which a multiplicity of dispersed wills, with heterogeneous aims, are welded together with a single aim, as the basis of an equal and common conception of the world' (Gramsci, 1971: 349). The building, maintenance or subversion of a common conception of the world is an aspect of ideological struggle involving a transformation of understanding through criticism of the existing popular ideologies.

IDEOLOGY AND POPULAR CULTURE

Ideology is lived experience and a body of systematic ideas whose role is to organize and bind together a bloc of diverse social elements, to act as social cement, in the formation of hegemonic and counter-hegemonic blocs. Though ideology can take the form of a coherent set of ideas, it more often appears as the fragmented meanings of common sense inherent in a variety of representations.

For Gramsci, all people reflect upon the world and, through the 'common sense' of popular culture, organize their lives and experience. Thus, common sense becomes a crucial site of ideological conflict and, in particular, the struggle to forge 'good sense', which, for Gramsci, is the recognition of the class character of capitalism. Common sense is the most significant site of ideological struggle because it is the terrain of the 'taken-for-granted', a practical consciousness which guides the actions of the everyday world. More coherent sets of philosophical ideas are contested and transformed in the domain of common sense. Thus, Gramsci is concerned with the character of popular thought and popular culture.

> Every philosophical current leaves behind it a sediment of 'common sense'; this is the document of its historical effectiveness. Common sense is not rigid and immobile but is continually transforming itself, enriching itself with scientific ideas and with philosophical opinions which have entered ordinary life. Common sense creates the folklore of the future, that is as a relatively rigid phase of popular knowledge at a given place and time. (Gramsci, 1971: 362)

THE INSTABILITY OF HEGEMONY

Hegemony can be understood in terms of the strategies by which the world views and power of ascendant social groups (be they class, sexual, ethnic or nationally constituted) is maintained. However, this has to be seen in relational terms and as inherently unstable. Hegemony is a *temporary* settlement and series of alliances between social groups which is won and not given. Further, it needs to be constantly rewon, renegotiated, so that culture is a terrain of conflict and struggle over meanings. Hegemony is not a static entity but a series of changing discourses and practices intrinsically bound up with social power. Gramsci characterizes hegemony as 'a continuous process of formation and superseding of unstable equilibria . . . between the interests of the funda- mental group and those of the subordinate groups . . . equilibria in which the interests of the dominant group prevail, but only up to a certain point' (Gramsci, 1968: 182).

Since hegemony has to be constantly remade and rewon, it opens up the possibility of a challenge to it, that is, the making of a counter-hegemonic bloc of subordinate groups and classes. For Gramsci, such a counter-hegemonic struggle must seek to gain ascendancy within civil society (affiliations outside of formal state boundaries including the family, social clubs, the press, leisure activities, etc.) before any attempt is made on state power. Gramsci makes a distinction between the 'war of position', which is the winning of hegemony within the sphere of civil society, and the 'war of manoeuvre', which is the assault on state power. For Gramsci, success in 'the war of manoeuvre' is dependent on attaining hegemony through the 'war of position'.

GRAMSCIAN CULTURAL STUDIES

The introduction and deployment of Gramscian concepts within cultural studies proved to be of long-lasting significance (see Chapter 12), not least because of the central importance given to popular culture as a site of ideological struggle. In effect, Gramsci makes ideological struggle and conflict within civil society the central arena of cultural politics, with hegemonic analysis the mode of gauging the relevant balance of forces. Gramsci's argu- ment that 'it would be interesting to study concretely the forms of cultural organization which keep the ideological world in move- ment within a given country and to examine how they function in practice' (Gramsci, cited Bennett et al., 1981: 195–6) could be read as a virtual campaign slogan for cultural studies, at least until the debates about **poststructuralism** and **postmodernism** gained ascendancy (Chapters 5 and 12).

For example, early work on advertising was cast within the problematic of ideology and hegemony. Textual and ideological analysis of advertising stressed the selling not just of commodities but of ways of looking at the world. The job of advertising was to create an 'identity' for a product amid the bombardment of com- peting images by associating the brand with desirable human values. Buying a brand was not only about buying a product but about buying into lifestyles and values. As Winship argues 'A woman is nothing more than the commodities she wears: the lipstick, the tights, the clothes and so on are "woman"' (Winship, 1981: 218).

For Williamson (1978), objects in advertisements are signifiers of meaning which we decode in the context of known cultural systems associating products in adverts with other cultural 'goods'. While an image of a particular product may denote only beans or a car, it is made to connote 'nature' or 'family' so that advertising creates a world of differences between products and lifestyles which we 'buy into'. In buying the products we buy the image and so contribute to the construction of our identities through consumption. For Williamson, advertising is ideological in its obscuring of economic inequality at the level of production by images of free and equal consumption.

The problem of ideology

Although neo-Gramscian hegemony theory has been a strong mode of analysis within cultural studies since the late 1970s, it has not gone unchallenged. Collins (1989) rejects the notion of hegemony on the grounds that culture no longer has a dominant centre in terms of either production or meaning. Rather, culture is heterogeneous in terms both of the different kinds of texts produced and the different meanings that compete within texts. Abercrombie et al. (1980) reject what they call the 'dominant ideology thesis' on the grounds that there is no coherent dominant culture and that power is primarily economic and social not cultural. That is, the brute force of economic necessity is quite sufficient to explain the lack of radical working-class political activity without recourse to the concept of ideology.

IDEOLOGY AS POWER

The whole concept of ideology has come under scrutiny for it involves at least two central problems:

- the problem of *scope*;
- the problem of *truth*.

Early Marxist and sociological versions of the concept of ideology restricted its usage to ideas associated with, and maintaining the power of, the dominant class. Later, more extended versions of the concept added questions of **gender**, **ethnicity**, age, etc., to that of class. Giddens' argument that ideology be understood in terms of 'How structures of signification are mobilized to legitimate the sectional interests of hegemonic groups

(Giddens, 1979: 6) is a contemporary definition of ideology which follows these lines. In other words, ideology refers to the way meaning is used to justify the power of ascendant groups which encompasses classes but also includes social groups based on race, gender, age, etc.

While Giddens' definition of ideology refers only to the ideas of the powerful, other versions, including Althusser's, see ideology as justifying the actions of *all* groups of people. In other words, marginal and subordinate groups also have ideologies in the sense of organizing and justifying ideas about themselves and the world. Of course, this wider version of the concept of ideology can also embrace the narrower one in that we are all, as Foucault (1980) argued, implicated in power relations. The difference between the dominant and subordinate groups is therefore one of degrees of power and differing substantive world views, not of ideological versus non-ideological ideas.

IDEOLOGY AND MISRECOGNITION

The second fundamental problem with the concept of ideology refers to its epistemological status, that is, the relation of ideology to **truth** and knowledge. These questions will be discussed at greater length in Chapters 3 and 5. However, we may note that ideology has commonly been counterpoised to truth so that, for example, Althusser compares ideology with science, casting the former as 'misrecognition'. However, science is a mode of thinking and a set of procedures which produces certain kinds of knowledge; it is not an elevated God-like form of knowledge which produces objective truth beyond dispute. No universally accurate picture of the world is possible, only degrees of agreement about what counts as truth. For this reason, thinkers like Foucault (1980) and Rorty (1989, 1991a, 1991b) have rejected the concept of ideology altogether.

Foucault certainly regards knowledge as implicated with power, hence his concept of **power/knowledge**. By power/knowledge is meant a mutually constituting relationship between power and knowledge so that knowledge is indissociable from regimes of power. Knowledge is formed within the context of the relationships and practices of power and subsequently contributes to the development, refinement and proliferation of new techniques of power. However, no simple uncontaminated 'truth' can be counterpoised to power/knowledge for there is no truth outside of it.

Rorty (1989) understands knowledge to be a series of descriptions of the world which have practical consequences. They can be judged in terms of values but not in terms of absolute truths. For

Rorty, 'truth' is a social commendation, that which we think 'good', rather than universal knowledge. Consequently, while one can compare world views (ideologies) in terms of their values, consequences and social/historical conditions of production, we cannot do so in terms of ultimate truth versus untruth.

WHAT IS IDEOLOGY?

Assuming that ideology is not confined to questions of class, and few would argue that it should be, then ideology can be seen in the following ways:

- world views of dominant groups which justify and maintain their power and which are counterposed to truth;
- world views of any social groups which justify their actions and which are counterposed to truth;
- world views of dominant groups which justify and maintain their power but which cannot be counterposed to truth; however, they can be subject to redescription and thus do not have to be accepted;
- world views of any social groups which justify their actions but which cannot be counterposed to truth; however, they can be subject to redescription and thus do not have to be accepted.

It would be unwise to suggest that any particular version of ideology is the 'correct' one or even the most commonly deployed one within cultural studies. Rather, if writers use the concept it is beholden on them to clarify what they mean by the term. My own view is that it is untenable to counterpoise the concept of ideology to truth (see Chapter 3) and that all social groups have ideologies. In this sense, the only acceptable concept of ideology is one which is interchangeable with the Foucauldian notion of power/knowledge. As such, ideology cannot be seen as a simple tool of domination but should be regarded as discourses which have specific *consequences* for relations of power at all levels of social relationships (including the justification and maintenance of ascendant groups).

SUMMARY

The first story of cultural studies concerns the move from perceiving culture as the 'arts' to seeing culture as being 'ordinary', encapsulating 'a whole way of life', that is, from a broadly literary to an anthropological definition. The second story concerns the place of culture in a social formation, that is, the relationship of culture to other social practices such as the economic and the political. Cultural studies has rejected the idea of culture as *determined* by economic forces in favour of understanding it as an *autonomous* set of meanings and practices with its own logic. This logic is paralleled by the transformation of culture as a concept from the margins of the humanities and social sciences to one at its very heart.

Definitions of culture are all contestable, but a widely accepted way of understanding it within cultural studies is in terms of 'maps of meaning'. Cultural studies asks questions about which meanings are put in to circulation, by whom, for what purposes and in whose interests. For, as Fiske (1992) has argued, the concept of culture within cultural studies is above all a political one concerned with questions of *power*. Consequently, much of cultural studies has been centred on questions of power, knowledge, ideology and hegemony.

Considerations of meaning have led cultural studies to be concerned with how our maps are produced and hence to culture as a set of **signifying practices**, that is, the organization of signs that generate meaning. The primary sign system in operation is language, which has led theorists to the idea of discourses or regulated ways of speaking. In short, cultural studies, along with the whole of the humanities and social sciences, has taken a 'linguistic turn', the subject of Chapter 3.

3
Culture, Meaning, Knowledge: The Linguistic Turn in Cultural Studies

The significance of language for an understanding of **culture** and the construction of knowledge has risen to the top of the agenda within cultural studies and the 'human social sciences'. This is for two central and related reasons:

- Language is the privileged medium in which cultural meanings are formed and communicated.
- Language is the means and medium through which we form knowledge about ourselves and the **social** world.

Language is not a neutral medium for the formation and transfer of values, meanings and knowledges which exist beyond its boundaries; rather, language is *constitutive* of those very values, meanings and knowledges. That is, language gives meaning to material objects and social practices which are brought into view and made intelligible to us in terms which language delimits. Language is not best understood as an innocent reflection of non-linguistic meaning, nor simply in terms of the intentions of language users. Rather, language constructs meaning. It structures which meanings can or cannot be deployed under determinate circumstances by speaking subjects. To understand culture is to explore how meaning is produced symbolically through the **signifying practices** of language. This has been the domain of semiotics, broadly understood as the study of signs, and developed from the pioneering work of Saussure.

SAUSSURE AND SEMIOTICS

Saussure is a founding figure of **structuralism** because he explains the generation of meaning by reference to a system of structured differences in language. He explores the rules and conventions which organize language (*langue*) rather than the specific uses and utterances which individuals deploy in everyday life (*parole*). Saussure, and structuralism in general, is more concerned with the **structure**s of language than actual performance. Structuralism is concerned with how cultural meaning is produced, holding it to be structured 'like a language'. A structuralist understanding of culture is concerned with 'systems of relations' of an underlying structure which forms the grammar which makes meaning possible.

Signifying systems

Saussure (1960) argued that language does not reflect a pre-existent and external reality of independent objects but constructs meaning from within itself through a series of conceptual and phonic differences. In language, he argued, there are only differences without positive terms. For Saussure, a signifying system is constituted by a series of **signs** which are analysed in terms of their constituent parts, the **signifier** and the signified. A signifier is taken to be the form or medium of signs, for example a sound, an image, the marks that form a word on the page, while the **signified** has been understood in terms of concepts and meanings. The relationship between the sounds and marks of language, the signifiers, and what it is taken to mean, the signified, is not held in any fixed eternal relationship. Rather, their arrangement is *arbitrary* in the sense that the animal we call a 'cat' as it sits on the 'mat' could equally be signified by 'tac' and 'tam' or by 'el gato' and 'la estera'.

According to Saussure, meaning is produced through the process of selection and combination of signs along the syntagmatic and paradigmatic axis. The syntagmatic axis is constituted by the linear combination of signs which form sentences. Paradigmatic refers to the field of signs (i.e. synonyms) from which any given sign is selected. Meaning is accumulated along the syntagmatic axis, while selection from the paradigmatic field alters meaning at any given point in the sentence. Hartley (1982: 20) offers the following example:

(*Paradigmatic*)
Soldiers
Freedom fighters
Terrorists
$\longrightarrow \longrightarrow \longrightarrow \longrightarrow$ Today attacked $\longrightarrow$ (*Syntagmatic*) $\longrightarrow$
Volunteers   liberated
Gunmen

On the paradigmatic axis, the selection of freedom fighter or terrorist is of meaningful significance. It alters what we understand the character of the participants to be and will influence the combination along the syntagmatic axis since it is by convention unlikely, though grammatically acceptable, to combine terrorist with liberated.

The arbitrary character of the signifier–signified relationship suggests that meaning is fluid, being culturally and historically specific, rather than fixed and universal. However, the fact that terrorist and liberated is a rare combination also suggests that meaning is *regulated* under specific historical social conditions. As Culler puts it, 'Because it is arbitrary, the sign is totally subject to history and the combination at the particular moment of a given signifier and signified is a contingent result of the historical process' (Culler, 1976: 36).

Cultural codes

A 'classic' illustration of semiotic arguments concerns the organization and regulation of colours into the cultural **code** of traffic lights. Colours are breaks in the light spectrum which we classify with signs such as red, green, amber, and so forth. There is, of course, no universal reason why the sign 'red' should refer to a specific colour; rather, the relationship is arbitrary. The 'same' colour can be designated by the sign 'rojo'. It is central to Saussure's argument that red is meaningful *in relation* to the difference between red, green, amber, etc. These signs are then organized into a sequence which generates meaning through the cultural *conventions* of their usage within a particular context. Thus, traffic lights deploy 'red' to signify 'stop' and 'green' to signify 'go'. This is the cultural code of traffic systems which temporally fixes the relationship between colours and meanings. Signs become naturalized codes. The apparent transparency of meaning (we 'know' when to stop or go) is an outcome of cultural habituation, the effect of which is to conceal the practices of cultural coding.

Saussure's contribution was to the study of a narrowly defined field of linguistics. Nevertheless, he predicted the possibility of a wider 'science that studies the life of signs within society'. This because cultural objects convey meaning and all cultural practices depend on meanings generated by signs. Consequently, culture is said to work 'like a language' and all cultural practices are open to semiotic analysis. Thus, Barthes (1967, 1972) takes Saussure's approach, amends it, and applies it to the practices of **popular culture** with an eye to showing how such events generate meaning.

BARTHES AND MYTHOLOGY

Barthes argues that we can talk of two systems of **signification**: denotation and connotation. Denotation is the descriptive and literal level of meaning shared by virtually all members of a culture. Thus, 'pig' denotes the concept of a useful pink farm animal with a snout and curly tail, etc. At the second level, connotation, meanings are generated by connecting signifiers to wider cultural concerns: the beliefs, attitudes, frameworks and ideologies of a social formation. Meaning becomes a matter of the association of signs with other cultural codes of meaning. Thus, 'pig' may connote nasty police officer or male chauvinist according to the sub-codes or lexicons at work.

Meaning is said to multiply up from a given sign until a single sign is loaded with manifold meanings. Connotation carries expressive value arising from the cumulative force of a sequence (syntagmatically) or, more usually, by comparison with absent alternatives (paradigmatically). Where connotations have become naturalized as hegemonic, that is, accepted as 'normal' and 'natural', they act as conceptual maps of meaning by which to make sense of the world. These are **myths**. Though myths are cultural constructions, they may appear to be pre-given universal truths embedded in common sense. Myths are thus akin to the concept of **ideology**, which, it is argued, works at the level of connotation. Indeed, Volosinov (1973) was to argue that the domain of ideology corresponds to the field of signs. Where there are signs, so there is ideology.

For Barthes, myth is a second-order semiological system or metalanguage. It is a second language which speaks about a first-level language. The sign of the first system (signifier and signified) which generates denotative meaning becomes a signifier for a second order of connotative mythological meaning. Barthes (1972) represents this as a spatialized metaphor (Figure 3.1).

'Myth Today'

In his essay 'Myth Today', Barthes gives an often quoted example of the work of signification, myth and ideology. The example refers to the cover of the French magazine *Paris Match* featuring a young black soldier in French military uniform saluting the

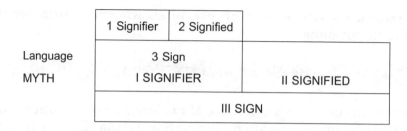

Figure 3.1   *Barthes: the signification of myth*

tricolour. His eyes are cast upward towards the French flag. On a denotative level this can be read as 'a black soldier salutes the French flag'. However, the repertoire of cultural codes available to Barthes and his contemporaries (which included French colonial history and their military involvement in Algiers) allowed him to interpret the image in more ideological way. That is, the connotations of the image suggest the loyalty of black French subjects to the French flag, undermining criticism of French imperial activity. As Barthes explains;

> I am at the barber's, and a copy of *Paris Match* is offered to me. On the cover, a young Negro in a French uniform is saluting, with his eyes uplifted, probably fixed on the fold of the tricolour. All this is the meaning of the picture. But, whether naïvely or not, I see very well what it signifies to me: that France is a great Empire, that all her sons, without colour discrimination, faithfully serve under the flag, and that there is no better answer to the detractors of an alleged colonialism than the zeal shown by this Negro in serving his so-called oppressors. (Barthes, 1972: 125–6)

According to Barthes, myth and ideology work by *naturalizing* the contingent interpretations of historically specific persons. That is, myth makes particular world views appear to be unchallengeable because natural or God-given. 'Myth has the task of giving an historical intention a natural justification, and making contingency appear eternal' (Barthes, 1972: 155). In another analysis, Barthes describes a French language advert thus:

> Here we have a Panzani advertisement: some packets of pasta, a tin, a sachet, some tomatoes, onions, peppers, a mushroom, all emerging from a half-open string bag, in yellows and greens on a red background. (Barthes, 1977: 33)

In his subsequent analysis, Barthes differentiates between a linguistic code (the French language, the Panzani label) and the visual code constructed from a series of signs. He highlights the visual signifier of 'a half-open bag which lets the provisions spill out over the table'. He reads this as 'a return from market', a signifier which implies 'freshness' and 'domestic preparation'. A second sign brings together 'the tomato, the pepper and the tri-coloured hues (yellow, green, red) of the poster; its signified is Italy or rather *Italianicity*' (Barthes, 1977: 34). The composition of the image suggest a still-life painting which adds to the Italianness of the image.

The work of Saussure and the early Barthes are amongst the founding texts of contemporary cultural studies and represent the move away from culturalism towards structuralism. Both were influential within cultural studies in helping critics break with notions of the text as a transparent bearer of meaning. They illuminated the argument that all cultural texts are constructed with signs. However, the structuralist view of language has itself been the subject of critique. In particular, the idea that signs can have stable meanings, which is implied by the idea of binary pairs and denotation, was to be undermined in the work of the later Barthes, Volosinov/Bakhtin and Derrida.

Polysemic signs

Instead of having one stable denotive meaning, signs are said by the later Barthes to be **polysemic**, that is, they carry many potential meanings. Consequently, texts can be interpreted in a number of different ways. Meaning requires the active involvement of readers and the cultural competencies they bring to bear on the text–image in order to temporally 'fix' meaning for particular purposes. Thus, interpretation of **texts** depends on readers' cultural repertoire and knowledge of social codes. These are differentially distributed along the lines of class, gender, nationality, etc.

This idea was carried forward within cultural studies through the work of Volosinov (1973) and his concept of the 'multi-accentuality' of the sign. For Volosinov, signs do not have one meaning but possess an 'inner dialectical quality' and an 'evaluative accent' which makes them capable of signifying a range of meanings. Signification changes as social conventions and social struggles seek to fix meaning. That is, the meanings of signs are not fixed but negotiable. They are fought over so that 'sign becomes the arena of class struggle' (Volosinov, 1973: 23). The ideological struggle is the contest over the significance of signs where power attempts to regulate and 'fix' their otherwise shifting meanings.

As Hall (1996e) argues, the thrust of Volosinov's (1973) writing echoes Bakhtin's (1984) argument that all understanding is dialogic in character. Bakhtin suggested that signs do not have fixed meanings; rather, sense is generated within a two-sided relationship between speaker and listener, addressser and addressee. Many critics hold that Bakhtin wrote under the name of Volosinov. In any case, both suggest that meaning cannot be guaranteed; it is not pure but always ambivalent and ambiguous. Meaning is the inherently unstable domain of contestation not the product of a finished secure language.

Volosinov's work enabled cultural studies to take on board the idea of the multi-accentuality of the sign. It highlighted a sense that meaning was the outcome of politics and the play of power. The inherent undecidability of meaning and the place of regulative power are also themes within poststructuralism, which has had an even more enduring influence within cultural studies.

Poststructuralism and intertextuality

The term **poststructuralism** implies 'after structuralism'. It embodies a notion of critique and absorption. That is, poststructuralism accepts and absorbs aspects of structural linguistics while subjecting it to a critique which, it is claimed, surpasses structuralism. In short, poststructuralism rejects the idea of an underlying structure which founds meaning including the idea that denotative meaning is itself clear, descriptive and stable. Rather, meaning is always deferred and in process. This is the position of the 'later' Barthes when he writes that

> a text is not a line of words releasing a single 'theological' meaning (the 'message' of the Author-God) but a multi-dimensional space in which a variety of writings, none of them original, blend and clash. The text is a tissue of quotations drawn from the innumerable centres of culture. (Barthes, 1977: 146)

In other words, textual meaning is unstable and cannot be confined to single words, sentences or particular texts. Meaning has no single originatory source, but is the outcome of relationships between texts, that is, **intertextuality**. There are no clear and stable denotative meanings (as in early Barthes) for all meaning contains traces of other meanings from other places.

These ideas make more sense if we explore the work of Jacques Derrida (1976), one of the most influential philosophers in cultural studies today. This poses a particular problem, for Derrida's work deliberately sets out to resist the stabilization of its meanings. Nevertheless, at the risk of simplification, I shall try to summarize key ideas in Derrida writings as they have been take up within cultural studies.

DERRIDA: TEXTUALITY AND *DIFFÉRANCE*
Nothing but signs

Derrida takes as axiomatic Saussure's claim (which he argues Saussure himself contradicts) that language is always a system of differential signs which generate meaning through difference rather than by correspondence with fixed transcendental meanings or referents to the 'real'. Consequently, 'From the moment that there is meaning there are nothing but signs. We think only in signs' (Derrida, 1976: 50). There is no original meaning outside of signs, which are a form of graphic 'representation', so that writing is in at the origins of meaning. We cannot think about knowledge, truth and culture without signs, that is, writing. For Derrida, writing is a permanent trace which exists *always already* before perception is aware or conscious of itself. Thus, Derrida deconstructs the idea that speech provides an identity between signs and meaning.

Derrida rehearses this argument in a number of places, for example against the opposition of nature and culture, wherein Derrida points out that nature is already a concept in language (i.e culture) and not a pure state of being beyond signs. Christianity is said to be based on the transcendental truth of the word of God. Yet the word of God is available only through the unstable signs of writing, that is, the Bible. Ultimately, Derrida argues, the very idea of literal meaning is based on the idea of the 'letter', which is writing. Literal meaning is thus underpinned by metaphor – its apparent opposite. As Derrida puts it, 'All that functions as metaphor in these discourses confirms the privilege of the logos and founds the 'literal' meaning then given to writing: a sign signifying itself signifying an eternal logos' (Derrida, 1976: 15).

Derrida critiques what he calls the 'logocentrism' and 'phonocentrism' of western philosophy. By 'logocentrism', Derrida means the reliance on fixed *a priori* transcendental meanings. That is, universal meanings, concepts and forms of logic which exist within human reason before any other kinds of thinking occurs, for example a universal conception of reason or beauty. By 'phonocentrism', Derrida means the priority given to sounds and speech over writing.

According to Derrida, Socrates held speech to be direct from the heart of truth and the self while writing was regarded as a form of sophistry and rhetoric. For Derrida this signals Socrates' attempt to find wisdom and truth through reason unmediated by signification. This privileging of speech, argues Derrida, allows philosophers to regard the formation of subjectivity as unmediated agency with 'the unique experience of the signified producing itself spontaneously from within itself' (Derrida, 1976: 20). This, Derrida argues, is the search for a universal transcendental truth which grounds itself as a source of the self, which is pure spontaneity. Derrida argues that the privileging of speech relies on the untenable idea that there is direct access to truth and stable meaning. This idea is fallacious because, in representing a **truth** which is argued to exist outside of **representation**, one must be re-representing it. That is, there can be no truth or meaning outside of representation. There is nothing but signs.

Différance

For Derrida, since meaning is generated through the play of signifiers not by reference to an independent object world, it can never be fixed. Words carry multiple meanings, including the echoes or traces of other meanings from other related words in other contexts. Language is non-representational and meaning is inherently unstable so that it constantly slides away. Thus, by *différance*, the key Derridean concept, is meant 'difference and deferral'. The production of meaning in the process of signification is continually deferred and supplemented in the play of more-than-one.

> Meaning is no longer fixed outside any textual location or spoken utterance and is always in relation to other textual locations in which the signifier has appeared on other occasions. Every articulation of a signifier bears a *trace* of its previous articulations. There is no fixed transcendental signified, since the meaning of concepts is constantly referred, via the network of traces, to their articulations in other discourses: fixed meaning is constantly *deferred*. (Weedon et al., 1980: 199)

Central to Derrida's project is the logic of the 'supplement' as a challenge to the logic of identity. While the latter takes meaning to be identical with a fixed entity to which a word refers, a supplement adds to and substitutes meanings. For example, writing supplements speech by adding to it and substituting for it, while the meaning of a word is supplemented by the traces of other words. Nevertheless, even this use of 'the supplement' is problematic for it assumes that the supplement adds to an already existent self-present original meaning. Instead, the supplement is always already part of the thing supplemented. Meaning is always displaced and deferred. The continual supplementarity of meaning, the continual substitution and adding of meanings through the play of signifiers, challenges the identity of noises and marks with fixed meaning.

Derrida's postcards

In *Le Carte Postal* (1980), Derrida plays with the idea of postcards and postal systems which act as metaphors for the generation and circulation of meaning. The postcard motif allows Derrida to challenge the idea that meaning operates within a closed circuit where intentions and messages are unambiguously sent and received. Rather, postcards may go astray, they may reach persons and generate meanings other than those which were intended. In this way the idea of 'true' meaning or communication is displaced for meanings circulate without any absolutely authorized source or destination. Reason is unable to permanently fix and define the meaning of concepts. The particular character of postcard writing as destined for a specific person who understands Derrida's cryptic messages suggests the irreducible specificity of writing.

Strategies of writing

By writing, Derrida means not simply text on a page but what he calls *arche-writing* in which there is no 'outside' of the text. Writing is always already part of the outside of texts and texts are constitutive of their outsides. It is in this sense that there is nothing outside of texts or nothing but texts (by which is not meant that there is no external material world), so that texts are constitutive of practices.

Writing plays an important part in Derrida's work. First, writing is seen not as secondary to speech (as self-present meaning) but a necessary part of speech and meaning. Not only is writing always already inside speech but, since writing is 'a sign of a sign', then the meaning of words cannot be stable and identical with a fixed concept but must be deferred by dint of the traces of other words. Second, the meaning and truth claims of philosophy (and of any other forms of knowledge) are always dependent on writing and subject to the rhetorical claims, metaphors and strategies of writing. Truths are not outside of a writing which tries to express them; rather, the strategies of writing are constitutive of any truth claims and can be deconstructed in terms of those strategies.

Deconstruction

Derrida is widely associated with the practice of **deconstruction**. To deconstruct is to take apart, to undo, in order to seek out and display the assumptions of a text. In particular, deconstruction involves the dismantling of hierarchical binary oppositions such as speech/writing, reality/appearance, nature/culture, reason/ madness, etc., which serve to guarantee truth through excluding and devaluing the 'inferior' part of the binary. Thus within the conventions of western culture, speech is privileged over writing, reality over appearance, men over women. Deconstruction seeks to expose the blind-spots of texts, the unacknowledged assumptions through which they operate. This includes those places where a text's rhetorical strategies work against the logic of its own arguments, that is, the tension between what a text means to say and what it is constrained to mean. For example, Saussure claims that the relationship between the signifier and signified is arbitrary. However, in deconstructing Saussure's writing, Derrida attempts to show that his text operates with a different logic in which speech is privileged over writing and the arbitrary character of the sign is implicitly abandoned.

In deconstructing the binaries of western philosophy and attacking the 'metaphysic of presence' (i.e. the idea of a fixed self-present meaning), Derrida must use the very conceptual language of the western philosophy he seeks to undo. In Derrida's view there is no escape from Reason, that is, from the very concepts of philosophy. To mark this tension, which can be exposed by a strategy of reversal (i.e. putting writing before speech, appearance before reality) but not overcome or replaced, Derrida places his concepts 'under erasure'.

To place a word **under erasure** is to first write the word and then cross it out, leaving both the word and its crossed-out version. For example, Reason R̶e̶a̶s̶o̶n̶. As Spivak explains. 'Since the word is inaccurate, it is crossed out. Since it is necessary, it remains legible' (Spivak, 1976: xiv). The use of accustomed and known concepts 'under erasure' is intended to destabilize the familiar as at one and the same time useful, necessary, inaccurate and mistaken. Thus does Derrida seek to expose the *undecidablity* of metaphysical oppositions, and of meaning as such, by arguing within and against philosophy and its attempts to maintain its authority in matters of truth by dictating in advance what shall count as topics, arguments and strategies.

Derrida and cultural studies

Derrida's work is complex, subtle, difficult and open to contested interpretations. For some (e.g. Norris, 1987) Derrida is taken to be an 'argumentative' philosopher who operates with a transcendental logic, that is, one which seeks to find the conditions for the existence of logic, the presuppositions on which reason is based. For others (notably Rorty, 1991b), Derrida is a poetic writer who displaces one intellectual world by another, giving us new ideas and new visions by making us dissatisfied with the old ways of thinking. For Rorty, Derrida makes the whole concept of representation unusable since there is never a stable referent to be represented nor any truth which is not re-presentation. Others, for example Hall (1997a), continue to use the term 'representation', while highlighting its constructed character.

Cultural studies has taken from Derrida the key notions of writing, intertextuality, undecidablity, deconstruction, *différance*, trace and supplement, all of which stress the instability of meaning, its deferral through the interplay of texts, writing and traces. Consequently, no categories have essential universal meanings but are social constructions of language. This is the core of the **anti-essentialism** prevalent in cultural studies. That is, words have no universal meanings and do not refer to objects that possess essential qualities. For example, since words do not refer to essences, identity is not a fixed universal 'thing' but a description in language (Chapter 6).

FOUCAULT: DISCOURSE, PRACTICE AND POWER

Alongside Derrida, Michel Foucault is the most influential anti-essentialist, poststructuralist thinker in cultural studies at present, and his work is cited in many chapters of this text. Here we will focus on his conception of language and practice, which coheres around the concepts of discourse, discursive practice and discursive formation.

Foucault (1972) argues against formalist theories of language which conceive of it as an autonomous system with its own rules and functions (i.e. structuralist semiotics). He also opposes interpretative or hermeneutic methods which seek to disclose the 'hidden' meanings of language. Instead, he is concerned with the description and analysis of the surfaces of discourse and their effects.

Foucault is determinedly historical in his insistence that language develops and generates meaning under specific material and historical conditions. He explores the particular and determinate historical conditions under which statements are combined and *regulated* to form and define a distinct field of knowledge/ objects requiring a particular set of concepts and delimiting a specific 'regime of truth' (i.e. what counts as truth). Foucault attempts to identify the historical conditions and determining rules of formation of regulated ways of speaking about objects.

Discursive practices

If, for Derrida, meaning has the potential to proliferate into infinity, Foucault explores how, through the operation of power in social practice, meanings are temporarily stabilized or regulated into a discourse. For Foucault, **discourse** 'unites' both language and practice and refers to the production of knowledge through language which gives meaning to material objects and social practices. Though material objects and social practices 'exist' outside of language, they are given meaning or 'brought into view' by language and are thus discursively formed. Discourse constructs, defines and produces the objects of knowledge in an intelligible way while excluding other forms of reasoning as unintelligible.

Where discourses provide ways of talking about a particular topic in similar ways with repeated motifs or clusters of ideas, practices and forms of knowledge across a range of sites of activity, we may speak of a **discursive formation**. A discursive formation is a pattern of discursive events which refer to, or bring into being, a common object across a number of sites. They are regulated maps of meaning or ways of speaking through which objects and practices acquire meaning. For example, Foucault's (1973) study of discourses of madness included:

- statements about madness which give us knowledge concerning madness;
- the rules which prescribe what is 'sayable' or 'thinkable' about madness;
- subjects who personify the discourses of madness, i.e. the 'madman';
- the processes by which discourses of madness acquire authority and truth at a given historical moment;

- the practices within institutions which deal with madness;
- the idea that different discourses about madness will appear at later historical moments, producing new knowledge and a new discursive formation.

Discourse and discipline

Foucault argued that discourse regulates not only what can be said under determinate social and cultural conditions but who can speak, when and where. Consequently, much of his work is concerned with the historical investigation of **power**. Foucault (1977) has been a prominent theorist of the 'disciplinary' character of modern institutions, practices and discourses. In particular, the 'regimes of truth' (what counts as truth) of modernity involve relations of **power/knowledge**. Foucault concentrates on three disciplinary discourses;

- the 'sciences', which constitute the subject as an object of inquiry;
- 'dividing practices', which separate the mad from the sane, the criminal from the law-abiding citizen and friends from enemies;
- technologies of the self, whereby individuals turn themselves into subjects.

Disciplinary technologies arose in a variety of sites, including schools, prisons, hospitals and asylums. They produced what Foucault called 'docile bodies' that could be 'subjected, used, transformed and improved' (Foucault, 1977: 198). Discipline involves the organization of the subject in space through dividing practices, training and standardization. It produces subjects by categorizing and naming them in a hierarchical order through a rationality of efficiency, productivity and 'normalization'. By 'normalization' is meant a system of graded and measurable categories and intervals in which individual subjects can be distributed around a norm. For example, western medicine and judiciary systems have increasingly appealed to statistical measures and distributions to judge what is normal. This leads, for example, not only to classifications of what is sane and mad but to degrees of 'mental illness'. Classificatory systems are essential to the process of normalization and thus to the production of a range of subjects.

The metaphor of disciplinary power commonly associated with Foucault is the 'Panopticon'. This is a prison design consisting of a courtyard with a tower in the centre capable of overlooking the surrounding buildings and cells, which have a window facing the tower. The inmates of the cells are visible to the observer in the tower but the latter is not seen by the inmates. The cells became 'small theatres, in which each actor is alone, perfectly individualized and constantly visible' (Foucault, 1977: 200). The idea of the Panopticon is a metaphor (it is doubtful that the design was materialized) for a continuous, anonymous and all-pervading power and **surveillance** operating at all levels of social organization.

The productivity of power

For Foucault, power is distributed throughout social relations and is not to be reduced to centralized economic forms and determinations nor to its legal or juridical character. Rather, power forms a dispersed capillary woven into the fabric of the entire social order. Further, power is not simply repressive but is *productive*; it brings subjects into being. Power is implicated in 'generating forces, making them grow, and ordering them, rather than one dedicated to impeding them, making them submit, or destroying them' (Foucault, 1980: 136). For example, Foucault argues against the 'repressive hypothesis' that discourses of sexuality are repressed. Instead, he suggests that there has been an 'incitement to discourse', a proliferation of discourses about sex in, amongst others, medicine, Christianity and population studies. These discourses about sex analyse, classify and regulate sexuality in ways which produce sexed subjects, making sexuality a cornerstone of subjectivity.

Foucault establishes a mutually constituting relationship between power and knowledge so that knowledge is indissociable from regimes of power. Knowledge is formed within the practices of power and is constitutive of the development, refinement and proliferation of new techniques of power. For example, psychiatry emerges through the practices of trying to understand and control 'madness' at the same time that it classifies madness, thereby bringing new forms of discipline and new kinds of subject into being. Hence the analytic term 'power/knowledge' (Foucault, 1980).

The subjects of discourse

For Foucault, bodies are 'subject to' the regulatory power of discourse by which they become 'subjects for' themselves and others. Here, Foucault is concerned with subjectivity as formed within the **subject positions** of discourse. The speaking subject is not the author or originator of a statement but depends on the prior existence of discursive positions which 'can be filled by virtually any individual when he formulates the statement; and in so far as one and the same individual may occupy in turn, in the same series of statements, different positions, and assume the role of different subjects' (Foucault, 1972: 94).

Foucault provides us with useful tools for understanding the way the social order is constituted by discourses of power which produce subjects who fit into, constitute and reproduce that order. Nevertheless, for some critics, Foucault deprives the self of any form of **agency**. However, in his later work, he does turn to questions of how subjects are 'led to focus attention on themselves, to decipher, recognize and acknowledge themselves as subjects of desire' (Foucault, 1985: 5); that is, how one recognizes oneself as a subject for oneself involved in practices of self-constitution, recognition and reflection.

This concern with self-production as a discursive practice is centred on the question of ethics as a mode of 'care of the self'. For Foucault, ethics is concerned with practical advice as to how one should concern oneself with oneself in everyday life. It centres on the 'government of others and the government of oneself' and forms part of our strategies for 'conduct about conduct' and the 'calculated management of affairs' (Foucault, 1979, 1984a, 1984b). (See Chapters 6 and 8.)

POST-MARXISM AND THE DISCURSIVE CONSTRUCTION OF THE 'SOCIAL'

The considerable influence of Foucault within cultural studies might be taken to mark the abandonment of its Marxist legacy. Foucault was opposed to what he saw as the economic **reductionism** and historical *telos* (or inevitable unfolding of a purposeful history) of **Marxism**. However, Laclau and Mouffe (1985), amongst others, have been involved in the critique and reconstitution of Marxism, sometimes called **post-Marxism**, through the application of poststructuralist theory to Marxism (Hall, 1997b).

Deconstructing Marxism

Laclau and Mouffe are particularly critical of the **essentialism**, **foundationalism** and reductionism of Marxism (see Chapter 12). They reject the idea that there are any essential, universal concepts (such as class, history, mode of production) which refer to unchanging entities in the world. Further, discursive concepts are not to be reduced to or explained solely in terms of the economic base as in reductionist forms of Marxism. Instead, Laclau and

Mouffe argue, along with Foucault, that discourse constitutes the objects of its knowledge. Consequently, they analyse the 'social' (a concept they reject as being not a proper object of analysis) in terms of the discursive construction of reality. For them, 'society' is an unstable system of discursive differences in which socio-political identities represent the open and contingent articulation of cultural and political categories.

Class, which in Marxism is conceived of as an essential unified identity between a signifier and a specific group of people who share socio-economic conditions, is seen by Laclau and Mouffe as the effect of discourse. Class is not simply an objective economic fact but a discursively formed collective subject position. Class consciousness is neither an inevitability nor a unified phenomenon. Classes, while sharing certain common conditions of existence, do not automatically form a core, unified class consciousness but are cross-cut by conflicting interests. Class and class consciousness, which are formed and unformed in the course of actual historical development, are cross-cut by concerns of gender, race and age. Thus, not only is subjectivity constituted by the positions from which discourse obliges us to speak, but subjects are not unitary wholes. They are fragmented subjects who take up plural subject positions.

For Laclau and Mouffe, the 'social' involves multiple points of power and antagonism rather than cohering around class conflict as in Marxism. The complex field of multiple forms of power, subordination and antagonisms are not reducible to any single site or contradiction. Consequently, any radical politics cannot be premised on the domination of any particular political project (e.g. the proletariat of Marxism) but must be constructed in terms of the recognition of **difference** and the identification and development of points of common interest. Laclau and Mouffe are critical of universal Reason and argue that all progressive values must be defended within the pragmatic context of particular moral traditions without appeal to absolute standards of legitimation. The formulation of what is equitable involves, for them, the recovery of modern political ideas of democracy, justice, tolerance, solidarity and freedom. Laclau and Mouffe could be said to be both modern and postmodern (Chapter 5) in their pursuit of radical democracy (Chapter 12).

The articulated social

Laclau and Mouffe argue that the 'social' is to be thought of not as a totality but as a set of contingently related aggregates of difference articulated or 'sutured' together. Laclau (1977) argues that there are no necessary links between discursive concepts, and that links which are forged are temporary and connotative. They are said to be articulated together and bound by the power of custom and opinion. Indeed, it is hegemonic practice which seeks to fix meaning 'for all time'. What we take to be the common-sense meanings of conceptual links are the outcome of a 'politics of articulation' (see Chapter 12).

The concept of **articulation** suggests that those aspects of social life (identities or nation or society) which we think of as a unity (and sometimes as universals) can be thought of as representing a temporary stabilization or arbitrary closure of meaning. As Hall suggests:

> the term [articulation] has a nice double meaning because 'articulate' means to utter, to speak forth, to be articulate. It carries that sense of language-ing, of expressing, etc. But we also speak of an 'articulated' lorry (truck); a lorry where the front (cab) and the back (trailer) can, but need not necessarily, be connected to one another. The two parts are connected to each other, but through a specific linkage that can be broken. An articulation is thus the form of the connection that *can* make a unity of two different elements, under certain conditions. It is the linkage which is not necessary, determined, absolute and essential for all time. You have to ask, under what circumstances can a connection be forged or made? The so-called 'unity' of a discourse is really the articulation of different, distinct elements which can be rearticulated in different ways because they have no necessary 'belongingness'. The 'unity' which matters is a linkage between the articulated discourse and the social forces with which it can, under certain historical conditions, but need not necessarily, be connected. (Hall, 1996b: 141)

Put this way, it is possible to regard both individual **identity** and **social formations** as the unique historically specific articulations of discursive elements. For example, since there is no necessary or automatic connection between the various discourses of identity (e.g. of class, gender and race), working-class black women do not necessarily share the same identity and identifications any more than all middle-class white men. Accordingly, the task of cultural studies is to analyse the articulations that have taken place illustrating how various contingent practices are 'put together' with each other through the operation of power.

Through the work of Derrida, Foucault, Laclau and Mouffe the idea that **subjectivity** is a discursive construction has become widely accepted within cultural studies. However, for some critics (Hall, 1996a), the stress on the discursive 'outside' does not fully explain the affective 'inside', that is, why particular subject positions are 'taken up' as the target of emotional investment by some subjects and not by others. Consequently, a number of cultural critics have turned to **psychoanalysis** to assist them in constructing an adequate account of language, subjectivity and identity. In particular, the work of Lacan, which seeks to unite poststucturalist understandings of language with Freudian psychoanalysis, has been influential, if contentious.

LANGUAGE AND PSYCHOANALYSIS: LACAN

According to Freud (1977), the self is constituted in terms of an ego, or conscious rational mind, a superego, or social conscience, and the unconscious, the source and repository of the **symbolic** workings of the mind which functions with a different logic from reason (according to Lacan, the unconscious is structured like a language). The self is by definition fractured into the ego, superego and unconscious, so that the unified narrative of the self is something we acquire over time through entry into the symbolic order of language and culture. Through processes of **identification** with others and with the subject positions of social discourses we create an identity which embodies an illusion of wholeness.

According to Freud, the libido or sexual drive does not have any pre-given fixed aim or object. Rather, through fantasy, any object, which includes persons or parts of bodies, can be the target of desire. Consequently, an almost infinite number of sexual objects and practices are within the domain of human sexuality. Freud's work is concerned to document and explain the *regulation* and repression of this 'polymorphous perversity' through the resolution (or not) of the Oedipus complex into 'normal' heterosexual gendered relationships. It is in this sense that 'anatomy is destiny', for it is hard to escape the regulatory discourses that constitute bodily difference and the signification of **sex** and **gender**.

The mirror phase

In Lacan's (1977) reading of Freud, the resolution of the Oedipus complex marks the formation of the unconscious as the realm of the repressed and the very possibility of gendered subjects established through entry into the symbolic order. Prior to the resolution of the Oedipus complex, infants are said to be unable to differentiate themselves from the surrounding world of objects, including other persons. Pre-Oedipal infants experience the world in terms of sensory exploration and auto-eroticism. The primary focus at this stage is the mother's breast as a source of warmth, comfort and food, a relationship which the child cannot control. Infants begin to regard themselves as individuated persons during what Lacan calls the 'mirror phase'. This involves identification with another person, primarily the mother, as being 'one' and/or recognition of themselves in a mirror as 'one'. However, since for Freud and Lacan we are fragmented subjects, such recognition of wholeness is 'misrecognition' and part of the infants' 'imaginary relations'.

The Oedipus complex involves a boy's desire for his mother as the primary love object, a desire which is prohibited by the symbolic order in the form of the incest taboo. Specifically, the father represents to boys the threat of castration which such prohibited desire brings forth. Consequently, boys shift their identification from the mother to father, who is identified with the symbolic position of power and control (the Phallus). For girls, this involves the acceptance that they have already been castrated. This leads to fury and partial identification with the mother as a gendered role together with the association of fathers with authority, domination and, indeed, mastery. For Lacan, meaning is generated along a system of differences and the Phallus is the primary universal or transcendental signifier. This arguably makes 'woman' a secondary signifier, an adjunct to the symbolic man which acquires meaning by way of difference from masculinity.

The symbolic order

Language plays a critical role in Lacanian theory. Language formation is motivated by the pleasure which comes through feelings of control, and language acquisition represents the wish to regulate desire through occupying the place of symbolic power. In fact, language is the manifestation of the *lack* which Lacan sees at the core of subjects. Specifically, this is the lack of the mother as a result of separation at the mirror phase and, more generally, the lack that human subjects experience by virtue of the prior existence of a symbolic order which they cannot control. Language is the symbolization of desire in a never-ending search for control.

It is through entry into the symbolic order that subjects are formed. Outside of the symbolic order lies only psychosis. For Lacan, the symbolic order is the overarching structure of language and received social meanings. It is the domain of human law and culture whose composition is materialized in the very structure of language which forms the subject positions from which one may speak. Crucially, these are gendered subject positions as the

Phallus serves to break up the mother–child dyad and stands for entry into the symbolic order. Indeed, it is the Phallus as 'transcendental signifier' which enables entry to language (for both sexes) and, by standing in for the fragmented subject, allows the construction of a narrative of wholeness. The symbolic Phallus is the privileged and universal signifier because it is the law of the Name-of-the-Father (resonant of God as the place of creation and power in Judaic–Christian culture) which organizes the symbolic order and the infant's entry into it (since it is the symbolic father that prohibits desire for the mother).

The unconscious as 'like a language'

The unconscious is the site for the generation of meaningful representations which, in Lacanian terms, is structured 'like a language'. Not only is language the only route to the unconscious, but the unconscious is a site of signification, that is, meaningful activity which works 'like a language'. In particular, the mechanisms of condensation and displacement, which Freud saw as the most important of the 'primary processes', are held by Lacan to be analogous to the linguistic functions of metaphor and metonymy.

Condensation is the mechanism by which one idea comes to stand for a series of associated meanings along a chain of signifiers, for example *rose* – as perfumed and petalled, as vagina, as female. Rose signifies female. Likewise, metaphor involves the replacement of one signifier by another – rose for female. While meaning is never fixed (or denotative) because generated through difference/*différance*, nevertheless, under the force of repression, a signifier comes to acquire the status of a signified. A conscious idea represents, as metaphor, a whole chain of unconscious meanings.

Displacement involves the redirection of energy due to one object or idea onto another. Thus objects are, in Freud's language, 'cathected' with psychic energy. Metonymy is a process whereby a part stands for the whole. It is the displacement of energy and therefore meaning along a chain of signifiers, for example burning cars as a metonym for urban riots and subsequently the 'state of the nation'. While meaning is differed, because generated by difference, displacement/metonymy is motivated by the desire for satisfaction that such a fixing could bring. It involves the attempt to control the symbolic and overcome lack. The continual sliding of meaning is prevented, or temporarily stabilized, by its metonymic organization around key cultural *nodal points* which structure (and gender) the unconscious.

Problems with Lacan

Although influential in cultural studies, the Lacanian reading of Freud poses a number of unanswered questions:

- Is the unconscious 'like a language' or is it a language?
- Is structuring of the symbolic order by the Phallus and the regulation of our entry into it by the law of the father a universal human condition, or is it culturally and historically specific? Is Lacanian theory **phallocentric**?
- How can gendered subjects be the outcome of subjection to the symbolic order and yet, at the same time, be a condition of the resolution of the Oedipus complex, which relies on male–female difference?
- Is it possible to struggle against, and change, the language and ideology of **patriarchy**, or are we forever formed in this way?

These questions are of particular significance for **feminism**. Indeed much of the debate which surrounds issues of language and subjectivity from a psychoanalytic perspective has been taken forward by feminist theorists. Feminism has been both attracted and repelled by psychoanalysis (and Lacan specifically) because this work seems to offers an account of the constitution of gendered subjects (Mitchell, 1974) yet places the formation of subjectivity in a set of universal, ahistorical and patriarchal (i.e. male-dominated) processes (see Chapter 8).

Others have attacked psychoanalysis *per se* as being at best unnecessary and at worst a misguided and disciplinary mythology. For example, Rose follows Foucault in arguing that psychoanalysis is a particular way of understanding persons, carved out at the end of the nineteenth century, which, given its historical specificity, cannot be used 'as the basis for an investigation of the historicity of being human' (Rose, 1996: 142).

Whatever its strengths and weaknesses, psychoanalysis must be taken as a historically specific account of human sexuality and subjectivity if it is to maintain its connections with the idea of 'polymorphous perversity' and social regulation. The particular kinds of psychic resolutions which psychoanalysis describes are not universals of the human condition but particular to specific times and places.

LANGUAGE AS USE: WITTGENSTEIN AND RORTY

The work of Derrida, Foucault and Lacan represents the influence of poststucturalist theories of language and representation within cultural studies. However, there is another tradition which, though different in some respects, shares and indeed prefigures the anti-representationalist, anti-essentialist stance of post-stucturalism. This tradition is personified by the philosopher Wittgenstein and the American tradition of pragmatism developed by Dewey and James of which Rorty is the foremost contemporary exponent. Though less influential in cultural studies than poststructuralism, they are of growing significance, especially in relation to debates about **postmodernism** (Chapter 5).

Wittgenstein's investigations

LANGUAGE AS A TOOL

In his *Philosophical Investigations* Wittgenstein suggests that looking for universal theoretical explanations for language is not the most profitable way to proceed. For Wittgenstein, language is not a metaphysical presence but a tool used by human animals to co-ordinate their actions in the context of social relationships. 'The meaning of a word is its use in the language' (Wittgenstein, 1953: §43: 20e). What is important is that we ask 'in what special circumstances this sentence is actually used. There does it make sense' (Wittgenstein, 1953: §117: 48e). To see language as a tool is to suggest that we do things with language. Language is action and a guide to action. Language, in the context of social usage, can be temporarily stabilized for practical purposes.

There are similarities between the writings of Derrida and Wittgenstein. For example, both stress:

- the non-representational character of language;
- the arbitrary relationship between signs and referents;
- the contextual nature of 'truth'.

However, Wittgenstein more than Derrida underlines the pragmatic and social character of language, including the significance of social relationships (which sometimes slips away from the latter). For Wittgenstein, while the meanings of language do derive from relations of difference, meanings are given a degree of stability by social convention and practice. The endless play of signification which Derrida explores is regulated and partially stabilized through pragmatic **narratives**.

For Wittgenstein, a meaningful expression is one that can be given a use by living human beings. That is, language is directly implicated in human 'forms of life'. Thus, in so far as the meaning of the word 'table' is generated through the relationship of signifiers –

table, desk, counter, console, etc. – it is unstable. Nevertheless, it is stabilized by social knowledge of the word 'table', of what it is used for, when, under what circumstances and so forth; in other words, by the pragmatic narratives or **language-games** the word 'table' appears in.

LANGUAGE-GAMES

Let us consider Wittgenstein's discussion of the word 'game', where he suggests that, in looking at games,

> you will not see something that is common to all, but similarities, relationships, and a whole series of them at that. . . . Look for example at board-games, with their multifarious relationships. Now pass to card-games; here you find many correspondences with the first group but many common features drop out, and others appear. When we pass next to ball-games, much that is common is retained, but much is lost. . . . And the result of this examination is: we see a complicated network of similarities overlapping and criss-crossing: sometimes overall similarities, sometimes similarities of detail. (Wittgenstein, 1953: 31e–32e)

The meaning of the word 'game' does not derive from some special or essential characteristic of a game but arises through a complex network of relationships and characteristics, only some of which are ever present in a specific game. Thus, games are constituted by a set of 'family resemblances'. Members of a family may share characteristics with one another without necessarily sharing any specific feature in common. In this sense the word 'game' is relational: the meaning of card-game depends on its relations to board-game and ball-game. Further, the word 'game' itself gains its meaning from its place in a specific language-game of games and of the relation of the word 'game' to things that are not games.

Nevertheless, as Wittgenstein argues, when it comes to explaining the word 'game' to others, we are likely to show them different games and to say this is what games are. In doing so, we draw boundaries for specific purposes and give examples not as 'meanings' generated by an abstract and reified 'language', but as practical explanation for specific purposes. In a sense, to know what games are is to be able to play games. While language-games are rule-bound activities, those rules are not abstract components of language (as in structuralism) but *constitutive rules*, rules which are such by dint of their enactment in social practice. The rules of language constitute our pragmatic understandings of 'how to go on' in society.

One of the better-known 'uses' of Wittgenstein (within cultural studies) is that of the postmodern philosopher Lyotard. He argues that Wittgenstein has shown that 'there is no unity of language, but rather islets of language, each governed by a system of rules untranslatable into those of others' (Lyotard, 1984: 61). That is, truth and meaning are constituted by their place in specific local language-games and cannot be universal in character. Knowledge is specific to language-games. Consequently, postmodern philosophy embraces local, plural and heterogeneous knowledges, rejecting grand narratives or big totalizing explanatory stories (notably Marxism). In Lyotard's interpretation this implies the 'incommensurability' or untranslatability of languages and cultures. From this follows the celebration of difference and 'local' knowledge regimes. However, Rorty (1991a), also influenced by Wittgenstein, argues that we should see language as a practice which utilizes skills. Though exact translation of languages or cultures is not feasible, we can learn the skills of language to make cross-cultural communication possible.

Rorty and the contingency of language

For Rorty (1980, 1989, 1991a, 1991b), human beings use noises and marks, which we call language, to co-ordinate action and to adapt to the environment. Here Rorty is making the Wittgensteinian point that language is a tool used by a human organism and that 'pairing off the marks and noises it makes with those we make will prove a useful tactic in predicting and controlling its future behaviour' (Rorty, 1989: 52). In this view, the relationship between language and the rest of the material universe is one of causality and not of adequacy of representation or expression. That is, we can usefully try to explain how human organisms come to act or speak in particular ways which have casual relationships, but we cannot usefully see language as representing the world in ways which more or less correspond to the material world.

ANTI-REPRESENTATIONALISM
For Rorty, '*no* linguistic items represent *any* non-linguistic items' (Rorty, 1991a: 2). That is, no chunks of language line up with or correspond to chunks of reality. There is no Archimedean place where one could independently verify the truth of a particular description of the world (if truth is taken to be the correspondence between the world and language). There is no God-like vantage

point from which to survey the world and language separately in order to establish the relationship between them for we cannot escape using language itself if we try and establish such a relationship. While we can describe this or that discourse, chunk of language, as being more or less useful and as having more or less desirable consequences, we cannot do so by reference to its correspondence with an independent reality but only in relation to our *values*.

Rorty argues that there is no 'skyhook – something which might lift us out of our beliefs to a standpoint from which we glimpse the relations of those beliefs to reality' (Rorty, 1991a: 9). However, that is not to say that no material reality exists or that by dint of being 'trapped' in language we are somehow out of sync with material reality (as sceptics might claim). On the contrary, since language is a tool for adapting to and controlling the environment, we are in touch with reality in all areas of culture as long as one takes this to mean 'caused by and causing' and not 'representing reality'. Since language is not understood in terms of representation, it makes no sense, and is not useful, to think of language as being out of phase with the environment. As Rorty argues:

> We need to make a distinction between the claim that the world is out there and the claim that truth is out there. To say that the world is out there, that it is not our creation, is to say, with common sense, that most things in space and time are the effects of causes which do not include human mental states. To say that truth is not out there is simply to say that where there are no sentences there is not truth, that sentences are elements of human languages, and that human languages are human creations. Truth cannot be out there – cannot exist independently of the human mind – because sentences cannot so exist, or be out there. The world is out there, but descriptions of the world are not. Only descriptions of the world can be true or false. The world on its own – unaided by the describing activities of human beings – cannot. (Rorty, 1989: 69)

TRUTH AS SOCIAL COMMENDATION

Rorty holds that most of the beliefs that we claim to be 'true' are indeed 'true'. However, truth is not a statement about correspondence between language and reality. To say that most of our beliefs are true is to say that we use a coherent pattern of noises and actions which line up with those of others and which enable us to co-ordinate actions with others. That is, 'true' is not an epistemological term referring to the relationship between language and reality but a consensual term referring to degrees of agreement and co-ordination of habits of action. Truth is social commendation. It is what we take to be good. To say that something is not true is to suggest that there is a better way of describing things, where 'better' refers to a value judgement about the consequences of describing the world in this way (including its predictive power).

Truth, knowledge and understanding are located within particular language-games. Truth is the literalization (or temporary fixing through social convention) of metaphors within a language-game into what Rorty calls a 'final vocabulary'. What we take to be true and good is the consequence of our particular form of **acculturalization**. As Rorty puts it,

> one consequence of antirepresentationalism is the recognition that no description of how things are from a God's-eye-view, no skyhook provided by some contemporary or yet-to-be developed science, is going to free us from the contingency of having been acculturated as we were. Our acculturation is what makes certain options live, or momentous, or forced, while leaving others dead, or trivial, or optional. We can only hope to transcend our acculturation if our culture contains (or, thanks to disruptions from outside or internal revolt, comes to contain) splits which supply toeholds for new initiatives. (Rorty, 1991a: 13–14)

DESCRIBING AND EVALUATING

For Rorty, the contingency of language and the **irony** which follows (irony here means holding to beliefs and attitudes which one knows are contingent and could be otherwise, i.e. they have no universal foundations) lead us to ask about what kind of human being we want to be (for no transcendental truth and no transcendental God can answer this question for us). This takes the form of questions about us as individuals – who do I want to be? – and questions about our relations to other human beings – how shall I relate to others? These are pragmatic questions which bring forth political–value responses and not metaphysical or epistemological questions bringing forth truth–correspondence answers.

The consequences of an anti-representational view of language is to put aside appeals to truth as correspondence in favour of appeals to the pragmatic consequences of discourse and action. Truth, then, is, in William James' phrase, 'what it is good for *us* to believe'. The evaluation and justification of claims about the self and courses of action are not to be done from the viewpoint of absolute metaphysical truth but rather on the basis of the desirability of their pragmatic consequences judged in relation to our values. Since there may be a gap between actual good and possible better, 'good' emerges through comparison between different *actual practices*. That is, there is room for new ways of looking at things which may have consequences judged to be better when compared with other actual ways of doing things. In order for truth as acculturation not to become narrow loyalty to a particular culture or way of being, Rorty argues that it is desirable to open ourselves up to as many possible descriptions and redescriptions of the world as possible. Hence, Rorty defends political–cultural pluralism and the enlargement of the self through the weaving in of new attitudes and beliefs.

One of the pragmatic consequences of multiple descriptions of the world is the greater likelihood of finding useful ways of adapting to and shaping our environment. A second significant consequence is that of listening to the voices of others who may be suffering, where the avoidance of suffering is taken to be the paramount political virtue. A third consequence is the idea that individuals grow through the acquisition of new vocabularies. Both individual **identity projects** and the **cultural politics** of collectivities require us to forge new languages or final vocabularies, new ways of describing ourselves, which recast our place in the world, with desirable consequences. We do not need universal foundations to validate political values or political action; rather, political projects can be justified in terms of pragmatism related to our values (Chapter 12).

DISCOURSE AND THE MATERIAL

Some critics have feared that a stress on discourse and the constitutive character of language, the core argument of this chapter, is a form of idealism. Idealism is a view which regards the world as formed by language and mind outside of any material considerations. In its extreme form, 'everything is discourse'. However, this is not what has been argued here. The materiality of the world is one of those things which is, in the Wittgensteinian sense, beyond doubt. That is, we cannot function without that assumption. As Wittgenstein argues, we may in principle imagine that every time we open a door there will be a bottomless chasm beneath us. However, it makes no sense to do so; it is unintelligible to us.

As Wittgenstein and Rorty argued, language can be understood as a series of marks and noises made by human animals by which they attempt achieve their purposes. Knowledge is a matter not of getting a true or objective picture of reality, but of learning how best to cope with the world. We produce various descriptions of the world and use those which seem best suited to our purposes.

We have a multiplicity of vocabularies because we have a multiplicity of purposes. Once we drop the idea that language 'represents' the world and adopt the metaphor of language as a tool with which we act in the world, then it makes no sense to suggest that language could be out of phase with the environment. Since language does not represent the material world, it cannot misrepresent it.

Indissolubility

For Foucault, material objects and social practices are given meaning and brought into view by language. They are discursively formed. Discourse constructs, defines and produces the objects of knowledge in an intelligible way while excluding other ways of reasoning as unintelligible. This, for Foucault, is a historical and material process for language generates meaning under determinate conditions. As Butler (1993) argues, discourse and materiality are indissoluble. She argues that not only is discourse the means by which we understand what material bodies are, but, in a sense, discourse brings material bodies into view in particular ways. For example, sexed bodies are discursive constructions, but indispensable ones, which form subjects and govern the materialization of bodies such that 'bodies will be indissociable from the regulatory norms that govern their materialization and the signification of those material effects' (Butler, 1993: 2).

SUMMARY

Language is a central concern of cultural studies. It is the means and medium for the generation of significance or meaning. The concept of meaning is core to the explication of culture. To investigate culture is to explore how meaning is produced symbolically in language as a signifying system. Here, meaning is generated through difference, the relation of one signifier to another, rather than by reference to fixed entities in an independent object world.

If meaning resides in a chain of signifiers, that is to say, 'bad' has meaning only in relation to evil–naughty–disagreeable, etc., then meaning has the potential to proliferate into infinity. Meaning is never fixed but always in motion and continually supplemented. Hence, the key Derridean concept of différance – 'difference and deferral' – which centres on the instability and undecidability of meaning. However, while this has proved to be a productive poetic of language, it was also argued that, in social practice, meanings are temporarily stabilized. For Wittgenstein, this occurs through language use, social convention and the embedding of words in pragmatic narratives. For Rorty, it involves the production of contingent 'final vocabularies'. For Foucault, it is the regulation of meaning by power into discourse and discursive formations.

Culture can be regarded as regulated maps of meaning constituted by criss-crossing discourses through which objects and practices acquire significance. Culture is a snapshot of the play of discourses within a given time and space, a map which temporarily freezes 'meaning-in-motion'. Cultures and cultural identities are temporarily stabilized at key 'nodal points', which, in modern western societies, have historically formed around class, gender, ethnicity and age. The processes by which meaning becomes temporarily fixed are questions of power and cultural politics (Chapter 12).

Part Two

Part Two

4

A New World Disorder?

There is a widespread perception that we are living through a period of radical change in our social orders. Old and trusted maps are felt to be giving way to the uncertainties of a global disorder. These multidimensional and interlinked changes concern the economy, technology, **politics**, **culture** (Chapter 5) and **identities** (Chapter 6). Above all, changes are not confined to specific nation-states but are implicated in processes of globalization which question the very concept of bounded societies and cultures. The complexity of the changes taking place has led to a reconsideration of questions of social determination; in particular, a recognition of complex overlapping and over-determined causes which are chaotic rather than linear and in which culture plays a decisive role.

A good deal of these changes, especially at the level of the technological and economic, have been theorized outside of the domain of **cultural studies**. This is reflected in the choice of writers deployed in the chapter. However, these changes form the context in which cultural studies of the 1990s developed and much of the vocabulary – post-Fordism, post-industrial society, post-modernization, etc. – has been absorbed into cultural studies. Further, cultural studies has tried to grasp these changes at the level of culture through exploration of consumer culture, global culture, cultural imperialism, postcoloniality, etc.

ECONOMY, TECHNOLOGY AND SOCIAL CLASS
Fordism

The post-1945 economies of the western world, and especially of Britain and America, are argued to have been dominated by 'Fordism' as an economic practice and Keynesianism as the economic policy of nation-states. Together, these practices add up to more than just an economic strategy for they constitute the organizing principles and cultural relations of an entire **social formation**. Although there were variations between economies and nation-states, the broad parameters of Fordism–Keynesianism were marked by large-scale production of standardized goods in the context of mass consumption. This required a system of relatively high wages, at the least for core workers, in order to sustain the purchasing of high-volume production. Of course, this was not the land of milk and honey for, allied to a relatively well-paid core labour force was a low-wage sector in which women and people of colour were overrepresented.

Central to the mass production and mass consumption of consumer goods was a developing culture of promotion and advertising which supported the selling process. Further, full employment strategies were pursued not just as a social 'good' but as a means of keeping spending power at levels which met the capacity for production. Efficiency was sought through the techniques of 'scientific management' (Taylor, 1911), which stressed:

- the organization of the division of labour to allow for separation of tasks;
- the use of time and motion studies to measure and describe work tasks;
- the use of financial incentives as the prime form of worker motivation.

As a mode of economic regulation, a degree of planning and management was required to maintain the stability of Fordism. This came about through the domination of world currencies by the USA, a degree of inter-state co-operation and the role of the state as a corporate policy maker and economic manager. This was a period in which the state played a significant interventionist role as creator of social welfare provisions, as corporate conflict resolver and as a significant direct employer.

Though strategies took different forms in various countries, Britain of the 1960s was not atypical in experiencing an economic boom, especially in the South East and Midlands, with particularly heavy investment in cars and engineering. In this context, the labour movement was able to take successful industrial action to push up wages in a process dubbed 'wage drift'. Politically, the 1950s and early 1960s were marked by successive Conservative election victories requiring large sections of the working class to vote for them. Some critics hailed a process of 'embourgeoisement' (see Goldthorpe and Lockwood, 1968) marked by the acquisition of incomes comparable to the middle-class by manual workers and the adoption by them of middle-class lifestyles and values. So solid did this picture of industrial prosperity appear that it was argued by some commentators to represent the very logic of industrialization for all societies world-wide (Kerr et al., 1973).

Many of the elements of the economic and social configuration described as Fordism are now thought to have changed irrevocably. Though these changes have been given a variety of names, the three most influential (and overlapping) characterizations are known as **post-Fordism**, the post-industrial society and disorganized capitalism. To characterize change with these concepts is to refer to shifts at the leading edges of the economy and culture. It does not imply that all production or cultural forms follow this model; rather, it represents the direction of change.

Post-Fordism

As described by Harvey (1989), the Fordist regime began to experience problems which came to a head during the early 1970s (he gives the 1972 oil crisis as the key moment). In particular, a system geared towards mass production and consumption faced the difficulties of saturated western markets with a consequent crisis of overproduction. This did not mean that everybody could have all the consumer goods that they wished for; rather, the spending power of consumers had reached its limit. In addition, western economies were facing increased price competition from Japan and the Newly Industrialized Countries (NICs), including Taiwan, Korea and Singapore. This, combined with the success of the Oil Producing and Exporting Countries (OPEC) in pushing up world oil prices and the failure to stabilize the world financial markets as US hegemony weakened, led to economies blighted by stagflation (economies with nil growth but high inflation levels).

The more or less global recession which followed proved difficult to escape because of the rigidity of Fordism in relation to:

- long-term and large-scale fixed capital investments which were built on the assumption of stable mass markets;
- the organization of labour markets in terms of job specialization and demarcation;
- state commitments to welfare spending involving large budget deficits.

In response, there was a perceived need by corporations to reintroduce growth and increase the rate of profit through more flexible production techniques involving new technology, the reorganization of labour and a speed-up of production/consumption turnover times.

On the level of production, the move from Fordism to post-Fordism involves a shift from mass production of homogeneous goods to small batch customization; that is, from uniformity and standardization to flexible, variable production for niche markets. Further, the costs involved in holding large buffer stocks within Fordist production processes was reduced through the system of Just-in-Time (JIT) stock management to ensure that supplies are delivered only when required. JIT and economically viable small batch production rely on the use of new technology, for example the use of computers to order stock or to amend the machinery of production to change the 'run' capacity and/or colour, shape, style and size of the product. Further, since post-Fordism is based on the sub-contracting out of whole areas of the production process to horizontally related 'independent' companies, information technology is used to co-ordinate operations.

REORGANIZING LABOUR

Post-Fordism involves a restructuring of the labour process. It aims at multi-skilling workers and eliminating rigid job demarcation lines to create a more horizontal labour organization with an emphasis on worker co-responsibility. Under the influence of Japanese economic success, quality control shifts from post-production testing into the very process of manufacturing. This requires the labour force to take responsibility for quality and 'continuous improvement' as a central part of their role. In some cases this involves 'quality circles' of workers who share ideas for the improvement of product calibre.

The expensive labour training required for multi-skilling leads companies to offer the core workforce higher long-term job security rather than waste their investment through high labour turnover. In the classical imagery of post-Fordism/Japanization, this is epitomized by the Nissan or Toyota life-long 'company worker'. However, even if this is the case for the core workforce, about which there is doubt, such privileges do not extend to the large periphery workforce upon which post-Fordism depends. Thus, a good deal of the production process, particularly in the horizontally related supplier companies, is handled by part-time, short contract, low-paid temporary workers whose hours yo-yo from week to week. Women, people of colour and young people are overrepresented in the 'peripheral' labour force.

Outside of Japan, critics' attention has focused upon a range of 'silicon valleys' and on a region of Northern Italy (Emilia Romagna or Third Italy) where the global fashion producer Benetton was held to be the 'ideal-type' post-Fordist company (Murray, 1989a, 1989b). Here was an organization which had established a world-wide network of retail franchise operations but which employed only 1500 workers in the core company, many of them highly skilled designers and marketing professionals. Rather than employ a large direct workforce, production and marketing depended on the use of information technology and a chain of sub-contractors to give Benetton flexibility and fast market-response times. For example, direct electronic links to their retail franchises gave the company up-to-date sales information enabling the core operation to respond rapidly to customer demand and subsequently to alter orders from sub-contractors.

THE REGULATION SCHOOL

Post-Fordism refers not just to the working practices of flexible specialization but to a new 'regime of accumulation' and an associated 'mode of social and political regulations', that is, a stabilizing of the relationship between consumption and accumulation, or how much companies retain and how much consumers spend. Such an analysis implies a relationship between conditions of production and social/political relations and lifestyles. This argument follows the 'regulationist' approach of Aglietta (1979), which stresses the role of social and cultural relations, rather than the 'hidden hand' of the free market, in stabilizing the advanced capitalist economies. This includes the role the state plays in mediating production and demand.

For some writers, including Aglietta, the changes in working practices which have been described here as post-Fordism are better seen as neo-Fordism, that is, as an *extension* of Fordist practices aimed at giving it new life. Neo-Fordism involves:

- the diversification of companies into new products;
- internationalization in search of new markets;
- economies of scale;
- the intensification of labour through the intensive application of new technology and automation.

It seems likely that Fordist, neo-Fordist and post-Fordist practices are co-existing globally within and across sectors of specific economies. However, I have concentrated on post-Fordism as the position which has been most widely discussed and adopted within cultural studies.

'NEW TIMES'

The new configuration of production, politics, consumption, lifestyles, identities and aspects of everyday private life constitutes a condition which has been dubbed 'New Times' (Hall and Jacques,

1989). The 'New Times' approach explores a wide-ranging set of cultural, social and economic issues and the connections between them. These include:

- flexible manufacturing systems;
- the customization of design and quality;
- niche marketing;
- consumer lifestyles;
- globalization;
- new social and political movements;
- state deregulation and privatization of welfare;
- the cultural configurations of postmodernism;
- the reconfiguration of class structures.

In this context, the old certainties that linked economy, culture and politics together through the figure of **class** are put into doubt. It has been argued that we are witnessing a terminal decline in the manual working class, a rise in service and white-collar work, and an increase in part-time and 'flexible' labour leading to new social divisions expressed as the two-thirds:one-third society. That is, two-thirds of the population are relatively well-off while one-third is either engaged in de-skilled part-time work or forms a new 'underclass' of the unemployed and unemployable. At the same time, it is argued, the **cultural identities** and political allegiances of class factions are increasingly unpredictable. The starkest vision of these changes has come from theorists of the **post-industrial society** and the more lavish thinkers of postmodernization.

Post-industrial society and the reconfiguration of class identities

For Bell (1973), a post-industrial society is characterized by the shift from industrial manufacturing to service industries centred on information technology. This gives a key role to knowledge production and planning. In this view, technological change is the driving force of social change as information exchange and cultural production displace heavy industry at the heart of the economy. New production processes, and a general shift of emphasis from production to consumption, make information technology and communications *the* industries of the future. Central to these processes are the role and capabilities of computers in managing the increase in volume, speed and distance with which increasingly complex information is generated and transferred.

Pivotal to conceptions of the post-industrial society is the place of knowledge, the shifts taking place in the kinds of work people do and the related changes in the occupational structure as manual jobs give way to white-collar, professional and service work (Allen, 1992; Burnham, 1941). There has been both a sectoral redistribution of labour from the primary and secondary sectors to the service sector and a shift in the style or organization of labour towards white-collar work increasingly organized on craft rather than industrial lines. For Bell, the new class structure is centrally connected to the growing importance of knowledge and technical skills in post-industrial society. That is, 'the major class of the emerging new society is primarily a professional class, based on knowledge rather than property' (Bell, 1973: 374).

THE RISE OF THE SERVICE CLASS

There is little doubt that the western world has seen a decline in the industrial manufacturing sectors of its economies and a rise in the service sectors with a comparable alteration in employment patterns. Thus, the proportion of administrative, professional and technical workers in America and the UK steadily rose until it formed nearly a third of the total workforce (Bell, 1973; Goldthorpe, 1982). This service class are not primarily involved in the direct production of commodities. Rather, they sell their skills and depend on their market power. They usually have a high degree of autonomy, working either as professional 'experts' or in directing the labour of others. Though they do not own the means of production, they may be shareholders and/or possess the ability, at least at the top of the spectrum, to manage the strategic direction of powerful companies.

Bell describes a class structure constituted by a professional class, a technician and semi-professional class, a clerical and sales class, and a class of semi-skilled and craft workers. Noticeably absent is the manual working class, to whom critics such as Gorz (1982) have said 'farewell'. Gorz's central argument is that, in the context of automation and post-industrial economies, new technologies have changed the employment patterns of societies, removing the majority of the population from working-class manual jobs and its associated class identity. Instead of *a* working class, we have a new cash-oriented post-industrial 'working' class, a secure and privileged labour 'aristocracy' and an unemployed underclass. In a similar move, Touraine (1971), like Bell, places the control of information and knowledge at the heart of new social conflicts. Consequently, the dominant class is that group able to access and control information. Technocrats and bureaucrats are counterpoised to workers, students and consumers.

Disorganized capitalism

Theories of the post-industrial or information society have proved to be useful in pointing to key changes in western economies and societies. However, they are also problematic in a number of respects:

- For many commentators, the scale, scope and range of the changes described are overstated geographically (different regions and countries experience change differently) and in absolute terms. Critics suggest that the changes described are confined to specific sectors of the economy and are not as widespread as they have been purported to be. For example, while there has been a shift towards information and service work, the standard capitalist patterns of labour organization still hold sway.
- While there has indeed been a growth in a service class, this category homogenizes a very diverse set of workers from office clerks and shop workers through to lawyers and the chief executive officers of major multi-national corporations. This seems too heterogeneous a set of occupational and cultural modes to be regarded as one class. Indeed, increased fragmentation and stratification are markers of the new class formations.
- Post-industrial society theorists rely on forms of technological determinism. That is, changes are explained by prioritizing technology as the motor of change without considering that the development and deployment of technology must be understood within a cultural, social and economic context. Not only is the very desire to develop technology cultural, but its deployment is dictated as much by questions of profit and loss as by the technology *per se*.

In contrast to post-industrial society theorists, Lash and Urry (1987) have wed economic, organizational and technological change to the restructuring and regeneration of global capitalism. Given its legacy of **Marxism**, and thus the significance of **capitalism** as a category, Lash and Urry's vision of 'disorganized capitalism' has been more readily absorbed into cultural studies than post-industrial society theory. As they argue:

> what is meant here by 'disorganized capitalism' is radically different from what other writers have spoken of in terms of 'post-industrial' or 'information' society. Unlike the post-industrial commentators we think that capitalist social relations continue to exist. For us a certain

level of capital accumulation is a necessary condition of capitalism's disorganized era in which the capitalist class continues to be dominant. (Lash and Urry, 1987: 5)

ORGANIZED CAPITALISM

Lash and Urry's work centres on a discussion of world-wide capitalism where none of the changes in economy, technology and class composition are confined to any single nation-state but are instead a part of the processes of globalization. According to Lash and Urry (1987), from the mid-1870s onwards, the western world developed a series of industrial economies as part of what they call 'organized capitalism'. This was marked by:

- the concentration and centralization of industrial, banking and commercial capital in the context of increasingly regulated markets;
- the separation of ownership from control in business, including the development of complex bureaucratic managerial hierarchies involving new sectors of managerial, scientific and technological intelligentsia – this is held to be part of the greater ideological significance given to technical rationality and the glorification of science;
- the growth of employment in large plants and of the collective power of labour;
- the increased size and role of the state in economic management and conflict resolution;
- the concentration of industrial capitalism within relatively few nation-states, who in turn sought overseas expansion and the control of world markets;
- the development of extractive/manufacturing industry as the dominant sector, together with the growth of very large industrial cities.

DECONCENTRATION AND DEINDUSTRIALIZATION

In contrast, 'disorganized capitalism' involves a world-wide deconcentration of capital through globalized production, financing and distribution. Further, the growth of capitalism in the 'developing world' has led to increasing competition for the West in the extractive and manufacturing industries. This has shifted the occupational structure of First World economies towards the 'service' sector. Thus, western economies have experienced a decline in the extractive/manufacturing sectors as economies are deindustrialized, leading directly to the decrease in the absolute and relative size of the core working class along with the emergence of a service class. This sectoral reorganization leads to a reduction in regional and urban concentration together with a rise in flexible forms of work organization and a decline in national bargaining procedures.

These changes in economic practices and class composition have, it is argued, an affinity with alterations in political thinking as manifested in the increased independence of large corporations from state regulation, the breakdown of state corporatist authority and challenges to the centralized welfare provision. The change in the role of the state is an aspect of the general decline in the salience and class character of politics and political parties. This arises from an educationally based stratification system which disorganizes the links between occupation and class politics.

Patterns of consumption

Thus far, analysis has focused on changes centred on the structure and character of work. However, we also need to consider the linkage between changing class identities and patterns of consumption, a theme absorbed into cultural studies via theorists of **postmodern** culture (see Chapter 5). Here we are concerned with two crucial dimensions. First, the rising absolute consumption levels available to labour; second, class fragmentation and the consumer orientation of the working class. Thus, the majority of the population of western societies have sufficient housing, transportation and income to be in a post-scarcity situation. Consequently, it is argued, workers' identifications and identities shift from location in the sphere of production to that of consumption. While the service class continue to enjoy more consumer items and services than the working class, their experiences are of a shared *qualitative* character. This consumption-centredness of the working class becomes the medium and instrument of their fragmentation as they are detached, through their incomes and consumption capabilities, from the underclass while becoming increasingly internally stratified through 'taste' preferences (Crook et al., 1992).

POSTMODERNIZATION

One of the more influential, if extravagant, positions is that of the postmodern thinker Baudrillard (1983a, 1983b, 1988). He argues that objects in consumer societies are no longer purchased for their use value but as commodity-signs in a society marked by increased **commodification**. For Baudrillard, no objects have an essential value; rather, use value itself is determined through exchange, making the cultural meaning of goods more significant than labour value or utilization. Commodities confer prestige and signify social value, status and power in the context of cultural meanings which derive from the wider 'social order'. Thus, **codes** of similarity and difference in consumer goods are used to signify social affiliation. Objects 'speak of a stratified society' and culture takes over, absorbs and abolishes the social as a separate sphere of interaction.

In this view, the greater part of consumption is the consumption of signs, which are embedded in the growth of commodity-culture, niche marketing and the creation of 'lifestyles'. In a process that Crook et al. (1992) call postmodernization (hypercommodification and hyperdifferentiation), all spheres of life are penetrated by commodification. External validation collapses and choice between values and lifestyles becomes a matter of taste and style rather than 'authentic' socially formed cultural authority. Style is not constrained by formal canons or the mores of social strata but operates within a self-referential world of commodities.

For Featherstone (1991), this represents a consumer culture in which the creation of lifestyles is centred on the consumption of aesthetic signs associated with a relative shift in significance from production to consumption. Indeed, 'it is important to focus on the growing prominence of the *culture* of consumption and not merely regard consumption as derived from production' (Featherstone, 1991: 13). That is, the culture of consumption has its own logic which is not reducible to production and which loosens the connections between social class groups and lifestyles/identities. Featherstone suggests that we are moving towards a society without fixed status groups in which the adoption of styles of life fixed to specific social groups and divisions is becoming irrelevant as they give way to lifestyles in which 'the new heroes of consumer culture make a lifestyle a life project and display their individuality and sense of style in the particularity of the assemblage of goods, clothes, practices, experiences, appearance and bodily dispositions they design together into a lifestyle' (Featherstone, 1991: 86).

The question of determination

The arguments presented as post-Fordism, post-industrial society, disorganized capitalism and postmodernization are not simply descriptions of changes in our contemporary world but are explanations that impute causes and determinations to sequences of events. Given its tendency to explain changes in culture in terms of changes in the economy, the power of the post-Fordist argument is jeopardized by an implicit economic **reductionism**. However, Hall rejects the idea that the post-Fordist paradigm involves economic reductionism. Instead, he argues, it is 'as much a description of cultural as of economic change' (Hall, 1989). While modern culture is, he suggests, 'relentlessly material in its practices', the material world of commodities 'is profoundly cultural', not least in the penetration of production processes by design, style and aesthetics. Indeed, 'rather than being seen as merely reflective of other processes – economic or political – culture is now regarded as being as *constitutive* of the social world as economic or political processes' (Du Gay et al., 1997: 4, my emphasis).

While Hall argues for the **articulation** of a 'circuit of culture' (where each moment is necessary for the next but does not determine its form), the Baudrillard–Crook–Featherstone formulation tends towards the 'end of the social' where 'culture takes over'. That is, they posit the decline of independently formed **social** relations of co-presence in the face of mediated cultural meanings and relationships of identification. For Crook et al., the relationship between economic, social, political and cultural practices should be seen as one of interpenetration and indeed the transgression by *cultural* meaning of the boundaries between them. Thus:

- Models in which cultural processes appear as functions of 'deeper' economic or social dynamics cease to apply.
- Freed from their subordination, cultural components proliferate, split off and recombine.
- Cultural dynamics not only reverse conventional hierarchies of material and ideal determination but play a crucial role in disrupting the autonomous developmental logic's of economy, polity and society. (Crook et al., 1992: 229)

For Hall (1988, 1989, 1997b) it is not so much the collapse of the social that is at stake, but the re-articulation of the social and cultural whereby material goods double up as social signs. Here, an increasingly differentiated socially organized market yields a 'pluralization of social life [which] expands the positionalities and identities available to ordinary people' (Hall, 1988: 129). For example, Mort (1989) explores the way in which advertising and consumer culture endorse and constitute new identities such as 'career women', 'new man', Yuppies and a whole range of youth-oriented identities.

An alternative way to conceive of the determinations within social formations is to see their operation as 'rhizomorphic'. In contrast to the 'root and branch' approach, in which the metaphor of the tree predominates, with causality running in straight lines, 'To be rhizomorphous is to produce stems and filaments that seem to be roots, or better yet connect with them by penetrating the trunk, but put them to new uses' (Deleuze and Guattari, 1988: 15). Burrows, 'in all their functions of shelter, supply, movement, evasion, and breakout' (Deleuze and Guattari, 1988: 7), not to mention their interconnected layout, are rhizomorphic in character, as are the bulbs and tumours of potatoes. In any case, the contemporary, chaotic, rhizomorphic, cultural arrangement that we are witnessing cannot be confined to the boundaries of nation-states; they are part of the new world disorder of globalization.

GLOBALIZATION

According to Robertson (1992), the concept of globalization refers us to an intensified compression of the world and our increasing consciousness of the world, that is, the ever-increasing abundance of global connections and our understanding of them. This 'compression of the world' can be understood in terms of the institutions of modernity, while the reflexive 'intensification of consciousness of the world' can be perceived beneficially in cultural terms.

The dynamism of modernity

Modernity is a post-middle ages, post-traditional order marked by change, innovation and dynamism. For Giddens (1990, 1991), the institutions of **modernity** (Chapter 5) consist of capitalism, industrialism, surveillance, the nation-state and military power. Thus, the modern world is marked by a complex of armed industrial capitalist nation-states involved in systematic monitoring of their populations. Globalization is grasped in terms of the world capitalist economy, the global information system, the nation-state system and the world military order. The institutions of modernity are said to be inherently globalizing because they allow for the separation of time-**space** and the 'disembedding', or lifting out, of social relations developed in one locale and their re-embedding in another.

A number of factors structure the patterns of time-space distanciation, that is, the processes by which societies are 'stretched' over shorter or longer spans of time and space. Of particular significance is the development of abstract clock time. This allows time, space and place (locales) to be separated from each other, enabling social relations to develop between people who are not co-present. At the same time, the development of new forms of communication and information control allow transactions to be conducted across time and space so that any given place is penetrated and shaped by social influences quite distant from it. For example, the development of money and electronic communications allows social relations to be stretched across time and space in the form of financial transactions conducted twenty-four hours a day throughout the globe.

Giddens likens the institutions of modernity to an uncontrollable juggernaut of enormous power which sweeps away all that stands before it. In this view, modernity originates in Western Europe and rolls out across the globe. This characterization of the relationship between modernity and globalization has been subject to the criticism that it is Eurocentric, envisaging only one kind of modernity, that of the West. Featherstone (1995) argues that modernity should be seen not only in temporal terms (i.e. as an epochal social transformation) but also in spatial and relational terms. Different spatial zones of the globe have, he argues, become modern in a variety of ways, requiring us to speak of global modernities in the plural.

Featherstone suggests that Japan does not fit neatly into a tradition–modernity–postmodernity linear development. Likewise, Morley and Robins argue that 'What Japan has done is to call into question the supposed centrality of the West as a cultural and geographical locus for the project of modernity' (Morley and Robins, 1995: 160). Japan has a growing lead in new technologies, owns significant parts of the Hollywood culture industries, has pioneered post-Fordist production techniques and is the largest creditor and net investor in the world. That is, Japan has its own specific version of the modern (and postmodern).

Global economic flows

Many of the processes of globalization are economic in character. Thus, one half of the world's largest economic units are constituted by 200 transnational corporations who produce between a third and a half of world output (Giddens, 1989). Automobile parts, chemicals, construction and semi-conductors are amongst the most globalized industries (Waters, 1995). For example, 90 per cent of semi-conductor production is carried out by ten transnational corporations whose geopolitical centre has increasingly shifted from the USA to Japan. World-wide financial transactions are conducted twenty-four hours a day enabled by the capabilities of new technologies in information transfer. Indeed, the financial sector is the most globalized of all economic practices. As the collapse of the European Exchange Rate Mechanism, Black Monday on the stock exchange and the so-called 'Asian economic meltdown' have demonstrated, states are at the mercy of the global financial markets. Globalization is, in part, constituted by planetary-scale economic activity which is creating an interconnected, if uneven, world economy.

The emergence and growth of global economic activity is not entirely new. Since at least the sixteenth century there has been an expansion of European mercantile trade into Asia, South America and Africa. However, what makes the contemporary manifestation of globalization notable is its scope and pace. It is widely held that since the early 1970s we have witnessed a phase of *accelerated* globalization marked by a new dimension of time-space compression. This was propelled by transnational companies' search for new sources of profit in the face of the crisis of Fordism. Global recession hastened a renewed globalization of world economic activity involving the speed-up of production and consumption turnover assisted by the use of information and communication technology (Harvey, 1989). Thus, accelerated globalization refers to a set of related economic activities understood as the practices of capitalism in its 'disorganized' era.

Global cultural flows

Globalization is not just an economic matter but is concerned with issues of cultural meaning. While the values and meanings attached to **place** remain significant, we are increasingly involved in networks which extend far beyond our immediate physical locations. We are not of course part of a world state or unitary world culture, but we can identify global cultural processes, of cultural integration and disintegration, which are independent of inter-state relations.

According to Pieterse, one can differentiate between a view of culture as bounded, tied to place and inward-looking, and one in which culture is seen as an outward-looking 'translocal learning process'. He suggests that:

> Introverted cultures, which have been prominent over a long stretch of history and which overshadowed translocal culture, are gradually receding into the background, while translocal culture made up of diverse elements is coming to the foreground. (Pieterse, 1995: 62)

Cosmopolitanism, argues Hebdige (1990), is an aspect of day-to-day western life. Diverse and remote cultures have become accessible, as signs and commodities, via our televisions, radios, supermarkets and shopping centres. Patterns of population movement and settlement established during colonialism and its aftermath, combined with the more recent acceleration of globalization, particularly of electronic communications, have enabled increased cultural juxtapostioning, meeting and mixing. This suggests the need to escape from a model of culture as a locally bounded 'whole way of life' (Chapter 2).

Clifford (1992) has argued that we should 're-place' culture by deploying metaphors of travel rather than those of location. Clifford includes peoples and cultures which travel and places/ cultures as sites of criss-crossing travellers. There is a sense in which this has always been the case. Britain has a population drawn from Celts, Saxons, Vikings, Normans, Romans, Afro-Caribbeans, Asians, etc. Likewise the USA, whose diverse peoples have a heritage derived from native American Indians, the English, French, Spanish, Africans, Mexicans, Irish, Poles and many more. However, the accelerated globalization of late modernity has increased the relevance of the metaphor of travel because *all* locales are now subject to the influences of distant places.

Disjunctive flows

A counterpoint to the stress on travel and movement is a certain re-emergence of the politics of place. Attachment to place can be seen in the renewal of forms of Eastern European nationalism, neo-fascist politics and to some degree Islamic fundamentalism. Consequently, globalization is far from an even process of western expansion driven by economic imperatives. Appadurai (1993) has argued that contemporary global conditions are best characterized in term of the *disjunctive* flows of ethnoscapes, technoscapes, finanscapes, mediascapes and ideoscapes. That is, globalization involves the dynamic movements of ethnic groups, technology, financial transactions, media images and ideological conflicts which are not neatly determined by one harmonious 'master plan'. Rather, the speed, scope and impact of these flows are fractured and disconnected.

Metaphors of uncertainty, contingency and chaos are replacing those of order, stability and systematicity. Globalization and global cultural flows cannot be understood through neat sets of linear determinations but are better comprehended as a series of overlapping, overdetermined, complex and chaotic conditions which, at best, cluster around key 'nodal points'. Unpredictable and elaborate overdeterminations have led 'not to the creation of an ordered global village, but to the multiplication of points of conflict, antagonism and contradiction' (Ang, 1996: 165). This argument, in emphasizing cultural diversity and fragmentation, runs counter to the common idea that globalization is a uniform process of cultural homogenization.

Homogenization and fragmentation

CULTURAL IMPERIALISM AND ITS CRITICS

The cultural homogenization thesis proposes that the globalization of consumer capitalism involves a loss of cultural diversity. It stresses the growth of 'sameness' and a presumed loss of cultural autonomy which is cast as a form of **cultural imperialism**. This argument revolves around the domination of one culture by another, usually conceived of in *national* terms. The principal agents of cultural synchronization are said to be transnational corporations (Hamelink, 1983). Consequently, cultural imperialism is the outcome of a set of economic and cultural processes implicated in the reproduction of global *capitalism*. In this context, Robins argues that: 'For all that it has projected itself as trans-historical and transnational, as the transcendent and universalizing force of modernization and modernity, global capitalism has in reality been about westernization – the export of western commodities, values, priorities, ways of life' (Robins, 1991: 25).

Herbert Schiller (1969, 1985), a leading proponent of the cultural imperialism thesis, argues that the global communications industries are dominated by US-controlled corporations. He points to the interlocking network that connects US television, defence sub-contractors and the Federal government. Schiller's case is that the mass media fit into the world capitalist system by providing ideological support for capitalism and transnational corporations in particular. They act as vehicles for corporate marketing along with a general 'ideological effect' which purportedly produces and reinforces locals attachment to US capitalism.

There are three central difficulties with the 'globalization as cultural imperialism' argument:

- It is no longer the case, if it ever was, that the global flows of cultural **discourses** are constituted as one-way traffic.
- In so far as the predominant flow of cultural discourse remains from West to East and North to South, this is not necessarily a form of domination.
- It is unclear that globalization is a simple process of homogenization since the forces of fragmentation and hybridity are equally as strong.

No doubt the first waves of economic, military and cultural globalization were part of the dynamic spread of western modernity. Given that these institutions originated in Europe, we would have to say that modernity is a western project. The early phases of globalization certainly involved western interrogation of the non-western 'other' (Giddens, 1990). Further, as the phase of mercantile expansion gave way to more direct colonial control, European powers sought to impose their cultural forms in tandem with military and economic power.

Colonial control manifested itself as military dominance, cultural ascendancy and the origins of economic dependency. Occupied lands were converted into protected markets for imperial powers as well as sources of raw materials. Though the early twentieth century saw a series of successful anti-colonial struggles and independence movements, the economies of these countries were already integrated into the world economic order as subordinate players (Frank, 1967; Wallerstein, 1974) albeit in an uneven fashion (Worsley, 1990).

HYBRIDITY AND COMPLEX CULTURAL FLOWS

European colonialism has left its cultural mark across the globe. Nowhere was this more compelling than in South African apartheid, where a white God and the European sword combined to enforce and justify domination. European culture is evident in South Africa through language, sport, architecture, music, food, painting, film, television and the general sense amongst whites that European culture represents high culture. It is not coincidental that in a country with a wide variety of languages, English provides the most common shared point of translation.

Nevertheless, the impact of 'external' cultural influences on South Africa is more complex than the idea of a simple cultural imperialism. Consider the prevalence and popularity of American-inspired Hip-Hop and Rap music amongst black South Africans. South African rappers take an apparently non-African musical form and give it an African twist to create a form of hybridization which is now being exported back to the West. Rap, which was described here as American, can be said to have travelled to the US from the Caribbean and can trace its roots/routes back to the influence of West African music and the impact of slavery. Any idea of clear-cut lines of demarcation between the 'internal' and 'external' are swept away. Rap has no obvious 'origin' and its American form is indebted to Africa. In what sense, then, can its popularity in Soweto be called cultural imperialism?

The concept of cultural imperialism depends at heart on a notion of imposition and coercion, but if Africans listen to some forms of western music, watch some forms of western television and buy western-produced consumer goods, which they enjoy, how can this be maintained as domination without resort to arguments that rely on 'false' consciousness (Tomlinson, 1991)? Rhizomorphic and disjunctive global cultural flows are characterizable less in terms of domination and more as forms of cultural **hybridity**.

That globalization is not a monolithic one-way flow from the West-to-the-rest can be seen in the impact of non-western ideas and practices on the West. For example:

- the global impact of 'World Music';
- the export of telenovelas from Latin American to the USA and Europe;
- the creation of ethnic **diasporas** through population movement from South to North;
- the influence of Islam, Hinduism and other world religions within the West;
- the commodification and sale of 'ethnic' food and clothing.

This adds up not only to a general decentring of western perspectives about 'progress' but to the deconstruction of the very idea of homogeneous national cultures (Chapter 7).

The current phase of accelerated globalization is not so much one-directional as 'a process of uneven development that frag- ments as it co-ordinates – introduces new forms of world inter- dependence, in which, once again there are no "others"'. This involves 'emergent forms of world interdependence and planetary consciousness' (Giddens, 1990: 175). For Giddens, not only can the other 'answer back', but mutual interrogation is now possible (Giddens, 1994). Indeed, for Appadurai, existing centre–periphery models are inadequate in the face of a new 'complex, overlapping, disjunctive order' in which,

> for people of Irian Jaya, Indonesianisation may be more worrisome than Americanisation, as Japanisation may be for Koreans, Indianisa- tion for Sri Lankans, Vietnamisation for Cambodians, Russianisation for the people of Soviet Armenia and the Baltic Republics. (Appadurai, 1993: 328)

GLOCALIZATION

Capitalist modernity does involve an element of cultural homo- genization for it increases the levels and amount of global co- ordination. However, mechanisms of fragmentation, hetrogeniza- tion and hybridity are also at work so that: 'It is not a question of *either* homogenization or hetrogenization, but rather of the ways

Conclusion –
very
forward.

in which both of these two tendencies have become features of life across much of the late-twentieth-century world' (Robertson, 1995: 27).

Bounded cultures, **ethnic** resilience and the re-emergence of powerful nationalistic sentiments co-exist with cultures as 'trans-local learning processes' (Pieterse, 1995). The global and the local are mutually constituting. As Robertson (1992) argues, much which is considered to be local, and counterpoised to the global, is the outcome of translocal processes. Nation-states were forged within a global system and the contemporary rise in nationalist sentiment can be regarded as an aspect of globalization.

Further, the current direction of global consumer capitalism is such that it encourages limitless needs/wants whereby niche markets, customization and the pleasures of constant identity transformation give rise to heterogeneity (Ang, 1996). Thus, the global and the local are relative terms. The idea of the local, specifically what is considered to be local, is produced within and by globalizing discourses, including capitalist marketing strate-gies which orientate themselves to differentiated 'local' markets. An emphasis on particularity and diversity can be regarded as an increasingly global discourse. Thus, 'the expectation of identity declaration is built into the general process of globalization' (Robertson, 1992: 175). Robertson adopts the concept of **glocal-ization**, in origin a marketing term, to express the global pro-duction of the local and the localization of the global.

CREOLIZATION

In this spirit, Ashcroft et al. (1989) argue that the hybridization and creolization of language, literature and cultural identities becomes a common theme in **postcolonial** literature, marking a certain meeting of minds with postmodernism. Neither the colonial nor colonized cultures and languages can be presented in 'pure' form, nor separated from each other, giving rise to hybridity. This challenges not only the centrality of colonial culture and the marginalization of the colonized but the very idea of 'centre' and 'margin'.

In a Caribbean linguistic contexts, increasing significance has been attributed to the idea of the 'Creole continuum'; that is, a series of overlapping language usages and code switching which deploys the specific modes of other languages, say English and French, while inventing forms particular to itself. Creolization stresses language as a cultural practice over the abstractions of grammar or any idea of 'correct' usage.

Creolization suggests that claims of cultural homogenization are not a strong basis for the arguments of cultural imperialism. Much of what is cast as cultural imperialism may be understood instead as the creation of a layer of western capitalist modernity which overlays, but does not necessarily obliterate, pre-existing cultural forms. Modern and postmodern ideas about time, space, rationality, capitalism, consumerism, sexuality, family, gender, etc., are placed alongside older discourses, setting up ideological competition between them. The outcome may be both a range of hybrid forms of identity *and* the production of traditional, 'fundamentalist' and nationalist identities. Nationalism and the nation-state continue to co-exist with cosmopolitanism and the weakening of national identities. The processes of reverse flow, fragmentation and hybridization are quite as strong as the push towards homogenization.

GLOBALIZATION AND POWER

Though the concepts of globalization and hybridity are more adequate than that of cultural imperialism, because they suggest a less coherent, unified and directed process, this should not lead us to abandon the exploration of power and inequality. The fact that **power** is diffused, or that commodities are subversively used to produce new hybrid identities, does not displace our need to examine it. As Pieterse argues:

> Relations of power and hegemony are inscribed and reproduced *within* hybridity for wherever we look closely enough we find the traces of asymmetry in culture, place, descent. Hence hybridity raises the question of the terms of the mixture, the conditions of mixing and mélange. At the same time it's important to note the ways in which hegemony is not merely reproduced but *refigured* in the process of hybridization. (Pieterse, 1995: 57)

For example, the cultural hybridity produced by the black diaspora does not obscure the power that was embedded in the moment of slavery nor the economic push–pull of migration. As Hall (1992b) argues, diaspora identities are constructed within and by cultural power. 'This power', he suggests, 'has become a constitutive element in our own identities' (Hall, 1992b: 233). Thus, the **cultural identities** of rich white men in New York are of a very different order to those of poor Asian women in rural India. While we are all part of a global society whose consequences no one can escape, we remain unequal participants and globalization remains an uneven process.

MODERNITY AS LOSS

Tomlinson (1991) makes the case for seeing the spread of western modernity as cultural *loss* in that it provides inadequate qualitative, meaningful and moral points of reference and experience. Tomlinson follows Castoriadis in suggesting that the western concept of development stresses 'more of everything', particularly more material goods, without offering significant cultural values which might suggest where more is undesirable or where growth might mean personal and meaningful experience. Further, the idea of cultural imperialism has strength where people are denied a cultural experience, for example where particular social groups or local concerns fail to be represented in the media as a result of multinational control of the economics of production.

However, recognition of imbalance or loss is not the same as viewing the process of globalization as a one-way process of imperialism. As Tomlinson argues:

> Globalization may be distinguished from imperialism in that it is a far less coherent or culturally directed process. For all that it is ambiguous between economic and political senses, the idea of imperialism contains, at least, the notion of a purposeful project; the intended spread of a social system from one centre of power across the globe. The idea of globalization suggests interconnection and interdependency of all global areas which happen in a far less purposeful way. It happens as the result of economic and cultural practices which do not, of themselves, aim at global integration, but which nonetheless produce it. More importantly, the effects of globalization are to weaken cultural coherence in all individual nation-states, including the economically powerful ones – the imperialist powers of a previous era. (Tomlinson, 1991: 175)

Globalization is in part supra-national, operating at a level 'above' the nation-state. As such, it has consequences for the nation-state and its political forms. Thus, it is argued, we are witnessing decisive political changes which include alterations in the role of the state, shifts in political ideologies and the emergence of New Social Movements (NSMs).

THE STATE, POLITICS AND NEW SOCIAL MOVEMENTS

According to Giddens (1985), the modern nation-state is a container of power constituted by a political apparatus recognized to have sovereign rights within the borders of a demarcated territorial area and possessing the ability to back these claims with military power. The state specializes in the maintenance of order through the rule of law and the monopoly of legitimate violence.

Many citizens of nation-states have positive feelings of commitment to their **national identity**. While the political processes of states have varied across time and space, some form of representative democracy is a marker of liberal democracies. In addition, a significant number of post-war states built up an edifice of welfare provision and have played an important role in corporate economic management. In short, the modern state can be seen to have three critical functions:

- external defence;
- internal **surveillance**;
- the maintenance of **citizenship** rights.

The decline of the nation-state and the end of history?

According to a number of commentators (Crook et al., 1992; Held, 1991; Hertz, 1957), aspects of the state's functions are in decline. For example, it is argued to be increasingly difficult to legitimize the deployment of vast resources for military purposes when nuclear warfare makes military strategies a high-risk option. The state is, in this respect, unable to fully defend its citizens and military force is increasingly irrelevant, other than as a last resort, to the solving of key economic, political and diplomatic problems. This is particularly so in the context of a post-cold war demilitarization in which states, especially those of the former Soviet bloc, are unable to bear the costs of maintaining massive military capabilities (Shaw, 1991). In terms of its more obviously political functions:

> There are four significant elements in this unravelling of the state: a horizontal redistribution of power and responsibility to autonomous corporate bodies; a vertical redistribution of power and responsibility to local councils, civic initiatives, and extra-state run enterprises; and an externalization of responsibility by shifting to supra-state bodies. (Crook et al., 1992: 38)

In Britain, decentralizing tendencies have been manifested through government privatization of major public utilities – gas, water, electricity and telecommunications – along with significant sections of the civil service. Though there are differences in the scale and scope of privatization/deregulation in different countries, the general principles have 'been followed in over 100 countries' (Crook et al., 1992: 99), including the USA, Australia, Germany, Sweden and Poland, amongst others. In addition to the selling of state assets, decentralization has included giving schools more local autonomy and radically reducing the state's commitments to health and social security. Indeed, a growth in private health insurance and personal pension schemes marks the arrival of a 'post-welfare paradigm' (Bennett, 1990: 12).

Above all, the nation-state is embroiled in the multi-faceted processes of globalization which can be argued to 'be corroding important functions of the modern nation-state: namely, its competence; its form; its autonomy; and its authority or legitimacy' (McGrew, 1992).

FORM AND COMPETENCE

States are increasingly unable to manage and control their own economic policy or to protect citizens from global events such as environmental disasters. That is, the state's *competence* is undermined, which, in turn, leads to the development of inter-governmental or supra-governmental agencies which alter the *form* and scope of the state. International organizations engaged in economic and political practices which reduce the state's competence and adjust its form include, amongst others:

- the International Monetary Fund;
- the G8 summits of major economic powers;
- the European Union;
- the European Court of Human Rights;
- the United Nations;
- the International Energy Agency;
- the World Health Organization.

AUTONOMY

The globalization of economic and political processes means that the state is increasingly unable to maintain direct control of policy formation, but must be an actor on the international stage of compromise and capitulation. That is, the *autonomy* of the state is increasingly restricted. Held argues that globalization exhibits

a set of forces which combine to restrict the freedom of action of governments and states by blurring the boundaries of domestic politics, transforming the conditions of political decision making, changing the institutional and organizational context of national polities, altering the legal framework and administrative practices of governments and obscuring the lines of responsibility and accountability of national states themselves. These processes alone warrant the statement that the operation of states in an ever more complex international system both limits their autonomy and impinges increasingly upon their sovereignty. Any conception of sovereignty which interprets it as an illimitable and indivisible form of public power is undermined.

Sovereignty itself has to be conceived today as already divided among a number of agencies, national, regional and international, and limited by the very nature of this plurality. (Held, 1991: 222)

LEGITIMATION

If the competence and autonomy of the state is being slowly undermined and at least some of its powers are transferred to supra-state bodies, then the state cannot fully carry out its modern functions. It may then suffer a crisis of *legitimation*. Since the state cannot do what it is expected to do, people may lose faith in it.

Some critics (Gilpin, 1987) do not accept that the nation-state is being eroded and argue that international co-operation between states and trans-state agencies *increases* the state's ability to direct its own fate. Further, nationalism and state military power play significant roles in international relations and show little sign of withering away. International diplomacy still operates through states rather than by-passing them. The position regarding the internal powers of the state is also ambiguous. On the one hand, states like Britain have privatized and deregulated in a process of decentralization, but, on the other hand, have taken increased authoritarian powers over questions of 'law and order', morality and internal surveillance (Gorden, 1988; Hall, 1988). Though the state is changing its form, transferring some of its powers to supra-state bodies and undergoing a degree of 'legitimation crisis', this is far from total and there seems to be little prospect of the state disappearing in the immediate future.

THE FALL OF COMMUNISM

Thus far, discussion has centred on the liberal-democratic states of Europe, Australia and North America. However, sweeping political and economic changes also took place in Eastern Europe in the 1980s and 1990s. During the 1970s and 1980s all the communist states experienced economic and social crises which included falling production, food and consumer goods shortages, declining welfare services, crime, alcoholism, political dissent and mass dissatisfaction. Subsequently, the anti-totalitarian social and political movements of Eastern Europe, spearheaded by Poland's Solidarity movement, took advantage of the space opened up by Soviet liberalization under Gorbachev to oust the communist establishments.

Most of the regimes of Eastern Europe have moved with varying degrees of speed towards forms of representative democracy, espoused consumer capitalism and sought to join NATO and the European Union. Though Russia has embraced the West less enthusiastically than Poland or the Czech Republic, nevertheless, Coca Cola and McDonald's are symbolically established in the heart of Moscow. Does this represent the final global triumph of liberal democracy and consumer capitalism?

THE END OF HISTORY?

The idea that the triumph of liberal democracy and capitalism is a permanent state of affairs was forwarded and popularized by Fukuyama, who argued for 'the end of history as such; that is, the end point of mankind's ideological evolution and the universalization of Western liberal democracy as the final form of human government' (Fukuyama, 1989: 3). What he means by the 'end of history' is not the end to the occurrence of events, but the universal triumph of the *idea* of liberal democracy as the only viable political system (Fukuyama, 1992). The end of history is the end of ideological competition, given that 'a remarkable consensus has developed in the world concerning the legitimacy and viability of liberal democracy' (Fukuyama, 1989: 22). Though Fukuyama does not expect social conflict to disappear, he argues that grand political ideologies will give way to economic management and technical problem solving in the context of liberal-democratic states and capitalist economic and social relations.

Held (1992) raises questions about the core of Fukuyama's thesis. He argues that liberalism should not be treated as the 'unity' which characterizes Fukuyama's argument. Fukuyama neither differentiates nor decides between different versions of liberalism, ignoring ideological contestation within it. Further, argues Held, Fukuyama does not explore potential tensions between the 'liberal' and 'democratic' components of liberal democracy, for example between individual rights and public accountability. In addition, Fukuyama fails to investigate the degree to which market relations, and the inequities of power and wealth to which they give rise, inhibit liberty and democracy. That is, social inequality can itself be regarded as an outcome of market power which is to the detriment of equal citizenship. Thus, 'it is far from self-evident that the existing economic system is compatible with the central liberal concern to treat all persons as "free and equal"' (Held, 1992: 24).

Held suggests that global economic inequalities, along with national, ethnic, religious and political ideologies, will continue to generate conflict that could give rise to new mass-mobilizing forces capable of legitimating new kinds of regime. However, it is difficult at present to see from where, within liberal democracies, alternative economic and political *systems* are going to be generated from, either ideologically or in terms of social actors capable of system change. Held's criticisms of Fukuyama do not disrupt the claim that liberal democracy has triumphed as an *idea*. The demise of a 'revolutionary politics' which would realize an alternative system seems to be marked by:

- the decline of socialism as an alternative systemic **ideology**;
- the collapse of communism;
- the decline of the working class as a numerical and political force;
- the increasing disconnection between class and politics;
- the rise of social and cultural movements, including ecology politics and feminism, whose political claims are reformist (in the best sense).

Globally, capitalism has triumphed. It is hard to see what an alternative could or will be other than liberal and social-democratic regulatory tinkering. This is not to suggest (as would classical modernization theory) that all societies will follow the western path. There will no doubt be regional variations and the character of capitalism and political forces will take on different configurations in different parts of the world. However, it is to suggest that capitalism has achieved global **hegemony** and that liberal democracy has triumphed in the West. This directs political activity to reformist changes within the system (see Chapter 12) and/or to New Social Movements as pressure groups.

New Social Movements

New Social Movements (NSMs) appeared in modern western societies during the 1960s when they were associated with the student movement, anti-Vietnam War protests, civil rights struggles and the women's movement. NSMs are commonly seen as encompassing **feminism**, ecology politics, peace movements, youth movements and the politics of cultural identity (Chapters 6–9). They are separated from the traditional class politics of labour movements.

DISPLACING CLASS?

According to Touraine (1981) and Melucci (1980, 1981, 1989), contemporary radical politics is becoming detached from class determinations and is organized through New Social Movements. As characterized by these writers, NSMs are increasingly strident social and political collectivities based outside of the workplace. The collective identity formation of NSMs involves the accomplishment of perceived commonalty, cohesion and continuity. This is achieved through the marking of social boundaries as an aspect of collective action, which, as a provisional and ongoing form of identification, has to be continually produced and reproduced over time and across space. As Melucci argues, 'Collective identity formation is a delicate process and requires continual investments' (Melucci, 1989: 34).

The forms of collective identity at the heart of New Social Movements are not those of orthodox class **identification**. Indeed, the rise of NSMs appears to correlate with a decline in the predictability of the relationship between class and political allegiance. Thus, 'studies of voting behaviour and political activism showed a steady decline in allegiance between the major classes or occupational categories on the one hand and the major political parties on the other. . . . Since the late 1960s . . . the class voting index has been in steady decline' (Crook et al., 1992: 139). It is also argued that there is a reduction in trust for the major political parties and an interest in more direct forms of political action. This involves a wider repertoire of strategy and tactics than the corporatist politics of compromise and negotiation had allowed for.

It would be mistaken to see New Social Movements as entirely replacing class politics or as an outcome of the disappearance of class. Nevertheless, it is possible to see them as a partial response to changes in the social formation. For example, Touraine identifies a general disintegration–decomposition of industrial society, along with a decline in the workers' movement and the primacy of class politics, as contributing to New Social Movements. Though characterized by Touraine as a part of the class struggle, NSMs are distanced in language, style and class composition from the traditions of the industrial era.

> . . . in a society where the largest investments no longer serve to transform the organization of labour, as in industrial society, but to create new products, and beyond that, new sources of economic power through the control of complex systems of communication, then the central conflict has shifted. (Touraine, 1985: 4)

For Touraine, conflict has been displaced from the opposition of manager and worker to a wider struggle for control over the direction of social, economic and cultural development. In particular, the axis of conflict has shifted to questions of identity, self-actualization and 'post-materialist' values.

LIFE-POLITICS

According to Giddens (1992), the 'emancipatory politics' of modernity is concerned with liberation from the constraints which limit life-chances. That is, 'emancipatory politics' directs its attention to the exploitative relations of class and the freeing of social life from the fixities of tradition. This includes an ethics of justice, equality and participation. In contrast, given a degree of release from material deprivation, 'life-politics' is more concerned with self-actualization, choice and lifestyle. Life-politics revolves around the creation of justifiable forms of life that will promote self-actualization in a global context. They are centred on the ethics of 'How shall we live?'

> Life-politics concerns political issues which flow from processes of self-actualisation in post-traditional contexts, where globalising influences intrude deeply into the reflexive project of the self and conversely where processes of self-realisation influence global strategies. (Giddens, 1992: 214)

For Giddens, the more we 'make ourselves', the more the questions of 'what a person is' and 'who I want to be' are raised in the context of global circumstances that no one can escape. For example, the recognition of the finite character of global resources and the limits of science and technology may lead to a de-emphasis on economic accumulation and the need to adopt new lifestyles. Likewise, developments in biological science lead us to ask questions about what life is, the rights of the unborn, claims on the body and the ethics of genetic research. This **reflexivity**, involving the re-moralizing of social life, lies behind many contemporary New Social Movements.

SYMBOLIC COMMUNITIES

According to Melucci, the organizational characteristics of New Social Movements are distinct from those which marked class politics, being less committed to working within the established political system. Further, though the achievement of specific instrumental goals do form a part of their agenda, NSMs are more concerned with their own autonomy and the value orientation of wider social developments. Melucci casts them as having a 'spiritual' component centred on the body and the 'natural' world, which acts as a source of moral authority.

New Social Movements are more preoccupied with direct democracy and member participation than with representative democracy. They are commonly marked out by their anti-authoritarian, anti-bureaucratic and even anti-industrial stance, alongside their loose, democratic and activist-oriented organizational modes. The boundaries between particular movements are blurred in terms of value-orientation, specific goals and overlapping flexible and shifting 'membership'. In so far as we can speak of membership at all, it is the very act of participation which bestows it.

New Social Movements often engage in 'direct action', though it is aimed not at the authority and personnel of orthodox representative politics (e.g. Members of Parliament or Congress), but at other actors or institutions in civil society such as companies, research establishments, military bases, oil rigs, road building projects, and so forth. New Social Movements challenge the cultural codes of institutionalized power relations through **symbolic** events and evocative language which lend themselves coherent form as an 'imagined community'.

NSM's symbolic politics are readily disseminated by the mass media, for whom such activities and emblems are good dramatic news events. The images generated by New Social Movements are core to their activities and blur the boundaries between their form and content. That is, many of the activities of New Social Movements are media events designed to give them popular appeal. The symbolic languages of these movements are **polysemic** and broad enough to suit the imprecision of their aims while forming the basis of an alliance or imagined community constituted by a range of otherwise disparate people. In this sense, more than traditional modern party politics, New Social Movements are expressly a form of **cultural politics** (Chapter 12).

SUMMARY

This chapter has described aspects of the changing world in which contemporary cultural studies operates and in which it seeks to intervene. This is an uncertain world in which metaphors of ordered and determinate relations between the economic, social, political and cultural have given way to more chaotic, rhizomorphic and disjunctive relations.

Culture, it is said, has come to play an increasingly significant role in a new globalized disorder. Indeed, Waters argues that not only is globalization most advanced in the sphere of culture, but because signs can more easily span time and space than material goods and services, 'we can expect the economy and the polity to be globalized to the extent that they are culturalized, that is, to the extent that the exchanges that take place within them are accomplished symbolically' (Waters, 1995: 9).

It was argued that while forces of cultural homogenization are certainly in evidence, of equal significance is the place of heterogenization and localization. Consequently, globalization and hybridity are preferred concepts to imperialism and homogeneity at the dawn of the twenty-first century. The themes of hybridity and creolization have been explored within cultural studies in relation to identities, music, youth culture, dance, fashion, ethnicity, nationality, language and the very concept of culture (all are said to be hybridized). Hybridity is one of the repeated motifs of contemporary cultural studies from Derridean deconstruction (the end of binaries where each is within the other) through post-modernism to explorations of ethnicity and postcoloniality.

We explored changes in the basis of the major world economies from Fordism to post-Fordism and emergence of post-industrial societies. This included a degree of class decomposition, the rise of consumer culture and new forms of lifestyle and identities. It was argued that there has been a decline in the predictability of the relationship between class and political allegiance and a rise in New Social Movements. We also reviewed arguments which pointed to a decline in the role and competence of the nation-state. It was suggested that these developments could be understood in the context of disorganized capitalism.

Many commentators agree on the broad components of these social and cultural change. However, there is disagreement about their scope and significance. In particular, there has been considerable debate about whether we are experiencing an epochal shift from modernity to **postmodernity**, or, at the very least, the rise of a cultural and epistemological 'structure of feeling' that we can call postmodern. These themes form the basis of Chapter 5.

5
Enter Postmodernism

The proliferation of books on the subject of postmodernism might be regarded as simply an academic fashion. However, it is also a significant response to substantive changes in the organization and enactment of our social worlds. In other words, there are material grounds for taking these debates seriously. Much of the primary theoretical work on postmodernism has been produced by writers with no direct affiliation to **cultural studies** as a 'discipline'. Nevertheless, the debates and conceptual maps which developed as postmodernism emerged have been filtered into cultural studies. They form the context in which contemporary cultural studies has been developing and permeate the 'sites' of cultural studies' investigations (Chapters 6–12). The postmodern influence in cultural studies underscores a certain break with its Marxist legacy.

DEFINING THE TERMS

Postmodern theory makes little sense outside of the associated concepts of **modernity** and **modernism**. Unfortunately, there is no consensus about what the pertinent concepts mean. I take modernity and **postmodernity** to be terms which refer to historical and sociological configurations. That is, they are periodizing concepts which attempt to broadly define the *institutional* parameters of social formations. In contrast, modernism and **postmodernism** are *cultural* and *epistemological* concepts. They concern:

- cultural formations and cultural experience, for example modernism as the cultural experience of modernity and postmodernism as a cultural sensibility associated with high or postmodernity;
- artistic and architectural styles and movements, that is, modernism as a style of architecture (Le Corbusier) or writing (Joyce, Kafka, Brecht) and postmodernism in film (*Blue Velvet*, *Bladerunner*), photography (Cindy Sherman) or the novel (E.L. Doctorow, Salman Rushdie).
- a set of philosophical and epistemological concerns and positions, that is, thinking about the character of knowledge and truth. Modernism

is associated with the Enlightenment philosophy of Rousseau and Bacon along with the socio-economic theory of Marx, Weber, Habermas and others. Postmodernism in philosophy has been associated with thinkers as diverse as Lyotard, Baudrillard, Foucault, Rorty and Bauman, not all of whom would welcome that characterization. In broad terms, enlightenment thought seeks after universal truths while postmodernism points to the socio-historical and linguistic specificity of 'truth'.

THE INSTITUTIONS OF MODERNITY

Modernity is an historical period following the middle ages. It is a post-traditional order marked by change, innovation and dynamism. The institutions of modernity can be seen, at least in the account of Giddens (1990), to consist of:

- industrialism (the transformation of nature; development of the created environment);
- surveillance (control of information and social supervision);
- capitalism (capital accumulation in the context of competitive labour and product markets);
- military power (control of the means of violence in the context of the industrialization of war).

The industrial revolution

The industrial revolution in Britain transformed a pre-industrial society with low productivity and zero growth rates into a society with high productivity and increased growth. Between 1780 and 1840 the British economy changed significantly. There was a shift from domestic production for immediate use to mass consumer goods production for exchange, and from simple family-centred production to a strict impersonal division of labour deploying capital equipment. The population trebled and the value of economic activity quadrupled (Hobsbawm, 1969). Changes also occurred in personal, **social** and political life. For example, alterations in working habits, time organization, family life, leisure activity, housing and the shift from rural to urban living.

Surveillance

The emergence of an industrial labour process entailed an increase in the size and division of labour, mechanization and the intensification of work. The workshop and factory were utilized as a means of exerting discipline and the creation of new work habits

(Thompson and McHugh, 1990), that is, they marked new forms of **surveillance**. As Giddens puts it, 'who says modernity says not just organizations, but organization – the regularized control of social relations across indefinite time-space distances' (Giddens, 1990: 91). Surveillance refers to the collection, storage and retrieval of information, direct supervision of activities and the use of information to monitor subject populations. Though modernity does not invent surveillance *per se*, it introduces new, more complex and extensive forms, including shifts from personal to impersonal control. Bureaucratization, rationalization and professionalization form the core institutional configurations of modernity (Dandeker, 1990).

The dynamism of capitalist modernity

The industrial organizations of modernity have been organized along capitalist lines. In the *Communist Manifesto*, first published in 1848, Marx characterized the processes of inquiry and innovation which marked capitalist modernity as the

> Subjection of nature's forces to man [*sic*], machinery, application of chemistry to industry and agriculture, steam navigation, railways, electric telegraphs, clearing of whole continents for cultivation, canalization of rivers, whole populations conjured out of the ground – what earlier century had even a presentiment that such productive powers slumbered in the womb of social labour? (Marx and Engels, 1967: 12)

Subsequently, the productive dynamism of capitalism spawned not just coal but nuclear power, not just trains but rockets, not just filing cabinets but computers and e-mail. Capitalism is restless in its search for new markets, new raw materials, new sources of profit and capital accumulation. It is inherently globalizing. Today the economies of all countries are integrated into the world capitalist economic order (Wallerstein, 1974).

The dynamism of modernity is such that it spreads out from its European base to encompass the globe. The western originating institutions of modernity are dynamic and globalizing because, as Giddens writes:

> The dynamism of modernity derives from the *separation of time and space* and their recombination in forms which permit the precise time-space 'zoning' of social life; the *disembedding* of social systems (a phenomenon which connects closely with the factors involved in time-space separation); and the *reflexive ordering and reordering* of social relations in the light of continual inputs of knowledge affecting the actions of individuals and groups. (Giddens, 1990: 16–17)

Modernity fosters relations between 'absent' others, transactions are conducted across time and space and any given place is penetrated and shaped by social influences quite distant from it, that is, social relations are disembedded or 'lifted out' from a local context and restructured across time and **space**. Giddens cites, in particular, **symbolic** tokens (e.g. money) and expert systems. Thus the development of money and professional knowledge allows social relations to be stretched (or distanciated) across time and space.

Modern life involves the constant examination and alteration of social practices in the light of incoming information about those practices. This **reflexivity** involves the use of knowledge about social life as a constitutive element of it and refers to the constant revision of social activity in the light of new knowledge; for example the collection of statistical information about populations by governments and commerce in order to facilitate planning and marketing.

The nation-state and military power

Today we understand the world as divided into discrete nation-states. However, the nation-state is a relatively recent modern contrivance in which most of the human beings who have walked the earth neither participated in nor identified with. The modern nation-state is a container of power constituted by a political apparatus recognized to have sovereign rights within the borders of a demarcated territorial area and possessing the ability to back these claims with military power. Since the discourse of nationalism is a global one and nation-states emerged in relation to each other, we may speak of a world-wide nation-state system (Giddens, 1985).

Nations are not just political formations but systems of cultural representation by which national identity is continually reproduced through discursive action. National identity is a form of imaginative **identification** with the nation-state expressed through symbols and discourses which narrate and creates the idea of origins, continuity and tradition (Bhabha, 1990; Hall, 1992b).

The state specializes in the maintenance of order through the rule of law and the monopoly of legitimate violence. The combination of state military power, political ambition and the emotional investments of national identity have underpinned modern twentieth-century warfare. As Giddens (1985) argues, wars are now fought with industrialized, i.e. modern, armies whose soldiers are trained, disciplined and bureaucratized and whose arms supplies are produced in factories owned by capitalist corporations who engage in international arms trading.

MODERNISM AND CULTURE

The processes by which industrialism, capitalism, surveillance and the nation-state emerged we may call 'modernization'. 'Modernism' refers to the human cultural forms bound up with this modernization (Berman, 1982). Here we are concerned with modernism as a cultural experience or 'structure of feeling' (Williams, 1981).

Modernism as a cultural experience

For Berman (1982), cultural modernism is an experience in which 'All that is solid melts into air', a phrase from Marx suggesting change and uncertainty. Thus, industry, technology and communications systems transformed the human world and continue to do so at a breathless pace. However, while such transformations hold out the promise of the end of material scarcity, they also carry a 'darker side'. For example, electronics are the basis of modern information technologies which are at the heart of global wealth production, communications networks and personalized information and entertainment systems. However, they are also the foundations of modern weapons systems and surveillance techniques from ICBMs to high street CCTV.

> To be modern is to find ourselves in an environment that promises us adventure, power, joy, growth, transformation of ourselves and our world – and at the same time, that threatens to destroy everything we have, everything we know, everything we are. (Berman, 1982: 15)

RISK, DOUBT AND REFLEXIVITY

Modernists have displayed an optimistic faith in the power of science, rationality and industry to transform our world for the better. Not that modernism is a culture of certainty; on the contrary, the very dynamism of modernity is premised on the perpetual revision of knowledge. Modern institutions are based on the principle of doubt, so that all knowledge is formed as a hypothesis open to revision (Giddens, 1990, 1991). Indeed, Giddens (1994) sees modernism as a 'risk culture'. This does not, he argues, mean that modern life is inherently more risky as such.

Rather, it is a reference to the way in which risk calculations play a central part in the strategic thinking of both institutions and the lives of ordinary people.

The ambiguity, doubt, risk and continual change which are markers of modernism are manifested in the constitution of the self. 'Tradition' values stability and the place of persons in a normatively ordered and immutable cosmos, a firmness of parameters in which things are as they are because that is how they should be. By contrast, modernism values change, life planning and reflexivity. In the context of tradition, **self-identity** is primarily a question of social position, while for the modern person it is a 'reflexive project'; that is, 'the process whereby self-identity is constituted by the reflexive ordering of self-narratives' (Giddens, 1991: 244). By **identity project** is meant the idea that identity is not fixed but created and built on, always in process, a moving towards rather than an arrival. For modernism, the self is a question not of surface appearance but of the workings of deeper structures so that metaphors of *depth* predominate. This is manifested by the ideas and concepts of **psychoanalysis** (including, of course, the unconscious).

Faust is one of the emblematic modern figures because he was determined to *make himself* and his world even at the cost of a deal with the Devil. According to Harvey, Faust can be regarded as the literary archetype of the dilemma of modern development, the interplay of creation and destruction. Faust is:

> An epic hero prepared to destroy religious myths, traditional values and customary ways of life in order to build a brave new world out of the ashes of the old, Faust is, in the end, a tragic figure. Synthesizing thought and action, Faust forces himself and everyone else (even Mephistopheles) to extremes of organization, pain, and exhaustion in order to master nature and create a new landscape, a sublime spiritual achievement that contains the potentiality for human liberation from want and need. (Harvey, 1989: 16)

THE *FLÂNEUR*

A crucial figure of modernism is Baudelaire's *flâneur*. A *flâneur*, or stroller, walks the anonymous spaces of the modern city, experiencing the complexity, disturbances and confusions of the streets with their shops, displays, images and variety of persons. This perspective emphasizes the *urban* character of modernism. For Baudalaire (1964), the *flâneur* was one of the heroes of modern life, taking in the fleeting beauty and vivid, if transitory, impressions of the crowds, seeing everything anew in its immediacy, yet with a certain detachment.

The *flâneur* was urban, contemporary and stylish, themes which are pursued by Simmel (1978) in relation to the modern concern with fashion. For Simmel, fashion represents a balancing act between individuation and absorption into the collective. It is marked as peculiarly modern by its rapid change and plurality of **styles** which form a blueprint for the stylization of the self as a project. As Featherstone comments, this

> directs us towards the way in which the urban landscape has become aestheticized and enchanted through architecture, billboards, shop displays, advertisements, packages, street signs, etc., and through the embodied persons who move through these spaces: the individuals who wear, to varying degrees, fashionable clothing, hair styles, make-up, or who move, or hold their bodies, in particular stylized ways. (Featherstone, 1991: 76)

THE DARK SIDE OF MODERNITY

Modernism's self-image is one of excitement, the promise of technological progress and the etching away of tradition in favour of the new. This is a world of social progress, urban development and the unfolding of the self. However, just as Faust was a troubled, destructive and tragic figure, so modernity is marked by the poverty and squalor of industrial cities, two destructive world wars, death camps and the threat of global annihilation. Simmel (1978) argued that, while, on the one hand, individual liberty was increased, people also had to submit to a rigorous discipline and urban anonymity. This was a theme pursued by Weber (1948, 1978), whose views on the development of modern bureaucracy summed up his deep ambivalence towards the modern world.

For Weber, the march of bureaucracy was an aspect of the wider spread of secular rationality and rational decision-making procedures based on calculability, rules and expert knowledge. This was bound up with the 'disenchantment' of the world in favour of economic and technical progress. The Weberian version of bureaucracy stresses impersonality, the allocation of functions, rule systems, and the processes of documentation. A bureaucracy is constituted by a framework of rule-governed and ordered activities which continue irrespective of individuals and independently of their personal characteristics. It relies on fixed and official jurisdictional areas supervised by a stable authority. Weber was convinced of the inexorable advance of bureaucracy, its rationality and efficiency, as well as its encroachments on individual self-expression: bureaucracy as the 'iron cage' of material 'progress'.

In sum, modernism as a 'structure of feeling' involves pace, change, ambiguity, risk, doubt and the chronic revision of knowledge. These are underpinned by the social and cultural processes of individualization, differentiation, commodification, urbanization, rationalization, bureaucratization. However, the concept of modernism also carries a narrower focus on the aesthetic forms associated with artistic movements dating from the nineteenth century.

Modernism as aesthetic style

Key modernist figures include Joyce, Woolf, Kafka and Eliot in literature, along with Picasso, Kandinsky and Mirò in art. While it would be better to talk of modernis*ms* rather than modernism, general themes of artistic modernism include:

- aesthetic self-consciousness;
- an interest in language and questions of representation;
- a rejection of realism in favour of an exploration of the uncertain character of the 'real';
- a jettisoning of linear narrative structures in favour of montage and simultaneity;
- an emphasis on the value of aesthetic experience drawn from romanticism;
- an acceptance of the idea of depth and universal mytho-poetic meaning;
- the exploration and exploitation of fragmentation;
- the value and role of avant-garde high culture.

Modernism rejects the idea that it is possible to represent the 'real' in any straightforward manner. **Representation** is not an act of mimesis or copying of the real but an aesthetic expression or conventionalized construction of the 'real'. In the context of an uncertain and changing world, modernist literature saw its task as finding the means of expression with which to capture the 'deep reality' of the world. Hence the concern with aesthetic self-consciousness, that is, an awareness of the place of form, and particularly language, in constructing meaning. This is manifested in the experimental approach to aesthetic style characteristic of modernist work, which seeks to express depth through fragmentation.

THE PROBLEMS OF REALISM

Since modernism accepts the meaningfulness of a reality which lies beneath or beyond appearance, it dispenses with the idea of naturalism/realism as a form which unproblematically represents the real. For modernists, the problem with **realism** is that it purports to 'show things as they really are' rather than acknowledging its own status as an artifice. Further, the narrative structures of realism are organized by a 'meta-language' of **truth** which privileges and disguises the editorial position rather than letting different discourses 'speak for themselves' and compete for allegiance (MacCabe, 1981).

For modernists, what is required is practices which reveal their own techniques and allow for reflection upon the very processes of **signification**. Thus, modernism's stories do not follow the established conventions of linear causality or the 'ordinary' flow of everyday time. If any one style can be said to encapsulate modernism it is the use of montage; that is, the selection and assemblage of shots or representations to form a composite of juxtaposed ideas and images which are not 'held together' by realist notions of time and motivation. According to the pioneering filmmaker Eisenstein, 'while the conventional film directs emotion, intellectual montage suggests an opportunity to direct whole thought processes as well' (Eisenstein, 1951: 62). Eisenstein's techniques aimed not to conceal an edit but to use that moment to create an intellectual collision between juxtaposed ideas and images which are symbolic in character. For Jean-Luc Godard, meanwhile, montage is used to explore the fragmented multiple discourses of the real and to encourage audiences to examine the very process by which meaning is constructed.

FRAGMENTATION AND THE UNIVERSAL

Modernism incorporates the tension between fragmentation, instability and the ephemeral, on the one hand, with a concern for depth, meaning and universalism, on the other. Though modernist writers have commonly rejected universalism founded on God, they have propounded the universals of a humanism grounded in mythic-poetic narratives (which art has the function of uncovering and constructing). Art replaces God as the **foundational** narrative of human existence. For example, Joyce's *Ulysses* is regarded as archetypal of high modernist novels because of its stream of consciousness, non-realist **narrative** style. In doing so, Joyce attempts to represent the real in new ways using language to capture the fragmented character of the self. Yet, while Joyce would have agreed with Nietzsche that 'God is dead', and that there can be no cosmic universals, there is nevertheless a sense that art can draw on, and reconfigure, universal mythic-poetic meanings. Thus, a day in the life one Dubliner is framed in terms of the universalist Ulysses of Greek myth.

THE CULTURAL POLITICS OF MODERNISM

One route to understanding modernism as **cultural politics** is to explore the debates about form in the work of Lukács (1972, 1977), Adorno (1977; Horkeimer and Adorno, 1979) and Brecht (1964, 1977). Lukács opposes modernism on the grounds that its concern with fragmentation, alienation and angst merely reflects the surface appearance of the world. Modernism represents for Lukács a retreat into the subjective world of angst in which the exterior world is an unchangeable horror (e.g. Kafka). Lukács charges modernism with formalism, that is, an obsession with form lacking significant content. Instead, he champions a realism which, he argues, goes beyond the world of appearance to express the true nature of reality, its underlying trends, characteristics and structures.

Although influenced by Lukács, Adorno (1977) takes up a position diametrically opposed to him. For Adorno, the modernist works of Kafka, Beckett and Schoenberg amongst the most radical of art forms as they 'arouse the fear that existentialism merely talks about'. Modernism highlights the alienating features of capitalism and engenders a critical activity on the part of audiences. In particular, it is the 'negativity' of modernism, its refusal to be incorporated by the dominant language of contemporary culture, which allows it to stand as a beacon of hope and a symbol of non-accommodation.

Brecht complicates the distinction between modernism and realism for he takes up the 'demystifying' purposes Lukács attributes to realism ('discovering the causal complexes of society'), while allying them to modernist techniques. Brecht argues that, since reality changes, so the political purposes of realism have to be expressed through new, modern, forms. Brecht is laying claim to be the new, true and popular realist by using modernist forms. For example, the 'alienation device' (addressing the audience directly, singing spectacles, alluding to the constructed characteristics of plays, etc.) aims to change the relationship between the stage and the audience, leading to reflection on meaning and the processes of signification.

MODERNISMS

The Lukács–Adorno–Brecht debates highlight the need to talk about modernisms rather than modernism. Any concept that can put Joyce, Kafka, Picasso and Brecht all in the same basket is operating at a high level of generality. However, we may say that modernism makes the whole idea of representation problematic and deploys non-linear, non-realist modes while retaining the idea of the real. While modernism rejects metaphysical foundations, it replaces them with narratives of progress and enlightenment which Art functions to illuminate. By Art is meant the work of a high culture demanding reflection and engagement from its audience. Thus, modernism retains the distinction between good and bad art, between popular culture and high culture. Further, whatever the differences between Lukács, Adorno, Brecht, Godard, Joyce and Eisentein, they do share the modern conception that the world is knowable and that true knowledge of it is possible. Indeed, perhaps the single biggest divide between modernism and postmodernism lies in its conceptualization of truth and knowledge, that is, questions of **epistemology**.

MODERN AND POSTMODERN KNOWLEDGE

The condition of modernity has been associated with an emancipatory project through which enlightenment reason would lead to certain and universal truths. This would lay the foundations for humanity's forward path of progress. That is, enlightenment philosophy and the theoretical discourses of modernity have championed 'Reason' as the source of progress in knowledge and society.

The enlightenment project

Enlightenment thought is marked by its belief that Reason can demystify and illuminate the world over and against religion, myth and superstition. Enlightenment thinkers hailed human creativity, rationality and scientific exploration as the epistemological underpinnings of the break with tradition which modernity heralds. The 'project of modernity' also has, at its best, a moral-political agenda that is encapsulated in the French Revolutionary slogan 'Equality, Liberty, Fraternity'. In both the scientific project and the moral-political project, enlightenment philosophy sought universal truths; that is, knowledge and moral principles which applied across time, space and cultural difference.

Enlightenment philosophy can be explored through the writings of key eighteenth century philosophers like Voltaire, Rousseau, Hume and Bacon. However, I am using two more recent and apparently contradictory streams of thought, Taylorism and Marxism, to illustrate the practical implications of enlightenment epistemology.

SCIENTIFIC MANAGEMENT

F.W. Taylor developed his ideas during the late 1880s and published his *Principles of Scientific Management* in 1911, in which he claims, on the basis of scientific knowledge, to provide the *one* best way of organizing production processes to achieve efficiency. We may summarize Taylor's main arguments thus:

- the organization of the division of labour to allow for separation of tasks and functions;
- the use of time and motion studies to measure and describe work tasks;
- the prescription of tasks to workers in minute degrees;
- the use of incentive schemes and money as motivation;
- the importance of management in planning and control.

The organization of production along Taylorist lines was manifested in the standardization and mechanization of factory assembly lines associated with the early days of the Ford motor company. However, the influence of Taylorism has spread much further afield than the factory. It can be seen in managerial control strategies of service industries, education systems, state administration and even mass party politics. For Braverman (1974), Taylorism is best explored as an **ideology** of management and control which, in modified form, became the orthodox doctrine of technical control in both capitalism and Soviet communism. In short, Taylorism is that which Habermas (1972) calls the 'instrumental rationality' underpinning domination. That is, Taylorism puts the logic of rationality and science to work in the service of the regulation, control and domination of human beings. While promising material benefits, Taylorism expresses a 'dark side' of enlightenment thought.

MARXISM AS ENLIGHTENMENT PHILOSOPHY

Braverman and Habermas draw considerable intellectual resources from **Marxism**, which can also be regarded as a child of enlightenment thought. For Marx, in producing the means of subsistence through labour, 'man [*sic*] opposes himself to nature' and 'by acting on the external world and changing it, he at the same time changes his own nature' (Marx, 1961: 102). Labour is socially organized into a mode of production understood in terms of the organization of the means of production (factories, machinery, etc.) and the specific social relations of reproduction which arise from it.

Capitalism is a system of production premised upon the private ownership and control of the means of production through which the bourgeoisie are able to extract from the proletariat a quantity of 'surplus value' which they appropriate. The proletariat are separated from the means of production and from the products of their own labour. Though labour epitomizes the human potential to be creative, it has become 'alien' through its subordination to capital accumulation. Capitalism, through engendering **class** conflict, sows the seeds of its own destruction and supplanting by socialist and communist modes of production. That is, the proletariat's historical role is to overthrow capitalism and in doing so liberate all people as a new society based on need rather than exploitation is brought into being.

With its stress on scientific thought, historical progress, human creativity and the emancipatory role of the proletariat, Marxism is a form of enlightenment thought. However, for Habermas (1972, 1987), it differs from Taylorism in being not so much instrumental rationality as *critical* rationality. That is, Marxism deploys the logic of rationality in the service of critiquing capitalism and liberating human beings from exploitation and oppression. Nevertheless, its arguable that Marxism also contains the 'dark side' of enlightenment thinking. Marxism continues the form of rationality by which humans seek to conquer and control nature. Thus, Adorno accused Marx of wanting to turn the whole world into a factory through the continual expansion of our productive capacities.

SCIENTIFIC LAWS AND THE PRINCIPLE OF DOUBT

One reading of Marx posits human history as the unfolding of an inevitable developmental logic leading from feudalism to communism. History in this sense has its own *telos*, or inevitable point to which it is moving, governed by the *laws* of human evolution and progress. This mechanical reading of Marxism underpins the idea of a vanguard party (the Leninist communist party) which has true knowledge of history and 'knows best' how to guide us. In other words, one can argue that the seeds of Soviet totalitarianism are inherent in the epistemological base of Marxism as a philosophy of history. In this sense, Taylorism and Marxism share a common epistemology based on the enlightenment principles of science and true knowledge. The idea that there could be 'laws of history' is a manifestation of the scientism of Marxism, that is, its wish to be emulate the (alleged) scientific certainty of physics and chemistry. The confidence of modern science allows it to hail itself as 'progress', symbolized by medicine, despite the now constant threat of nuclear annihilation.

Yet modernism is again ambiguous for it is far from clear that science does proceed through laws of certainty. For Popper (1959), science proceeds through experimentation and the principle of falsification. The Einsteinian paradigm which predominates is one of relativity. Kuhn (1962) noted the way in which science periodically overthrows its own paradigms. Giddens (1991) regards modern science as premised on the methodological principle of doubt and the chronic revision of knowledge. Enlightenment science may have begun with the search for certain laws but is now beset with doubt and chaos.

Enlightenment thought in its many manifestations promises increased levels of material production and the abolition of want and suffering. It promotes the development of medicine, universal education, political freedom and social equality. However, the dark side of modernity is regarded by some thinkers as not merely an aberration or side-effect of enlightenment thinking but as inherent in it. Thinkers as diverse as Adorno, Nietzsche, Foucault, Lyotard and Baudrillard have criticized the impulses of modernity for heralding not progress but domination and oppression. The modern world is seen as having to give a rational account of everything, 'interrogating everything' as Foucault describes it. In this characterization, Reason leads not to alleviation of material needs or philosophical enlightenment but to control and destruction. Reason can, at the very least, be argued to have turned out to be selective and unbalanced.

The critique of the enlightenment

In their book *Dialectic of Enlightenment*, Horkheimer and Adorno (1979) argue that enlightenment rationality is a logic of domination and oppression. The very impulse to control nature through science and rationality is, they argue, an impulse to control and dominate human beings. In this view enlightenment thinking is inherently an instrumental rationality whose logic leads not only to industrialization but to the concentration camps of Auschwitz and Belsen. Epistemologically speaking, Horkheimer and Adorno characterize enlightenment thinking as positing an 'identity' between thought and its objects which seeks to capture and subsume all that is different from itself. They regard enlightenment reason as turning rationality into irrationality and deception as it eliminates competing ways of thinking and claims itself as the sole basis for truth. As Best and Kellner put it:

In their [Horkheimer and Adorno's] interpretation, a synthesis of instrumental rationality and capitalism employed sophisticated modes of mass communication and culture, a bureaucratized and rationalized

state apparatus, and science and technology to administer consciousness and needs to ensure social integration so that individual would
act in conformity with the system's dictates. (Best and Kellner, 1991:
218)

NIETZSCHE: TRUTH AS A MOBILE ARMY OF METAPHORS

Though Horkheimer and Adorno's critique of enlightenment
thought remains pertinent, the work of Foucault has been more
influential within cultural studies. Foucault is indebted to the
philosopher Nietzsche, for whom knowledge is a form of the 'will
to power'. The idea of a pure knowledge is impermissible because
reason and truth is 'nothing more than the expediency of a certain
race and species – their utility alone is their truth' (Nietzsche,
1967: §515). Nietzsche characterizes truth as a 'mobile army of
metaphors and metonyms', that is, sentences are the only things
that can be true or false. Knowledge is a question not of true
discovery but of the construction of interpretations about the
world which are taken to be true. For Nietzsche, truth is not a
collection of facts, for there can be only interpretations and there
is 'no limit to the ways in which the world can be interpreted'. In
so far as the idea of truth has an historical purchase, it is the
consequence of power, that is, of whose interpretations count as
truth. Consequently, Nietzsche rejects the enlightenment philosophy of universal reason and progress.

FOUCAULT'S ARCHAEOLOGY

Foucault's early work deploys a methodological approach described
as *archaeology*. By this he means the exploration of the specific
and determinate historical conditions under which statements are
combined and regulated to form and define a distinct field of
knowledge/objects requiring a particular set of concepts and
delimiting a specific 'regime of truth' (i.e. what counts as truth).
Foucault attempts to identify the historical conditions and
determing rules of formation of regulated ways of speaking about
objects, that is, discursive practices and **discursive formations**.
  Foucault (1972, 1973) argues that in the transition from one
historical era to another the social world is no longer perceived,
described, classified and known in the same way. That is, **discourse** is *discontinuous*, it is marked by historical breaks in
understanding, changes in the way objects are conceptualized and
understood. Different historical eras are marked by different
epistemes, or configurations of knowledge that shape the social
practices and social order of particular historical periods. For

example, Foucault points to a rupture in the understanding of madness wherein modern reason breaks off its dialogue with madness and seeks to set up oppositions between madness and reason, the sane and the insane. History is not to be explained in terms of connections across historical periods (though breaks are never complete and are to be understood on the basis of that which already exists), nor in terms of the inevitable movement of history from locatable origins towards a predetermined destiny. Foucault's stress on discontinuity is an aspect of his questioning of the modern themes of genesis, teleology, continuity, totality and unified subjects.

FOUCAULT'S GENEALOGY

While archaeology suggests excavation of the past in one specific site, **genealogy** (Foucault's name for his later approach) takes the form of tracing the historical continuities and discontinuities of discourse. Here Foucault emphasizes the material and institutional conditions of discourse and the operations of **power**. While archaeology digs up the local sites of discursive practice, genealogy examines the way in which discourse develops and is brought into play under specific and irreducible historical conditions through the operations of power.

> . . . 'archaeology' would be the appropriate method of the analysis of local discursivities, and 'genealogy' would be the tactics whereby on the basis of the descriptions of these local discursivities, the subjected knowledges which were released would be brought into play. (Foucault, 1980: 85)

> [Genealogy] must record the singularity of events outside of any monotonous finality . . . it must be sensitive to their recurrence, not in order to trace the gradual curve of their evolution, but to isolate the different scenes where they engage in different roles . . . it depends on a vast accumulation of source material. (Foucault, 1984a: 76)

Foucault's genealogical studies examine prisons, schools and hospitals in order to show the operations of power and discipline in the formation and use of knowledge, including the construction of the subject as an 'effect' of discourse (Chapter 6). Foucault argued that discourse regulates not only what can be said under determinate social and cultural conditions but who can speak, when and where. Specifically, the 'regimes of truth' of modernity involve relations of **power/knowledge** whereby knowledge is a form of power implicated in the production of subjectivity. Crucially, Foucault argues that criticism is no longer going to be practised in the search for formal structures with universal value, but rather as a historical investigation into the events that have led us to constitute ourselves and to recognize ourselves as subjects of what we are doing, thinking, saying. In that sense, this criticism is not transcendental, and its goal is not that of making a metaphysics possible: it is genealogical in its design and archaeological in its method. Archaeological – and not transcendental – in the sense that it will not seek to identify the universal structures of all knowledge or all possible moral action, but will seek to treat the instances of discourse that articulate what we think, say, and do as so many historical events. And this critique will be genealogical in the sense that it will not deduce from the form of what we are what is impossible for us to do and know; but it will separate out, from the contingency that has made us what we are, the possibility of no longer being, doing, or thinking what we are, do, or think. (Foucault, 1984b: 45–6)

BREAKING WITH THE ENLIGHTENMENT

Foucault's thinking breaks with the premises of 'classical' enlightenment thought in five key ways:

- Knowledge is not metaphysical, transcendental or universal. Rather it is specific to particular times and spaces. Foucault talks not of truth *per se*, but of 'regimes of truth', that is, the configurations of knowledge that 'count as truth' under determinate historical conditions.
- Knowledge is perspectival in character. There can be no one totalizing knowledge which is able to grasp the 'objective' character of the world. Rather, we both have and require multiple viewpoints or truths by which to interpret a complex heterogeneous human existence.
- Knowledge is not regarded as a pure or neutral way of understanding. It is implicated in regimes of power.
- Foucault breaks with the central enlightenment metaphor of 'depth'. He argues against interpretative or hermeneutic methods which seek to disclose the hidden meanings of language. Foucault is concerned with the description and analysis of the surfaces of discourse and their effects under determinate material and historical conditions.
- Foucault casts doubt on the enlightenment understanding of progress. Knowledge as discourse does not unfold as an even historical evolution but is discontinuous. That is, Foucault identifies significant epistemological breaks in knowledge across time and rejects any notion of *telos* or the inevitable direction of human history.

However, the idea that there is a clear, distinctive and final break between enlightenment and post-enlightenment thought, or between the modern and postmodern, is challenged by Foucault when he suggests that we do not have to be 'for' or 'against' the enlightenment. It is a question not of accepting or rejecting enlightenment rationality but of asking:

> What is this reason that we use? What are its historical effects? What are its limits, and what are its dangers? [If] philosophy has a function within critical thought, it is precisely to accept this sort of spiral, this sort of revolving door of rationality that refers us to its necessity, to its indispensability, and at the same time to its intrinsic dangers. (Foucault, 1984c: 249)

Postmodernism as the end of grand narratives

While Foucault does not designate himself a postmodern thinker, others, most notably Lyotard (1984), have embraced the perspectival conception of knowledge and the term 'postmodern' with greater alacrity. Lyotard argues that 'there is no unity of language, but rather islets of language, each governed by a system of rules untranslatable into those of others' (Lyotard, 1984: 61). Truth and meaning are constituted by their place in specific local **language-games** and cannot be universal in character. For Lyotard, the postmodern condition is neither a periodizing concept (i.e. the postmodern is not an historical epoch) nor does it refer to the institutional parameters of modernity and postmodernity. Rather it is

> the condition of knowledge in the most highly developed societies. I have decided to use the word postmodern to describe that condition. . . . [It] designates the state of our culture following the transformations which, since the end of the nineteenth century, have altered the rules for science, literature, and the arts. (Lyotard, 1984: xxiii)

For Lyotard, modern knowledge rests on its appeal to meta-narratives, that is, grand historical stories which claim universal validity. By contrast, the postmodern, in arguing that knowledge is specific to language-games, embraces local, plural and hetero-geneous knowledges. The postmodern condition involves a loss of faith in the foundational schemes that have justified the rational, scientific, technological and political projects of the modern world. This is what Lyotard describes as 'incredulity toward metanarra-tives', by which he means that there remain no viable meta-narratives (or elevated standpoints) from which to judge the universal truth of anything. For Lyotard, we should resist the totalizing terror of such dogmas in favour of the celebration of difference and understandings from within particular knowledge regimes.

THE END OF EPISTEMOLOGY

For postmodernism, no universalizing epistemology is possible because all truth claims are formed within discourse. There is no access to an independent object world free from language and no Archimedean vantage point from which to neutrally evaluate claims. There are no universal philosophical foundations for human thought or action and all truth is culture bound. Indeed, Rorty suggests that the concept of truth has no explanatory power, being at best a degree of social agreement from within a particular tradition. He recommends that we abandon epistemology, recognizing 'truth' as a form of social commendation (Rorty, 1989, 1991a); a condition which Foucault described as 'being-in-the-true'.

Gergen (1994) argues that no epistemological position, including modern science and postmodernism, is able to give universal grounding for its own truth claims. However, the *consequences* of adopting a modern or postmodern epistemology are different. According to Gergen, modern truth claims are universalizing: they assert their truths for all people in all places, with potentially disastrous consequences in which the bearers of 'truth' know best. In contrast, Gergen suggests that the consequence of saying that truths are only truths within the language-games in which such truths are founded is to accept the legitimacy of a range of truth claims, discourses and representations of 'reality'.

RELATIVISM OR POSITIONALITY?

For some commentators, postmodernism is a form of relativism, that is, the existence of a series of truth claims of equal epistemological status which leads us to an inability to make judgements between forms of knowledge. Gergen embraces the term 'relativism' arguing that truth is/should be an outcome of debates between competing claims. Rorty rejects relativism as self-contradictory in favour of the culturally specific character of truth, what cultural studies would call positionality. He argues there is no standpoint from which one can see across different forms of knowledge and regard them of equal value. Rather, we are always positioned *within* acculturalized knowledge, so that the true and the good are what we believe. For Rorty, the true and the good are judged in terms of pragmatism, that is, the consequences of adopting certain kinds of understanding. Such judgements can be made by reference only to our *values* and not to a transcendental truth. For example, science does not generate universal truths about the world. Rather, through a set of pragmatic procedures, it produces forms of knowledge which allow us to predict and control our environments to a greater degree with more or less desirable consequences.

THE PROMISE OF POSTMODERNISM (OR MODERNITY AS AN UNFINISHED PROJECT?)

For Bauman (1991), postmodernism has the potential to give voice to a liberatory politics of difference, diversity and solidarity. He argues that the condition of postmodernity is the modern mind reflecting upon itself from a distance and sensing the urge to change. The uncertainty, ambivalence and ambiguity of the postmodern condition, argues Bauman, open up the possibility of grasping contingency as destiny, by which we may create our own futures. To do so we must transform tolerance into solidarity,

> not just as a matter of moral perfection, but a condition of survival. . . . Survival in the world of contingency and diversity is possible only if each difference recognizes another difference as the necessary condition of the preservation of its own. Solidarity, unlike tolerance, its weaker version, means a readiness to fight; and joining the battle for the sake of the other's difference, not one's own. Tolerance is ego-centred and contemplative; solidarity is socially oriented and militant. (Bauman, 1991: 256)

Politics without foundations

There are no guarantees nor universal foundations for such a project. It remains only a possibility inherent in postmodern culture. As Bauman argues, liberty remains truncated, diversity thrives only so far as the market drives it, tolerance slips into indifference and consumers replace citizens. Yet, he suggests, postmodern culture implies the need for **politics**, democracy, full-blown **citizenship** and the potential withdrawal of consent from the political edifice of the state. The postmodern mentality demands that modernity fulfil the promises of its, albeit distorted, reason.

Critics of postmodernism fear that the abandonment of foundationalism leads to irrationalism and the inability to ground any radical politics. Yet, one may argue, to accept the legitimacy of a range of truth claims is in itself a political position for it signals support for pragmatic postmodern cultural pluralism. Thus, Rorty (1991a) would agree with Laclau and Mouffe (1984) that we do not require universal validations and foundations to pursue a pragmatic improvement of the human condition on the basis of the values of our own tradition.

These are themes of the politics of **difference** (Chapter 12) whose coalition politics is part of a long-term strategy conducted in civil society, that is, clubs, pubs, schools, factories and of course the media, aimed at winning minds and changing legislation. It can be seen in terms of the politics of **race**, of **feminism**, of queer politics, amongst others, and the interconnections and alliances that can be built within and across those boundaries.

Modernity as an unfinished project

Postmodern 'epistemology' has not gone unchallenged. The doubt and uncertainty which characterizes contemporary knowledge is seen by Giddens (1990, 1991) as the condition not of postmodernity but of a 'radicalized modernity'. In his view, relativity, uncertainty, doubt and risk are core characteristics of late or high modernity. Similarly, Habermas (1987, 1989) sees the political project of modernity as ongoing. The basis of his argument is the distinction he makes between 'instrumental reason' and 'critical reason'. He is censorious of enlightenment reason for the instrumentality by which the 'lifeworld' is colonized by 'system imperatives', that is, the subordination of social-existential questions to money and administrative power. In this sense, Habermas views Reason as unbalanced and selective. However, the enlightenment also has a critical side which for him is the basis of an emancipatory project which remains unfinished.

Pursuing the tradition of critical theory, Habermas has sought grounds for the validation of evaluative judgement and claims to human emancipation. He does so by arguing that all human interaction presupposes language, and that in the structure of speech we may find the essential grounding conditions for all forms of social organization. When we speak, suggests Habermas, we are making four validity claims: to comprehensibility, truth, appropriateness and sincerity. These, he argues, imply both the logical justification of truth and the social context for their rational debate. Habermas postulates the existence of an 'ideal speech situation' in which competing truth claims are subject to rational debate and argument. In an 'ideal speech situation' truth is not subject to the vested interests and power-plays of truth-seekers but emerges through the process of argumentation.

The public sphere

For Habermas, our very ability to make truth claims is dependent on a democratically organized **public sphere** which approximates an 'ideal speech situation'. The notion of a public sphere is traced historically by Habermas as a realm which emerged in a specific phase of 'bourgeois society'. It is a space which mediates between society and the state where the public organizes itself and in which 'public opinion' is formed. Habermas describes the rise of literary clubs and salons, newspapers, political journals and institutions of political debate and participation in the eighteenth century. This public sphere was partially protected from both the church and the state by the resources of private individuals and was in principle, though not in practice, open to all. Within this sphere individuals were able to develop themselves and engage in rational debate about the direction of society.

Habermas goes on to document the decline of the public sphere in the face of the development of capitalism towards monopoly and the strengthening of the state. The increased **commodification** of life by giant corporations transforms people from rational citizens to consumers of, amongst other things, the non-rational products of the advertising and public relations industries. In a parallel erosion of the public sphere, the state has taken increased power in the economic realm as a corporate manager and in the private realm through the management of welfare provision and education.

The concept of the public sphere in the work of Habermas is a philosophical, historical and normative one. On the historical level there has been considerable criticism of the historical accuracy of the concept (Curran, 1991) and of the male gender bias of the bourgeois public sphere (Fraser, 1995b). Others (Thompson, 1995) have suggested that the modern media have actually expanded the public sphere. More philosophically, some postmodern critics, particularly Lyotard (1984), argue that Habermas reproduces the totalizing discourse of 'Enlightenment Reason', ignoring its repressive character. Honneth (1985) has countered that Lyotard has a mistaken interpretation of Habermas' discursive ethics, whose purpose lies not in the final determination of common needs, but in intersubjective agreement about the very social norms which allow different needs to be articulated and realized. By this he means that Habermas is stressing the importance of the democratic process rather than the outcome of that process.

A normative project

Whatever the historical problems with Habermas' work, as a *normative* position the idea of a public sphere retains an appeal. Postmodernists, poststructuralists and neo-pragmatists would all think Habermas mistaken in his attempt to construct a universal and transcendental rational justification for the public sphere. However, the concept retains normative political leverage for it can be justified on the pragmatic grounds of cultural pluralism (rather than epistemological grounds). That is, the public sphere (or spheres) should be able to accommodate difference as a vital principle. The emancipatory project of modernity and the public sphere might best served by a commitment to 'postmodern' public spheres based on difference, diversity and solidarity.

POSTMODERN CULTURE

Even if one agrees with Habermas that modernity has not yet passed, or with Giddens (1990) that most of the elements described as postmodern were already existent in the modern, there have been significant *cultural* changes in contemporary life which have been described in the language of the 'postmodern'. Given that these social and cultural changes are at the leading edge of the society and are pointing to its future (or are already the dominant configuration), we may refer to living in a 'postmodern era'. This does not necessarily represent a sharp break with the modern but rather suggests a transitional period of changing economic, social and cultural patterns which are shaping the contours of the future. The postmodern does not have to mean postmodernity (as an historical period) but rather indicates a 'structure of feeling' (Williams, 1979, 1981) and a set of *cultural* practices. Core to the postmodern 'structure of feeling' is:

- a sense of the fragmentary, ambiguous and uncertain nature of living;
- an awareness of the centrality of contingency;
- a recognition of cultural difference;
- an acceleration in the pace of living.

The reflexive postmodern

Without the certainties of traditional religious and cultural beliefs, modern life may appear as a series of proliferating choices to be made without foundations. This encourages us to be more reflexive about ourselves, having no certainties on which to fall back. Reflexivity can be understood as 'discourse about experience' (Gergen, 1994: 71). To engage in reflexivity is to partake in a range of discourses and relationships while constructing further discourses about them. Reflexivity enables increased possibilities for the playful self-construction of multiple identities. It also requires that we compare our traditions with those of others; consequently, postmodern culture invites the 'other' of modernity, those voices which had been suppressed by the modern drive to extinguish difference, to find ways to speak. Such voices include those of feminism, ethnic **diasporas**, ecologists, ravers and travellers.

Reflexivity encourages an ironic sense of the 'said before', the feeling that one cannot invent anything new but merely play with the already existent. Eco (cited in Collins, 1992: 333) gives a good example of this with the person who cannot, without irony, say 'I love you' but prefaces it with the words 'As Barbara Cartland would say'. The thing is said, but the unoriginality acknowledged. Indeed, **irony**, understood as a reflexive understanding of the contingency of one's own values and culture, is the key sensibility of postmodernism. A widespread awareness of the history of film, television, music and literature promotes this feeling. For example, television has a history and repeats that history within and across channels thus 'television produces the conditions of an ironic knowingness' (Caughie, 1990: 54).

Two riders need to be attached to the notion of reflexive post-modern culture as a liberatory one:

- Increased social and institutional reflexivity is manifested in the desire of institutions to know more about the workforce, the customers and the clients. This involves increased forms of surveillance, from cameras in shopping centres and 'quality management' at work, to the increased significance of marketing.
- The experience of postmodern culture cannot be assumed to be the same for all people regardless of class, **ethnicity**, **gender**, nationality, etc. A more finely grained sociological analysis would need to take account of the variable experiences of postmodern culture.

Postmodernism and the collapse of cultural boundaries

Lash (1990) identifies the shift from the 'discursive' to the 'figural' as core to the postmodern turn. By this he means that the signifying logics of the modern and postmodern work in different ways. For Lash, the modernist 'regime of signification' prioritizes words over images, promulgates a rationalist world view, explores the meanings of cultural texts and distances the spectator from the cultural object. In contrast, the postmodern 'figural' is more visual, draws from everyday life, contests rationalist views of culture and immerses the spectator in his/her desire for the cultural object. The increasing prominence of the postmodern 'figural' is integral to the 'aestheticization of everyday life' and to the erosion of the cultural boundaries of modernity.

Thus, postmodern culture is marked by the blurring and collapse of the traditional boundaries between **culture** and art, high and low culture, commerce and art, culture and commerce. For example, the rise in visibility and status of **popular culture**, hastened by the electronic media, has meant that the distinction between high and low culture is no longer viable. 'High culture becomes just one more sub-culture, one more opinion, in our midst' (Chambers, 1986: 194). Further, the collapse of attempts to sustain art/high culture:commercial/low culture distinctions, combined with the recognition of **active audiences**, has undone the obviousness of the critique of commodity culture by both the political 'right' and 'left'.

BRICOLAGE AND INTERTEXTUALITY

The postmodern is marked by an historical blurring. That is, representations of the past and present are displayed together in a **bricolage** which juxtaposes previously unconnected signs to produce new codes of meaning. Bricolage as a cultural style is a core element of postmodern culture and observable in architecture, film and popular music video. Shopping centres have made the mixing of styles from different times and places a particular 'trade mark', while MTV is noted for the blending of pop music from a variety of periods and locations. There has also been a notable collapse or blurring of **genre** boundaries within cultural products. *Bladerunner* and *Blue Velvet* are frequently cited as films which mix the genres of noir, horror, sci-fi, etc. Further, they are double-coded (Jencks, 1986), allowing them to be understood both by the literati and by a popular audience.

Postmodern culture is marked by a self-conscious **intertextuality**, that is, citation of one text within another. This involves explicit allusion to particular programmes and oblique references to other genre conventions and styles. For example, reference to a bar in Boston where everyone knows your name in both *Hill Street Blues* and *St. Elsewhere*, or to *Twin Peaks* in *Northern Exposure*. It may also be seen in the reworking of noir conventions in *Pulp Fiction* and the recycling of the 'road movie' in *Wild at Heart* and *True Romance*. This intertextuality is an aspect of enlarged cultural self-consciousness about the history and functions of cultural products.

THE AESTHETICIZATION OF EVERYDAY LIFE

The blurring of the boundaries between art and culture, culture and commerce, allied to the prominence of the image, have arguably resulted in an aestheticization of urban life. Featherstone (1991) argues that this takes three critical forms:

- artistic subcultures which sought to efface the boundaries between art and everyday life;
- the project of turning life into a work of art;
- the flow of signs and images which saturate the fabric of everyday life.

Identity projects and the aestheticization of daily life are linked in consumer culture through the creation of lifestyles centred on the consumption of aesthetic objects and **signs**. This is related to a relative shift in importance in society from production to consumption along with **post-Fordist** flexible forms of production which make small batch production, customization and niche marketing viable.

POSTMODERN AESTHETICS IN TELEVISION

Television is at the heart of image production and the circulation of a collage of stitched-together images core to postmodern cultural style. The variety of juxtapositions of images and meanings in television creates an electronic bricolage in which unexpected associations can occur. This is an outcome of the flow of a given channel and a reflection of multi-channel diversity. The ability of viewers to zip and zap, channel change and fast forward constitutes a bricolage 'strip text' (Newcombe, 1988) wherein adopting the 'appropriate' reading attitudes and competencies is itself an aspect of postmodern culture.

Stylistically, the markers of the postmodern have been seen as aesthetic self-consciousness, self-reflexiveness, juxtaposition/montage, paradox, ambiguity, uncertainty and the blurring of the boundaries of genre, style and history. While postmodernism in the arts is seen as reaction against modernism, postmodern television takes on and makes popular modernist techniques, including montage, rapid cutting, non-linear narrative techniques and the de-contextualization of images.

THE POSTMODERN DETECTIVES

The American TV 'detective' series *Twin Peaks* and *Miami Vice* are widely regarded as indicative of postmodern style. *Twin Peaks* was 'double-coded' in the commonly understood manner of postmodern texts. It involved a combination of **codes** which enabled it to engage with a 'concerned minority' familiar with an 'expert' language and a wider popular audience. *Twin Peaks* was postmodern in its multi-generic form, whereby the conventions of the police series, science fiction and soap opera were blended together in a way which was sometimes to be taken seriously and at other times regarded as humorous ambivalent parody. This was accompanied by a series of tonal variations including pathos and camp, seriousness and humour which encourages the shifting of subject position and oscillation of emotional involvement in one series that a 'strip text' might create across an evening (Collins, 1992). Further, *Twin Peaks* was an example of the postmodern **'semiotics** of excess'. It was brimming over with meanings which seemed 'irrelevant' to the solving of the crime or the forward movement of the narrative but which formed a spectacle or a diversion.

For Kellner (1992), *Miami Vice* was postmodern in two fundamental ways:

- its aesthetic style by, which the lighting, camera work, rock music, bright colours and exotic terrain led to 'aesthetic spectacles that are intense, fascinating, and seductive. . . . Image frequently takes over from narrative and the look and feel become primary, often relegating story-line to the background' (Kellner, 1992: 148–9);
- its polysemic nature, involving shifting and conflicting identities, meanings and ideologies. The two main detective protagonists, Crockett and Tubbs, slip in and out of various identities, suggesting that identity is a construction not a given, a game of style and choice.

THE CARTOON POSTMODERN

The Simpsons has made a 'dysfunctional' American family the ironic heroes of a series which is double-coded in its appeal to children and adults. It is entertainment and a subtle reflection on American cultural life. In accordance with contemporary postmodern culture, the television set is at the heart of the Simpsons' life and its audience. The programme requires us to have a self-conscious awareness of other television and film genres as it makes a range of intertextual references. For example, *Itchy and Scratchy*, the Simpson children's favourite cartoon, parodies *Tom and Jerry*, mocking the double standard by which television violence is simultaneously condemned and enjoyed.

The postmodern markers of ambivalence, irony and intertextuality are equally evident in the popular show *South Park*, which parodies a series of cultural stereotypes. We are presented with a range of small-minded racist and sexist characters in conjunction with a series of stereotypes of race, gender, age, body size, etc.

Yet, the show manages to undermine the stereotypes by making us laugh at them. The representation of the African-American chef as the sexy black soul singer, the Barry White of *South Park*, parodies the 'original' image as itself a stereotype. This is given an added intertextual dimension and ironic twist by the voice of Isaac Hayes, known for the theme song to the blaxploitation *Shaft* movie. The show walks the line between offending everyone and undermining the offence. It takes nothing seriously while making serious statements about, for example, the use of television as a child-minder.

Evaluating postmodern culture

Just as *South Park* divides public opinion as much loved and much hated, so the significance or insignificance of postmodern culture has been hotly debated. For some critics, contemporary culture is depthless and meaningless, while for others it is to be welcomed as a new and popular form of transgressive culture.

DEPTHLESS CULTURE

For Baudrillard, postmodern culture is constituted through a continual flow of images which establishes no connotational hierarchy. Postmodern culture is argued to be flat and one dimensional; it is literally and metaphorically 'superficial'. In this vein, Grossberg describes *Miami Vice* as 'all on the surface. And that surface is nothing but a collection of quotations from our own collective historical debris, a mobile game of trivia' (Grossberg, 1987: 29). Here is a culture in which no objects have an 'essential' or 'deep' value; rather, value is determined through the exchange of symbolic meanings. That is, commodities have sign value which confers prestige and signifies social value, status and power. A commodity is not an object with use value but a commodity-sign. 'Floating free' from objects, signs are able to be used in a variety of associations, as illustrated every day in television advertising. As Featherstone suggests, 'consumption . . . must not be understood as the consumption of use-values, a material utility, but primarily as the consumption of signs' (Featherstone, 1991: 85).

IMPLOSIONS AND SIMULATIONS

Baudrillard's world is one in which a series of modern distinctions have broken down (sucked into a 'black hole', as he calls it), collapsing the real and the unreal, the public and the private, art and reality. For Baudrillard, postmodern culture is marked by an all-encompassing flow of fascinating simulations and images, a

hyperreality in which we are overloaded with images and information: 'It is reality itself today that is hyperrealist . . . it is quotidian reality in its entirety – political, social, historical and economic – that from now on incorporates the simulating dimension of hyperrealism. We live everywhere in an "aesthetic" hallucination of reality' (Baudrillard, 1983a: 148).

The 'hyper' prefix signifies 'more real than real'. The real is produced according to a model which is not a given but artificially reproduced as real, a real retouched in a 'hallucinatory resemblance' with itself. The real implodes on itself. Implosion in Baudrillard's work describes a process leading to the collapse of boundaries between the real and simulations. This includes that between the media and the social, so that 'TV is the world'. Television simulates real-life situations, not so much to represent the world as to execute its own. News re-enactments of 'real-life' events blur the boundaries between the 'real' and the simulation, 'entertainment' and 'current affairs'.

According to Baudrillard, the postmodern world of communication saturation represents an over-intense advance of the world upon the consciousness of subjects which he describes as 'schizophrenic'. There is an overexposure or explosion of visibility by which all becomes transparency and immediate visibility, which Baudrillard calls 'obscenity'. The television screen is the central metaphor as the schizoid subject of 'obscenity' becomes 'a pure screen, a switching centre for all the networks of influence' (Baudrillard, 1983: 148).

THE CULTURAL STYLE OF LATE CAPITALISM

For Jameson (1984), who draws on the work of Baudrillard, postmodernism is implicated in a depthless sense of the present and a loss of historical understanding. We live in a postmodern hyperspace in which we are unable to place ourselves, the specific manifestations of which include:

- the cannibalization of styles from past and present;
- the loss of authentic artistic style in favour of pastiche;
- the transformation of representations of the world into images and spectacles;
- the breakdown of a firm distinction between high and low culture;
- the culture of the simulacrum or copy (for which no original existed);
- the fashion for nostalgia in which history is the object not of representation but of stylistic connotation.

Jameson's description of the postmodern world as one marked by fragmentation, instability and disorientation is one that has much in common with Baudrillard. However, he parts company on the level of explanation. Jameson is at pains to point out that postmodernism has genuine historical reality. He argues that postmodern cultural practices are not superficial but expressive of developments and experiences in a deep 'reality'. For Jameson, postmodernism is expressive of a world system of multinational or late capitalism and represents the cultural style of late capitalism operating in a new global space. It is late capitalism which, by extending commodification to all realms of personal and social life, transforms the real into the image and simulacrum.

TRANSGRESSIVE POSTMODERNISM

In contrast to the negative evaluations of Baudrillard and Jameson, Kaplan (1987) claims a transgressive and progressive role for postmodern culture and its collapsing of boundaries. She argues that the postmodern music video offers, in **deconstructionist** mode, no assured narrative position for the viewer, undermining the status of representation as real or true. This parallels Hutcheon's (1989) argument that postmodernism makes the whole idea of representation problematic even as it is complicit with it. She suggests that postmodernism 'takes the form of self-conscious, self-contradictory, self-undermining statement. It is rather like saying something with inverted commas around what is being said' (Hutcheon, 1989: 1). Postmodernism is ironic knowingness because it explores the limitations and conditions of its own knowing.

Collins (1992) argues that postmodernism acknowledges multiple **subject positions** and **identities** while actively encouraging a conscious moving in and out of positions, a playing with meaning and form. For Collins, Jameson's characterization of postmodernism as 'camp' recycling, pastiche and a loss of historical depth 'fails to account for the diversity of possible strategies of rearticulation'. These range from simple revivalism and nostalgia to 'the radicalized cover versions of pop standards by the Sex Pistols or The Clash, in which the past is not just accessed but "hijacked", given an entirely different cultural significance' (Collins, 1992: 333).

Finally, the commodity-signs which for Baudrillard are at the core of a depthless culture form the raw material from which, for Chambers (1987, 1990), active and meaning-oriented consumers construct **multiple identities**. Here, consumers are bricoleurs, selecting and arranging elements of material commodities and meaningful signs into a personal style. Thus, the postmodern can be read as the democratization of culture and of new individual and political possibilities.

ot diffs
between mod
+ postmod

SUMMARY

Modernity and postmodernity are periodizing concepts which refer to historical epochs. They are abstractions which broadly define the institutional parameters of social formations. In this sense, modernity is marked by the post-middle ages rise of industrial capitalism and the nation-state system. These institutions of modernity are associated with the social and cultural processes of individualization, differentiation, commodification, urbanization, rationalization, bureaucratization and surveillance.

Modernism and postmodernism are cultural and epistemological concepts. As cultural concepts, they concern the experience of day-to-day living and artistic styles/movements. However, the distinction between modernism and postmodernism is less than clear. For example, it was argued that the experience of living with modernity involves pace, change, ambiguity, risk, doubt and the chronic revision of knowledge. Yet, a sense of a fragmentary, ambiguous and uncertain world involving high levels of reflexivity is also a marker of postmodern culture. The stress on contingency, irony and the blurring of cultural boundaries is more obviously a marker of the postmodern. Modernism as an artistic movement and philosophy upholds the high–popular distinction in a way that postmodernism does not. At postmodernism's outer edge, theorists point to the collapse of the modern distinction between the real and simulations.

As a set of philosophical and epistemological concerns, modernism is associated with the enlightenment philosophy of rationality, science, universal truth and progress. In contrast, postmodern philosophy has been associated with a questioning of these categories. Not depth but surface, not truth but truths, not objectivity but solidarity or social commendation (Rorty), not universalism or foundationalism but historically specific 'regimes of truth' (Foucault). However, while Lyotard calls these philosophical positions postmodern, Foucault questioned the need to be either for or against the enlightenment. Rorty has regretted using the term 'postmodern' (since the post-enlightenment philosophy he espouses can be traced back at least as far as Nietzsche), while Giddens argues that postmodern culture is an expression of 'radicalized modernity'.

Disagreements and debates centre on whether we should describe the features of contemporary life as modernity or postmodernity, whether or not the artistic projects of modernism and postmodernism are worlds apart, or whether they share features and whether it is valuable to describe the prevailing culture as postmodern. While many regard the questioning of the philosophical foundations of modernity as pointing to the democratic acceptance of difference and the reflexive ability to create ourselves, others have viewed it with trepidation. They have feared the inability to ground cultural politics, seeing postmodernism as a form of irrationalism which opens the door to the unfettered imposition of power. Likewise, while some writers see consumer capitalism as releasing the possibility for creative play and identity construction, others regard it as furthering the domination of global corporate power.

Part Three

SITES OF CULTURAL STUDIES

Part Three

6

Issues of Subjectivity and Identity

This chapter examines debates in cultural studies about subjectivity and cultural identity, exploring the assumptions of the western 'regime of the self'. Fuelled by political struggles as well by philosophical and linguistic concerns, 'identity' emerged as the central theme of cultural studies in the 1990s. The politics of feminism, of ethnicity and of sexual orientation, amongst others, have been high-profile concerns intimately connected to the politics of identity. In turn, these struggles for and around identity necessarily raised the question: what is identity?

SUBJECTIVITY AND IDENTITY

The concepts of **subjectivity** and **identity** are closely connected and virtually inseparable. However, we may take subjectivity to refer to the condition of being a person and the processes by which we become a person, that is, how we are constituted as subjects. As subjects, that is, as persons, we are 'subject to' social processes which bring us into being as 'subjects for' ourselves and others. The conceptions we hold of ourselves we may call **self-identity**, while the expectations and opinions of others form our **social identity**. Both take narrative or story-like form. To ask about subjectivity is to pose the question: what is a person? To explore identity is to enquire: how do we see ourselves and how do others see us?

Personhood as a cultural production

Subjectivity and identity are contingent culturally specific productions. What it means to be a person is social and cultural 'all the way down'. That is, identities are wholly social constructions and cannot 'exist' outside of cultural representations and **acculturalization**. There is no known culture that does not use the pronoun 'I' and which does not therefore have a conception of self and personhood. However, the manner in which 'I' is used, what it means, does vary from culture to culture. The individualistic sense of uniqueness and self-consciousness which is widespread in western societies is not shared to the same extent by people in cultures where personhood is inseparable from a network of kinship relations and social obligations.

The cultural repertoire of the self in the western world describes us as having a true self, an identity which we possess and which can become known to us. We take identity to be *expressed* through forms of representation which are recognizable by ourselves and by others. That is, identity is an essence which can be signified through **signs** of taste, beliefs, attitudes and lifestyles. Identity is deemed to be both personal and social and to mark us out as the same and different from other kinds of people. We may agree that identity is concerned with sameness and difference, with the personal and the social and with forms of **representation**. However, we will question the assumption that identity is either something we possess or a fixed thing to be found. Identity is best understood not as a fixed entity but as an emotionally charged description of ourselves.

Essentialism and anti-essentialism

The western search for identity is premised on the idea that there is such a 'thing' to be found, that identity exists as a universal and timeless core of the self which we all possess. We might say that persons have an 'essence' of the self which we call identity. Such **essentialism** assumes that descriptions of ourselves reflect an essential underlying identity. By this token there would be a fixed essence of femininity, masculinity, Asians, teenagers and all other social categories.

In contrast, it has been argued here that identity is cultural 'all the way down', being specific to particular times and places. This suggests that forms of identity are changeable and related to definite social and cultural conjunctures. The idea that identity is plastic is underpinned by arguments referred to as **anti-essentialism**. Here words are not taken as having referents with essential or universal qualities, for language 'makes' rather than 'finds' (Chapter 3). Identity is not a thing but a description in language. Identities are discursive constructions which change their meanings according to time, place and usage.

Self-identity as a project

For Giddens (1991), self-identity is constituted by the ability to sustain a **narrative** about the self, thereby building up a consistent feeling of biographical continuity. Identity stories attempt to answer the critical questions: 'What to do? How to act? Who to be?' The individual attempts to construct a coherent identity narrative by which 'the self forms a trajectory of development from the past to an anticipated future' (Giddens, 1991: 75). Thus, 'Self-identity is not a distinctive trait, or even a collection of traits, possessed by the individual. It is *the self as reflexively understood by the person in terms of her or his biography*' (Giddens, 1991: 53).

Giddens' argument conforms to our common-sense notion of identity, for he is saying that self-identity is what we as persons think it is. However, he is also arguing that identity is not a collection of traits that we possess; it is not something we have, nor an entity or a thing to which we can point. Rather, identity is a mode of thinking about ourselves. However, what we think we are changes from circumstance to circumstance in time and space. This is why Giddens describes identity as a *project*. By this he means that identity is something we create, something always in process, a moving towards rather than an arrival. An **identity project** builds on what we think we are now in the light of our past and present circumstances, together with what we think we would like to be, the trajectory of our hoped-for future.

Social identities

Though self-identity may be conceived of as *our* project, it is a sociological truism that we are born into a world that pre-exists us. We learn to use a language that was in use before we arrived and we live our lives in the context of social relationships with others. In short, we are constituted as individuals in a social process using socially shared materials. This is commonly understood as socialization or acculturalization. Without acculturalization we would not be persons as we understand that notion in our everyday lives. Without language the very concept of personhood and identity would be unintelligible to us.

There are no transcendental or ahistorical elements to what it is to be a person. Identity is wholly social and cultural, for the following reasons:

- The very notion of what it is to be a person is a cultural question. For example, individualism is a marker of specifically modern societies.
- The resources that form the material for an identity project, namely language and cultural practices, are social in character. Consequently, what it means to be a woman, a child, Asian or elderly is formed differently in different cultural contexts.

The resources we are able to bring to an identity project depend on the situational power from which we derive our cultural competencies within specific cultural contexts. It matters whether we are black or white, male or female, African or American, rich or poor, because of the differential cultural resources to which we will have had access. Here identity is a matter not only of self-description but also of social ascription.

> *Social identities* . . . are associated with normative rights, obligations and sanctions which, within specific collectivities, form roles. The use of standardized markers, especially to do with the bodily attributes of age and gender, is fundamental in all societies, notwithstanding large cross-cultural variations which can be noted. (Giddens, 1984: 282–3)

In sum, identity is about sameness and difference, about the personal and the social, 'about what you have in common with some people and what differentiates you from others' (Weeks, 1990: 89).

THE FRACTURING OF IDENTITY

In a seminal article on 'the question of cultural identity', Stuart Hall (1992b) identified three different ways of conceptualizing identity, which he calls (a) the enlightenment subject, (b) the sociological subject and (c) the postmodern subject. The purpose of this section is to expand upon those conceptualizations of identity, tracing the development of the fractured, decentred or postmodern subject.

The enlightenment subject

The notion of persons as unique unified agents has been allied to the Enlightenment, a philosophical movement associated with the idea that reason and rationality form the basis for human progress. The enlightenment subject

> was based on a conception of the human person as a fully centred, unified individual, endowed with the capacities of reason, consciousness and action, whose 'centre' consisted of an inner core. . . . The essential centre of the self was a person's identity. (Hall, 1992b: 275)

This is a view, known as the Cartesian subject and conjoined with Descartes' famous declaration 'I think, therefore I am', which placed the rational, conscious *individual* subject at the heart of western philosophy. Here the mind is regarded as having inherently *rational* capacities which allow it to experience the world and make sense of it according to the actual properties of that world.

Conceiving of the subject in this way is a matter not simply of philosophy but of the wider cultural processes of subject and identity formation, for it is central to the current western account of the self to see persons as unified and capable of organizing themselves. For example, morality talk, which in western culture seeks to make intelligible and manageable the moral and ethical dilemmas that face us, is centrally concerned with questions of individual responsibility for actions. Indeed, individual responsibility is embodied in the law which holds persons accountable for their actions. It is also manifested in the organization of academic knowledge into discrete subjects whereby the domain of psychology is held to be the workings of the individual mind and western medicine treats individual ailments. Economic theory, though concerned with social processes, has the rational, self-interested, choice-making individual at its centre.

The sociological subject

We have noted that identities are not self-generating or internal to the self but are cultural 'all the way down' because constituted through the processes of acculturalization. This socialized self Hall calls the sociological subject, where

> the inner core of the subject was not autonomous and self-sufficient, but was formed in relation to 'significant others', who mediated to the subject the values, meanings and symbols – the culture – of the worlds he/she inhabited. (Hall, 1992b: 275)

Our first 'significant others' are likely to be family members, from whom we learn, through praise, punishment, imitation and language, 'how to go on' in social life. Thus a key assumption of the sociological view of the subject is that people are social creatures whereby the social and the individual constitute each other. Though the self is conceived as possessing an inner unified core, this is formed *interactively* between the inner world and the outside social world. Indeed, the internalization of social values and roles stabilizes the individual and ensures that individual persons 'fit' the social structure by being stitched or 'sutured' into it.

The postmodern subject

The intellectual movement from the 'enlightenment' subject to the 'sociological' subject represents a shift from describing persons as unified wholes who ground themselves, to regarding the subject as socially formed. The social subject is not the source of itself, nor is it a 'whole' by virtue of the truism that people take up a variety of social positions. Nevertheless, the subject is seen as having a 'core self' able to **reflexively** co-ordinate itself into a unity. According to Hall's schema, the decentred or **postmodern** self involves the subject in shifting, fragmented and **multiple identities**. Persons are composed not of one but of several, sometimes contradictory, identities.

> The subject assumes different identities at different times, identities which are not unified around a coherent 'self'. Within us are contradictory identities, pulling in different directions, so that our identifications are continually being shifted about. If we feel that we have a unified identity from birth to death, it is only because we construct a comforting story or 'narrative of the self' about ourselves. (Hall, 1992b: 277)

Social theory and the fractured subject

Hall argues that five major 'ruptures in the discourses of modern knowledge' have contributed to our understanding of the subject as decentred. These are:

- Marxism;
- psychoanalysis;
- feminism;
- the centrality of language;
- the work of Foucault.

THE HISTORICAL SUBJECT OF MARXISM

Marxism, it is argued, displaces any notion of a universal essence of personhood which is the possession of each individual because 'men [sic] make history, but only on the basis of conditions not of their own making'. In other words, a historically specific mode of production and social relations constitutes subjects in particular ways so that what it is to be a person cannot be universal. Rather, the production of subjectivity is located in a social formation of a definite time and place with specific characteristics.

Thus, a feudal mode of production is based on the power of barons who own land and serfs (or lease it to peasants), so that the identities of barons and serfs are quite different, not only from each other, but from the social relations and identities formed within a capitalist mode of production wherein capitalists (and shareholders) employ the 'free' labour of the working class. What it means to be a baron, a serf, a capitalist and a worker are quite different because of the specific form of social organization of which they are a part.

Hall's interpretation of the Marxist subject could be held to be a simple sociological one were it not for the significance he attributes to the Althusserian reading of Marx, in which the place of ideology in the constitution of subjects is central. By the concept **ideology** is meant structures of signification or 'world views' which constitute social relations and legitimate the interests of the powerful. Crucially, for Althusser, the subject formed in ideology is not a unified Cartesian subject but a shattered and fragmented one.

For Althusser, classes, while sharing certain common conditions of existence, do not automatically form a core unified class consciousness but are cross-cut by conflicting interests and are formed and unformed in the course of actual historical development. Though I share similar working conditions with my neighbour, we do not share a homogeneous working-class identity, because I am male and she is female, I am black and she is white, I am a liberal and she is a nationalist. The general point here is that subjects are formed through difference, constituted by the play of signifiers, so that what we are is in part constituted by what we are not. In this context, Hall's Marxism points to the historically specific character of identity and to a fractured subject formed in ideology.

PSYCHOANALYSIS AND SUBJECTIVITY

Hall attributes the next of his decentrings to Freud and the 'discovery' of the unconscious through **psychoanalysis**. For Hall (1996a), psychoanalysis has particular significance in shedding light on how **identifications** of the 'inside' link to the regulatory power of the discursive 'outside'. Hall, along with many feminists, deploys psychoanalysis to link the 'inside' with the 'outside', stressing the processes by which discursively constructed subject positions are taken up (or otherwise) by concrete persons' fantasy identifications and emotional 'investments' (Henriques et al., 1984). Indeed, this contention is central to Hall's whole conceptualization of 'identity' as

> the point of suture, between on the one hand the discourses and practices which attempt to 'interpellate', speak to us or hail us into place as the social subjects of particular discourses, and on the other hand, the processes which produce subjectivities, which construct us as subjects which can be 'spoken'. Identities are thus the points of temporary attachment to the subject positions which discursive practices construct for us. (Hall, 1996a: 5–6)

According to Freud, the self is constituted in terms of an ego, or conscious rational mind, a superego, or social conscience, and the unconscious, the source and repository of the symbolic workings of the mind which functions with a different logic from reason. This view of personhood immediately fractures the unified Cartesian subject. It suggests that what we do and what we think are the outcome not of a rational integrated self but of the workings of the unconscious which are normally unavailable to the conscious mind in any straightforward fashion. The self is by definition fractured into the ego, superego and unconscious; the unified narrative of the self is something we acquire over time through entry into the symbolic order of language and culture. That is, through processes of identification with others and with social discourses we create an identity which embodies an illusion of wholeness.

For its supporters (Chodorow, 1978, 1989; Mitchell, 1974; J. Rose, 1997) the great strength of psychoanalysis lies in its rejection of the fixed nature of subjects and sexuality. Instead it concentrates on the construction and formation of subjectivity. Psychoanalysis also points us to the psychic and emotional aspects of identity through the concept of identification. By contrast, Nikolas Rose (1996) argues that psychoanalysis is an historically specific way of understanding persons which cannot be used to investigate the historicity of being human. He argues that 'the "interiority" which so many feel compelled to diagnose is not that of a psychological system, but of a discontinuous surface, a kind of infolding of exteriority' (Rose, 1996: 142). That is, the 'inside' is formed by the discourses which circulate on the 'outside'.

FEMINISM AND DIFFERENCE

Feminism is a plural field of theory and politics which has competing perspectives and prescriptions for action. In general terms, feminism asserts that sexual difference is a fundamental and irreducible axis of social organization. Feminism is centrally concerned with sex as an organizing principle of social life which is thoroughly saturated with power relations subordinating women to men.

For Hall, **feminism** constitutes a further decentring influence on conceptions of the subject because of its challenge, through the slogan and practice of the 'personal is political', to the distinction between the 'inside' and 'outside'; the public and the private. For example, domestic violence may occur in the private domain, but is of public concern and social causality. Feminism has interrogated the question of how we are formed as sexed subjects in the context of gendered families so that the 'inside' of gender is formed by the 'outside' of the family. Thus, what it is to be a person cannot be universal or unified since, at the very least, identity is marked by sexual difference.

In particular, poststructuralist and postmodern feminism (Nicholson, 1990; Weedon, 1997) argues that sex and gender are social and cultural constructions which are not reducible to biology. This is an anti-essentialist stance which argues that femininity and masculinity are not essential universal and eternal categories but are discursive constructions. As such, poststructuralist feminism is concerned with the cultural construction of subjectivity *per se* and with a range of possible masculinities and femininities. What distinguishes poststructuralism is the emphasis on language, which is also central to Hall's account of fractured identity.

LANGUAGE AND IDENTITY

As argued in Chapter 3, language is not a mirror which reflects an independent object world ('reality'), but a resource in 'lending form' to ourselves and our world out of the contingent and disorderly flow of everyday talk and practice (Shotter, 1993). Here, identity is not a fixed, eternal thing, nor an inner essence of a person to which words refer, but a regulated way of 'speaking' about persons. The idea that identities are discursive constructions is underpinned by a view of language in which there are no essences to which language refers and therefore no essential identities. That is, representation does not 'picture' the world but constitutes it for us. This is because of the following:

■ Signifiers generate meaning not in relation to fixed objects but in relation to other signifiers. According to **semiotic** theory, meaning is generated through relations of **difference**. Thus, 'good' is meaningful in relation to 'bad'.

■ The relationship between the sounds and marks of language, the **signifiers**, and what they are taken to mean, the **signifieds**, is not held in any fixed, eternal relationship.

■ To think about an independent object world is to do so in language. It is not possible to escape language in order to be able to view an independent object world directly. Nor can we attain a God-like vantage point from which to view the relationship between language and the world.

■ Language is relational in character. Words generate meaning not by reference to some special or essential characteristic of an object or quality but through the network of relationships of a **language-game** in use.

- Any given word includes the echoes or traces of other meanings from other related words in a variety of contexts. Meaning is inherently unstable and constantly slides away. Hence, **différance**, 'difference and deferral', by which the production of meaning is continually deferred and added to (or supplemented) by the meanings of other words.

This view of language has important consequences for understanding the self and identity. It cannot now be said that language directly *represents* a pre-existent 'I'. Rather, language and thinking *constitute* the 'I', they bring it into being through the processes of **signification**. Just as one cannot have an 'I', nor can one 'have' an identity. Rather, one is constituted through language as a series of discourses. Language does not express an already existent 'true self' but brings the self into being. Descartes' famous phrase 'I think, therefore I am' now becomes deeply problematic. 'I think, therefore I am' suggests that thinking is separate from and represents the pre-existent 'I'. However, since there is no 'I' outside of language, then thinking *is* being; 'I' is a position in language.

Although language generates meanings through a series of unstable and relational differences, it is also regulated within discourses which define, construct and produce their objects of knowledge. Consequently, what we can say about the identity characteristics of, for example, men is socially circumscribed. Identities are discursive constructions which do not refer to an already existent 'thing'. Identities are both unstable *and* temporarily stabilized by social practice and regular, predictable behaviour. This is a view influenced, as Hall argued, by the work of Foucault.

THE FOUCAULDIAN SUBJECT

Foucault is said to have produced a '**genealogy** of the modern subject'. That is, he has traced the derivation and lineage of subjects in and through history. Here, the subject is radically historicized, that is, the subject is wholly and only the product of history. For Foucault, subjectivity is a discursive production. That is, discourse (as regulated ways of speaking/practice) enables speaking persons **subject positions** from which to make sense of the world while 'subjecting' speakers to those discourses. A subject position is that perspective or set of regulated discursive meanings from which discourse makes sense. To speak is to take up a pre-existent subject position and to be subjected to the regulatory power of that discourse.

Foucault describes a subject which is the product of **power** through the individualization of those subject to it. For Foucault, power is not simply a negative mechanism of control but is *productive* of the self. The disciplinary power of schools, work organizations, prisons, hospitals, asylums and the proliferating discourses of sexuality produce subjectivity by bringing individuals into view. They fix them in writing via the discourses of, for example, medicine. For Foucault, genealogy's task 'is to expose the body totally imprinted by history and the processes of history's destruction of the body' (Foucault, 1984a: 63). The body is the site of disciplinary practices which bring subjects into being, these practices being the consequences of specific historical discourses of crime, punishment, medicine, science, sexuality, and so forth. Hence, power is generative; it is productive of subjectivity.

Foucault concentrates on three disciplinary discourses: the 'sciences', which constitute the subject as an object of inquiry; technologies of the self, whereby individuals turn themselves into subjects; and 'dividing practices', which separate the mad from the insane, the criminal from the law-abiding citizen, and friends from enemies. Disciplinary technologies, which arose in a variety of sites, including schools, prisons, hospitals and asylums, produced what Foucault called 'docile bodies' that could be 'subjected, used, transformed and improved' (Foucault, 1977: 198).

Discipline involves the organization of the subject in space through dividing practices, training and standardization. It brings together knowledge, power and control. Discipline produces subjects by categorizing and naming them in a hierarchical order through a rationality of efficiency, productivity and 'normalization' (Chapter 3). In this way we are produced and classified as particular kinds of people. Classificatory systems are essential to the process of normalization and thus to the production of a range of subjects. For example, schools demand that we be in certain places at specific times (classrooms and timetables), supervise our activities and grade us in relation to others by judging our (alleged) abilities (e.g. examinations).

Discourses of disciplinary and bio-power can be traced historically. Consequently, we can locate particular kinds of 'regimes of the self' in specific historical and cultural conjunctures. That is, different types of subject are the outcome of particular historical and social formations. Foucault attacks the 'great myth of the interior' and sees the subject as an historically specific production of discourse with no transcendental continuity from one subject position to another. This is an anti-essentialist position in which the subject is not unified but fractured.

The articulated self

For Stuart Hall, the cumulative effect of Marxism, psychoanalysis, feminism, theories of language and the work of Foucault is to **deconstruct** the essentialist notion of the unified agent who possesses a fixed identity as a referent for the pronoun 'I'. Instead, anti-essentialist conceptions of identity within cultural studies stress the decentred subject, the self as made up of multiple and changeable identities.

ANTI-ESSENTIALISM AND CULTURAL IDENTITY

Hall (1990) has usefully summarized the essentialist and anti-essentialist positions from which **cultural identity** can be understood. In the essentialist version identity is regarded as the name for a collective 'one true self' and is thought to be formed out of a common history, ancestry and set of **symbolic** resources. Through such optics it is possible to speak of a 'British identity' expressed through the symbol of the 'Union Jack', memories of the Second World War and collective rituals such as the FA Cup Final, the opening of Parliament and the nightly news. The underlying assumptions of this view are that collective identity exists, that it is 'a whole' expressed through symbolic representation. By this token there would be an essence of, for example, Black identity based on similarity of experience.

By juxtaposing 'British' and 'black', the assumptions of an essentialist argument are immediately made problematic for it might have been assumed that a British identity was a white Anglo-Saxon one. The presence of a substantial black (and Asian, Jewish, Chinese, Polish, etc.) population in Britain makes such an assumption impossible to sustain. Indeed it redefines what it means to be British. Being British can involve being black with the capability to trace one's ancestry back to Africa. However, just as the concept of British identity is problematic, so too is that of black identity. It is possible not only to argue for cultural identifications that *connect* black populations in Africa, America, the Caribbean and Britain, but also to trace the lines of *difference*. To be black British is not the same as being black African or black American.

Hall's anti-essentialist position regarding cultural identity stresses that as well as points of similarity, cultural identity is organized around points of difference. Cultural identity is seen not as a reflection of a fixed, natural, state of being but as a process of *becoming*. There is no essence of identity to be discovered; rather, cultural identity is continually being produced within the vectors of similarity and difference. Cultural identity is not an essence but a continually shifting position, and the points of difference around which cultural identities could form are multiple and proliferating. They include, to name but a few, identifications of class, gender, sexuality, age, ethnicity, nationality, political position (on numerous issues) morality, religion, etc., and each of these discursive positions is itself unstable. The meaning of Americanness, Britishness, Blackness, masculinity, and so forth, are subject to continual change since meaning is never finished or completed. Identity then becomes a 'cut' or a snapshot of unfolding meanings; it is a strategic positioning which makes meaning possible. This anti-essentialist position does not mean that we cannot speak of identity. Rather, it points us to the political nature of identity as a 'production' and to the possibility of multiple, shifting and fragmented identities which can be articulated together in a variety of ways.

THE ARTICULATION OF IDENTITIES

Laclau (1977) has argued that there are no *necessary* links between discursive concepts. Those which are forged are temporary, being articulated and bound together by connotative or evocative links which power and tradition have established. The concept of **articulation** suggests that those aspects of social life, for example identities, which we think of as unified and eternal can be thought of as the unique historically specific temporary stabilization or arbitrary closure of meaning.

Hall (1996b) suggests that an articulation is a connection that *can* make a unity of two different elements under certain conditions. The apparent 'unity' of identity is really the articulation of different and distinct elements which, under other historical and cultural circumstances, could be re-articulated in different ways. Thus, individuals are the unique historically specific articulation of discursive elements which are contingent but also socially determined or regulated. Since there is no *automatic* connection between the various discourses of identity, class, gender, race, age, etc., they can be articulated together in different ways. Thus, all middle-class white men do not necessarily share the same identity and identifications any more than all working-class black women do.

Hall illustrates his argument with the case of Clarence Thomas, an African-American US Supreme Court judge with conservative political views. Judge Thomas was accused of sexual harassment by Anita Hill, a black woman and former colleague of Thomas. As Hall puts it:

> Some blacks supported Thomas on racial grounds; others opposed him on sexual grounds. Black women were divided, depending on whether their 'identities' as blacks or women prevailed. Black men were also divided, depending on whether their sexism overrode their liberalism. White men were divided, depending, not only on their politics, but on how they identified themselves with respect to racism and sexism. White conservative women supported Thomas, not only on political grounds, but because of their opposition to feminism. White feminists, often liberal on race, opposed Thomas on sexual grounds. And because Judge Thomas is a member of the judicial elite and Anita Hall, at the time of the alleged incident, a junior employee, there were issues of social class position at work in these arguments too. (Hall, 1992b: 279–80)

Hall is making the point that identities are contradictory and cross-cut or dislocate each other. No single identity can, he argues, act as an overarching organizing identity; rather, identities shift according to how subjects are addressed or represented. We are constituted by fractured multiple identities. This signals to Hall (1996a) the 'impossibility' of identity as well as its 'political significance'. Indeed, in the plasticity of identity lies its political significance, for the shifting and changing character of identities marks the way that we think about ourselves and others. Contestation over identity and subjectivity concerns the very way that we are formed as human subjects, that is, the kinds of people we are becoming.

SITES OF INTERACTION

Giddens (1991) argues that the multiple narratives of the self are not the outcome of the shifting meanings of language *alone* but are also the consequence of the proliferation and diversification of social relationships, contexts and sites of interaction (albeit constituted in and through discourse – see Chapter 10). For example, compared to the eighteenth-century peasant, modern persons have a much wider scope of relationships, **spaces** and **places** in which to interact. These include spaces and relationships of work, family and friends, but also the global resources of television, e-mail and travel. The proliferation and diversification of contexts and sites of interaction prevent easy identification of particular subjects with a given, fixed, identity, so that the same person is able to shift across subject positions according to circumstances.

We might say that discourse, identities and social practice in time-space form a mutually constituting set implicated in the cultural politics of identity and the constitution of humanity as a form of life.

AGENCY AND THE POLITICS OF IDENTITY
The question of agency

Though the argument that identities are fractured discursive constructions is widely held within cultural studies, it is not without its problems. In particular, if subjects and identities are the product of discursive and disciplinary practices, if they are social and cultural 'all the way down', how can we conceive of persons as able to act and engender change in the social order? Since subjects appear within these arguments to be 'products' rather than 'producers', how shall we account for the human agency required for a cultural politics of change?

FOUCAULT AND THE PROBLEM OF AGENCY

Foucault concentrates the mind on issues of discourse, discipline and power. Subjects are understood as discursive constructions and the products of power, where discourse regulates what can be said about persons under determinate social and cultural conditions. Specifically the 'regimes of truth' (what counts as truth) of a disciplinary modernity involve relations of **power/knowledge** whereby knowledge is a form of power implicated in the production of subjectivity. As such, Foucault provides us with useful tools for understanding the connections between subjectivity/identity and the social order.

However, he does not provide us with an understanding of how and why particular discourses are 'taken up' by some subjects and not by others, or how a subject produced through disciplinary discursive practices can resist power (Hall, 1996a). That is, he does not provide us with an understanding of the emotional investments by which subjects are attached to discourse nor with a theory of agency. In this context, Foucault's description of subjects as 'docile bodies' whereby subjects are the 'effect' of discourse has been of concern to feminists and others involved in identity politics for he appears to rob subjects of the agency required for political action.

It is arguable that Foucault's later work centred on 'techniques of the self' does reintroduce agency and the possibility of **resistance** and change. Here, Foucault explores how subjects are 'led to focus attention on themselves, to decipher, recognize and acknowledge themselves as subjects of desire' (Foucault, 1987: 5); that is, how the self recognizes oneself as a subject involved in practices of self-constitution, recognition and reflection. This concern with self-production as a discursive practice is centred on the question of ethics as a mode of 'care of the self'.

According to Foucault, ethics are concerned with practical advice as to how one should concern oneself with oneself in everyday life, for example what it means to be a 'good' person, a self-disciplined person, a creative person, and so forth. They centre on the 'government of others and the government of oneself', so that ethical discourses, which circulate independently of any given particular individual, are ways by which we constitute ourselves, bring ourselves into being (Foucault, 1979, 1984b, 1986). Ethical discourses construct subject positions which enable agency to occur. More broadly, one can argue that regulatory discourses construct subject positions of agency. That is, agency is a discursive construction exemplifying the productive character of power.

GIDDENS AND STRUCTURATION THEORY

The case for conceiving of subjects as active and knowledgeable agents has consistently been put by Giddens, who has been a steadfast critic of Foucault for effacing agents from the narratives of history. Giddens, drawing from Garfinkel (1967), argues that social order is constructed in and through the everyday activities and accounts (in language) of skilful and knowledgeable actors or members. The resources that actors draw on, and are constituted by, are social in character, and indeed social **structure** (or regular patterns of activity) distributes resources and competencies unevenly between actors. That is, regularities or structural properties of social systems, which are distinct from any given individual, operate to structure what an actor is. For example, patterns of expectations about what it means to be a man or a woman, and the practices associated with gender, construct men and women differently as subjects. Gendered subjectivity then enables us to act in specifically gendered ways, for example as a mother or father.

Structuration theory (Giddens, 1984) centres on the way agents produce and reproduce social structure through their own actions. Regularized human activity is not brought into being by individual actors as such, but is continually re-created by them via the very means whereby they express themselves as actors. That is, in and through their activities agents reproduce the conditions that make those activities possible. Having been constituted as a man or a woman by gendered expectations and practices, having learned to be a father or mother, we then act in accordance with those rules, reproducing them again.

In this context, Giddens (1984) discusses Willis' (1977) *Learning to Labour*, wherein 'the lads' are active, knowledgeable agents who resist forms of school-based power on the basis of their class affiliations and expectations. However, through the very activity of resistance they unintentionally produce and reproduce their subordinate class position in the labour process. The lads resist school because they do not see schooling as relevant to their future lives since they expect to do working-class jobs (which they value); this leads to 'failure' at school, so that working-class jobs are precisely what they are then restricted to doing. In this way, Giddens seeks to demonstrate how persons can both be active, knowledgeable agents *and* be constituted by and reproduce social structures of, for example, class, gender and ethnicity.

THE DUALITY OF STRUCTURE

Central to Giddens' theory of structuration is the concept of the 'duality of structure', by which structures are not only constraining but enabling. Here, individual actors are determined by social forces which lie beyond them as individual subjects. However, those social structures enable subjects to act. For Giddens, identities are posed as an issue both of agency (the individual constructs a project) *and* of social determination (our projects are socially constructed and social identities ascribed to us).

For example, what it means to be a mother in a given society may mean that we cannot undertake paid employment, that is, we are constrained. However, the structures of motherhood also allows us to act as a 'mother', to be close to our children, to form networks with other mothers, and so forth. Likewise with language: we are all constructed and constrained by language, which pre-exists us, yet language is also the means and medium of self-awareness and creativity. That is, we can only say what is sayable in language, yet language is the medium by which we can say anything at all.

We noted that for Foucault the subject is the 'effect' of historically specific discourses and disciplinary practices. We also observed that Foucault's work has difficulties explaining the mechanisms by which particular subjects 'take up' certain discourses and how agency could be possible. Yet, Foucault also proposed a form of agency through a discursively constructed ethics centred on the care of the self. Indeed, agency can be said to be a subject position within discourse. Although Giddens tends to stress agency and Foucault discipline and determination, both suggest that it might be possible to think of subjects as being determined as has having agency. To grasp this possibility, we need to be clearer about what is meant by the concept of agency.

The concept of agency

The concept of agency has commonly been associated with notions of freedom, free will, action, creativity, originality and the very possibility of change through the actions of free agents. However, we need to differentiate between a metaphysical or 'mystical' notion of free agency in which agents are self-constituting (i.e. bring themselves into being out of nothingness) and a concept of agency as *socially produced* and enabled by differentially distributed social resources, giving rise to various degrees of the ability to act in specific spaces. For example, that an aspect of my identity is tied up with teaching and writing is not something which a pre-linguistic 'I' simply chose; rather, it is the outcome of the values and discourses of my family and educational experiences which in turn enable me to carry out those activities as an agent. There is, then, a difference between conceptions in which acts are made by agents who are free in the sense of 'not determined' and **agency** as the socially constituted capacity to act.

The notion that agents are free in the sense of undetermined is untenable for two reasons:

- In what could an undetermined or uncaused human act consist? It would have to be something created spontaneously from nothing – a metaphysical and mystical form of original creation.
- There is enough historical and sociological work available, not least from Foucault and Giddens, to show that subjects are determined, caused and produced, by social forces which lie outside of themselves as individuals. We are all subject to the 'impress of history' (Rorty, 1989).

AGENCY AS MAKING A DIFFERENCE

It is possible to argue that agency consists of acts which make a pragmatic difference. Here, agency means the enactment of X rather than Y as a course of action. Of course, precisely because agency is socially and differentially produced, some actors have more domains of action than others. Those whose acculturalization has led them to be highly educated in a formal sense or who have accrued wealth may have more options for action than others. The idea of agency as 'could have acted differently' avoids some of the problems of 'free as undetermined' because the pathways of action are themselves socially constituted.

CHOICE AND DETERMINATION

To enact X rather than Y does not mean that we have chosen it *per se*. We have simply acted. Nevertheless, questions of choice and determination remain at the heart of the debates about agency. There are a number of points to be considered here:

- As novelist Milan Kundera comments, 'We can never know what to want, because, living only one life, we can neither compare it with our previous lives nor perfect it in our lives to come' (Kundera, 1984: 8). We face a series of contingent choices and can have no certain foundations on which to base those choices.

- When we compare the outcomes of past actions, we are making *value judgements* about what is the best course of action, values in which we have been previously socially constituted. The basis for our choice does not spring out of thin air but has been determined or caused by the very way we are constituted as subjects, by where, when and how we came to be who we are.

- One of the implications of Freud's work is the idea that we act and choose in ways which are determined by psychic and emotional narratives which we cannot bring wholly to consciousness. Acts are determined to some degree from outside of the consciousness of the agent.

- A good deal of the actions of modern life are routine in character and are not thought about in a conscious discursive way but are part of taken-for-granted acts of 'going on'. Often, we do not make self-conscious choices at all but follow a socially determined routinized path.

- There is a sense in which we can never have 'objective' knowledge of the conditions of our own actions because we cannot step outside of those circumstances in order to compare our pristine selves with those conditions. Whatever we have to say about ourselves and the conditions of our existence is always already from within our socially constituted selves. The best we can do is to produce another story about our selves.

In sum, *agency is determined*. It is the socially constructed capacity to act and nobody is free in the sense of undetermined (in which event, one could not 'be' at all). Nevertheless, agency is a culturally intelligible way of understanding ourselves, and we clearly have the existential experience of facing and making choices. We do act even though those choices and acts are determined by social forces, particularly language, which lie beyond us as individual subjects. The existence of social structures (and of language in particular) is arguably a condition of action; it enables action so that neither human freedom nor human action can consist of an escape from social determinants.

MODES OF DISCOURSE

It is felicitous to consider freedom and determination as different *modes of discourse* and discursively constructed experience.

- Since we cannot escape language to achieve a God-like vantage point on an independent reality, it is pointless to ask whether people are 'really' free or 'really' determined in any absolute metaphysical sense. Rather, discourses of freedom and discourses of determination are different socially produced narratives about human beings which have different purposes and are applicable in different ways.
- We act with the idea of freedom, and the notion of determination 'all the way down' has no bearing on this existential experience. In other words, it plays no part in our everyday practices.
- Since discourses of freedom and discourses of determination are socially produced for different purposes in different realms, it make sense to talk about freedom from political persecution or economic scarcity without the need to say that agents are free in some undetermined way. Rather, such discourses are comparing different social formations and determinations and judging one to be better than another on the basis of our socially determined values.

ORIGINALITY

To hold subjectivity and identity to be contingent and determined does not mean that we are not original. While identity is a social and cultural accomplishment, our individuality can be understood in terms of the specific ways in which the social resources of the self are arranged. That is, while we are all subject to the 'impress of history', the particular form that we take, the specific arrangements of discursive elements, is unique to each individual for we have all had unique patterns of family relations, of friends, of work and of access to discursive resources. Further, it is possible to see the processes of the unconscious workings of the mind as a unique source of creativity where each human being is a 'tissue of contingencies' (Rorty, 1991b). For example, dreams can be seen as unique creative associations produced by specific individuals so that no two people dream the same dream in its exactness. The self is original like the moving elements of a kaleidoscope or like a snowflake constructed from the common ingredients that make up snow.

INNOVATION AND CHANGE

The determined or caused contingency of the self does not make the question of *innovative acts* especially problematic for they can be understood as the practical outcomes of unique combinations of social structures, discourses and psychic arrangements. Innovation is not a quality of the act but is a retrospective judgement by us on the form and outcomes of that act made in relation to other acts in specific historical and cultural conjunctures. Innovation is also a question of performance-in-context in so far as innovative acts are the consequence of discourses formed in one sphere of cultural life transported into another. For example, discourses of individuality and creativity formed in and through artistic practices or in the domain of leisure activities may have innovative and disturbing consequences in the context of discipline-oriented work organizations, schools or in families structured around an ideology of parental authority and control.

Innovation and change are possible because we are unique interdiscursive individuals and because the discourses which constitute society are themselves contradictory. In the context of contemporary western societies, it is intelligible to say that we can 're-articulate' ourselves, re-create ourselves, form ourselves anew in unique ways. This does not mean that we are not caused or determined but that we make ourselves singular by making new languages. We produce new metaphors to describe ourselves with and expand our repertoire of alternative descriptions (Rorty, 1991a). In so far as this applies to individuals, so it applies also to social formations. Social change becomes possible through rethinking the articulation of the elements of 'societies', redescribing the social order and the possibilities for the future.

Since, as Wittgenstein (1953) argued, there is no such thing as a private language, rethinking is a social and political activity. Change occurs through rethinking and redescribing, along with the material practices which are implicated in them. Rethinking ourselves, which emerges through social practice and more often than not through social contradiction and conflict, brings new political subjects and practices into being. For example, speaking of Rastafarians in Jamaica, Hall (1996b) argued that they became political subjects by learning to speak a new language, which was adapted from the Bible and shaped to their own purposes.

The concepts of agency, originality and innovation are important because they underpin the possibility of a politics of identity and social change. That is, **identity politics** rests on the notion that human beings can act purposefully and creatively. However, we must ask about what the politics of identity can mean in the

light of anti-essentialist arguments. That is, what can the politics
of identity be about if there is no such thing as identity?

Anti-essentialism, feminism and the politics of identity

The politics of feminism (see Chapters 8 and 12) provides a good
example of identity politics for it is based on the category of
'woman' which is said to give rise to shared interests. Some feminist writing has assumed a commonality of interests founded on a
shared biology. However, such biological essentialism is bedevilled
by problems.

BIOLOGY AS DISCOURSE

It is difficult to see how, on the basis of biology, women could form
a politics of common interest. It does not follow that because
women have similar bodies that they share cultural or political
interests. Rather, women are divided by class, ethnicity, nationality and other cultural forms and practices. For example, one of
the criticisms of western feminism is that a broadly middle-class
western movement does not articulate the interest of black women
or women in the developing world. Further, there is in principle
no access to biological truths which lie outside of cultural discourses. All knowledge, which includes understandings of biology
and shared interests, must, by necessity, be formed in language
and subject to discursive resources. There is no biology which is
not itself a social and cultural classifacatory construction. Since
there is no biology outside of discourse, it is difficult to see how
women's politics can be based on shared essential or 'real' biology.

   This does not mean that 'everything is discourse' and that there
are no bodies as such. The materiality of bodies is one of those
things which is, in the Wittgensteinian sense, beyond doubt. That
is, we cannot function without that assumption. As Wittgenstein
argues, we may in principle imagine that every time we open a
door there will be a bottomless chasm beneath us, but it makes no
sense to do so; it is unintelligible to us.

   As Butler (1993) argues, discourse and the materiality of bodies
are indissoluble. Not only is discourse the means by which we
understand what bodies are, but discourse brings bodies into view
in particular ways: 'In other words, "sex" is an ideal construct
which is forcibly materialized through time. It is not a simple fact
or static condition of a body, but a process whereby regulatory
norms materialize "sex" and achieve this materialization through
a forcible reiteration of those norms' (Butler, 1993: 1–2). The

discourse of sex is one which, through repetition of the acts it guides, brings sex into view as a necessary norm. Sex is a construction, but an indispensable one which forms subjects and governs the materialization of bodies.

SEX AND GENDER

Most feminist writing has relied not on biological determinism but on a conceptual division between **sex** and **gender**, where the former is the biology of the body and the latter the cultural assumptions and practices which govern the social construction of men, women and their social relations. Subsequently it is argued that it is the social, cultural and political discourses and practices of gender which lie at the root of women's inequality. This is what Nicholson (1995) has called the 'coat-rack' view of self-identity, by which the body is held to be a rack upon which cultural meanings are thrown. As she argues, 'one crucial advantage of such a position for feminists was that it enabled them to postulate both commonalities and differences among women' (Nicholson, 1995: 41). Further, since gender is a cultural construct, it is open to change.

However, if we accept Butler's argument that sex and the body are discursive constructs, then the sex–gender difference breaks down since both are socially constructed.

> In this alternative view the body does not disappear from feminist theory. Rather, it becomes a variable rather than a constant, no longer able to ground claims about the male/female distinction across large sweeps of history but still there as always a potentially important element in how the male/female distinction *gets played out in any specific society*. (Nicholson, 1995: 43–4, my emphasis)

Of course, most societies continue to operate with a binary male–female distinction, attaching to it cultural expectations which are detrimental to women. However, the cultural variations that exist between women, based not only on differences of class, ethnicity, age, etc., but also on differences about what it means to be a woman, suggest that there is no universal cross-cultural category of 'woman' that is shared by all women. Further, acceptance of the idea that sex is a cultural construct leads to the blurring of the male/female distinction, allowing for ambiguous and dual sexualites. In short, neither biological nor cultural essentialism can found a feminist politics based on a universal identity of woman.

IS A UNIVERSAL FEMINISM POSSIBLE?

Some of these issues are raised by Kaplan (1997) in her discussion of the film *Warrior Marks* directed by the African-American Alice Walker and the Kenyan-born British Asian Pratibha Parmar. The film was a graphic critique of clitoridectomies in Africa which aimed to dramatize the terror and pain involved while educating women about its dangers. In doing so, the film claims that clitoridectomies are a form of torture and child abuse in violation of universal women's rights (as affirmed by the 1995 Beijing Women's Conference). However, the adult African women in the film confidently defend clitoridectomies as a necessary part of their traditions and sacred practices. While sympathetic to the anti-clitoridectomy theme, Kaplan raises a number of potential criticisms of the film, including the arguments that it:

- makes its points at the expense of the African women;
- reproduces the imperialist tradition of teaching Africans a 'better' way of living;
- relies on established stereotypes of Africans as exotic and savage;
- assumes a global women's rights and is thus essentialist.

How can there be a universal or global feminism when there is an unbridgeable difference between these western African-American and British-Asian feminists and the African women in the film? There would appear to be no agreed rules or point of potential arbitration for coming to agreement as to what would constitute justice or women's rights and interests. By implication, universal women's rights are either impossible or, if declared, another version of the imperialist representation of western categories as applicable at all times and in all places.

Since all knowledge is positional or culture-bound, cultural and political discourses can in the abstract be said to be incommensurable, there being no metalanguage of translation. Feminism cannot bridge cultures but must be satisfied with being specific to times and places. However, we can recognize others as language users. If we consider languages (as culture and knowledge) as not constituted by untranslatable and incompatible rules but as learnable skills then incommensurable languages could only be unlearnable languages. As Davidson (1984) avers, it makes no sense to say that another's language is unlearnable (and therefore untranslatable) for we would in the first place have had to have learned enough of the others' language to recognize them as language users at all. Hence we need to encourage *dialogue* and the attempt to reach pragmatic agreements. There is no *a priori* reason why this should succeed – agreement may never be reached – but there is no *a priori* reason why it should fail either (Rorty, 1991a). Given the poverty, inequality and violence that women across the globe endure, it is difficult to believe that agreement could not reached on a range of practical issues.

THE PROJECT OF FEMINISM

None of this means that the project of feminism is not valid. Nor is it being suggested that women are not subject to patterns of gender inequality. Rather, it is to argue for the 'replacement of claims about women as such or even women in patriarchal societies with claims about women in particular contexts' (Nicholson, 1995: 59). Nicholson goes on to argue that we should regard the meaning of the word 'woman' not in the singular but as part of a language-game of different and overlapping meanings. Consequently, feminism is conceived of as a coalition politics formed amongst women who come to believe that they share particular interests in specific contexts. The meaning of 'woman' in feminist politics has to be forged rather than taken as a given. The politics of identity has to be *made* rather than found.

In a not dissimilar vein, Rorty argues that feminism represents the redescription of women as subjects. The critical point of Rorty's argument is that

> injustices may not be perceived as injustices, even by those who suffer them, until somebody invents a previously unplayed role. Only if somebody has a dream, a voice, and a voice to describe the dream, does what looked liked nature begin to look like culture, what looked liked fate begin to look like a moral abomination. For until then only the language of the oppressor is available, and most oppressors have had the wit to teach the oppressed a language in which the oppressed will sound crazy – *even to themselves* – if they describe themselves as oppressed. (Rorty, 1995: 126)

The contention is that the language of feminism brings oppression into view and expands the logical space for moral and political deliberation. Feminism does not need essentialism at all. What is required is a 'new language' in which the claims of women do not sound crazy but come to be accepted as 'true' (in sense of a social commendation). Feminism involves not less distorted perception but a language with consequences which serve particular purposes and values. The emergence of such a language is not the discovery of universal **truth** but part of an evolutionary struggle which has no immanent teleology, that is, no future predetermined destiny to which it must evolve.

CREATING 'NEW LANGUAGES'

Like Nicholson, Rorty regards feminism as creating 'women's experience' by creating a language rather than by finding what it is to be a woman or unmasking truth and injustice. As such, feminism is seen as a form of 'prophetic pragmatism' which imagines, and seeks to bring into being, an alternative form of community. Feminism forges a moral identity for women as women by gaining linguistic authority over themselves rather than assuming that there is an essential identity for women waiting to be found.

In her discussion of Rorty's arguments, Fraser (1995a) suggests that he locates redescriptions exclusively in individual women. In contrast, she suggests that such redescriptions form part of a *collective* feminist politics which must involve argument and contestation about which new descriptions will count and which women will be empowered. Thus, Fraser links feminism to the best of the democratic tradition and to the creation of a 'feminist counter-sphere' of collective debate and practice. In doing so, she begins to address the question of *how* a politics of identity can bring about change, in a way which is underplayed in Rorty's argument. These themes are taken up and elaborated in Chapter 12.

Challenging the critique of identity

The anti-essentialist conception of identities which locates them as discursive constructs is the dominant strain of thinking in contemporary cultural studies. However, there is a stream of thought within cultural studies that opposes, or at least seeks to modify, such conceptions.

- It is argued that a discourse-centred conception of society and identities collapses the notion of the social into language. Critics argue that everything becomes discourse and there is no material reality. However, to say that we can only have knowledge of the material world through discourse is not to say that such a material world is not present. There are indeed aspects of the world which 'are the effects of causes which do not include human mental states' (Rorty, 1989). However, we can only know them through language. Discourse and materiality are, *pace* Butler, indissociable. Indeed, what could the social consist of outside of the discursive, and how could we know?
- It is argued that discourse-based theories efface human agency, that is, human beings are seen as 'effects' of discourse. However, we tackled this question earlier in the chapter by arguing that agency is

the socially constructed capacity to act. Discourse enables action by providing subject positions of agency.

- It is suggested that anti-essentialist arguments about identity are of no *practical* value. We require, it is said, a more constructive and positive account of the politics of identity based on a **strategic essentialism** in which we act *as if* identities were stable entities for specific political and practical purposes. This point requires further elaboration.

STRATEGIC ESSENTIALISM

Appiah (1995) has suggested that while we can make the argument for 'African identity' being a discursive device which can be 'deconstructed', this does not mean that people do not mobilize round the idea of African identity or pan-Africanism as the means for political change and improvement. Nor does it mean that pan-Africanism may not provide a valuable device for the improvement of the human condition. Indeed, he suggests that deconstructing identities from within the academy is simply of little relevance to most people's lives or to the practice of most forms of political action.

That argument has some merit for practical purposes. Indeed, strategic essentialism may be what in practice happens. Hall (1993) has argued that any sense of self, of identity, of communities of identification (nations, ethnicities, sexualities, classes, etc.) and the politics that flow from them are fictions marking a temporary, partial and arbitrary closure of meaning. Some kind of strategic cut or temporary stabilization of meaning is necessary in order to say or do anything. As Hall remarks, 'politics, without the arbitrary interposition of power in language, the cut of ideology, the positioning, the crossing of lines, the rupture, is impossible' (Hall, 1993: 136).

Strategic essentialism is open to the criticism that at some point certain voices have been excluded. Thus, the strategic essentialism of feminism, that it takes women to be an essential category for tactical reasons, may lead to some women, for example black or Hispanic women, saying to white women, 'you have not taken account of our differences as well as our similarities with you'. Likewise, pan-Africanism may lead to the obscuring of difference and the exclusion of certain voices. In particular, 'strategic essentialism' begs the question of where to draw the tactical line. Who, for example, is African or a woman? Strategic essentialism tends towards ethnic or gender 'absolutism' and bypasses the **hybrid** and syncretic character of contemporary culture and identities (Chapter 7).

SUMMARY

Identity concerns both self-identity and social identity. It is about the personal and the social, about ourselves and our relations with others. It has been argued that identity is wholly cultural in character and does not exist outside of its representation in cultural discourses. Identity is not a fixed thing which we possess but a becoming. It is a strategic cut or temporary stabilization in language. We may understand identity as regulatory discourses to which we are attached through processes of identification or emotional investment.

The self has been understood as multiple, fragmented and decentred. This is an outcome of the instability of language, our constitution by multiple discourses and the proliferation of social relationships and sites of activity. None of these arguments need efface human agency, provided that one understands agency as itself a socially constructed and differentially distributed set of capabilities to act. Nor do anti-essentialist arguments preclude identity politics, where such a politics is constituted through redescriptions in language and temporary strategic coalitions of people who share at least some *values*.

Ethnicity, Race and Nation

I n this chapter we will be concerned with ethnicity, race and nationality as forms of **cultural identity**. These are regarded as discursive–performative constructions (Chapter 6). That is, ethnic, racial and national identities are contingent and unstable cultural creations with which we identify. They are not universal or absolute existent 'things'. However, as regulated ways of speaking about ourselves, identities are not arbitrary either for they are temporarily stabilized by social practice. Indeed, race, ethnicity and nationality are amongst the more enduring 'nodal points' of **identity** in modern western societies.

RACE AND ETHNICITY

The concept of **race** bears the traces of its origins in the biological discourses of social Darwinism which stress 'lines of descent' and 'types of people'. Here race refers to alleged biological and physical characteristics, the most obvious of which is skin pigmentation. These attributes, frequently linked to 'intelligence' and 'capabilities, are used to rank 'racialized' groups in a hierarchy of social and material superiority and subordination. These racial classifications, constituted by and constitutive of **power**, are at the root of racism.

Racialization

The idea of 'racialization' or 'race formation' encompasses the argument that race is a social construction and not a universal or essential category of biology or culture. Races, it is argued (Hall, 1990, 1996d, 1997c), do not exist outside of **representation** but are formed in and by it in a process of social and political power struggle. Thus, observable characteristics are transformed into signifiers of race, including the spurious appeal to essential biological and cultural difference. As Gilroy argues:

> Accepting that skin 'colour', however meaningless we know it to be, has a strictly limited material basis in biology, opens up the possibility

of engaging with theories of signification which can highlight the elasticity and emptiness of 'racial' signifiers as well as the ideological work which has to be done in order to turn them into signifiers of 'race' as an open political category, for it is struggle that determines which definitions of 'race' will prevail and the conditions under which they will endure or wither away. (Gilroy, 1987: 38–9)

In Britain, America and Australia the historical formation of 'race' is one of power and subordination so that people of colour have occupied **structurally** subordinate positions in relation to every dimension of 'life-chances'. British Afro-Caribbeans, African-Americans and Australian Aboriginal peoples have occupied lower paid, less skilled jobs, have been disadvantaged in the housing market, at school and in media and cultural representations. In this context, race formation or racialization has been inherently racist for it involves forms of social, economic and political subordination which are lived through the categories and **ideology** of race.

Different racisms

As a discursive construct, the meanings of 'race' change and are struggled over so that different groups are differentially racialized and subject to different racisms. For example, British Asians have historically been subject to different forms of stereotyping and have occupied a different place in the social and racial hierarchy from British Afro-Caribbeans. While British Asians may be second-class citizens, black Britons are on the third rung of the ladder. British Asians are stereotyped as doctors and shopkeepers while young Afro-Caribbean men in Britain are cast in the role of criminals.

The meanings of race differ over time and across space. For example, it has been argued (Barker, 1982) that the 'new racism' in Britain relies not on biological discourses of superiority, as in South African apartheid, but on cultural differences which exclude black people from being fully a part of the *nation*. In addition, the meanings of race differ between, say, America and Britain. In Britain, the relatively homogeneous white character of the *in situ* population was disturbed in the 1950s by the arrival of migrants from the Caribbean and Indian sub-continent, making questions of national identity a crucial category through which racialization operated. However, West (1992) has argued that the history of the modern United States begins with the dispossession and genocide of native American peoples and continues through the long history of slavery. Thus, questions of race are posed at the very inception of the US in ways which are more long-standing, but less concerned with nationality, than in Britain.

The concept of ethnicity

Ethnicity is a cultural concept centred on the sharing of norms, values, beliefs, cultural symbols and practices. The formation of 'ethnic groups' relies on shared cultural signifiers which have developed under specific historical, social and political contexts and which encourage a sense of belonging based, at least in part, on a common mythological ancestry. However, following **anti-essentialist** arguments (Chapter 6), it is clear that ethnic groups are not based on primordial ties or universal cultural characteristics possessed by a specific group but are formed through discursive practices. Ethnicity is formed by the way we speak about group identities and identify with the signs and symbols which constitute ethnicity.

Ethnicity is a *relational* concept concerned with categories of self-identification and social ascription. What we think of as our identity is dependent on what we think we are *not*. Serbians are not Croatians, Bosnians or Albanians. Consequently, ethnicity is best understood as a process of boundary formation constructed and maintained under specific socio-historical conditions (Barth, 1969). Of course, to suggest that ethnicity is not about pre-given cultural difference but a process of boundary formation and maintenance does not mean that such distinctiveness cannot be socially constructed around signifiers which do connote universality, territory and purity, for example metaphors of blood, kinship and homeland.

A culturalist conception of ethnicity is a valiant attempt to escape the racist implications which are inherent in the historically forged concept of race. As Hall writes,

> If the black subject and black experience are not stabilized by Nature or by some other essential guarantee, then it must be the case that they are constructed historically, culturally and politically – the concept which refers to this is 'ethnicity'. The term ethnicity acknowledges the place of history, language and culture in the construction of subjectivity and identity, as well as the fact that all discourse is placed, positioned, situated, and all knowledge is contextual. (Hall, 1996c: 446)

However, the concept of ethnicity is not without its problems of usage and it remains a contested term. For instance, white Anglo-Saxons frequently use the concept of ethnicity to refer to *other* people, usually with different skin pigmentation, so that Asians, Africans, Hispanics and African-Americans are ethnic groups but the English or white Anglo-Saxon Americans or Australians are not. Here whiteness is seen as a taken-for-granted universal while anyone else is held to have been constituted ethnically. In contrast, it is important to maintain that white English, American or Australian people *do* constitute ethnic groups. As Dyer has argued, studying whiteness 'is about making whiteness strange rather than treating it as a taken for granted touchstone of human ordinariness' (Dyer, 1997). Nevertheless, as he notes, the recognition that whiteness is a historical invention does not mean that it can simply be wished away.

Ethnicity and power

One problem with the cultural concept of ethnicity is that questions of power and racism may be sidelined. Ethnicity can be deployed, as in some discussions about multiculturalism, to suggest that a **social formation** operates with plural and equal groups rather than hierarchical racialized groups. Consequently, hooks (1990) and Gilroy (1987) prefer the concept of 'race', not because it corresponds to any biological or cultural absolutes, but because it connotes, and refers investigation to, issues of power. In contrast, Hall (1996c) looks to a reworking of the concept of ethnicity in which we are all held to be ethnically located (Hall, 1996c).

Ethnicity is constituted through power relations between groups. It signals relations of marginality, of the centre and the periphery, in the context of changing historical forms and circumstances. Here, the centre and the margin are to be grasped through the politics of representation, for, as Brah argues: 'It is necessary for it to become axiomatic that what is *represented* as the "margin" is not marginal at all but is a *constitutive effect of the representation itself*. The "centre" is no more a centre than is the "margin"' (Brah, 1996: 226).

Discourses of ethnic centrality and marginality are commonly **articulated** with those of nationality. For example, the nations of the industrialized West are often regarded as 'the centre' in relation to a 'periphery' of 'developing' nations. Further, history is littered with examples of how one ethnic group has been defined as central and superior to a marginal 'other'. While Nazi Germany, apartheid South Africa and 'ethnic cleansing' in Bosnia are clear-cut examples, the metaphor of superiority and subordination is no less applicable to contemporary Britain, America and Australia. Thus, race and ethnicity have been closely allied to nationalisms which conceive of the 'nation' as a shared culture requiring that ethnic boundaries should not cut across political ones (though of course they do).

NATIONAL IDENTITIES
The nation-state

The modern nation-state is a relatively recent invention, for most of the human species have never participated in any kind of state nor identified with one. The nation-state, nationalism and **national identity** as collective forms of organization and identification are not 'naturally' occurring phenomena but contingent historical–cultural formations.

The nation-state is a **political** concept which refers to an administrative apparatus deemed to have sovereignty over a specific **space** or territory within the nation-state system. National identity is a form of imaginative **identification** with the symbols and discourses of the nation-state. Thus, nations are not simply political formations but systems of cultural representation through which national identity is continually reproduced as discursive action. The nation-state as a political apparatus and a symbolic form has a temporal dimension in that political structures endure and change while the **symbolic** and discursive dimensions of national identity narrates and creates the idea of origins, continuity and tradition.

Though we speak of the nation-state, it is necessary to disentangle the couplet since national cultural identities are not coterminous with state borders. Various global diasporas – African, Jewish, Indian, Chinese, Polish, English, Irish etc. – attest to national and ethnic cultural identities which span the borders of nation-states. Further, few states have ethnically homogeneous populations. Smith (1990) not only distinguishes between *civic/political* conceptions of nations and *ethnic* ones, but is able to list over sixty states which are constituted by more than one national or ethnic culture.

Narratives of unity

Cultures are not static entities but are constituted by changing practices and meanings which operate at different social levels. Any given national culture is understood and acted upon by different social groups, so that governments, ethnic groups and classes may perceive it in divergent ways. At which level should a national culture be identified? Which set of values within those groups are the **authentic** ones? Further, any ethnic or class group will be divided along the lines of age and gender (Tomlinson, 1991). Representations of national culture are snapshots of the symbols and practices which have been foregrounded at specific historical conjunctures for particular purposes by distinctive groups of people. National identity is a way of unifying cultural diversity so that, as Hall argues,

> Instead of thinking of national cultures as unified, we should think of them as a discursive device which represents difference as unity or identity. They are cross-cut by deep internal divisions and differences, and 'unified' only through the exercise of different forms of cultural power. (Hall, 1992b: 297)

That unity is constructed through the **narrative** of the nation by which stories, images, symbols and rituals represent 'shared' meanings of nationhood (Bhabha, 1990). National identity is an identification with representations of shared experiences and history told through stories, literature, **popular culture** and the media. Narratives of nationhood emphasize the traditions and continuity of the nation as being 'in the nature of things' along with a foundational myth of collective origin. This in turn both assumes and produces the linkage between national identity and a pure, original people or 'folk' tradition.

The imagined community

National identities are intrinsically connected to, and constituted by, forms of communication. For Anderson (1983), the 'nation' is an 'imagined community' and national identity a construction assembled through symbols and rituals in relation to territorial and administrative categories.

> It is *imagined* because the members of even the smallest nation will never know most of their fellow members, meet them, or even hear of them, yet in the minds of each lives the images of their communion. . . . The nation is imagined as *limited* because even the largest of them, encompassing perhaps a billion living beings, has finite, if elastic boundaries, beyond which lie other nations. . . . It is imagined as *sovereign* because the concept was born in an age in which Enlightenment and Revolution were destroying the legitimacy of the divinely ordered, hierarchical dynastic realm. . . . Finally, it is imagined as a *community* because, regardless of the actual inequality and exploitation that may prevail in each, the nation is always conceived as a deep, horizontal comradeship. Ultimately, it is this fraternity that

makes it possible, over the past two centuries, for so many millions of people, not so much to kill, as willingly to die for such limited imaginings. (Anderson, 1983: 15–16)

According to Anderson, the mechanized production and **commodification** of books and newspapers, the rise of 'print capitalism', allowed vernacular languages to be standardized and disseminated, providing the conditions for the creation of a national consciousness. Thus, 'Print language is what invents nationalism, not a particular language per se' (Anderson, 1983: 122). For the first time it was possible for the mass of people within a particular state to understand each other through a common print language. The processes of print **capitalism** thus 'fixed' a vernacular language as the 'national' language and made possible a new imagined national community. Communication facilitates not just the construction of a common language but also a common recognition of time, which, within the context of **modernity**, is an empty universal concept measurable by calendar and clock. For example, the media encourage us to imagine the simultaneous occurrence of events across wide tracts of time and space, which contributes to the concept of nation and to the place of states within a spatially distributed global system.

Criticisms of Anderson

Useful though Anderson's account is in linking forms of national identity with modes of communication, his work falls short, as Thompson (1995) points out, of specifying exactly how new print forms give rise to national sentiments. Nor does he deal adequately with the various ways in which divergent social groups use media products and decode them in different ways. At best, Anderson shows how print media established the necessary conditions for national identity and the nation-state.

Anderson tends to overstate the unity of the nation and the strength of nationalist feeling and thus covers over differences of class, gender, ethnicity, and so forth. Indeed, the proliferation and diversification of contexts and sites of interaction, constituted in and through discourse, prevent easy identification of particular subjects with a given, fixed, identity. Consequently, in the context of the accelerated **globalization** of late modernity (Chapter 4), we have begun to talk about **hybrid** cultural identities rather than a homogeneous national or ethnic cultural identity. Further, the instability of meaning in language, **différance**, leads us to think of culture, identities and identifications as always a place of borders and hybridity rather than fixed stable entities (Bhabha, 1994).

DIASPORA AND HYBRID IDENTITIES

Stable identities are rarely questioned; they appear as 'natural' and taken for granted. However, when 'naturalness' is seen to dissolve, we are inclined to examine these identities anew. As Mercer (1992) has argued, identity is hotly debated when it is in crisis. Globalization provides the context for just such a crisis since it has increased the range of sources and resources available for identity construction. Patterns of population movement and settlement established during colonialism and its aftermath, combined with the more recent acceleration of globalization, particularly of electronic communications, have enabled increased cultural juxtaposing, meeting and mixing.

According to Pieterse, it is necessary to differentiate between 'culture' as bounded, that is, tied to place and inward-looking, from 'culture' as an outward-looking 'translocal learning process'. He argues that introverted cultures are receding into the background as diverse translocal cultures come to the fore (Pieterse, 1995).

Bounded societies and states, though very much still with us, are cut across by the circulation of global cultural discourses. Thus, Clifford (1992), amongst others, has argued that culture and cultural identities can no longer be adequately understood in terms of **place**, but are better conceptualized in terms of travel. This includes peoples and cultures which travel and places/ cultures as sites of criss-crossing travellers.

The idea of diaspora

In this context, new prominence is being given to the old concept of **diaspora**, which focuses attention on travel, journeys, dispersion, homes and borders in the context of questions about who travels, 'where, when, how and under what circumstances' (Brah, 1996: 182). Thus, 'diasporic identities are at once local and global. They are networks of transnational identifications encompassing "imagined" and "encountered" communities' (Brah, 1996: 196). Diaspora is a *relational* concept referring to 'configurations of power which differentiate diasporas internally as well as situate them in relation to one another' (Brah, 1996: 183).

Diaspora space as a conceptual category is 'inhabited' not only by those who have migrated and their descendants, but equally by those who are constructed and represented as indigenous. In other words, the concept of *diaspora space* . . . includes the entanglement, the intertwining of the genealogies of dispersion with those 'staying put'. The diaspora space is the site where *the native is as much a diasporian as the diasporian is a native*. (Brah, 1996: 209)

According to Gilroy (1997), the divided network of related peoples which form the diaspora is one 'characteristically produced by forced dispersal and reluctant scattering'. It 'connotes flight following the threat of violence', so that 'diaspora identity is focused less on the equalizing, proto-democratic force of common territory and more on the social dynamics of remembrance and commemoration defined by a strong sense of the dangers involved in forgetting the location of origin and the process of dispersal' (Gilroy, 1997: 318).

The Black Atlantic

The concept of diaspora helps us to think about identities in terms of contingency, indeterminacy and conflict; of identities in motion rather than of absolutes of nature or culture. Routes rather than roots. A 'changing same' of the diaspora which involves 'creolized, syncretized, hybridized and chronically impure cultural forms' (Gilroy, 1997: 335). As an example, Gilroy (1993) introduces the concept of the Black Atlantic. Black identities cannot be understood, he argues, in terms of being American or British or West Indian. Nor can they be grasped in terms of ethnic absolutism (that there is a global essential black identity); rather, they should be understood in terms of the black Diaspora of the Atlantic. Here, cultural exchange within the black Diaspora produces hybrid identities and cultural forms of similarity and difference within and between the various locales of the diaspora. As Gilroy (1987) argues, black self-identities and cultural expressions utilize a plurality of histories.

Blackness is not a pan-global absolute identity for the cultural identities of black Britons, black Americans and black Africans are different. Nevertheless, Gilroy points to *historically* shared cultural forms within the Black Atlantic. Despite the different meanings and history of 'race' which have operated in Britain, America, Africa and the Caribbean, 'It may be that a common experience of powerlessness somehow transcending history and experienced in *racial* categories; in the antagonism between white and black rather than European and African, is enough to secure affinity between these divergent patterns of subordination' (Gilroy, 1987: 158–9). For example, Rap and Hip-Hop, American–Caribbean hybrids, have become the prominent musical forms of the Black Diaspora and a point of identification within the Black Atlantic.

Types of hybridity

The concept of hybridity has proved useful in highlighting cultural mixing and the emergence of new forms of identity. However, we need to differentiate between types of hybridity and to do so with reference to the specific circumstances of particular social groups. Pieterse (1995) has suggested a distinction between structural and cultural hybridization. The former refers to a variety of social and institutional *sites* of hybridity, for example border zones or cities like Miami or Singapore. The latter distinguishes cultural *responses*, which range from assimilation, through forms of separation, to hybrids that destabilize and blur cultural boundaries. Pieterse argues that structural hybridization, which increases the range of organizational options to people, and cultural hybridization, which involves the opening up of 'imagined communities', are signs of increased boundary crossing. However, they do not represent the erasure of boundaries so that we need to be sensitive both to cultural *difference* and to forms of identification that involve recognition of *similarity*.

This requires us to recognize the *range* of cultural and national identities which are formed and unformed over time and across a variety of spaces. We might in theory think of at least six different kinds of cultural juxtaposing (Barker, 1997a, 1997b):

- Two distinct cultural traditions are kept separate in time and/or space. We would define ourselves as Asian *or* British, Mexican *or* American. This is the domain of nationalism and ethnic absolutism.
- Two separate cultural traditions are juxtaposed in time and space. We would define ourselves as Asian *and* British, Mexican *and* American, moving between them as situationally appropriate.
- Cultures are translocal and involve global flows. Hybridization occurs out of recognition of difference and produces something new. We are 'British Asian' or 'Mexican American'.
- Cultural traditions develop in separate locales but develop identifications based on perceived similarity and commonalty of tradition and circumstance. For example, an essentialist version of pan-global black or Hispanic nationalism.

- One cultural tradition absorbs or obliterates the other and creates effective similarity. This could involve assimilation (my parents are Asian but I am British) or cultural domination and imperialism (one tradition is wiped out).
- New forms of identity are forged out of shared concerns along the axis of class, ethnicity, gender, age, etc. This is an anti-essentialist position in which similarity is forged strategically. For example, a strategic alliance in which black and Asian people share a common anti-racist strategy. Equally, strategic identifications and alliances occur on other axes, such as gender, so that a shared feminism might be more significant than ethnic difference.

The hybridity of all culture

The concept of hybridity remains problematic in so far as it assumes or implies the meeting or mixing of completely separate and homogeneous cultural spheres. To think of British Asian or Mexican American hybrid forms as the mixing of two separate traditions is problematic because neither British, Asian, Mexican nor American culture is bounded and homogeneous. Each category is always already a hybrid form which is also divided along the lines of religion, class, gender, age, nationality, and so forth. Hybridization is the mixing of that which is already a hybrid. All cultures are zones of shifting boundaries and hybridization (Bhabha, 1994). Nevertheless, the concept of hybridity has enabled us to recognize the production of new identities and cultural forms, for example 'British Asians' and British Banghra. Thus, the concept of hybridity is acceptable as a device to capture cultural change by way of a strategic cut or temporary stabilization of cultural categories.

Hybridity and British Asians

In Britain, the 'place' and cultures of Asians in relation to Anglo-Saxon and Afro-Caribbean Britons have raised issues of purity and hybridity. Ballard (1994) documents the emergence, since the early 1950s, of *desh pardesh*, a phrase with the double meaning of 'home from home' and 'at home abroad'. He emphasizes:

- the determination of arrivals from South Asia to pursue their own self-determined goals;
- the diverse and heterogeneous character of South Asian ethnicities in Britain;
- the changing dispositions involved in the settlers' adaptive strategies.

The already complex nature of South Asian settler cultural identities is indicated by the diverse 'origins' of direct migrants, who came from the distinct geographical areas of the Punjab, Gujarat and Sylhet, each of which is cross-cut by differences of religion, caste, class, age and gender, as well as by an urban–rural distinction. To this we may add the presence of 'twice migrants' who arrived in Britain by way of East Africa.

FROM 'SOJOURNERS TO SETTLERS'

According to Ballard, migrants from South Asia to Britain transformed themselves from 'sojourners to settlers', that is, from a temporary entrepreneurial disposition involving the primacy of earning and saving money, to become permanent settlers constructing families, houses, businesses and cultural institutions. However, even when settler status was taken on board, clear boundaries were drawn between themselves and their white neighbours. In particular, the maintenance of *izzat*, or personal honour, required them to keep their distance from a culture which seemed to have little sense of family, of sexual morality, of respect for elders or personal hygiene. Indeed, 'those who mimicked English ways too closely began to be accused of being *be-izzat* – without honour' (Ballard, 1994: 15).

SWITCHING CULTURAL CODES

The emergence of British-born young 'Asians' gave rise to a generation which was much more deeply involved in transactions across ethnic boundaries than were the original migrants. Young British Asians went to school with white and Afro-Caribbean Britons, shared leisure sites, watched television and were frequently bilingual. Though British Asians have often been characterized as being 'between two cultures' (Watson, 1977) or caught up in a process of 'cultural conflict', we would be better to see these young people as skilled operators of cultural **code** switching. This is so, Brah (1996) argues, for a number of reasons:

- the notion of 'two cultures' is incorrect because both 'British' and 'Asian' cultures are heterogeneous and stratified;
- there is no reason to see cultural encounters as necessarily involving clashes or conflicts;
- the relationship between 'British' and 'Asian' cultures is not a one-way process but multi-directional;
- while some Asians may experience dissonance, there is no evidence to suggest that this is widespread;
- inter-generational difference should not be conflated with conflict.

British Asian young people have developed their own home-grown syncretic or hybrid cultural forms along with political and cultural discourses of 'British Asianness'. In her study of Asian youth in Southall (London), Gillespie (1995) shows how young people constituted themselves, to varying degrees, as British Asian. Under some circumstances this involved identification with Britishness, at other times with aspects of Asian culture (neither being homogeneous). The circumstances of the Gulf War opened up ambiguities and insecurities around those points of identification. On the one hand some young Asians identified with an Islamic 'developing nation' in conflict with the West. On the other hand they wanted to remain within the boundaries of Britishness, the place of their birth and upbringing. The young people shifted from one position to another as they determined it to be situationally appropriate. This shifting within and between the discourses of Britishness and Asianness was further complicated by religious and geographical differences within Asian culture and by age, gender and class.

MULTIPLE IDENTITIES

The differences within the community studied by Gillespie prevent easy identification of particular subjects with a given, fixed identity. Thus, a British Asian girl might identify herself with Asianness to argue that traditional clothes should be respected or to suggest that Asians are misrepresented on television. Yet, in the context of a discussion about relationships, she might speak from a position of western **feminism** to argue against the traditional **patriarchal** practices of some Asian men. On another occasion she may position herself as a young person, irrespective of ethnicity or gender, as she adopts the fashion and music of a specific youth subculture. One such range of shifting identity positions is put by a young singer:

> I rap in Bengali and English. I rap on everything from love to politics. I've always been into rapping . . . it was rebellious, the lyrics were sensational. I could relate to that, I could identify with it. Like living in the ghetto and that. . . . It's from the heart. It's: 'I'm Bengali, I'm Asian, I'm a woman, and I'm living here.' (cited Gardner and Shukur, 1994: 161)

The **subject positions** of this young woman involve the articulation of positions drawn from a variety of discourses and sites. At the very least she has identifications with being Bengali, English, a woman, with youth culture and with Rap, an American–Caribbean hybrid, now appropriated as Anglo-Bengali. She is involved not only in shifting identifications but in enacting a hybrid identity which draws on multiplying global resources. Thus, identities are never either pure or fixed but formed at the intersections of age, **class**, **gender**, race and nation.

INTERSECTIONS AND BOUNDARY CROSSINGS

According to Hall, the end of **essentialism** 'entails a recognition that the central issues of race always appear historically in articulation, in a formation, with other categories and divisions and are constantly crossed and recrossed by the categories of class, of gender and ethnicity' (Hall, 1996d: 444). We may consider this process in three fundamental ways:

- the **multiple identities** of the postmodern subject, that is, the weaving of the patterns of identity from discourses of class, race, gender, etc.;
- the construction of one discourse in terms of metaphors drawn from another, that is, the construction of nation through gendered metaphors or of race in terms of class – for example, the idea of 'race' is connected to the idea of the ascent of 'Man', ethnic groups may be derided as effeminate, nations are gendered as female, and absolute ethnic differences are premised on the idea of blood lines and thus women's bodies;
- the capability of persons to move across discursive and spatial sites of activity which address them in different ways. As Rose has argued, people

> live their lives in a constant movement across different practices that address them in different ways. . . . [T]he existence of contestation, conflict and opposition in practices which conduct the conduct of persons is no surprise and requires no appeal to the particular qualities of human agency. . . . [I]n any one site or locale, humans turn programmes intended for one end to the service of others. One way of relating to oneself comes into conflict with others. (Rose, 1996: 140–1)

In this context, the social position of British Asian girls is significant because they are arguably 'special' by virtue of living across cultural boundaries and, as girls, being somewhat marginalized within male-dominated cultures. In a study of the moral discourses produced by British Asian girls watching television soap opera (Barker, 1998) it was argued that the contradictory subject positions they took up, while an aspect of logical tensions in moral discourses themselves, were also the outcome of the proliferation of discursive resources stemming from different conventions, sites and practices which were in contradiction with each other.

Gillespie (1995) discusses the way that young Asian girls use *Neighbours* to explore the rules surrounding male–female relationships and teenage romance. This is especially significant for girls since *Neighbours* portrays young women with a greater degree of freedom than many British Asian girls can themselves expect. *Neighbours* offers the pleasure of seeing more assertive women and provokes discussion about gender roles.

WEAVING THE PATTERNS OF IDENTITY

We can thus conceive of persons as operating across and within multiple subject positions constituted by the intersections or criss-crossing of discourses of race, gender, age, nation, class, etc. Further, we do not *have* a weave of multiple beliefs, attitudes, language, etc.; we *are* such a weave. Nevertheless, some critics have worried that the critique of essentialism robs us of the tools to combat racism because the very category of race seems to disappear. However, to abandon an essentialist universal condition called 'race' does not mean that the social and historical construction of race, the racialization of specific groups of human beings, need also be lost. On the contrary, the critique of essentialist arguments exposes the radical contingency of identity catagories, helping to combat the **reduction** of people to race by encouraging us to see all people as multifaceted. Thus:

> Employing a critique of essentialism allows African-Americans to acknowledge the way in which class mobility has altered collective black experience so that racism does not necessarily have the same impact on our lives. Such a critique allows us to affirm multiple black identities, varied black experience. It also challenges colonial imperialist paradigms of black identity which represent blackness one-dimensionally in ways that reinforce and sustain white supremacy. . . . When black folks critique essentialism, we are empowered to recognize multiple experiences of black identity that are the lived conditions which make diverse cultural productions possible. When this diversity is ignored, it is easy to see black folks as falling into two categories: nationalist or assimilationist, black-identifiers or white-identified. (hooks, 1990: 28–9)

As hooks submits, one of the benefits of casting off essentialism, and thus black absolutism or nationalism, is that black women do not have to subsume their critique of black masculinity. It is not a betrayal of black people to put forward a black feminist critique of black male macho (Wallace, 1979) nor a betrayal of women to critique white feminism from the perspective of black women (Carby, 1984; hooks, 1990). Rather, these are the processes of articulation and coalition building which are core to **cultural politics** (Chapter 12).

Anti-essentialist arguments suggest that social categories do not reflect an essential underlying identity but are constituted in and through forms of representation. Thus, a consideration of ethnicity and race directs us to issues of identity, representation, power and politics. For example, what kinds of representations are constructed of whom, by whom and for what purposes?

RACE, ETHNICITY, REPRESENTATION

Representation involves questions of inclusion and exclusion and as such is always implicated in questions of power. Nevertheless, Dyer (1977) points us to a useful distinction between types and **stereotypes**. The former act as general and necessary classifications of persons and roles according to local cultural categories. The latter are regarded as vivid but simple representations which reduce persons to a set of exaggerated, usually negative, characteristics

Stereotyping commonly involves the attribution of negative traits to persons who are different from ourselves. This points to the operation of power in the process of stereotyping and to its role in the exclusion of others from the social, symbolic and moral order. Dyer suggests that 'types are instances which indicate those who live by the rules of society (social types) and those whom the rules are designed to exclude (stereotypes)' (Dyer, 1977: 29). Stereotypes concern those excluded from the 'normal' order of things and simultaneously establish who is 'us' and who is 'them'. Thus, 'stereotyping reduces, essentializes, naturalizes and fixes "difference"' (Hall, 1997c: 258).

Within the West, people of colour have been represented as a series of *problems*, objects and victims (Gilroy, 1987). Black people are constructed as the object rather than subject of history. Unable to think or act for themselves, people of colour are not held to be capable of initiating activity or of controlling their own destiny. Subsequently, as objects and aliens from another place, black people pose a series of problems for white people, for example as a foreign contaminating cultural presence or as the perpetrators of crime.

Savages and slaves

In Britain and America the more obvious racist stereotypes echo colonial and slave history, respectively. Hall (1997c) argues that a central component of British imperial representations of black people was the theme of non-Christian savages requiring civilizing by British missionaries and adventurers. These images were subsequently transformed into what he calls 'commodity racism', whereby 'Images of colonial conquest were stamped on soap boxes . . . biscuit tins, whisky bottles, tea tins and chocolate bars' (McClintock, 1995, cited Hall 1997c: 240). Representations of white colonial power and black 'savagery' were gendered in that the heroes of imperial Britain were male while the commodities on which such images appeared were frequently domestic and targeted at women.

> Soap symbolized this 'racializing' of the domestic world and the 'domestication' of the colonial world. In its capacity to cleanse and purify, soap acquired, in the fantasy world of imperial advertising, the quality of a fetish object. It apparently had the power to wash black skin white as well as being capable of washing off the soot, grime and dirt of the industrial slums and their inhabitants – the unwashed poor – at home, while at the same time keeping the imperial body clean and pure in the racially polluted contact zones 'out there' in the Empire. In the process, however, the domestic labour of women was often silently erased. (Hall 1997c: 241)

Plantation images

American plantation images share the British concern with the binary of white civilization and black 'naturalness' and 'primitivism'. African-Americans were represented as naturally incapable of the refinements of white civilization. They were by nature lazy and best fitted for subordination to whites. The social and political subordination of black people was represented as part of the inescapable God-given order of the universe. Not that American racial stereotypes were the same as those in Britain. On the contrary, we need to recognize the existence and emergence of different historically specific forms of racism and of the subtle typologies within given cultural contexts. In America, Bogle (1973) argues that five distinct stereotypes which derive from plantation and slave images are to be found in film:

- *Toms* (good blacks, submissive, stoic);
- *Coons* (slapstick entertainers, gamblers, 'no-account' 'niggers');
- *the Tragic Mulatto* (beautiful, sexy, exotic mixed-race women 'stained' with black blood);
- *Mammies* (the big, strong, bossy house servant devoted and subservient to the white family);
- *Bad Bucks* (big, strong, violent, oversexed male renegades).

The criminalization of black Britons

In Britain, Gilroy (1987) has charted the transformations of racism in relation to the law. He argues that in the 1950s anxiety about black criminality within the police, judiciary and press was relatively low, concerning only the alleged association of black people with prostitution and gambling. This imagery of sexual squalor was combined throughout the late 1950s and early 1960s with the theme of housing shortages and overcrowding. During the late 1960s and the 1970s racial discourse centred on immigration, the 'alien presence' in Britain and the 'threat' to the national culture and law which this was claimed to pose. By this time, the idea that there was something intrinsically criminal about black culture had begun to take hold and the imagery of black youth as dope-smoking muggers and/or urban rioters came to the fore. Hedonism, evasion of work and the criminality of black **culture** became the closely entwined motifs of British media racism.

Hall et al. (1978) argued that in covering stories about 'mugging', journalists reproduce the assumption that street crime is solely the work of young black men. Journalists seek the views of the police, politicians and judges, who declare that not only is street crime on the increase, but that something must be done about it in the form of heavier policing and harsher sentences. The news media report these comments as common-sense concern about rising crime and its association with black youth. Subsequently, the circle becomes complete when judges cite news coverage of crime as the expression of public concern, using it to justify the harsher sentences and increased police activity which they and politicians had called for. Given that increased police activity is directed to areas in which young black men live, because they are seen as the perpetrators of crime, confrontation between the police and black youth increases.

Orientalism

Racism is a matter not simply of individual psychology or pathology, but of patterns of cultural representation deeply ingrained within the practices, discourses and subjectivities of western societies. Said (1978) illuminates this 'structural' and societal character of racism in his discussion of Orientalism. He argues that cultural–geographical entities such as the 'Orient' are not inert facts of nature, but historically specific, discursive constructions which have a history, tradition, imagery and vocabulary that have given it a particular kind of reality and presence with the West.

Orientalism is a set of western **discourses** of power which have constructed an Orient – have Orientalized the Orient – in ways which depend on and reproduce the positional superiority and hegemony of the West. For Said (1978) Orientalism is a general group of ideas impregnated with European superiority, racism and imperialism which are elaborated and distributed through a variety of texts and practices. Orientation is argued to be a system of representations that brought the Orient into Western learning (Said, 1978). These include Flaubert's encounter with an Egyptian courtesan, which produced an influential image of the Oriental woman who never spoke for herself, never showed her emotions and lacked **agency** or history, that is, the sexually beguiling dark maiden of male power-fantasy. In contrast, the Oriental male is seen as wily, fanatical, cruel and despotic.

In this respect, the contemporary elevation of 'Islam' to the role of chief bogeyman in western news follows a well-worn path. As Said (1981) has argued, western media have represented Islamic peoples as irrational fanatics led by messianic and authoritarian leaders. Much news coverage in the West has been devoted to the states of Iran, Iraq and Libya (with a special emphasis on their alleged sponsoring of terrorism), to the *fatwa* declared by Ayatollah Khomeini against Salman Rushdie, and to the Gulf War, and Saddam Hussein in particular. Responsibility for the Gulf War and subsequent conflicts over UN weapons inspections have been placed firmly on the shoulders of Saddam Hussein, who has been cast in the role of 'evil emperor'. Morrison (1992) confirms that, during the Gulf War, Hussein was the political leader most referred to by television news. Television plays an important part in contemporary culture, being the major disseminator of cultural representations, including those concerned with race and ethnicity.

Television and the representation of race and ethnicity

WHITES ONLY

On one level, people of colour have simply been ignored by television. In America, it was not until the late 1960s and early 1970s that we find any black families in television drama (Cantor and Cantor, 1992). The Kerner Commission, set up to examine the unrest that spread across urban America in the 1960s, argued that the US news media 'has too long basked in a white world, looking out of it, if at all, with white men's eyes and a white perspective' (Kerner Commission, 1968: 389). This reflected what the commission called 'the indifference of white America'.

In 1980s Britain the Commission for Racial Equality (1984) noted that while in the USA black people were being seen more frequently on television, in the UK only 5 per cent of dramatic characters were black and only three of sixty-two non-white appearances constituted leading roles. For example, one criticism of British soap operas has been the representation of community as, on the whole, exclusively white, heterosexual and working class. The high-rating soap opera *Coronation Street* has had few black characters, somewhat odd for a programme with realist pretensions located in multicultural Manchester. Nor have the US soaps *Dallas*, *Dynasty*, *Days of Our Lives*, *The Bold and the Beautiful*, *Melrose Place*, etc., a good record of representing the multi-ethnic population of America. The invisibility of black people within the media is not only incompatible with the democratic role of the media but arguably promotes white ignorance about black people and black cultures. By ignoring black people, media coverage places them outside of mainstream society, signalling them as peripheral and irrelevant.

STEREOTYPED REPRESENTATIONS

As media representations of people of colour increased in volume during the 1980s and 1990s, so attention focused on the *kinds of representations* which are constitutive of ethnicity and race. For example, black people in Britain have frequently been represented by news media as a problem. In particular, young black men have been associated with crime and civil disorder. In many 'comedy' programmes images drawn from a colonial past have been deployed to suggest stupidity and ignorance. *Mind Your Language*, set in an English language class, reduced every single non-white community to a stereotype through the "joke" that all-foreigners-are-hilarious-because-they-talk-funny (Medhurst, 1989).

In America, the first television programme to feature African-Americans was *Amos 'n' Andy*, a 'comedy' which became a symbol for the degradation of black people through the use of 'humour' based on stereotypes. Indeed, the American film and television industry has a long history of presenting stereotypical images of black people drawn from the plantation tradition of the 'Sambo' and 'Brute' slave through the smooth liberals of the sixties to the 'Superspade' detectives of the mid-seventies.

> Yet whether Sambo or Superspade, the black image on screen has always lacked the dimension of humanity. With all too few exceptions this human dimension has been lacking in the movie treatment of the black ever since the 1890s, when the first motion picture was produced. (Leab, 1975: 5)

SIGNS OF CHANGE

These racist representations of people of colour are not to be lightly dismissed. However, an understanding of the contemporary representation of race requires recognition that change has occurred. Campbell (1995) reports that in forty hours of American local news 'there was no evidence of intentional, blatant bigotry' and few examples of what he calls 'old-fashioned racism' (but a good deal of more subtle modern racism). More generally, there have been attempts to construct representations of Britain and America as multicultural societies. Here a more pluralistic society is depicted in which the cultures and customs of different ethnic groups add to the richness and variety of society. In Britain, *Empire Road* and *Desmond's*, both comedies, centred on black family life and tried to be funny without the use of racist humour, while *Goodness Gracious Me* is a showcase of British Asian humour. The soap opera *EastEnders* has portrayed a wider cross-section of ethnic communities and characters than had previously been the case. In the USA, meanwhile, the black Huxtable family (*The Cosby Show*) were the focal point of what was at one time the most popular prime-time comedy on television. At the same time, *EastEnders* and *The Cosby Show* have also had their critics in terms of the representation of race (see pp. 217 and 214 respectively).

MENACE TO SOCIETY

Nevertheless, racism continues to be treated as an issue of personal illiberality rather than of structured inequality, while insufficient attention is given to the specificity of black culture. Contemporary representations of race in television continue to associate people of colour, specifically young men, with crime and social problems. According to Martindale (1986) and Campbell (1995), the most common portrayal of African-Americans in newscasts is as criminals connected to guns and violence. Poor blacks in particular are constructed as a 'menace to society', having moved beyond the limits of acceptable behaviour through their association with crime, violence, drugs, gangs and teenage pregnancy. For Gray (1996) this was typified by the CBS documentary *Vanishing Family: Crisis in Black America*, which, he argues, associated normalcy with the (white) nuclear family and turned African-American families into problems. The documentary depicted a number of caring and conscientious young African-American women struggling to raise young children while a breed of feckless men hung around on street corners.

Gray makes the significant point that what might be regarded as 'positive' representations of African-Americans do not always function positively, particularly when juxtaposed to other images of black people in the context of a wider set of representations of race. Though the programme contained reference to what the television presenter called 'successful strong black families in America', these functioned to shift blame away from the structural and systematic character of racial inequality in America, redirecting blame onto alleged individual weakness and moral deficiencies of poor black people. Thus, the meanings of 'blackness' are cumulative and **intertextual**. The association of black people with crime and their depiction as a constant social problem is in contrast with, and arguably reinforced by, the more positive *assimilationist* imagery of contemporary sitcoms.

ASSIMILATIONIST STRATEGIES

The Cosby Show's Huxtable family (along with talk show hosts such as Oprah Winfrey) represent middle-class achievement and social mobility. In line with the American Dream, they suggest that success is open to all who are talented and work for it. Consequently, African-American poverty must be at best an outcome of individual weakness and at worst a collective aspect of African-American culture, for why else would black people be overrepresented in all the statistics of poverty and urban deprivation? As Jhally and Lewis argue, 'The Huxtables' success implies the failure of a majority of black people . . . who have not achieved similar professional or material success' (Jhally and Lewis, 1992: 137). Accordingly, while middle-class black American sitcoms stress material success and the values of hard work, education, honesty and responsibility, Gray argues that 'many individuals trapped in the underclass have the very same qualities but lack the options and opportunities to realize them' (Gray, 1996: 142).

Entman (1990) suggests that similar assimilationist strategies operate in local news, notably the use of black anchors contributes to the idea that racism no longer exists in America. Not only does the presence of black authority figures on the screen suggest that racism has been relegated to the dustbin of history, but their adoption of majority cultural views lends credence to the assimilationist vision. This argument is supported by Campbell (1995) by way of his qualitative analysis of local American news coverage of the Martin Luther King holiday celebrations. With one notable exception, news coverage depicted racism as a thing of the past and the holiday a celebration of King's success rather than as a reminder to us of the failure of his historic vision to be materialized in the day-to-day reality of American life.

THE AMBIGUITIES OF REPRESENTATION

The representation of people of colour in America and Britain is riven with contradictions. Black people are, at one and the same time, characterized as at the poles of criminality and middle-class success. Race is held to be a current 'problem' and yet racism is held to be a thing of the past. As Hall remarks:

> people who are in any way significantly different from the majority – 'them' rather than 'us' – are frequently exposed to this *binary* form of representation. They seem to be represented through sharply opposed, polarized, binary extremes – good/bad, civilized/primitive, ugly/excessively attractive, repelling-because-different/compelling-because-strange-and-exotic. And they are often required to be *both things at the same time*! (Hall, 1997c: 229)

Ambiguity and ambivalence are foregrounded when the attempt is made to represent black people 'positively'. For example, the prominence give to African-American and black British sports men and women in the Olympics or in basketball and football is double-edged. On the one hand this is a celebration and acceptance of black success. On the other hand it is part of a process by which black success is *confined* to sport and black people depicted in stereotypical fashion as primarily physical rather than mental beings.

In the world of entertainment and music, Hip-Hop, Rap and their associated videos have become one of television's most prominent genres. Rap can be said to depict the 'cultural reality' of black people's (but especially men's) experience in relation to the police, challenging what are seen as unjust authoritarian practices. Indeed, hooks suggests that:

> It is no accident that 'rap' has usurped the primary position of rhythm and blues music among young black folks as the most desired sound or that it began as a form of 'testimony' for the underclass. It has enabled underclass youth to develop a critical voice, as a group of young black men told me, a common literacy. Rap projects a critical voice, explaining, demanding, urging. (hooks 1990: 75)

Yet Rap has also been criticized as insular, sexist, misogynist and violent even as it reformulates and extends popular music. Rap is critical and reactionary at the same time.

> As a cultural forum, rap itself is a contested terrain between different types of rap with competing voices, politics and styles . . . some rap glorifies a gangster lifestyle, drugs, and misogynistic attitudes, other rap artists contest these problematic interventions, using rap to articulate quite different values and politics. (Kellner, 1995: 176)

THE NEW GHETTO AESTHETIC

Ambiguities are evident in a series of black-made films closely associated with Rap music, including the work of Marion Van Peebles (*New Jack City*) and John Singleton (*Boyz N the Hood*). Jacquie Jones (1996) describes them as 'The New Ghetto Aesthetic'. On the one hand these films are significant for being Hollywood films made by African-Americans. They have also been praised for their representation of the shocking life circumstances of some African-Americans. On the other hand, they arguably 'codify a range of behaviours as uncharacteristic of the black experience as those represented in films made by whites' (Jones, 1996: 41).

Two facets of these films might be regarded as particularly problematic:

- the depiction of black communities as being racked by crime and violence, whose causes lie with individual pathologies and whose solution is either more police or strong father figures;
- the portrayal of women in the standard bitch/ho mode, so that few are defined apart from their relationships with men.

While we get to know male characters in terms of their personal histories and emotional torments, women are frequently *reduced* to being only tough and/or sexy. Of significance is the gendered character of the representation of race, so that an exaggerated male macho style is held to be symbolic of black **resistance** to white power (hooks, 1992). For some black men the adoption of a hard and excessive form of masculinity has been a response to white power, offering a sense of self-worth and strength in the face of social disempowerment. This does not negate the undesirability of the bitch/ho binary or of 'Black Macho' (Wallace, 1979).

It is important to consider the *ambiguities* of representations of race so that debates are not reduced to a simple good/bad binary which elicits knee-jerk accusations of racism or demands for only positive images. After all, positive images, useful and desirable though they are in the context of stereotypes, do not necessarily undermine or displace the negative. Indeed, it is common to find that what is considered to be a 'positive' image by some is attacked by others. For example, the British soap opera *EastEnders* and the American series *I'll Fly Away* consciously attempted to engage with realistic and positive representations of black people but were nevertheless seen by some commentators as problematic.

EASTENDERS

As a consequence of deliberate policy, *EastEnders* deploys an array of black and Asian characters rarely before seen on British television. Rather than represent people of colour as 'a problem', black characters have been enabled to take up active and significant dramatic roles. *EastEnders* represents a multi-ethnic community in ways which do not reduce black and Asian characters to one-dimensional representatives of 'the black experience'. Further, the series contained the sympathetic representation of a mixed-race relationship/marriage which, according to Bramlett-Solomon and Farwell (1996), is virtually absent from US soaps. On the other hand, the serial has been attacked for stereotyping, for example, representing Asians as doctors and shopkeepers, and for ignoring the wider structural questions of racism by reducing it to individual character traits. It is also argued that the centrality of the white Beale family (and other traditional white East End characters) displaces black and Asian characters to the margins so that they can never be a part of the core of the drama (see Daniels and Gerson, 1989).

I'LL FLY AWAY

The debate about *I'll Fly Away* centred on the representation of the central character Lily Harper, including her relationship to other characters and to the politics of the civil rights movement. For Karen Smith (1996), the series offered a character who, though a maid, was most definitely not a 'mammy'. Rather, Lily Harper was portrayed as an independent-minded and wise woman active in the civil rights movement and not subordinated to the white family for whom she worked. Though Smith points out that other writers have indeed seen Lily Harper as a mammy, her core criticism is of the network, which promoted the series with 'out-of-context' images suggesting that Lily *was* a stereotyped black maid. In other words, the Lily Harper character became, through the intertextual array of representations for different purposes, a site of contradictory and ambiguous meaning construction.

THE QUESTION OF POSITIVE IMAGES

The incontestable abundance of cultural stereotypes has led many of those who suffer at their hands to seek more positive representations of people of colour and a range of other 'abjected' groups. The demand for positive images of people of colour is at heart a desire to show that black people are as 'good' or as 'human' as white people (West, 1993). However, while positive images have much to commend them in terms of the development of self-esteem, the strategy is beset by problems. Namely the following:

- It rests on an essentialist and homogenizing understanding of ethnic identity and as such obliterates differences of class, gender, sexuality, etc. That is, positive images of black people assume that all black people have essential qualities in common. They may not.
- It is impossible to know what an unambiguously positive image would consist of. We are unlikely ever to be able to agree on this, so that one person's commendable image is another's stereotype.
- The strategy rests on an **epistemology** of **realism** by which it is thought possible to bring representations of black people into line with 'real' black people. This is not viable, for the real is always already a representation.

These arguments form part of the wider debate about what representation 'does' (Chapter 3). The demand for positive images, when manifested as a call for accuracy in the representation of race, stumbles over the problem of knowing what the real or accurate is. Not only is race a cultural construction, but we cannot compare the real with representations. Representation is constitutive of race as cultural identity and not a mirror or a distortion of it. Consequently, no criteria can assess the accuracy of the representation of race.

More sustainable are arguments which revolve around the pragmatic social and political consequences of constructing and disseminating specific discursive constructions of the world. The role of criticism becomes the development of a more profound understanding of our cultural and symbolic processes and the way in which they are connected to social, political and economic *power*. The questions to be asked concern *consequences* rather than **truth**. Rather than seek only positive images, we require, argues Hall (1996d), a politics of representation which:

- registers the arbitrariness of signification;
- promotes representations which explore power relations;
- deconstructs black–white binaries;
- advances the willingness to live with difference.

This does not require universal epistemological justification for it is founded not on transcendental reason or representations of the 'real but on a tradition of cultural values which judges difference, diversity, solidarity equality and democracy to be desirable ends. It is based on pragmatic comparison with other forms of social organization and not on notions of accuracy. Consequently, while continuing to critique stereotyped representations of people of colour, the issue may be one not of positive images but of the representation of *difference* and *diversity*.

Postcolonial literature

Television remains the central representational form of popular western culture and is therefore a core concern of cultural studies. However, there is also a significant strand of work which explores issues of race, ethnicity and nation within literature. This includes the current interest in postcolonial literature as exemplified by Ashcroft et al. (1989) in *The Empire Writes Back*. More than three-quarters of the people living in the world today, the authors claim, have had their lives shaped by the experience of colonialism. For Ashcroft et al., postcolonial literature is that work produced by the peoples of former European colonies. While the term 'postcolonial' might refer to literature produced after colonization, it is taken here to include the colonial discourse itself, that is, the world both during and after European colonization. As such, **postcolonial** theory explores the discursive condition of postcoloniality, that is, the way colonial relations and their aftermath have been constituted through being spoken about. Postcolonial theory explores postcolonial discourses and their subject positions in relation to the themes of race, nation, subjectivity, power, subalterns, hybridity and creolization.

While this definition is useful in defining a broad area of study, it also opens up questions for exploration. For example, the degree to which a range of former colonies can now be considered postcolonial is varied and arguable (Williams and Chrisman, 1993). Though the literature of the USA might be seen as postcolonial in relation to Europe, American neo-colonial power with respect to Latin America makes generalization problematic. Further, many writers see black literature in the US as an aspect of internal colonialism/postcolonialism. We also need to distinguish the work produced in former white settler colonies – Australia, Canada and New Zealand – from the literature of black Africa or the Indian sub-continent.

MODELS OF POSTCOLONIAL LITERATURE

Ashcroft et al. (1989) highlight two important models of postcolonial literature, the 'national' model and the 'black writing' model. The national model centres on the relationship between a nation and its former colonizers. The paradigmatic case is the USA, where literature was a part of 'an optimistic progression to nationhood' based on difference from Britain. This involved a breaking away from metaphors of parent–child or stream–tributary which had placed American literature in a subordinate position.

However, debate rages about whether national culture is a legitimate conceptual tool or an essentialist device which unifies through the suppression of **difference** (e.g. of gender, class and ethnicity). Consequently, the other major exemplar cited by Ashcroft et al. (1989) is the 'black writing' model, which centres on the work of the African Diaspora of the Black Atlantic. This model can be extended to include other forms of writing, for example Australian Aboriginal writing or that of India, for the model is one based on ethnicity rather than nationality. It does not follow, of course, that this model escapes the problem of essentialism either.

Though it does a disservice to the complexity of the issues, we may for the current purposes reduce the themes of post-colonial literature and postcolonial theory to the two key concerns: domination–subordination and hybridity–creolization.

DOMINATION AND SUBORDINATION

Issues of domination and subordination surface most directly in terms of colonial military control, genocide and economic 'under-development'. In more cultural terms, questions arise about the denigration and subordination of 'native' culture by colonial power. This includes the very language of English literature. Is English, the language of a major colonial power, a suitable tool for postcolonial writers? On the one hand, it can be said to carry within itself the very assumptions and concepts of colonial power. On the other hand, English has a variety of global forms, leading postcolonial literature to be concerned with a range of Englishes. Depending on which side of the equation is stressed, a postcolonial writer might choose to either abrogate or appropriate English.

> The first, the abrogation or denial of the privilege of 'English', involves a rejection of the metropolitan power over the means of communication. The second, the appropriation and reconstitution of the language to new usages, marks a separation from the site of colonial privilege. Abrogation is a refusal of the categories of the imperial culture, its aesthetic, its illusory standard of normative or 'correct' usage and its assumption of a traditional and fixed meaning 'inscribed' in words. . . . Appropriation is the process by which the language is taken and made to 'bear the burden' of one's own cultural experience, or, as Rja Rao puts it, to 'convey in a language that is not one's own the spirit that is one's own'. (Ashcroft et al., 1989: 38–9)

Domination and subordination is a relationship which occurs not only between nations or ethnic groups but also within them. The emphasis on ethnicity in postcolonial theory literature can mask the power relations of gender. For example, images of women are significant bearers of the purity and reproduction of the nation. Further, women carry a double burden of being colonized by imperial powers and subordinated by colonial and native men. Indeed, Spivak (1993) has argued that the 'subaltern cannot speak', by which she means that poor women in colonial contexts have neither the conceptual language to speak nor the ear of colonial and indigenous men to listen. It is not that women cannot literally communicate but that there are no subject positions within the discourse of colonialism which allow them to articulate themselves as persons. They are thus condemned to silence.

HYBRIDIZATION AND CREOLIZATION

The theoretical critique of essentialism combined with the physical meeting and mixing of peoples throws the whole notion of a national or ethnic literature into doubt. Consequently, the hybridization and creolization of language, literature and cultural identities is a common theme of postcolonial literature and theory marking a certain meeting of minds with **postmodernism**. For example, the concept of the 'Creole continuum' highlights the overlapping language usages and code switching common to the Caribbean. Creolization stresses language as a cultural practice and the inventions of new modes of expression particular to itself.

Dialogue with the values and customs of the past allows traditions to be transformed, bringing forth the new. The meaning of old words is changed and new words brought into being. Neither the colonial nor the colonized cultures and languages can be presented in 'pure' form, nor can they be separated from each other (Bhabha, 1994). This gives rise to a hybridity which challenges not only the centrality of colonial culture and the marginalization of the colonized, but also the very idea of centre and margin as being anything other than 'representational effects'.

Postmodern Rushdie

The work of Salman Rushdie (e.g. *Midnight's Children*, *The Satanic Verses* and *The Moor's Last Sigh*) raises questions of hybridity and cultural representation through characters who cross or blur cultural boundaries. The non-linear narrative style of Rushdie's work derives from the oral storytelling traditions of

India, yet these very same techniques are part of Rushdie's challenge to the certainties of facts and historical narrative. That is, there are histories, not a history, which are written or told by specific people from particular perspectives. Such a challenge has often been taken as a mark of postmodernism and Hutcheon (1989) hails Rushdie's postmodern parody. On the other hand, Berman claims Rushdie for modernism, and in particular the struggle for 'visions of truth and freedom that all modern men and women can embrace . . . an inner dynamism and a principle of hope' (Berman, 1982: 54). It would seem that in exploring the boundaries of cultures, their mixing and meeting, Rushdie is at one and the same time traditional, modern and postmodern.

SUMMARY

It has been argued that ethnicity, race and nationality are discursive–performative constructions which do not refer to already existent 'things'. That is, they are contingent cultural categories rather than universal biological 'facts'. Ethnicity as a concept refers to the formation and maintenance of cultural boundaries and has the advantage of stressing history, culture and language. Race is a problematic idea because of its association with biological discourses of intrinsic and inevitable superiority and subordination. However, the idea of racialization or race formation has the advantages of stressing power, control and domination, for, as Jordan and Weedon (1995) have commented, while racism certainly is a discourse about difference, it is also most assuredly a discourse of brutality.

We noted the intersections between race, ethnicity, nation, class, age and gender so that cultural identities require to be understood in terms of the articulation of these criss-crossing discourses. The ideas of race, ethnicity and nation must be explored in terms of their reliance on each other, for example the ethnic purity of nations as posited by nationalist discourse and the role that gendered metaphors play in the construction of the nation, e.g. the fatherland, mother of the nation, etc.

The anti-essentialist argument by which identities are said to be formed within and through discourse makes the question of representation central to race, ethnicity and nation. We noted the systematic construction of black people as objects, victims and problems. In particular, we explored a range of discourses of race and ethnicity on television highlighting not only blatant forms of racism but the inherent ambiguity and ambivalence of representations. Considerable stress was placed on the idea of hybridity. Cultures and identities are increasingly hybridized as specific places are subject to distant influences and cultural mixing, for example the African Diaspora of the Black Atlantic and the literature of the postcolonial world. Above all:

If you go to analyze racism today in its complex structures and dynamics, one question, one principle above all, emerges as a lesson for us. It is the fear – the terrifying, internal fear – of living with *difference*. This fear arises as the consequence of the fatal coupling of difference and power. And, in that sense, the work that cultural studies has to do is mobilize everything that it can in terms of intellectual resources in order to understand what keeps making the lives we live, and the societies we live in, profoundly and deeply antihuman in their capacity to live with difference. (Hall, 1997d: 343)

8

Sex, Subjectivity and Representation

This chapter is concerned with sex and gender, that is, with the character of men and women in contemporary societies. In particular, we will explore the social construction of sexed subjects and the cultural representation of women. We focus on work influenced by feminism, poststructuralism and psychoanalysis as being the prevailing streams of thought within cultural studies on these questions.

FEMINISM AND CULTURAL STUDIES

To discuss questions of **sex** and **gender** is necessarily to engage with a large body of feminist theory, and it is impossible to conceive of a cultural studies which did not do so. However, while feminist thinking permeates cultural studies, not all forms of **feminism** are to be thought of as cultural studies and not all zones of **cultural studies** are concerned with questions of gender (though many feminists would argue that contemporary cultural studies is hindered by its production of ungendered understandings of culture). Consequently, this chapter does not purport to be a history, classification or analysis of the women's movement *per se* but an exploration of streams of thought within cultural studies concerned with sex, gender and feminism.

Franklin et al. (1991) point to a number of similarities of concern between cultural studies and feminism. They draw attention to the aspirations of feminism and cultural studies to connect with social and political movements outside of the academy and to their critical stance vis-à-vis more established disciplines such as sociology and English literature. This focus on knowledge production stems from a mutual suspicion of and challenge to established ideas of 'certain knowledge', asserting in its place the **positionality** of knowing. Gray describes this as 'Who can know what about whom, by what means and to what purposes' (Gray, 1997: 94). Thus, both feminism and cultural studies have sought to produce knowledges of and by 'marginalized' and oppressed groups with the avowed intention of making a political intervention. Consequently, cultural studies and feminism have shared a substantive interest in issues of power, representation, **popular culture**, subjectivity, identities and consumption.

The comfortable relationship between feminism and cultural studies which recognition of shared interests can bring, though now widely felt, has not always been the case. Hall describes feminism as 'A thief in the night, it broke in; interrupted, made an unseemly noise, seized the time, crapped on the table of cultural studies' (Hall, 1992a: 282). That is, feminism was not warmly welcomed, even by verbally sympathetic men, but had to make itself be heard in an overtly political way (Women's Study Group, 1978). In doing so, feminists put questions of sexuality, gender, subjectivity and power at the heart of cultural studies, displacing, but not abandoning, what had been the central issue of **class**.

Patriarchy, equality and difference

Feminism is a plural field of **theory** and **politics** which has competing perspectives and prescriptions for action. In general terms we may hold feminism to be asserting that sex is a fundamental and irreducible axis of **social** organization which, to date, has subordinated women to men. Thus, feminism is centrally concerned with sex as an organizing principle of social life which is thoroughly saturated with **power** relations. Feminists have argued that the subordination of women occurs across a whole range of social institutions and practices, that is, it is **structural**. This structural subordination of women has been described by feminists as **patriarchy**, with its derivative meanings of the male-headed family, mastery and superiority.

As a movement, feminism is concerned to construct political strategies by which to intervene in social life in pursuit of the interests of women. It has adopted a range of analyses and strategies of action which have been broadly categorized as liberal feminism, difference feminism, socialist feminism, poststructuralist feminism, black feminism and postcolonial feminism. These categories are not set in stone and indeed do a disservice to feminism in so far as they erect unhelpful and inflexible divisions. However, as explanatory devices they do point to variations in base assumptions and emphasis about what constitutes the interests of women. While one line of feminist thought regards women's interests as lying in the achievement of social 'equality' with men, another argues that they lie with the creative enablement and realization of their fundamental **difference** from men.

Liberal and socialist feminism

Liberal feminists regard differences between men and women as socio-economic and cultural constructs rather than the outcome of an eternal biology. They stress equality of opportunity for women in all spheres, which, within the liberal democracies of the West, is held to be achievable within the broad structures of existing legal and economic frameworks (e.g. Mackinnon, 1987, 1991). In contrast, socialist feminists point to the interconnections between class and gender, including the fundamental place of gender inequalities in the reproduction of **capitalism**. The subordination of women to men is seen as intrinsic to capitalism, so that the full 'liberation' of women would require the overthrow of capitalist organization and social relations. It is argued that women's domestic labour is core to the reproduction of the workforce both physically (feeding, clothing, care, etc.) and culturally (learning appropriate behaviour such as time-keeping, discipline, respect for authority, etc.). Further, women form a supply of cheap and flexible labour for capitalism which is more easily 'returned to the home' when required. Thus, core to socialist feminism is a stress on the 'dual role' (domestic labour and paid labour) of women in the reproduction of capitalism (Oakley, 1974).

Difference feminism

While liberal and socialist feminists stress equality and sameness, difference feminism asserts essential distinctions between men and women. These differences, regarded as fundamental and intractable, are variously interpreted as cultural, psychic and/or biological. In any case, difference is celebrated as representing the creative power of women and the superiority of their values over those of men (Daly, 1987; Rich, 1986). As such, difference feminism has developed a tendency towards separatism.

One criticism of difference feminism, and indeed the concept of patriarchy, is that the category of woman is treated in an undifferentiated way. 'The trouble with patriarchy', as Rowbotham (1981) argued, is that it obscures the differences between individual women and their particularities in favour of an all-embracing universal form of oppression. Not only do all women appear to be oppressed in the same way, but there is a tendency to represent them as helpless and powerless. These are assumptions challenged by black feminists, who have argued that a white middle-class movement has overlooked the centrality of race and colonialism.

Black and postcolonial feminism

Black feminists have pointed to the differences between black and white women's experiences, cultural representations and interests (Carby, 1984; hooks, 1992). They have argued that colonialism and racism have structured power relationships between black and white women, defining women as white. Gender intersects with race, ethnicity and nationality to produce different experiences of what it is to be a woman. In a **postcolonial** context, women carry the double burden of being colonized by imperial powers and subordinated by colonial and native men. Thus, Spivak (1993) holds that the 'subaltern cannot speak'. She is suggesting that poor women in colonial contexts have neither the conceptual language to speak nor the ear of colonial and indigenous men to listen. There are no subject positions within the discourse of colonialism which allow them to speak for themselves.

Poststructuralist feminism

Feminists influenced by **poststructuralist** and **postmodern** thought (Nicholson, 1990; Weedon, 1997) have argued that sex and gender are social and cultural constructions which are not to be explained in terms of biology nor to be reduced to functions of capitalism. This **anti-essentialist** stance suggests that femininity and masculinity are not universal and eternal categories but discursive constructions. That is, femininity and masculinity are ways of describing and disciplining human subjects. As such, poststructuralist feminism is concerned with the cultural construction of **subjectivity** *per se* including a range of possible masculinities and femininities. Femininity and masculinity, which are a matter of how men and women are represented, are held to be sites of continual political struggle over meaning. Given the stress on culture, representation, language, power and conflict, poststructuralist feminism has become a major influence within cultural studies. This includes poststructuralist psychoanalysis, which has been drawn upon to connect the 'inside' with the 'outside' of gender construction.

A note about men

This chapter is centred on women and the pertinent debates within feminism and cultural studies. However, years of reflection upon the social construction of gender have helped us to realize that men face significant problems in their lives, not least as an outcome of the incompatibility of hegemonic notions of masculinity and what is required to live contentedly in the contemporary social world. As a generalization, traditional masculinity has encompassed the values of strength, power, stoicism, action, control, independence, self-sufficiency, male camaraderie/mateship and work amongst others. Devalued were relationships, verbal ability, domestic life, tenderness, communication, women and children.

Real (1998) argues that 48 per cent of men in the USA are at some point in their lives implicated in depression, suicide, alcoholism, drug abuse, violence and crime. In Australia, the press (*The Sun Herald*, 29.08.99) reported a government health survey whose findings represent an enormous cost to the state and a human tragedy of vast proportions. The report suggests that men are more likely than women to:

- be obese;
- be diagnosed as having 'mental disorders' (e.g. Attention Deficit Disorder) as a child;
- be diagnosed as HIV positive (ten times higher);
- have an accident (five times higher);
- engage in high risk behaviour (e.g. dangerous levels of drinking or drug taking);
- be a victim of suicide (six times higher with 80 per cent of suicide victims being male and death rates highest among men aged 20–24 or 80 and above).

It is widely held that depression rooted in family life underpins young male suicide, masculine violence and alcoholism. Psychotherapeutic work (McLean et al., 1996; Real, 1998; Rowe, 1988, 1997) suggests that a good deal of men's problematic attitudes are rooted in low self-esteem, itself an outcome of family life and cultural expectations about masculinity; in particular the sense that men, in their own eyes, are insufficiently masculine, that they have failed to meet the social demands of what it means to be a man. This tendency may well be intensified in the context of a post-industrial world where traditional 'hard' male jobs like those in the steel industry are in decline with no obvious replacements for young men.

For Real (1998) men's violence, sex addiction, gambling, alcohol and drug abuse is a form of self-medication, an attempted defence, achieved through 'merging' or self-elevation, against covert depression stemming from shame and 'toxic' family relationships. To give up such bulwarks is to invite a flood of depression to overwhelm the self as the desperate game of propping up self-esteem collapses. For many men life becomes a restless search for love and the overcoming of feelings of inadequacy rooted in family experience.

Sexual abuse and post-traumatic stress syndrome mark the currently understood outer limits of psychological pain and damage. However, violence comes in many forms and for most men it is the less dramatic childhood injuries of 'petty' violence and neglect that take up residence in their minds. The stage is then set for the compulsive re-enactment of childhood routines which are broken only though a declaration of emotional independence and responsibility. If the shackles of noxious parenting are not cast off then further painful relationships and attempts at self-medication invariably follow.

MEN, ADDITION AND INTIMACY

In his analysis of the transformation of intimacy transpiring in the western world, Giddens (1992) argues that:

> Men are the laggards in the transitions now occurring – and in a certain sense have been so ever since the late eighteenth century. In Western culture at least, today is the first period in which men are finding themselves to be men, that is, as possessing a problematic 'masculinity'. In previous times, men have assumed that their activities constituted 'history', whereas women existed almost out of time, doing the same as they always had done. (Giddens, 1992: 59)

He argues that men's predominance in the public domain and their association with 'reason' has been accomplished at the cost of their exclusion from the transformation of intimacy. Intimacy is largely a matter of emotional communication and the difficulties men have talking about relationships, which requires emotional security and language skills, is rooted in a culturally constructed and historically specific form of masculinity. From birth, boys are treated by parents as independent and outgoing beings leading to a framework of masculinity which stresses externally oriented activity (e.g. work and sport) at the price of a masked emotional dependence on women and weak skills of emotional communication, i.e. of intimacy.

What men repress, or fail to acquire, is the emotional autonomy necessary for the development of closeness. That is, lacking competency in the vocabulary of intimacy, men are unable to name and speak about feelings or take responsibility for their own emotions. Instead, they seek to uphold the basic trust which fore-stalls anxiety and sustains ontological security through mastery and control of themselves, others (particularly women) and their environment.

Male violence can be regarded as a hyper-mastery born out of anxiety which self-assured routine competence and intimacy cannot assuage because they have not been attained. Addiction and other forms of compulsive behaviour offer a source of comfort and a defence against anxiety so that failure to engage in them produces an upsurge of anxiety and/or depression. For Giddens, 'Every addiction is a defensive reaction, and an escape, a recog-nition of lack of autonomy that casts a shadow over the com-petence of the self' (Giddens, 1992: 76). He argues that addictions as compulsive behaviour are narcotic like 'time-outs' which blunt the pain and anxiety of other needs or longings that cannot be directly controlled. Addiction is the 'other side' of the choice and responsibility which goes with the autonomous development of a self-narrative or identity in circumstances in which traditional giudance has collapsed making life-style decisions a potentially dread-full process of 'making oneself'.

The addictive experience is a search for the 'high' and giving up of the self which acts as a release from anxiety and marks a temporary abandonment of that reflexive concern generic to the circumstances which govern contemporary daily life. This sus-pension of the self is frequently followed by feelings of shame and remorse. Since addictions signal an incapacity to cope with certain anxieties they tend to be functionally interchangeable. That is, one may overthrow one addiction only to replace it with another.

If we are to promote the health and well-being of men, along with the women who live with them, then we have to understand how men see the world and their place in it. Understanding the scripts by which men operate in the world, and their implications for action, is necessary if, in the long term, we are to seek ways of changing constructs with negative consequences to more positive ones (Seidler, 1989).

We can only ever do this if we know what depression, violence, crime, drug abuse, etc. do for men, the part they play in their lives. This suggests the need for ethnographic research into the cultural construction of masculinity (Connell et al., 1982). We also need to explore the kinds of cultural representations of men and masculinity which constitute traditional forms of masculinity and those which signify cracks in that order and hence the possibility of change (Nixon, 1997).

SEX, GENDER AND IDENTITY

Identification of oneself as male or female is a foundation stone of a **self-identity** which is widely held to be the outcome of particular bodies and their attributes. Common sense encompasses a form of biological **reductionism** suggesting that the biochemical and genetic structures of human beings determine the behaviour of men and women in quite definite and specific ways. Men are commonly held to be more 'naturally' domineering, hierarchically oriented and power-hungry, while women are seen as nurturing, child rearing and domestically inclined.

There is a considerable body of evidence to suggest genetic and biochemical difference between men and women in relation to language ability, spatial judgement, agression, sex drive, ability to focus on tasks or to make connections across the hemispheres of the brain (Hoyenga and Hoyenga, 1993; Moir and Moir, 1998). 'Feminist' psychologist Diane Halpern begin her review of the literature holding the opinion that socialization practices were solely responsible for apparent sex differences in thinking patterns. However:

> After reviewing a pile of journal articles that stood several feet high and numerous books and book chapters that dwarfed the stack of journal articles, I changed my mind . . . there are real, and in some cases sizeable, sex differences with respect to some cognitive abilities. Socialization practices are undoubtedly important, there is also good evidence that biological sex differences play a role in establishing and maintaining cognitive sex differences, a conclusion I wasn't prepared to make when I began reviewing the relevant literature. (Halpern, 1992: xi)

Genetic science and biochemistry suggest that there are material, i.e. chemical, limits to behavioural possibilities. Today, few scientists dispute the influence of hormones on the formation of the foetus as male or female. Hormones are the switches that activate the genes which 'instruct' our brains and bodies as to its reproductive organs, testosterone levels, body fat, muscle development, bone structure, etc. It is also thought that those same hormones shape our brain structure so that men and women have different patterns of brain activity.

Yet, biology is itself a language and cultural classification system. Biochemistry and genetics are constituted by a particular type of vocabulary deployed for the achievement of specific purposes. The arguments of these sciences should be understood not as the revelation of objective truth or the correspondence of language with an independent object world but as the achieve-ments of agreed procedures. These procedures have enabled us to produce levels of predictability which have underpinned a consensus or solidarity amongst the scientific community leading them to call particular statements true. However, such truths are always provisional, for paradigm shifts in scientific thinking mean that the truths of today's ordinary science are revised and even overturned by tomorrow's conceptual revolution (Kuhn, 1962).

There is a philosophical case that the language of biochemistry could never explain causal connections to the categories of con-sciousness because in a more general sense the mental can never be reduced to the physical. There can be no causal laws which explain events under mental descriptions by those under physical descriptions (Davidson, 1980). There is no way to explain how electro-chemical activity is experienced by us as consciousness. Yet, in pragmatic terms, anti-depressant drugs can be successful in treatment depression while hormone treatment is the necessary and central plank in bodily sex-change strategies. The test is empirical and pragmatic, related to purposes and values not one of correspondence between the language of biochemistry and 'real' bodies. At the same time, what it *means* to be male or female remains a cultural question of signification and there is clear evidence that cultural attitudes about masculinity and femininity have changed over time (Giddens, 1992).

We may say that sex as biology and sex as the discursive–performative are different languages for different purposes. Both are social constructions which enable us to do different things. The language of biology enables us to make behavioural and bodily predictions and alterations through the use of drugs. The language of the discursive–performative helps to re-cast the symbolic, to rethink the way we talk about and perform 'sex' with consequences which we deem to be good, i.e. acceptance of a wider range of sexualities. The problems felt by men trapped in women's bodies may be usefully approached using the predictions made available to us through the language of biochemistry and drug therapy. They may also be advanced through therapeutic talk and the re-description of self in the symbolic domain (including dress and bodily movement).

Either way, biochemical arguments should not be used as an excuse not to test the limits of the culturally possible for it is a language whose utility belongs to a different domain.

Certainly Connell's conclusion is one that would find wide-spread support within cultural studies: 'there is no evidence at all of strong determination in this [biological] sense. . . . And the evidence of cross-cultural and historical diversity in gender is overwhelming' (Connell, 1995: 229). That is, cultural and language are of central significance in understanding sex and gender. At stake are the questions 'what is a woman?' and 'what is a man?'

Women's difference

An **essentialist** answer to the question 'what is a woman?' takes the category 'woman' as reflecting an underlying identity based on either biology or culture. Thus, Collard and Contrucci's (1988) ecofeminist *Rape of the Wild* relies on biological essentialism in its arguments that all women are linked by childbearing bodies and innate ties to the natural earth which support egalitarian, nurturance-based values. Likewise Rich (1986), who celebrates women's difference from men, locating its source in motherhood. This is condemned in its historical modes of oppression but celebrated for its female power and potentialities.

Nevertheless, most of the arguments which celebrate women-cultures are linguistic and cultural rather than biological, even as they are based on **signifiers** of the female body. For example, Daly's (1987) *Gyn/Ecology* links women to nature, stresses the material and psychological oppression of women and celebrates a separate woman-culture. Much of her argument revolves around the language used to describe women and its power over them. A clearly culturally founded argument for women's difference comes from Gilligan (1982) and her study of moral reasoning in which she argues that while men are concerned with an 'ethic of justice', women are more centred on an 'ethics of care'. Women, it is argued, develop for cultural reasons 'a different voice' from men which stresses context-specific forms of argument in contrast to the more abstract thinking of men.

Irigaray and womanspeak

A psychoanalytic–philosophical route to difference comes from Luce Irigaray, who theorizes a pre-symbolic 'space' or 'experience' for women which is unavailable to men. This is constituted by a feminine *jouissance* or sexual pleasure, play and joy, which is outside of intelligibility. Irigaray (1985a, 1985b) has been at the forefront of attempts to write the unwritable, to inscribe the feminine through *écriture feminine* (woman's writing) and *le parler femme* (womanspeak).

Irigaray speculates on the 'otherness' of the feminine, which she grounds in the female body. In particular, she turns to the mother–daughter relationship of the pre-Oedipal imaginary as the source of a feminine which cannot be symbolized (because it precedes entry into the symbolic order and the Law of the Father – see Chapters 1 and 6). For Irigaray, woman is outside the specular (visual) economy of the Oedipal moment and thus outside of representation (i.e. of the symbolic order). Given that the **symbolic** lacks a grammar which could articulate the mother–daughter relationship, the feminine can return only in its regulated form as man's 'Other'.

Irigaray proceeds by **deconstructing** western philosophy, which she reads as guaranteeing the masculine order and its claims to self-origination and unified agency. That is, western philosophy is said to be **phallocentric**. Irigaray explores the feminine as the constitutive exclusion of philosophy. Woman is not an essence *per se* but that which is excluded. The feminine is the unthinkable and the unrepresentable (other than as a negative of phallocentric discourse). Of course, in trying to read philosophical texts for their absences, Irigaray is faced with the problem of trying to critique philosophy for its exclusions while using the language of that philosophy. Her strategy is to 'mime' the discourse of philosophy, to cite it and talk its language but in ways which question the capacity of philosophy to ground its own claims. Womanspeak mimes phallogocentrism only to expose what is covered over (Irigaray, 1985b).

For Irigaray's supporters she represents a bold attempt to

- assert the specificity of the feminine;
- break with the logic of identity and of masculinity;
- celebrate the undefinable *jouissance* of women;
- tactically and successfully mime and expose phallocentric thinking.

As such, Irigaray offers a challenge to a masculine symbolic order through poetic writing. However, critics have accused her of essentialism through the assertion of the primacy of female biology and a distinct female imaginary. The positing of women as imaginative, poetic, feeling, etc., is said to mirror patriarchal **discourse** itself, which sees reason as male and emotion as female.

The social construction of sex and gender

In contrast to Rich, Daly and Irigaray, another strand of feminism rejects any form of essentialism, holding femininities and masculinities to be solely and only social constructions. Alcoff regards any emphasis on a special and benign female character as wrong not only because there is a lack of evidence for innate difference, but on the political grounds that 'it is in danger of solidifying an important bulwark for sexist oppression: the belief in innate "womanhood" to which we must all adhere lest we be deemed either inferior or not "true" women' (Alcoff, 1989: 104). Equality, rather than difference, is stressed in the work of Catherine Mackinnon (1987, 1991), who regards a woman-culture as 'making quilts'. She argues that women's subordination is a matter of social power founded on men's dominance of institutionalized hetero-sexuality. Though not all men have equal power and not all women are subject to the same forms of oppression, her summation of feminist arguments stresses equality: 'We're as good as you. Any-thing you can do, we can do. Just get out of the way' (Mackinnon, 1987: 32).

Scott has argued that the equality–difference debate relies on a false binary since it is possible for equality and difference to co-exist. 'Equality is not the elimination of difference, and difference does not preclude equality' (Scott, 1990: 137–8). That is, sameness is not the only ground for claims to equality; rather, difference is the condition for all identities and the very meaning of equality. We may struggle for equal opportunities but we should not expect or hope for sameness of outcome.

A good deal of sociological, cultural and feminist writing, including Mackinnon's, has sought to challenge biological deter-minism through the conceptual division between sex and gender. Sex is taken to be the biology of the body while gender refers to the cultural assumptions and practices which govern the social construction of men, women and their social relations. Subse-quently, it is argued that it is the social, cultural and political discourses and practices of gender which lie at the root of women's subordination. The sex–gender distinction constitutes the 'coat-rack' (Nicholson, 1995) view of self-identity by which the body is viewed as a framework upon which cultural meanings are thrown. It is argued that no fundamental sex differences exist and that those which are apparent are insignificant in relation to argu-ments for social equality. Further, since gender is a cultural construct it is said to be malleable in a way that biology may not be.

Sex as a discursive construct

The sex–gender distinction is now the subject of criticism. It is argued that sexual **identity** is not a reflection of a natural state of being but a matter of **representation**. The distinction between sex as biology and gender as a cultural construction is broken down on the grounds that there is in principle no access to biological 'truths' which lie outside of cultural discourses and therefore no 'sex' which is not cultural. Sexed bodies are always already represented as the production of regulatory discourses (see Butler's arguments later in the chapter). In this view, the body does not disappear:

> Rather, it becomes a variable rather than a constant, no longer able to ground claims about the male/female distinction across large sweeps of history but still there as always a potentially important element in how the male/female distinction gets played out in any specific society. (Nicholson, 1995: 43–4)

For poststructuralists, the cultural variations that exist between women (and between men) suggests that there is no universal cross-cultural category of 'woman' (or 'man') that is shared by all. Rather, there are multiple modes of femininity (and masculinity) which are enacted not only by different women, but, potentially by the same woman under different circumstances. The claim is that sex and gender are infinitely malleable in principle though in practice moulded and regulated into specific forms under particular historical and cultural conditions. As such, 'women are constantly confronted with the cultural task of finding out what it means to be a woman, of marking out the boundaries between the feminine and unfeminine' (Ang, 1996: 94).

SEXED SUBJECTS

Within cultural studies the argument that femininity and masculinity are malleable social constructions has taken its inspiration either from the work of Foucault (Weedon, 1997) or from psychoanalysis. We shall trace these apparently contradictory arguments (Foucault was opposed to psychoanalysis), culminating in Judith Butler's attempt to unite them.

Foucault: subjectivity and sexuality

For Foucault, subjectivity is a discursive production. That is, discourse (as regulated ways of speaking/practice) offers speaking persons **subject positions** from which to make sense of the world while 'subjecting' speakers to the rules and discipline of those discourses. A subject position is that perspective or set of regulated discursive meanings from which discourse makes sense. To speak is to take up a subject position and to be subjected to the regulatory power of that discourse.

Foucault propounds an anti-essentialist argument in which there are no universal ahistorical subjectivities. To be a man or a woman is not the outcome of biological determinism or universal cognitive structures and cultural patterns. Gender is historically and culturally specific, subject to radical discontinuities over time and across space. This does not mean that one can simply pick and choose genders or that gender is a matter of random chance. Rather, we are gendered through the power of regulated and regulatory discourses.

SEX AND THE DISCURSIVE CONSTRUCTION OF THE BODY

The body and sexuality are major themes in Foucault's work. He argued that sexuality was a focal point for the exercise of power and the production of subjectivity in western societies. Subjectivity is coterminous with sexuality as subjects are constituted through the production of sex and the control of the body. Thus:

> We, on the other hand, are in a society of 'sex', or rather a society 'with a sexuality': the mechanisms of power are addressed to the body, to life, to what causes it to proliferate, to what reinforces the species, its stamina, its ability to dominate, or its capacity for being used. Through the themes of health, progency, race, the future of the species, the vitality of the social body, power spoke of sexuality and to sexuality; the latter was not a mark or a symbol, it was an object or target. (Foucault, 1979: 147)

Foucault is concerned with 'the overall "discursive fact", the way in which sex is "put into discourse"' (Foucault, 1979: 11). He suggests that discourses of polymorphous sexualities have proliferated and been disseminated through medicine, the church, psychoanalysis, education programmes and demography. The proliferating discourses of sexuality *produce* particular subjectivities by bringing them into view via the discourses of, for example, medicine. These discourses analyse, classify and regulate sexuality in ways which produce sexed subjects and construct sexuality as the cornerstone of subjectivity.

Foucault argues that from the early eighteenth century onwards women's bodies were subject (to become a subject and to be subjected) to the discourse of modern science, which produced them as hysterical and nervous while reducing them to their reproductive system. Thus, there was

> a threefold process whereby the feminine body was analysed – qualified and disqualified – as being thoroughly saturated with sexuality; whereby it was integrated into the sphere of medical practices, by reason of a pathology intrinsic to it; whereby, finally, it was placed in

organic communication with the social body (whose regulatory fecundity it was supposed to ensure), the family space (of which it had to be a substantial and functional element), and the life of children (which it produced and had to guarantee, by virtue of a biologico-moral responsibility lasting through the entire period of the children's education): the mother, with her negative image of 'nervous women', constituted the most visible form of this hysterization. (Foucault, 1979: 104)

Foucault maintains that the confessional, developed by Catholicism, has been adapted and taken over by other institutions (e.g. therapy, or in more contemporary vein we might suggest TV talk shows such as *The Jerry Springer Show* and *The Oprah Winfrey Show*) to become the basis of discursive 'subjection'. However, wherever discursive power operates, so resistance is possible, not least through the production of 'reverse discourses'. For example, as medics and clerics put the idea of homosexuality into discourse, albeit to condemn, so the very discursive production of a homosexual subject position allowed homosexuals to be heard and to claim rights.

THE FEMINIST CRITIQUE OF FOUCAULT

Foucault has been subject to feminist criticism for neglecting 'to examine the gendered character of many disciplinary techniques' (McNay, 1992: 11). It is argued (Bartky cited McNay, 1992) that Foucault treats bodies as gender-neutral with little specificity beyond a male norm. He does not, for example, explore how men and women are related differently to the disciplinary institutions he describes. For example, it is argued, Foucault fails to consider the way the penal system treated male and female prisoners in different ways, that is, women's crime was understood as an inherent pathology unavailable to reform. While these criticisms have force, McNay (1992) tempers them by pointing out the dangers of positing a completely different history and experience of repression for women. While male and female bodies have been worked on in historically specific ways, this should not lead us, she argues, to propose an eternal and essential opposition between the sexes.

Foucault's description of subjects as 'docile bodies', whereby subjects are the 'effect' of discourse, has been of concern to feminists for it appears to rob subjects of the **agency** required for a politics based on women's action. However, it is arguable that Foucault's later work centred on 'techniques of the self' does reintroduce agency and the possibility of **resistance** and change. Foucault is led to consider how 'man [*sic*] proposes to think his own nature when he perceives himself to be mad; when he considers himself to be ill; when he conceives of himself as a living, speaking, labouring being' (Foucault, 1987: 6–7). This concern with self-production as a discursive practice is centred on the question of ethics as a mode of 'care of the self'.

ETHICS AND AGENCY

According to Foucault, morality is concerned with systems of injunction and interdiction constructed in relation to formalized codes. Ethics are concerned with practical advice as to how one should concern oneself with oneself in everyday life (Foucault, 1979, 1984b, 1986). While morality operates through a set of imposed rules and prohibitions, ethics are concerned with the actual practices of subjects in relation to the rules which are recommended to them. These rules are enacted with varying degrees of compliance and creativity.

Foucault explores the space between a system of laws and an individual's ethical practices which permit a degree of freedom to subjects in forming their individual behaviour. In particular, he points to an ethics of self-mastery and 'stylization' which is drawn from the character of relationships themselves rather than from external rules of prohibition. Thus does Foucault attribute a degree of individual autonomy and independence to subjects even while pointing to the indissociability of subjectivity from social and cultural constraints. McNay argues that this more dynamic conception of the self enables the exploration of a variety of sexualities and suggests a route for feminist political activity: 'Foucault's idea of practices of the self parallels developments in feminist analysis of women's oppression that seek to avoid positing women as powerless victims of patriarchal structures of domination' (McNay, 1992: 66).

Foucault's work has been criticized for its inability to explain why some discourses are 'taken up' by subjects and others are not. Consequently, some critics have looked for ways to connect the discursive 'outside' with the psychic 'inside'. For Stuart Hall (1995, 1996a), identity is the point of 'suture' between a domain of discursive operations and the realm of the imaginary or unconscious. Identities are forms in which we are obliged to act but which can never be adequate to the subject processes invested in them. Hall highlights the importance of thinking the **articulation** between the unconscious and political processes without being able to square them up or see them as equivalents. These arguments, he suggests, are learned from psychoanalysis and feminism.

Psychoanalysis, feminism and sexed subjectivity

REGULATING SEXUALITY

Amongst Freud's most oft quoted sayings are two apparently contradictory phrases whose interrogation may help us to grasp the implications of **psychoanalysis** for questions of sexual identity. On the one hand, Freud suggests that 'anatomy is destiny', but on the other describes human sexuality as involving 'polymorphous perversity', that is, the capability of taking on any number of forms.

According to Freud, the libido or sexual drive does not have any pre-given fixed aim or object. Rather, through fantasy, any object, which includes persons or parts of bodies, can be the target of desire. An almost infinite number of sexual objects and practices are within the domain of human sexuality. Subsequently, Freud's work is concerned to document and explain the *regulation* and repression of this 'polymorphous perversity' through the resolution (or not) of the Oedipus complex into the normative destiny of heterosexual gendered relationships.

Anatomy is argued to be destiny not because of genetic determination but because bodily differences are signifiers of sexual and social differentiation. Anatomy is destiny because it is hard to escape the regulatory scripts which surround bodily difference and which subordinate women to the political, economic and sexual power of men. It is quite clear that, as years of feminist writing have argued, bodies do matter.

CHODOROW: MASCULINITY AND FEMININITY

Freud shows, Chodorow (1978, 1989) argues, that while there is nothing inevitable about our sexual object choices and **identifications**, which are formed through a developmental process in the context of our first relationships, our sexualities are regulated in ways which are particularly costly for women. For Chodorow, the theory of the Oedipus complex is a demonstration of the reproduction of male dominance and male contempt for women.

Chodorow argues that in the context of patriarchy boys are treated as independent and outgoing persons by mothers while girls are loved more narcissistically as like the mother. Boys' separation involves identification with the father and symbolic Phallus as the domain of social status, power and independence. A form of masculinity is produced which stresses externally oriented activity, though at the price of covering over an emotional dependence on women and weaker skills of emotional communication. In contrast, girls have acquired a greater surety with the communicative skills of intimacy through introjection of, and identification with, aspects of their mothers' own narratives. The traditional cost is a greater difficulty with externally oriented autonomy.

These sexed subjectivities are not universals, for psychoanalysis shows us, argues Chodorow, that the formation of sexual love objects and of the relations between men and women is formed in the context of specific family configurations which, if challenged, can be changed. Over time, new forms of subject and new forms of masculinity and femininity could be forged.

PHALLOCENTRIC PSYCHOANALYSIS

There remains the vexed question of the phallocentric (i.e. male-centred) character of psychoanalysis, for example Freud's assertion that women would 'naturally' see their genitals as inferior or that genital heterosexual activity which stresses masculine power and feminine passivity is the normal form of sexuality. Further, in Lacan's reworking of Freud, the Oedipal moment marks the formation of the subject in the symbolic order and into the Law of the Father. The symbolic Phallus as signifier of the power of the symbolic order serves to split the subject from desire for the mother, enabling subject formation. It marks the necessary interruption of the mother–child dyad and the entry into the symbolic, without which there is only psychosis. Here the Phallus is a 'transcendental signifier' which covers over a sense of lack, allowing the subject to experience itself as a unity.

For some critics (Irigaray, 1985a, 1985b), the centrality of the Phallus to Lacan's argument renders 'woman' an adjunct term. That is, in Lacanian psychoanalysis the feminine is always repressed and entry into the symbolic always tied to the father/ Phallus. By contrast, Mitchell (1974) holds that if psychoanalysis is phallocentric, it is because the human social order it perceives and works through is 'patro-centric'. She stresses the Freudian emphasis on the *construction* and formation of subjectivity and sexuality, not on what a women is but on how she comes into being.

For Mitchell, psychoanalysis offers a deconstruction of the very formation of gendered identity in the psychic and symbolic domains of patriarchal societies. She argues that a feminist politics can interrogate and subvert the masculine phallic fantasies central to gender inequality. In doing so it can bring forth new structures of the unconscious, new mechanisms for the entry into culture and new subject positions. Chodorow (1978, 1989) argues that Freud's patriarchal assumptions are an expression of this value system and not inherent to psychoanalysis *per se*. Psychoanalysis could be cleansed of these assumptions and the historical specificity of its categories recognized and reworked. One may accept the historical primacy given to the Phallus but question the universality attributed to it in Lacanian theory.

Indeed, Rose (1997) argues for the fundamentally symbolic character of the Phallus in Lacan's work so that its function as a 'transcendental signifier' could be taken by other objects in alternative socio-cultural circumstances. It is, she says, the place of the Phallus in language and culture which counts, not any specific Phallus/penis or parent–child relationships. Thus, the particular kinds of psychic resolutions which psychoanalysis describes are not universals of the human condition but historically and culturally specific.

JULIA KRISTEVA

The semiotic and the symbolic

The Lacanian-influenced psychoanalyst who has perhaps attracted the most attention within feminist cultural studies is Julia Kristeva (see Kristeva, 1986c). This is for a number of reasons:

- Kristeva's work is centrally concerned with **signs/semiotics**, that is, with the symbolic order of culture.
- Her work is organized around questions of subjectivity and identity which have become critical issues for cultural studies.
- She is a practising psychoanalyst and is of interest as psychoanalysis undergoes a revival within cultural studies.
- Her work explores the way that psychic forces are intertwined with cultural **texts** through the identifications or investments that subjects make in texts and the place they have in the production of texts.

Kristeva distinguishes between the 'semiotic chora', which is pre-symbolic, and the 'thetic' or symbolic sphere. For Kristeva, subjects are 'always *both* semiotic *and* symbolic' (Kristeva, 1986a: 93). What she calls the 'subject-in-process' is an interplay between the 'semiotic' and the symbolic. Language, that is, the symbolic (thetic) is the mechanism by which the body can signify itself (as a signified ego) and involves the regulation of the (pre-symbolic) semiotic by the symbolic. Nevertheless, the semiotic returns in the symbolic order as a transgression of it.

Transgression is marked in certain kinds of (modernist) literary and artistic practice through the rhythms, breaks and absences in texts which reorder signs in time and space, that is, they develop a new language. Since the semiotic is associated with the pre-Oedipal relation with the mother's body (of plenitude and primary narcissism), one might expect that the revolutionary transformation of language which semiotic transgression of the symbolic brings about might be specifically associated with women. However, though there is a sense in which this is 'feminine', it is not the preserve of women *per se* for Kristeva holds a firmly anti-essentialist view of sexual identity.

Deconstructing sexual identity

Kristeva has argued that 'To believe that one "is a woman" is almost as absurd and obscurantist as to believe that one "is a man"' (cited Moi, 1985: 163). While we may identify with gendered identities and find it necessary for political reasons to continue to campaign as women (i.e. **strategic essentialism**,) one cannot *be* a woman. Sexual identities as opposites can only come into being after entry into the symbolic order, that is, sexual identity is not an essence but a matter of representation. According to Kristeva, a small child faces the choice of mother-identification, and subsequent marginality within the symbolic order, or father-identification, giving access to symbolic dominance but wiping out the plenitude of pre-Oedipal mother-identification. These choice face *both* male and female infants.

Consequently, degrees of masculinity and femininity are said to exist in biological men and women. Femininity is a condition or subject position of marginality which some men, for example avante-garde artists, can also occupy. Indeed, it is the patriarchal symbolic order that tries to fix all women as feminine and all men as masculine, rendering women as the 'second sex'. Kristeva advocates a position in which

> the very dichotomy man/woman as an opposition between two rival entities may be understood as belonging to *metaphysics*. What can 'identity', even 'sexual identity', mean in a new theoretical and scientific space where the very notion of identity is challenged? . . . What I mean is, first of all, the demassification of the problematic of *difference* . . . in order that the struggle, the implacable difference, the violence be conceived in the very place where it operates with the maximum intransigence, in other words, in the personal and sexual identity itself, so as to make it disintegrate in its very nucleus. (Kristeva, 1986b: 209)

Kristeva is suggesting that the struggle over sexual identities takes place within each individual. Rather than a conflict between two opposing male–female masses, sexual identity concerns the balance of masculinity and femininity within specific men and women. This struggle, she suggests, could result in the deconstruction of sexual and gendered identities understood in terms of marginality within the symbolic order. This stresses the singularity and multiplicity of persons as well as the relativity of symbolic and biological existence. 'The time has perhaps come to emphasize the multiplicity of female expressions and preoccupations' (Kristeva, 1986b: 193).

Kristeva contends not only that women occupy a range of subject positions but that a new symbolic space and subject position is opening itself. She explores the idea that a new generation of feminists is emerging who seek to reconcile the linear time of history and politics with the cyclical gestation time of motherhood. That is, the space is now available for women to intermingle motherhood (and difference) with the politics of equality and the symbolic order.

Judith Butler: between Foucault and psychoanalysis

Kristeva's attempt to deconstruct sexual identity is one shared by Judith Butler. Though Foucault rejected psychoanalysis as yet another network of disciplinary power, Butler has attempted to work with and between the work of Foucault and psychoanalysis. She accepts the Foucauldian argument that discourse operates as a normative regulatory power which produces the subjects it controls. However, she also suggests a return to psychoanalysis in order to pursue 'the question of how certain regulatory norms form a "sexed" subject in terms that establish the indistinguishability of psychic and bodily formation' (Butler, 1993: 22). Butler reads psychoanalysis in a way which opens up a space in which to discuss how regulatory norms are invested with psychic power through processes of identification.

In Foucauldian fashion, Butler argues that discourse defines, construct and produces bodies as objects of knowledge. Discourse is the means by which we understand what bodies are.

> The category of 'sex' is, from the start, normative; it is what Foucault has called a 'regulatory ideal'. In this sense, then, 'sex' not only functions as a norm, but is part of a regulatory practice that produces the bodies it governs, that is, whose regulatory force is made clear as a kind of productive power, the power to produce – demarcate, circulate, differentiate – the bodies it controls. Thus, 'sex' is a regulatory ideal whose materialization is compelled, and this materialization takes place (or fails to take place) through certain highly regulated practices. In other words, 'sex' is an ideal construct which is forcibly materialized through time. It is not a simple fact or static condition of a body, but a

process whereby regulatory norms materialize 'sex' and achieve this materialization through a forcible reiteration of those norms. (Butler, 1993: 1–2)

The discourses of sex are ones which, through repetition of the acts they guide, bring sex into view as a necessary norm. Sex is a construction, but an indispensable one which forms subjects and governs the materialization of bodies. This does not mean that 'everything is discourse'; rather, as Butler argues, discourse and the materiality of bodies are indissoluble.

THE PERFORMATIVITY OF SEX

Butler conceives of sex and gender in terms of citational **performativity**. The performative being 'that discursive practice which enacts or produces that which it names' (Butler, 1993: 13). This is achieved through citation and reiteration of the norms or conventions of the 'law' (in its symbolic, Lacanian sense). A perfomative is a statement which puts into effect the relation that it names, for example within a marriage ceremony 'I pronounce you . . .'.

Butler argues that judges in criminal and civil law do not originate the law or its authority but cite the conventions of the law which is consulted and invoked. This is an appeal to an authority which has no origin or universal foundations. Indeed, the very practice of citation produces the authority which is cited and reconstitutes the law. The maintenance of the law is a matter of reworking a set of already operative conventions and involves iterability, repetition and citationality.

For Butler, 'sex' is produced as a reiteration of hegemonic norms, a performativity which is always derivative. The 'assumption' of sex, which is not a singular act or event but an iterable practice, is secured through being repeatedly performed. Thus, the statement 'It's a girl' initiates a process by which 'girling' is compelled.

This is a 'girl', however, who is compelled to 'cite' the norm in order to qualify and remain a viable subject. Femininity is thus not the product of choice, but the forcible citation of a norm, one whose complex historicity is indissociable from relations of discipline, regulation, punishment. Indeed, there is not 'one' who takes on a gender norm. On the contrary, this citation of the gender norm is necessary in order to qualify as a 'one', to become viable as a 'one', where subject-formation is dependent on the prior operation of legitimating gender norms. (Butler, 1993: 232)

Performativity is not a singular act for it is always a reiteration of a set of norms. Nor should it be understood as a performance given by a self-conscious intentional actor. Rather, the performance of sex is compelled by a regulatory apparatus of heterosexuality which reiterates itself through the forcible production of 'sex'. Indeed, the very idea of an intentional sexed actor is a discursive production of performativity itself. 'Gender is *performative* in the sense that it constitutes as an effect that very subject it appears to express' (Butler, 1991: 24).

IDENTIFICATION AND ABJECTION

Butler combines this reworking of discourse and speech act theory with psychoanalysis to argue that the 'assumption' (taking on) of sex involves identification with the normative phantasm (idealization) of 'sex'. Sex is a symbolic subject position assumed under threat of punishment (e.g. of symbolic castration or abjection). The symbolic is a series of normative injunctions which secure the borders of sex (what shall constitute a sex) through the threat of psychosis and abjection (an exclusion, a throwing out, a rejection). For Butler, identification is understood as a kind of affiliation and expression of an emotional tie with an idealized fantasized object (person, body part) or normative ideal. It is grounded in fantasy, projection and idealization. However, identification is not an intentional imitation of a model or conscious investment in subject positions. Rather, it is indissoluble from the very formation of subjects and is coterminous with the emergence of the ego.

Identification constitutes an exclusionary matrix by which the processes of subject formation simultaneously produce a constitutive outside. That is, identification with one set of norms, say heterosexuality, repudiates another, say homosexuality. Indeed, Butler's work is concerned with abjection of gay and lesbian sexuality by the **hegemonic** heterosexual 'imperative'. She is also at pains to argue that identifications are never complete or whole. Since identification is with a *fantasy* or idealization, it can never be coterminous with 'real' bodies or gendered practices. There is always a gap or slipping away of identification. Like Rose (1997), psychoanalysis highlights for Butler the very *instability* of identity.

Identifications can be multiple and need not involve the repudiation of all other positions. Indeed, repudiated elements are always within the identification as that which is rejected but returns. Identifications of homosexuality are always within heterosexuality, and vice versa.

DRAG: RECASTING THE SYMBOLIC

Some feminists, for example Irigaray and to some extent Kristeva, regard resistance to heterosexual masculine hegemony as rooted in the pre-symbolic 'imaginary', that is, a zone outside of language. By contrast, Butler argues for the recasting the symbolic itself as that set of regulatory norms which govern sex. Though the symbolic regulates identificatory practices, this is never complete. It involves only *partial* identifications. Consequently, Butler is able to theorize a space for change in which the very notions of 'masculinity' and 'femininity' can be rethought.

Butler argues that drag can destabilize and recast gender norms through a re-**signification** of the ideals of gender (Butler, 1990). Through a miming of gender norms, drag can be subversive to the extent that it reflects on the performative character of gender. Drag suggests that all gender is performativity and as such destabilizes the claims of hegemonic heterosexual masculinity as the origin which is imitated. That is, hegemonic heterosexuality is itself an imitative performance which is forced to repeat its own idealizations. That it must reiterate itself suggests that heterosexuality is beset by anxieties that it can never fully overcome. The need for reiteration underlines the very insecurity of heterosexual identifications and gender positions. However, Butler's arguments are only indicative of one possible subversive activity for, as she points out, drag is at best always ambivalent and can be itself a reiteration and affirmation of the Law of the Father and heterosexuality.

THE DISCIPLINE AND THE FICTION OF IDENTITY

Ambivalence pervades Butler's discussion of identity categories *per se* and the notion of 'queer' in particular. The word 'queer' has been re-articulated and resignified by ACT-UP, Queer Nation and other communities of queer politics to deflect its injurious effects and turn it into an expression of resistance. However, Butler argues that identity categories of this type cannot be re-articulated (redefined) in any way. Nor can the effects of re-articulation be controlled for they are always open to further resignifications. Thus, the use of the term 'queer' as an affirmative has proved politically useful at the same time as it continues to echo its past. Further, Butler argues that we need to be attentive to the exclusions and abjections that *any* identity category enacts. This includes 'queer', for it establishes a false unity between men and women which may not resonate within all communities. For Butler, *all* identity categories are necessary fictions which, though we have to continue using them, should simultaneously be interrogated.

If we ask the question 'what is a woman?' we are enquiring about the character of sexual identity which we explored through the work of Irigaray, Nicholson, Kristeva, Butler, etc. For most of these writers, masculinity and femininity are not essential qualities of embodied subjects but matters of representation. They are ways of speaking about and disciplining bodies. This theme of representation is a trope of cultural studies which is also manifested in the study of gender in popular culture.

GENDER, REPRESENTATION AND MEDIA CULTURE

A good deal of feminist writing in the field of culture has been concerned with the representation of gender and of women in particular. As Evans (1997) comments, in the first place there was a concern to demonstrate that women had played a part in culture, and in literature in particular, in the face of their omission from the canon of good works. This was coterminous with a concern for the kinds of representations of women which had been constructed; that is, 'the thesis that gender politics were absolutely central to the very project of representation' (Evans, 1997: 72).

In early feminist studies the **realist** assumption was made that representation was a direct expression of social reality and/or a potential and actual distortion of that reality. That is, representations of women reflected male attitudes and constituted misrepresentations of 'real' women (see Tuchman et al., 1978). This is known as the 'images of women' perspective. However, later studies informed by poststructuralism regard all representations as cultural constructions and not as reflections of a real world. Consequently, concern centres on how representations signify in the context of social power with what consequences for gender relations. This exploration of 'women as a sign' (Cowie, 1978) we may call the 'politics of representation'.

Images of women

The concept of the **stereotype** occupies a prominent place within the images of women perspective. A stereotype involves the reduction of persons to a set of exaggerated, usually negative, character traits. 'Stereotyping reduces, essentializes, naturalizes and fixes "difference"' (Hall, 1997c: 258). Through the operation of power a stereotype marks the boundaries between the 'normal' and the 'abjected', 'us' and 'them'. Given the large body of work within the 'images' approach, the examples offered here should be regarded only as indicative of the kind of studies accomplished.

THE BITCH, THE WITCH AND THE MATRIARCH

Meehan (1983) analysed the stereotypes into which women are commonly cast on US television. Her study combined a quantitative analysis, which counted the number and kind of representations of women, with a qualitative interpretation of women's roles and power(lessness) within those representations. She suggested that representations on television cast 'good' women as submissive, sensitive and domesticated while 'bad' women are rebellious, independent and selfish. Meehan identifies the following as common stereotypes:

- *the imp*: rebellious, asexual, tomboy;
- *the good wife*: domestic, attractive, home-centred;
- *the harpy*: aggressive, single;
- *the bitch*: sneak, cheat, manipulative;
- *the victim*: passive, suffers violence or accidents;
- *the decoy*: apparently helpless, actually strong;
- *the siren*: sexually lures men to a bad end;
- *the courtesan*: inhabits saloons, cabarets, prostitution;
- *the witch*: extra power, but subordinated to men;
- *the matriarch*: authority of family role, older, desexed.

She concludes that 'American viewers have spent more than three decades watching male heroes and their adventures, muddied visions of boyhood adolescence replete with illusions of women as witches, bitches, mothers and imps' (Meehan, 1983: 131).

AFFIRMATION AND DENIAL

US television is not the only villain in the story: Gallagher's (1983) survey of women in the media suggests a consistent *global* depiction of women as **commodified** and stereotyped into the binary images of 'good' and 'bad'. For example, Krishnan and Dighe (1990) argue that affirmation and denial were the two main themes evident in their study of the representation of women on Indian television: affirmation of a limited definition of womanhood as passive and subordinate, being tied to housework, husbands and children; denial of the creativity, activity and individuality of women, particularly in relation to work and the public sphere.

They report that men in television fiction were the principal characters in much larger numbers than women (105 men to 55 women). Further, while men were represented in a range of occupations, most women (34) were depicted as housewives. Each of

Table 8.1   *Attributes of masculinity and femininity on Indian television*

Male characters	Female characters
self-centred	sacrificing
decisive	dependent
self-confident	anxious to please
seeing a place in the larger world	defining the world through family relations
rational and conniving	emotional and sentimental
dominant	subordinate
paternal	maternal

Source: Krishnan and Dighe, 1990

the principal characters was described on the basis of 88 polar opposite personality attributes and analysis revealed that the most common characteristics ascribed to men and women were as in Table 8.1.

Women were stereotyped into the idealized and deviant. The ideal woman was caring and maternal. She was supportive of men in their ambitions but had none of her own, being sacrificing, empathic and home-centred. As a passive wife/daughter she accepted male control and was devoted to the men in her life, defending even the most reprehensible of husbands in an unquestioning and submissive fashion. Deviant women were domineering of their husbands and did not remain at home to look after the family. In having personal ambitions, they broke up family ties, disrupted male bonding and were not sufficiently understanding or accommodating.

WOMEN OF BOLLYWOOD

According to Krishnan and Dighe (1990), the representation of the idealized woman on Indian television is embedded in and drawn from the Hindu *dharma shastras* or sources of tradition and right conduct such as the *Ramayana* and *Mahabharata*. These texts also provide the ideal moral universe and **ideological** structure for a series of popular Hindi films produced in Bombay which transform and rework their **narratives** and value systems (Mishra, 1985).

The title of the Hindi film *Suhaag* connotes a symbol of marriage, which is the continuing motif of a movie which acts as a guide to what constitutes a virtuous woman (Bahia, 1997; see also Dasgupta and Hedge, 1988, and Rajan, 1991, as sources of the following discussion). These include the characteristics of chastity, patience and selflessness, which are exemplified by the central character, 'Maa', who, abandoned by her villainous husband, brings up her sons without straying from traditional boundaries. Throughout the film it is Maa's role to bring up her sons in the correct and respectable way at whatever cost to herself. Despite her husband's lack of acknowledgement of her existence, when he later reappears Maa subordinates herself to him despite his continual betrayal of her trust. Above all things she must seek to save her marriage, without which she has no identity.

Where popular Hindi film has represented more independent and assertive women, they have frequently been depicted as coming to undesirable ends. For example, the film *Laadla* represents the independent, factory-owning woman Shittel as a heartless character with a reprehensible disregard for tradition. She declares that even after marriage she will remain number one with her husband below her. However, the independent woman must learn the errors of her ways: Shittel is rejected by her entire family before falling at her husband's feet to beg his forgiveness. In the final scene, dressed in a traditional sari serving her husband his lunch, she is represented as a much happier and more contented person.

THE TAMING OF THE SHREW

The critique of the cultural representation of women is not confined to popular culture but includes the 'Arts'. For example, McLuskie (1982) discusses how Shakespeare's *Taming of the Shrew* involves the treatment of women as commodities within a pattern of luxury consumption and aristocratic lifestyle. Shakespeare's work is culturally significant for its place in 'high' culture, which is assured through the education system. McLuskie argues that the whole notion of 'taming' is ideological as Petruchio tames Kate as he would an animal. All the 'jokes' are at Kate's expense and the play requires Petruchio's systematic destruction of her will through his puns. That he has the right to 'tame' Kate and that she is his property is made clear in the following extract from Petruchio:

> I will be master of what is mine own.
> She is my goods, my chattels; she is my horse,
> My household stuff, my field, my barn,
> My horse, my ox, my ass, my anything,
> And here she stands. Touch her whoever dare,
> I'll bring my action on the proudest he
> that stops my way in Padua. (III, ii, 229–35)

Further explorations of 'high' culture include Berger's (1972) discussion of Gainsborough's painting *Mr and Mrs Andrews*, which, he argues, represents the latter as an aspect of Mr Andrew's property, and Lovell's (1978) analysis of the novels of Jane Austen, which, she suggests, encapsulate the inferior position of women in the context of gentry conservatism.

THE PROBLEM OF ACCURACY

Illuminating though such studies are, the 'images of women' approach presents us with an **epistemological** problem for it asserts the **truth** and falsity of representations. For example, Gallagher (1983) describes the world-wide representation of women as demeaning, damaging and *unrealistic*. As Moi comments, an 'images of women' approach 'is equivalent to studying *false* images of women constructed by both sexes because the "image" of women in literature is invariably defined in opposition to the "real person" whom literature somehow never quite manages to convey to the reader' (Moi, 1985: 44–5). The central problem is that the 'real' is always already a representation (Chapter 3).

Consequently, later studies become concerned less with representational adequacy and more with a 'politics of representation' in which the marginality or subordination of women can be understood as a constitutive effect of representation realized or resisted by living persons. This approach explores the subject positions constructed by representations.

Subject positions and the politics of representation

A subject position is that perspective or set of regulated and regulatory discursive meanings from which the text or discourse makes sense. It is that subject with which we must identify in order for the discourse to be meaningful. In identifying with this subject position, the text subjects us to its rules; it seeks to construct us as a certain kind of subject or person. For example, in the context of advertising:

> Addressing us in our private personae, ads sell us, as women, not just commodities but also our personal relationships in which we are feminine: how we are/should be/can be a certain feminine woman, whose attributes in relation to men and the family derive from the use of these commodities. . . . A woman is nothing more than the commodities she wears: the lipstick, the tights, the clothes and so on are 'woman'. (Winship, 1981: 218)

Winship is arguing that advertising constructs subject positions for women which place them in the patriarchal work of domesticity, child care, beautification and 'catching men'. Women are to be mothers, housewives, sexually attractive, and so forth. The issue is not whether such imagery is 'true' or 'false' but what kinds of people it seeks to construct and with what consequences.

THE SLENDER BODY

Among the more powerful and influential representations of women that western culture promotes is the 'slender body' as a disciplinary cultural norm (Bordo, 1993). Slenderness and a concern with diet and self-monitoring are preoccupations of western media culture and its interest in a 'tighter, smoother, more constrained body profile'. Consequently, adverts target bulge, fat or flab and the desirability of flat stomachs and cellulite management. As Bordo (1993) argues, the slender body is a gendered body for the subject position of the slender body is female. Slenderness is a contemporary ideal for female attractiveness so that girls and women are culturally more prone to eating disorders than men.

Paradoxically, advertising culture offers us images of desirable foods while proposing that we eat low-calorie items and buy exercise equipment. In the face of this contradiction, Bordo argues, the capacity for self-control and the containment of fat is posed in moral as well as physical terms. The choice to diet and exercise is regarded as an aspect of self-fashioning requiring the production of a firm body as a symbol of gendered identity and the 'correct' attitude. The failure to exert such control, symbolically manifested in obesity and anorexia, is disciplined through, among other things, television talk shows which feature portrayals of 'eating disorders' or the struggles of the obese to lose weight. *The Oprah Winfrey Show*, for example, has placed the presenter's struggle with weight gain at the centre of its strategy to humanize her.

THE INDEPENDENT MOTHER

In arguing that texts construct subject positions about and for women, we should not imagine that these representations remain static. Thus Woodward (1997) discusses the changing representation of motherhood in contemporary culture. She notes the emergence of a new 'independent mother' representation which is not an idealized domesticated figure concerned only with child care but is supportive of autonomy and work for women/mothers. Woodward argues that the pleasures of this subject position lie in the fantasy of being a mother *and* having a career *and* being able to explore one's individuality *and* looking attractive.

REPRESENTING PERSONS WITH AIDS

Key issues of subject position, representation and sexuality have been explored in the context of a politics of AIDS which critiques the depiction of persons with AIDS (PWAs) as *victims* who are complicit in their own downfall. To reiterate, this is a question not so much of distortion and accuracy as of the politics of representation. Thus, 'we must recognize that every image of a PWA is a representation, and formulate our activists demands not in relation to the "truth" of an image, but in relation to the conditions of its construction and to its social effects' (Crimp, 1992: 126).

According to Benson (1997), the impact of AIDS cannot be accounted for simply in terms of its fatal effects for, though these have been devastating on specific populations, the total number of deaths has been small compared to other fatal diseases. For example, there have been some 10,000 AIDS deaths in Britain up until December 1994 while over 12,000 women die of breast cancer *each year*. At about 65 British deaths a year, AIDS is well below heart disease, cancers and road accidents as a cause of death (Benson, 1997). Thus, we have to pay attention to the cultural representation of AIDS, rather than fatalities as such, in considering why AIDS is a high-profile disease. This includes the anxieties about sexuality, especially about gay sexuality and gay culture, which have fuelled a 'moral panic' in relation to AIDS.

Resonating with the assertion that PWAs 'look like you and me' (Crimp, 1992), a good deal of media coverage of AIDS, including health promotion imagery, is intended to give out the 'big story' that AIDS is a grave danger to *heterosexuals*. Crimp (1992) argues that the typical portraits of PWAs, particularly as it relates to so-called 'risk' groups, are of gay men in tight 501s, prostitutes on the streets, Afro-Caribbeans and drug addicts who are depicted as an 'arm-with-a-needle-in-it'. These persons are contrasted to 'ordinary' heterosexuals – ordinary in that they are white, heterosexual and do not shoot drugs. In trying to convince the white heterosexual population that AIDS is a danger, heath promotion imagery stereotypes gays and other so-called 'risk' groups.

Even attempts to humanize PWAs and to help us understand suffering are riddled with problems. Crimp (1992) suggests the following:

- Images of PWAs tend to reinforce a sense of hopelessness. Whatever we learn about PWAs always includes the fact of their death or at least some kind of 'before' and 'after' imagery showing the ravages of the disease on their bodies. PWAs are presented as *passive victims*, whereas current treatment regimes are increasingly enabling PWAs to live longer, more productive lives. Lacking are any representations of people *living* with AIDS.

■ Images of PWAs nearly always involve a brutal invasion of privacy as they are exploited for a public spectacle and morality play.

■ PWAs are portrayed in terms of a narrative of their private tragedies and kept firmly within those bounds. Consequently:

> No one utters a word about the politics of AIDS, the most deliberate failure of public policy at every level of government to stem the course of the epidemic, to fund biomedical research into effective treatments, provide adequate health care and housing, and conduct massive and ongoing preventive education campaigns. (Crimp, 1992: 120)

As Benson (1997) suggests, there are serious issues of representation at stake here. How to address the fact that gay communities have borne the brunt of AIDS without depicting a 'gay plague'. How to acknowledge suffering without demonizing PWAs. How to talk about 'living with AIDS' when there is dying. A comparison with breast cancer is again illuminating. The understanding of breast cancer is framed by medical models, which, combined with the diversity of persons who are being treated for this condition, means that no dominant cultural representations have developed and been maintained. In contrast, PWAs are located both within a media moral panic and within a gay community for whom each death resonates. Thus, as Benson argues, 'the experience of cancer is individualized, AIDS collectivized' (Benson, 1997: 159). That collective is of course the gay community.

MADONNA'S PERFORMANCE

Not all representations offer subordinate subject positions, and theorists have been interested not only in subject positions which seek to fix the character of sexuality but also in those which destabilize them. Kaplan (1992), drawing on the work of Butler, explores the ambiguity of Madonna as a text which deconstructs gender norms. Her concern is not so much with the fabrication of fixed representations of women as with the exploration of sex as an unstable but regulated performance, that is, a politics of the signifier.

For Kaplan, Madonna is able to 'alter gender relations and to destabilize gender altogether' (Kaplan, 1992: 273). Not only do

Madonna's videos seek to empower women by exhorting them to take control of their lives, but they play with the **codes** of sex and gender to blur the boundaries of masculinity and femininity. Kaplan argues that Madonna's videos are implicated in the continual shifting of subject positions, involving stylized and mixed gender signs that question the boundaries of gender constructs. This, she argues, is a politics of representation which centres on sex and gender as unstable 'floating' signifiers.

Kaplan argues that Madonna's video 'Express Yourself' continually shifts the focus of the camera, and thus the audience, to adopt a variety of subject–viewer positions so that identification is dispersed and multiple. Body boundaries are violated and gender norms crossed. For example, Madonna mimes the male film maker Fritz Lang, only to open her jacket to reveal a bra. In 'Justify My Love', Madonna confuses the audiences as to the gender of a variety of lovers and couplings, while the movie *Truth or Dare* (released in the UK as *In Bed with Madonna*) pretends to reveal the 'truth' about Madonna, thus engaging in the politics of representation as truth, while placing her in a range of gendered identities. This includes a sequence where, as Cleopatra, Madonna simulates masturbation under the gaze of male eunuchs sporting huge conical breasts. Kaplan asks, 'Are the eyes male or female? Is it feminine to masturbate publicly, or does that action transgress feminine codes and reach over to masculinity? Such are the questions the performance provokes' (Kaplan, 1992: 275).

During 1998 Madonna was again at the centre of controversy when she appeared at an awards ceremony dressed in a version of 'traditional' Indian clothing. Madonna's appearance was met with protest from some Hindus for defiling sacred items by juxtaposing them with her bare nipples and dancing lasciviously. On the one hand, Madonna could be criticized for commodifying ethnic femininity and offending the religious beliefs of some Hindus. On the other hand, the very performativity of the ethnic and gender identity she enacted and re-signified could be said to be supportive of anti-essentialist ideas that all identities are performances and none can lay claim to **authenticity**.

THE QUESTION OF AUDIENCES

Much depends on how one reads Madonna's performance. While we have concentrated on forms of textual analysis focusing on the subject positions offered readers, a new range of reception studies has stressed the **active audience**. That is, the way viewers construct, negotiate and perform a multiplicity of meanings and gendered identities. Rather than regard audiences as reproducing textual subject positions and meanings, we need to consider what concrete people in specific locations actually do with texts.

For example, while soap opera does produce certain symbolic forms of gendered spectatorship, for example the subject position of 'ideal mother' (Modeleski, 1982), there is a difference between 'the analysis of spectatorship, conceived as a set of subject positions constructed in and through texts, and the analysis of social audiences, understood as the empirical social subjects actually engaged in watching television' (Ang, 1996: 112). Indeed, a number of studies of the soap opera audience confirm the general genre competencies of the audience and a sense of a collective, collaborative network of viewing (Ang, 1985; Buckingham, 1987; Hobson, 1982; Seiter, 1989). Topics of discussion included speculation about future developments and moral–ideological judgements about characters and their actions. We must be concerned, then, not simply with textual devices which produce a variety of modes of femininity and masculinity but with the extent to which textual subject positions are 'taken up' by concrete women and men (see Chapter 9).

SUMMARY

Within cultural studies, sex and gender are held to be social constructions intrinsically implicated in matters of representation. They are matters of culture rather than nature. Though there is a strand of feminist thinking which stresses the essential differences between men and women, cultural studies tends to explore the idea of the historically specific, unstable, plastic and malleable character of sexual identity. However, this does not mean that one can simply throw off sexual identities with ease and take on others, for, while sex is a social construction, it is one which constitutes us through the impositions of power and the identifications of the psyche. That is, social constructions are regulated and have consequences.

Since sexual identity is held to be not a universal biological essence but a matter of how femininity and masculinity are spoken about, then feminism and cultural studies must be concerned with matters of sex and representation. For example, cultural studies has explored the representation of women in popular culture and within literature to argue that women across the globe are constituted as the second sex, subordinated to men. That is, women have subject positions constructed for them which place them in the patriarchal work of domesticity and beautification or, increasingly (within the West), of being a mother and having a career and being able to explore one's individuality and looking attractive. Women in postcolonial societies carry the double burden of having being subordinated by colonialism and native men. Nevertheless, we also noted the possibility of destabilizing representations of sexed bodies (drag and Madonna).

While texts construct subject position, it does not follow that all women or men take up that which is offered. Rather, reception studies have stressed the negotiations between subject and text, including the possibility of resistance to textual meanings. Indeed, such studies have often celebrated the values and viewing culture of women. This shift from text to audience, from image to talk, is discussed in Chapter 9, where we explore the place of television as a textual resource for concrete persons who identify or otherwise with the subject positions texts offer.

9

Television, Texts and Audiences

The development and institutionalization of cultural studies has long been intertwined with that of media studies. In particular, television, the major form of communication in most western societies, is one of cultural studies' prolonged concerns. No other medium can match television for the volume of popular cultural texts it produces and the sheer size of its audiences.

Television is a resource open to virtually everybody in modern industrialized societies and an increasing one in the 'developing' world. It is a source of popular knowledge about the world and increasingly brings us into contact, albeit in a mediated way, with ways of life other than those into which we were born. Television is implicated in 'the provision and the selective construction of social knowledge, of social imagery, through which we perceive the "worlds", the "lived realities" of others, and imaginarily reconstruct their lives and ours into some intelligible "world-of-the-whole"' (Hall, 1977: 140).

There have always been grounds for exploring the economic and cultural significance of television. However, the case is particularly acute at present because of changes in the patterns of global communications. There has been a significant rise in transnational television. In turn, the globalization of the institutions of television raise crucial questions about culture and cultural identities. As Thompson has argued:

> We must not lose sight of the fact that, in a world increasingly permeated by the products of the media industries, a major new arena has been created for the process of self-fashioning. It is an arena which is severed from the spatial and temporal constraints of face-to-face interaction and, given the accessibility of television and its global expansion, is increasingly available to individuals world-wide. (Thompson, 1995: 43)

Television needs to be understood in terms of:

- texts (programmes);
- the relationship between texts and audiences (audience research);

- political economy (organizations/industry);
- patterns of cultural meaning.

This points to the desirability of a multidimensional and multi-perspectival approach to the understanding of television which would seek to avoid **reductionism** by grasping the connections between the economic, political, social and cultural dimensions of the medium.

TELEVISION AS TEXT: NEWS AND IDEOLOGY

News is one of the principal **texts** of television. It appears on just about every television network across the globe and is the subject of entire globally distributed channels, including Cable News Network (CNN). The production of news holds a strategic position in debates about television for its presumed, and often feared, influence on public life. This concern has been heightened by the emergence of global cross-border television.

Putting reality together

Television news is not a reflection of reality so much as 'the putting together of reality' (Schlesinger, 1978). News is not an unmediated 'window-on-the-world' but a selected and constructed representation constitutive of 'reality'. The selection of items for inclusion as news and the specific ways in which, once selected, a story is constructed are never neutral. They are always a particular version of events. News **narratives** concern explanations for the way things are. They offer us frameworks of understanding and rules of reference about the way the world is constructed. It follows that news selection criteria tell us about the ideological world view that is being assembled and disseminated. By **ideology** (Chapter 4) is meant structures of signification or 'world views' which constitute social relations in and through the operation of power.

The first selection concerns the topics that news covers. For Anglo-American news, Hartley (1982) identifies these as politics, the economy, foreign affairs, domestic affairs, sport and 'occasional' stories. These topics define the news paradigm, the significant omission being the domain of the personal/sexual. A second moment of selection concerns the constitution of the topic so that **politics** is defined as being about government and mainstream political parties with a stress on personalities. The economy is circumscribed as being about the stock exchange, trade figures, government policy, inflation, money supply, and so forth. Foreign affairs means inter-governmental relations, while domestic news is sub-divided into 'hard' stories – conflict, violence, industrial disputes – and 'soft' human interest stories. The category of 'sport' has traditionally been constituted by male professional sport.

For the manufacture of a story within a topic, we can turn to Galtung and Ruge's (1973) pioneering work on **news values**, that is, the values which guide the selection processes. Galtung and Ruge identify four prime news values of the *western* world:

- reference to elite nations;
- reference to elite persons;
- personalization;
- negativity.

While the unexpected is a significant news value, it is even more so if it has negative consequences involving elite persons of an elite nation. A scandal about the private life of the President of the USA is more 'newsworthy' than successful crop figures in Malawi.

The manipulative model

Explanations for how and why the news is ideological come in a variety of forms. In the manipulative model the media are seen as a reflection of a **class**-dominated society and ideology is consciously introduced by allocative controllers. This happens as a direct result of the concentration of media ownership in the hands of people who are part of the 'establishment' or by government manipulation and informal pressure. Though there have been examples of direct manipulation of the news, this is too crude a model of the media in the context of western plural democracies. This is so because of the quasi-independence granted to operational controllers and journalists, legal constraints placed on news organizations, and the sophistication of audiences.

The pluralist model

Western journalists and news organizations themselves often stress a pluralist model. This argument suggests that market forces lead to a plurality of outlets and to a multiplicity of voices addressing different audiences. Where concentration of media ownership occurs, this does not lead to direct proprietorial control because of the independence of professional staff. In so far as the media pay attention to some issues more than others, this is said to be determined by audience choice through the mechanisms of the market. Audiences, aware of a range of political views and presentational styles within the media, choose to buy or watch that which they already agree with.

While a pluralist model recognizes that the media are not simply manipulated by their owners, this paradigm arguably bends the stick too far. Not only does increasing media concentration belie arguments about pluralism, but there is considerable evidence of the systematic exclusion of some world views in favour of others (see 'Gulf War' news below). Further, the increasing reliance on advertising in television systems may lead to a stress on immediacy, entertainment and the omission of certain types of news programmes such as documentaries (Blumler, 1986; Dahlgren, 1995).

The hegemonic model

Within cultural studies the hegemonic model has been popular. While any given culture is constructed in terms of a multiplicity of streams of meaning, there is, it is argued, a strand of meanings which can reasonably be called ascendant or dominant (Hall, 1977, 1981; Williams, 1973). The process of making, maintaining and reproducing these authoritative sets of meanings and practices has, after Gramsci (1968), been dubbed cultural **hegemony** (see Chapter 2). Hegemony is won and not given; further, it needs to be constantly rewon and renegotiated, making **culture** a terrain of conflict and struggle over meanings.

Within a hegemonic model, ideology in news is held to be not the result of direct intervention by owners or even a conscious attempt at manipulation by journalists, but an outcome of the routine attitudes and working practices of staff. News journalists learn the conventions and codes of 'how things should be done', reproducing ideology as common sense. For example, Hall et al. (1978) argue that reliance on 'authoritative sources' leads to the media reproducing 'primary definers', accounts as news. Primary definers are taken to be politicians, judges, industrialists, the police, and so forth, that is, official agencies involved in the making of news events. In translating the primary definitions of news, the media, as secondary definers, reproduce the hegemonic ideologies associated with the powerful, translating them into popular idioms.

Hall et al. (1978) hold that in constructing stories about 'mugging', journalists reproduce the racist assumption that street crime is the work of young black men. Journalists seek the views of the police, politicians and judges, who declare that not only is street crime on the increase, but that something must be done about it in the form of heavier policing and harsher sentences. The news media report such comments as common-sense concern about rising crime and its association with black youth. The circle becomes complete when judges cite news coverage of crime as the expression of public concern, using it to justify the harsher sentences and increased police activity which they and politicians had called for. Subsequently, police activity is directed into areas in which young black men live, because they have been seen as the perpetrators of crime, fuelling confrontation between the police and black youth.

Agenda setting

In the hegemonic model of news, the media draw off and constitute consensual assumptions about the world in a process of agenda setting. They define what constitutes news; that which is important and that which is outside of the news paradigm. Hall et al. (1981) argue that though many current affairs programmes do offer balance in terms of the time given to different political views, the very field of 'politics' has already been set up as concerning established political procedures, that is, Parliament or Congress. Consequently, a balance of 'protagonists' and 'respondents' encompasses only those political **discourses** favouring the field of politics as currently structured. Green politics, revolutionary politics and **feminist** concerns with domestic life usually fall outside of the established view of what politics and balance are about.

Gulf War news

As an example of the ideological and agenda setting capacities of news, let us consider the coverage of the 1991 'Gulf War', which marked the arrival of Cable News Network (CNN) as a world-wide news service. The most enduring motif of the television Gulf War was that of technologically 'smart' weapons able to hit targets with pin-point accuracy, thereby confining the war to military engagements and minimizing casualties. However, there is another version of the 'truth' (Mowlana et al., 1992) which suggests that Iraq was subjected to carpet bombing of a greater tonnage than that which was dropped in the entire Second World War. Mowlana et al. (1992) claim that only 7 per cent of the tonnage dropped was 'smart', and of these 10 per cent missed their targets. Consequently, the

Iraqi infrastructure was destroyed to an extent which returned it to a pre-industrial era.

Though television coverage of the war was hailed as 24-hour live reporting, Morrison's (1992) content analysis of CNN, Sky News and UK terrestrial television confirms that over half of the coverage of the war was studio-based and that most of the images that were not from a studio were of military press conferences. As he argues, this is hardly the action of battle. Morrison goes on to document the evidence that only 3 per cent of the news coverage was of 'the results of military action in terms of human casualties' and only 1 per cent of the visual images of television were of 'death and injury'. Instead, much of the news coverage of the Gulf War, especially by CNN, made use of staged press conferences and tapes supplied by the military authorities, that is, the primary definers of news.

Though overt management of the news by military authorities was marked in the Persian Gulf, we should not overlook the cultural assumptions of western journalists, who, with few exceptions, could be expected to support the war. The influence of these western journalists extended well beyond the boundaries of the US and Europe. Sainath (1992) reports the attraction of CNN to Indian elites and the domination of Indian press and television by western pro-war sources. While state television did introduce an element of debate, it suffered from the domination of the screen by images supplied by the coalition authorities. 'Many of the journalists working on the programme were clearly against the war, but the footage was not' (Sainath, 1992: 71).

Arguably the greatest failing of television coverage of the Gulf War was its deficiency in providing adequate causal explanations. Rather, 'the event itself – war – appears to swamp the news and did so at the expense of discussion about either the initial invasion of Kuwait in August 1990, or the presentation of a historical perspective on the war' (Morrison, 1992: 68). By concentrating on the 'glamour' of high-tech weaponry and the immediate military objectives of the war, television arguably obscured the contestable reasons that lay behind the conflict.

Presentational styles

Television news is constituted not only by its choice of topics and stories but by its verbal and visual idioms or modes of address. Presentational styles have been subject to a tension between an informational–educational purpose and the need to entertainingly engage us. While current affairs programmes are often 'serious' in tone, with adherence to the 'rules' of balance, more popular programmes adopt a friendly, lighter, idiom in which we are invited to consider the impact of particular news items from the perspective of the 'average person in the street'. Political coverage has come to rely on the staged sound-bite, with politicians going to some length to provide television with a resonant phrase or telling image.

Dahlgren (1995) argues that growing commercial competition has tilted television towards popular formats. He cites increased use of faster editing tempos and 'flashier' presentational styles, including the use of logos, sound-bites, rapid visual cuts and the 'star quality' of news readers. A stress on immediacy in the presentation of news is a specific and recent development in global news. Electronic news gathering (ENG) technology allows television to bring edited accounts of global and local events to the screen almost as they happen, while lightweight cameras, digital video editing and the multiskilling of television personnel allow for speed and flexibility. Global television has thus shortened the 'threshold' time of what constitutes news.

Alongside these developments within the traditional news programme there has been a proliferation of new popular formats, including the tabloid-style news broadcast, the political talk show, the vox-pop audience participation format and the 'infotainment' magazine shows of breakfast and daytime television (Dahlgren, 1995). These programmes rely on a rapid turnover of items, emblematic visuals and a sense of proximity through the location of news in everyday experience (the human interest story). Popular formats can be said to enhance understanding by engaging an audience unwilling to endure the longer verbal orientation of older news formats. However, they arguably work to reduce understanding by failing to provide the structural contexts for news events. We quickly learn what has happened (or at least a version of it) but not why it has happened.

TELEVISION AS TEXT: SOAP OPERA AS POPULAR TELEVISION

Though news is an obvious arena of political and ideological interest, cultural studies has also been concerned with popular television, that is, game shows, police and hospital dramas, sport, music and soap opera. I take the latter as my example of a popular television form much explored within cultural studies.

Soap opera as a genre

The general features of soap opera as a **genre** can be summarized (see Allen, 1985, 1995; Ang, 1985; Buckingham, 1987; Dyer et al., 1981; Geraghty, 1991) thus:

- *Open-ended narrative forms*: Soap opera, as a long-running serial, has a potentially unlimited time period in which to tell its stories. There is not the sense of closure to be found in the feature film or the thirteen episode series.
- *Core locations*: Most soaps establish a sense of geographical space that the audience can identify with and to which the characters return again and again. Thus *Neighbours* utilizes the Melbourne suburbs while *Coronation Street* and *EastEnders* are set in fictionalized working-class areas of major British cities.
- *The tension between the conventions of realism and melodrama*: Soap opera utilizes the conventions of **realism** and melodrama and can be differentiated in terms of the balance struck between them. Realism refers to a set of conventions by which drama appears to be a representation of the 'real world' with motivated characters, recognizable locations and believable social problems. The narrative techniques deliberately hide and obscure their own status as constructs, denying their artificiality in order to present themselves as 'real'. In contrast, melodrama is constituted through a heightened sense of the dramatic, with a focus on emotions and 'life's torments', where characters have insufficient motivation from a 'realist' point of view. Reinforced by the use of a certain elevated acting style, dramatic music and lingering close-up shots, the story-lines contain a variety of twist and turns which would stretch the credibility of a realist narrative as viewers are propelled along a roller-coaster ride of emotional ups and downs.
- *The pivotal themes of inter-personal relationships*: Marriages, divorces, break-ups, new alliances, arguments, acts of revenge and acts of caring are at the core of the soap opera, providing the narrative dynamic and emotional interest. Given the stress in soaps on the personal sphere, it is understandable that the family forms the mythic centre of the soap opera. It is mythic because though 'family' is a major theme and most of the characters take up family roles (available in plot terms for a marriage, divorce, relationships), only a limited number of characters actually live in a conventional nuclear family. The imaginary ideal of the family is constantly shattered by the arguments, affairs and divorces which are so necessary a part of the soap opera.

While these features are markers of soap opera in general, it is important to recognize that they work in different ways under different national circumstances. For example, Geraghty (1991) draws attention to different treatments of 'the family' in US and British soaps. The former, she argues, adopt a patriarchal model of the family which centres on men's efforts to hold the family together in the face of crisis, where the family is intimately connected to questions of property, power and money. In British soaps, there is a tradition of strong women characters who offer selfless support to others, most notably a breed of feckless men, so that the moral and practical task of family survival falls on female shoulders.

Telenovelas

Contrasts and similarities are further evidenced within 'telenovelas', the Latin American serial form. During the late 1970s telenovelas became the dominant Latin American television export, representing 70 per cent of the total of hours sold abroad. Within Latin America they consistently get higher ratings than their imported American rivals (Rogers and Antola, 1985). The telenovela has 'family resemblances' with the Anglo-American soap opera. Both are long-running serial narratives produced for television, and both, with varying degrees of emphasis, employ melodramatic narrative modes. However, as Lopez (1995) reminds us, telenovelas have distinctive features which make them a specific genre. While the core of the telenovelas' universe is interpersonal relations, a feature they share with soap opera, this has not prevented them from incorporating more social realist themes than might be found in the American format (Vink, 1988).

Women and soap opera

The addressing and representation of women has been pursued by a number of feminist writers in relation to soap opera since it is frequently suggested that soap opera is a women's space in which women's motivations are validated and celebrated. It has been argued (Ang, 1985; Hobson, 1982; Geraghty, 1991) that the central themes of soap opera – interpersonal relationships, marriages, divorces, children, and so forth – chime with the traditionally domestic concerns of women so that soap opera is a space in which women's concerns and points of view are validated and from which women take pleasure.

Soap operas deploy a variety of strong and independent-minded women characters. However, while the private sphere may be celebrated, women are frequently confined. For example, the financially independent woman in the soap is a relatively recent and limited phenomenon. Additionally, the use of glamour and the physical appearance of women to enhance soaps is subject to the criticism that the representation of women is for the male gaze. Women may be strong in soaps, but that strength is frequently put at the service of the family and the men within it.

As commentators have argued, there is both protest and acceptance by women in soap opera (Geraghty, 1991). Indeed, television frequently involves *contradictory ideologies* which compete with each other. For example, in telenovelas women are presented, on the one hand, as adjuncts of men – they are economically and socially dependent on men so that daughters are directed to marry according to the fathers' wishes – while, on the other hand, they often depict women denouncing and resisting domination in a variety of ways (Vink, 1988). The family in soap opera is also handled in a contradictory way, idealized yet shown to be tearing itself apart. Women are the victims of the claustrophobia of family life and, in a sense, the saviours of that which is valuable about it, that is, the care and concern.

Soap opera and the public sphere

The emphasis on the family in soap opera may lead to the general exclusion of issues located in the **public sphere**. A potential ideological implication of which is that personal and family relations are deemed more important than wider **social** and **structural** issues. If we are happy in the family, nothing else matters, or it matters only in terms of its private implications for individuals. Whether it be in response to such criticism or not, soaps have begun to engage with public issues like racism, AIDS, crime and unemployment. While the increase in the range of characters in soap and the expansion of story-lines to include wider social issues are to be welcomed, Geraghty (1991) expresses concern that the increasing role of male characters and the entrance of the teenager as a key soap concern may be upsetting the particular orientation of soaps to women viewers, disrupting the pleasures they gain from them. For example, the courting of the male audience has lead to an increased use of crime series conventions and, Geraghty suggests, a shift in the **representation** of women towards pleasing the male eye.

THE ACTIVE AUDIENCE

No consideration of television would be complete without exploring the evidence provided by audience research. However, empirical evidence never simply 'speaks for itself' in an unambiguous way but is framed within particular theoretical perspectives. The concentration in this account is on the framework which has dominated audience research within the cultural studies tradition, namely (at least retrospectively) the **active audience** paradigm. This 'tradition' suggests that audiences are not cultural dopes but are active producers of meaning from within their own cultural context.

The active audience paradigm developed in reaction to the numerous ways in which audiences had been studied with the built-in assumption that watching television was passive in character with the meanings and messages of television unproblematicaly taken up by audiences; for example the considerable volume of research which understood viewing in behavioural terms, arguing that audiences imitated violence on television, or which used statistical correlations to 'prove' that watching television had certain 'effects' on audiences. It was also a reaction to a textual strand in cultural studies which implied that one could 'read off' audience understandings from a close examination of the meanings embodied in television texts.

The proponents of the active audience approach argued that not only was the behavioural evidence inconclusive and contradictory, with statistical correlations not in themselves evidence of causes, but that this was a fundamentally mistaken way to approach television audiences. It was argued that television audiences are not an undifferentiated mass of aggregated but isolated individuals. Rather, watching television is a socially and culturally informed activity which is centrally concerned with *meaning*. Audiences are active creators of meaning in relation to television (they do not simply accept uncritically textual meanings) and they do so on the basis of previously acquired cultural competencies forged in the context of language and social relationships. Further, it was argued that texts do not embody one set of unambiguous meanings but are themselves polysemic, that is, they are carriers of multiple meanings, only some of which are taken up by audiences. Indeed, differently constituted audiences will work with different textual meanings. Thus the active audience paradigm represented a shift of interest from numbers to meanings, from textual meaning to textual meanings and from the general audience to particular audiences.

There is now a good deal of mutually supporting work on television audiences within the cultural studies tradition from which the following conclusions can be drawn:

■ The audience is conceived of as active and knowledgeable producers of meaning not products of a structured text.

But . . .

- Meanings are bounded by the way the text is structured and by the domestic and cultural context of the viewing.
- Audiences need to be understood in the contexts in which they watch television in terms of both meaning construction and the routines of daily life.
- Audiences are easily able to distinguish between fiction and reality; indeed they actively play with the boundaries.
- The processes of meaning construction and the place of television in the routines of daily life alter from culture to culture and in terms of gender and class within the same cultural community.

The active audience paradigm is not the 'property' of Anglo-Saxon cultural studies. McAnany and La Pastina's review of twenty-six studies of telenovelas substantiates the argument that local organizational and cultural configurations mediate the understandings of soap operas generated by audiences. Their claim is that similar findings 'are apparent across a number of studies and are not or rarely contradicted by others' (McAnany and La Pastina, 1994: 3). In summary they suggest the following:

- Audiences are active and derive a variety of meanings from tele-novelas.
- Audiences make application to their lives.
- Audiences recognize the fictional nature of the genre and the functioning of its rules.
- The contextual variables of family, class, gender and neighbourhood qualify audiences' reaction.

Conclusions about the character of audiences have been reached by way of two mutually supporting routes: theoretical work and empirical research. On the theoretical front, two fields of study have proved to be particularly influential: the encoding–decoding model and literary reception studies.

Encoding–decoding

Hall (1981) conceives of the process of television encoding as an **articulation** of the linked but distinct moments of production, circulation, distribution and reproduction, each of which has its specific practices which are necessary to the circuit but which do not guarantee the next moment. Though meaning is embedded at each level, it is not necessarily taken up at the next moment in the circuit. In particular, the production of meaning does not ensure consumption of that meaning as the encoders might have intended because television messages, constructed as a **sign** system with multi-accentuated components, are **polysemic**. In short, television messages carry multiple meanings and can be interpreted in different ways. That is not to say that all the meanings are equal among themselves; rather, the text will be 'structured in dominance' leading to a 'preferred meaning', that is, the one the text guides us to.

The audience is conceived of as socially situated individuals whose readings will be framed by shared cultural meanings and practices. To the degree that audiences share cultural **codes** with producers/encoders, they will decode messages within the same framework. However, where the audience is situated in different social positions (e.g. of class and gender) with different cultural resources, it is able to decode programmes in alternative ways. Hall (1981) proposed, after Parkin, a model of three hypothetical decoding positions:

- the dominant–hegemonic encoding/decoding which accepts the 'preferred meanings';
- a negotiated code which acknowledges the legitimacy of the hegemonic in the abstract but makes its own rules and adaptations under particular circumstances;
- an oppositional code where people understand the preferred encoding but reject it and decode in contrary ways.

Hermeneutic theory

Work within the tradition of hermeneutics and literary reception studies further challenges the idea that there is one textual meaning associated with authorial intent and that textual meanings are able to police meanings created by readers/audiences (see Wilson, 1993). For Gadamer (1976) and Iser (1978), the relationship between the text and the audience is an interactive one in which the reader approaches the text with certain expectations and anticipations which are modified in the course of reading to be replaced by new 'projections'. Understanding is always from the position and point of view of the person who understands, involving not merely reproduction of textual meaning but the *production of new meaning* by the readers. The text may structure aspects of meaning by guiding the reader but it cannot fix meanings, which are the outcome of the oscillations between the text and the imagination of the reader.

These theoretical perspectives informed a series of empirical studies of television audiences. For the purposes of establishing and popularizing the active character of audiences within cultural studies, the early work of Morley and Ang proved to be critical.

The *Nationwide* audience

Morley's (1980) research into the audience for the British news 'magazine' programme *Nationwide* was based on Hall's encoding–decoding model. It aimed to explore the hypothesis that decodings varied by socio-demographic factors (class, age, sex, race) and by their associated cultural competencies and frameworks. Though not without its methodological problems, which Morley (1992) acknowledges, the study suggests a multitude of readings which cluster around key decoding positions constituted by class. For example, dominant decodings were made by a group of conservative print managers and bank managers while negotiated readings were made by a group of trade union officials. The latter's readings remained negotiated rather than oppositional because they were specific to a particular industrial dispute while remaining within the general discourse that strikes were a 'bad thing for Britain'. According to Morley, oppositional decodings were made by a group of shop stewards, whose political perspectives led them to reject wholesale the discourses of *Nationwide*, and by a group of black further education students, who felt alienated from the programme by virtue of its perceived irrelevance to their lives.

Watching *Dallas*

Ang's (1985) much discussed study of *Dallas* and its audience was carried out amongst women viewers in the Netherlands, involving a 'symptomatic' analysis (i.e. searching for the attitudes which lie behind texts) of letters written to her about watching the soap. Ang begins by exploring the tension between ideas of an active audience and the potential structuring of meaning by the text. Her central argument is that *Dallas* viewers are actively involved in the production of meaning and pleasure, which take on a range of manifestations not reducible to either the structure of the text, an 'ideological effect' or a political project.

Fiction, says Ang, is a way of enjoying the here and now and involves playing with feelings in a movement between involvement and distance, acceptance and protest. It is also an experience mediated by the 'ideology of mass culture', which places *Dallas* in an inferior relationship to other cultural activities. This led viewers to adopt a range of viewing positions: some felt guilty about watching *Dallas*; others adopted an ironic stance to stave off the contradiction of liking *Dallas* and seeing it as 'trash'; one group argued that it was acceptable to watch the programme if you were 'aware of the dangers'; while others, informed by an ideology of populism, defended themselves on the grounds that they had the right to hold whatever cultural tastes they so wished.

Ideology and resistance

It has often been assumed that the active nature of the audience undercuts the role of ideology in television, making reception less problematically tied to textual construction and issues of **power**. There has been a tendency to see the reproduction of ideology as associated with passive audiences and to link the active audience with **resistance** to ideology. However, while evidence suggests that television viewers understand a good deal about the grammar and production processes of television, that on the level of television *form* they are extremely sophisticated and literate, this does not necessarily prevent them from producing and reproducing forms of ideology.

For example, Liebes and Katz's (1991) study of *Dallas* suggests that while American viewers often had a good understanding of television form and production contexts, they nevertheless regarded *Dallas* as entertainment with no particular ideological stance, a view which is arguably itself ideological. Research carried out amongst British Asian teenage viewers of soap opera in the UK (Barker, 1998, 1999; Barker and Andre, 1996) suggested that they are both active *and* implicated in the reproduction of ideology about the family, relationships and gender. Indeed, audience activity is a *requirement* for the engagement with and reproduction of ideology.

The 'active audience' paradigm is now so well established and the evidence sufficiently strong that we may conclude with Silverstone (1994) that audiences are *always* active. While the active audience may well challenge ideological formations, this is to be determined empirically in given cases and not to be taken for granted. Audience activity can deconstruct ideology only when alternative discourses are available so that the self becomes a site of ideological struggle.

TELEVISION AUDIENCES AND CULTURAL IDENTITY

Watching television is constitutive of and constituted by forms of **cultural identity** (Chapter 6). Television is a resource for the construction of cultural identity just as audiences deploy their cultural identities and cultural competencies to decode programmes in their own specific ways. As television has become globalized, so the place of television in the constitution of **ethnic** and **national identities** has taken on a particular significance (Barker, 1999).

The export of meaning

The most famous large-scale study of national/ethnic cultural identity and television fiction viewing is Liebes and Katz's (1991) exploration of the reception of *Dallas* amongst viewers from a range of cultural and ethnic backgrounds. Of particular interest is the exploration of the *cross-cultural* dimensions of viewing, for the study involved 65 focus discussion groups from various ethnic communities. These were constituted by Arabs, Russian Jews, Moroccan Jews and Israeli kibbutz members in Israel, plus a group of Americans and Japanese situated in their country of origin. The study was looking for evidence of different readings of *Dallas* in terms of understanding and critical ability. It was assumed that members of the groups would discuss the text with each other and develop interpretations together based on mutual cultural understanding.

Liebes and Katz argue that their study provides evidence of divergent readings of *Dallas* narratives founded in different cultural backgrounds. In particular they explore the differences between 'referential' and 'critical' approaches to the programme across different groups. By 'referential' they mean an understanding of *Dallas* which reads the programme as if it were referring to 'reality'. By 'critical' they mean an awareness of the constructed nature of the programme evidenced through discussion of the mechanisms of narrative construction and the economics of the television industry. Overall, referential statements outweighed critical statements three to one.

Liebes and Katz argue there were distinct differences between ethnic groups in the levels of each type of statement, concluding that Americans and Russians were particularly critical. However, the critical awareness displayed by Americans was largely centred on questions of form and production context based on their greater understanding of the business of television. Americans were less critical in terms of themes/content, tending to assume that *Dallas* has no ideology but is 'merely' entertainment. In contrast, the Russians were more critical of the 'politics' of *Dallas*, seeing it as a distorted representation of the capitalist West. Arab groups were said to have a high sensitivity to the 'dangers' of western culture and of western 'moral degeneracy'.

The Liebes/Katz research into Dallas suggests a number of important connections between television and national/cultural identity. Most significantly we can draw the conclusion that audiences use their own sense of national and ethnic identity as a position from which to decode programmes. American television is not uncritically consumed by audiences with the destruction of 'indigenous' cultural identities as the inevitable outcome. Indeed, the very deployment of their own cultural identifications as a point of resistance also helps to constitute that very cultural identity through its enunciation.

Localizing the global

In a similar vein, Miller (1995) argues that it would be mistaken to think that a Trinidadian audience's engagement with the US soap opera *The Young and the Restless* is simply the consumption of American consumer culture. He recounts the ways in which the soap opera is 'localized', made sense of and absorbed into local practices and meanings. In particular the gossip and scandal (specifically that of a sexual nature) which are core concerns of the soap opera's narrative resonate with the Trinidadian concept of 'bacchanal', which, according to Miller, is a deeply rooted folk concept fusing ideas of confusion, gossip, scandal and truth. The concerns of the soap thus 'colludes with the local sense of truth as exposure and scandal' (Miller, 1995: 223). Miller's work is significant because it suggests that the study of the formal characteristics of narratives is insufficient, stressing the need to understand local processes of absorption and transformation, which by their very nature will be specific, contingent and unpredictable. The **cultural politics** of television are as significant at the level of consumption as they are in terms of production or text.

That television is uneven and contradictory in its impact is illustrated by Lull's research in China. According to Lull (1991, 1997), television was introduced into China by a government hoping to deploy it as a form of social control and cultural homogenization. However, it has turned out to play quite the opposite role. Although the Chinese government has attempted to use television to re-establish social stability after Tiananmen Square, it has instead become a central agent of popular resistance.

Television has amplified and intensified the diversity of cultural and political sentiments in China by presenting alternative views of life. Driven by the need to attract larger audiences, television has become a cultural and ideological forum of competing ideas as commercial and imported dramas have been juxtaposed with China's own economic difficulties. Further, not only are programmes themselves polysemic, but audiences have become adept at reading between the lines of official pronouncements. For Lull, the challenge to autocratic rule raised by the Chinese resistance movement, with its stress on freedom and democracy, could not have happened without television. In short, though television may circulate discourse on a global scale, its consumption and use as a resource for the construction of cultural identities always take place in a local context.

Audiences, space and identity

The significance of television lies not only in textual meanings and interpretations, but in its place within the rhythms and routines of everyday domestic life. In particular, watching television is something we commonly do in specific domestic spaces, for example the 'living room'. Thus, writers have begun to take an interest in the spaces in which television is watched, suggesting connections between spaces, activities and the construction of **identity**. Of particular interest has been;

- the manner in which broadcasting provides ritual social events wherein families or groups of friends watch together and talk before, during and after programmes;
- the connection between such rituals, the spaces in which they are watched and the production of cultural identities.

Space, as Massey (1994) argues, is not 'empty' but is produced culturally by social relations (Chapter 10). That is, the spaces of home, nation, classroom, front room, etc., are constructed in and through social relations and are invested with emotional commitment in order that space become place. The distinction between space and **place** is, according to Silverstone (1994), one marked by feeling. That is, places are spaces invested with human experiences, memories, intentions and desires which act as important markers of individual and collective identity.

NATIONAL SPACE

Trying to fix the meaning of space represents an attempt to anchor it to specific identities which are claimed as one's own, for example the nationalist claim to locate spaces as those of exclusive national identities through naming and fixing the meaning of space and place. Scannell (1988) has argued that broadcasting plays a role in the construction of national space by bringing major public events into the private worlds of viewers and in doing so constructs a national calendar which organizes, co-ordinates and renews a national public social world. Such events might include, the FA

Cup Final, Wimbledon, the opening of Parliament and the last night of the Proms in Britain and Congressional elections, the Superbowl and 4th July celebrations in America.

GENDERED SPACE

Gender identity is a site of potential conflict within the space nominated as home and which is commonly coded as feminine. Domestic routines and space are gendered together as social and cultural categories when, for example, kitchens are coded female and garages coded male. Within these gendered spaces, technologies 'fit' with and are absorbed into certain social/gender norms.

In a study of British 'housewives', Gray (1992) argues that the VCR as a whole was seen as both masculine and feminine by women but the timer function was seen as exclusively male. In particular, the technology of setting the timer on the video was regarded by the women in her study as technologically difficult, and thus male, despite women's routine use of equally complex washing machines. Similarly, Morley's (1986) study *Family Television* suggests that power and control over programme choice lies mostly with men. He argues that men and women have different viewing patterns and preferences. For example, men have more attentive viewing styles than women, who are engaged in other domestic activities. Drama and fiction feature more in the preferences of women than men, for whom sport and news are more central.

FAMILY SPACE AND GLOBAL SPACE

The connections between television, space and daily routines have been further explored by Lull (1991, 1997) in China, where limited domestic space means that the introduction of a television set into a household has considerable impact. When the television is on it cannot be escaped from, so that watching television has to be a collective family experience with family routines now including a specific time to watch TV. The arrival of television has altered family relationships, introducing potential conflict over what is watched, when and by whom. The regulation of children's viewing was a particular issue.

In contrast to Lull's stress on the home as a place, Meyrowitz (1986) is concerned with global space. He suggests that electronic media alter our sense of the 'situational geography' of social life so that we inhabit a virtual world-wide space in which new forms of **identification** are forged. The core of his argument is that electronic media break the traditional bonds between geographic place and social identity since mass media provide us with increasing sources of identification which are situated beyond the immediacy of specific places. Meyrowitz's arguments raise questions about television, culture and identity in the context of accelerated globalization.

THE GLOBALIZATION OF TELEVISION

By **globalization** (see Chapter 4) is meant a set of processes which are leading to the compression or shrinking of the world, that is, an ever-increasing abundance of global connections and our understanding of them. The globalization of television is a question of technology, economics, institutions and culture. Television may be considered global in respect of:

- the various configurations of public and commercial television, which are regulated, funded and viewed within the boundaries of nation-states and/or language communities;
- the technology, ownership, programme distribution and audiences of television, which operate across the boundaries of nation-states and language communities;
- the circulation by television of similar narrative forms and discourses around the world.

The globalization of television is an aspect of the dynamic expansionist logic of **capitalism** in its quest for new commodities and new markets. While there is money to be made from the production and sale of television programmes, these are also a means to sell the technological hardware of television, from satellites to sets, and to deliver audiences to advertisers. Television stands at the centre of wider commercial activities, being core to the expansion of consumer capitalism.

The political economy of global television

Political economy is concerned with power and the distribution of economic and social resources. For current purposes this translates into a concern with who owns and controls the production and distribution mechanisms of television, along with the consequences of those patterns of ownership and control for contours of the cultural landscape.

Murdock and Golding (1977) have argued that the ownership of communications by private capital is subject to a general process of concentration via conglomeration. This produces **multi-**

media corporations which are part of a wider process of capital conglomeration. Murdock (1990) distinguishes three basic kinds of conglomerates operating in the communications field: industrial conglomerates, service conglomerates and communications conglomerates. These operate in the context of changes in the communications industries centred on the processes of synergy, convergence and deregulation (Dyson and Humphreys, 1990).

SYNERGY AND TELEVISION OWNERSHIP

During the mid-1980s and 1990s there was a good deal of diversification by financial, computer and data processing companies into telecommunications, creating multi-media giants dominating sectors of the market. Companies needed the financial power that can come from mergers to undertake the massive investment needed to be players in the global market. Thus the 1989 merger of Time and Warner created the largest media group in the world with a market capitalization of $25 billion. This was followed in 1995 by Time Warner's acquisition of Turner Broadcasting (CNN). In late 1993 the merger of Paramount communications and Viacom, owner of MTV, saw the emergence of a $17 billion company, making it the fifth largest media group behind Time Warner, News Corporation, Bertelsmann and Walt Disney.

The prime reason for these developments is the search for **synergy**. This involves bringing together the various elements of television and other media at the levels of production and distribution so that they complement each other to produce lower costs and higher profits. The preoccupation with combining software and hardware can be seen when films are marketed simultaneously with pop music soundtracks and virtual reality video games all owned by the same company. This is now not so much the exception as the rule. No communications organization represents that synergy better than Rupert Murdoch's News Corporation.

The acquisition by News Corporation of the Hong Kong-based Star TV for $525 million gave Murdoch a satellite television footprint over Asia and the Middle East with a potential audience of 45 billion viewers. Allied to other television holdings, notably BskyB (UK) and Fox TV (USA and Australia), News Corp's television interests have a global reach of some two-thirds of the planet. Of significance is not just the spatial breadth of the corporations ownership but the potential link-ups between its various elements. In Twentieth-Century Fox and Star TV, Murdoch acquired a huge library of film and television product which he can channel through his network of distribution outlets. He hopes to create a lucrative global advertising market. At the same time, Murdoch can use his newspapers to promote his television interests by giving space in his press holdings to the sporting activities covered by his television channels.

CONVERGENCE AND TELEVISION TECHNOLOGY

One of the contemporary buzz words which illustrates the processes of synergy and convergence is the 'information super-highway', that is, television with built-in computers linked with cable which will allow us to order and pay for shopping, transfer e-money, keep an eye on our bank accounts, call up a selection of films, and search the world-wide web for information. PC-TV highlights the issue of technological **convergence**, that is, the process whereby technologies which had been produced and used separately merge into one. Convergence refers to the breakdown of boundaries between technologies, which is paralleled by organizational convergence, so that synergy is sought through mergers and take-overs, giving rise to multi-media corporations.

Technological convergence is enabled by digital technology. Digital technology organizes information electronically into bytes, or discrete bundles of information, which can be compressed during transmission and decompressed on arrival. This enables more information to travel via any given conduit (be that cable, satellite or terrestrial signals) at greater speed over larger distances. The impact of new technologies in general, and digital processes in particular, can be summed up in terms of speed, volume and distance. More information at greater speed over larger distances.

It is becoming apparent that the technologies having the most impact are those concerned with distribution. Organizations which control the distribution mechanisms are eclipsing the power of producers because no one is willing to commit expensive resources to a project which has not secured a distribution agreement. Satellites offer a much increased volume of TV signals either directly or via head stations of cable systems and, despite high start-up costs, have the potential to offer high-quality picture and sound on a much increased scale. Most of the present cable systems are based on the copper-based coaxial specification. However, the future of cable will lie with the use of fibre-optic cable with its far greater capabilities in terms of numbers of channels and the potential for interactive programmes.

Of course, the impact of cable and satellite technology has been distinct in different parts of the world. In India, commercial satellite television threatens the state-owned network's (Doordarshan) dominance, whereas in the USA Direct Satellite Broadcasting

(DBS) has had little impact, having been eclipsed by cable. While cable struggled in the UK, it has reached penetration rates of 95 per cent in the Netherlands – the most densely cabled country in Europe.

DEREGULATION AND REREGULATION

Synergy and convergence have been made to happen by the captains of industry and enabled by politicians. Though multi-media conglomerates have existed for many years, the scope of their activities has been allowed to widen by governmental relaxation of the regulations restricting cross-media ownership and the entry of new players. The 1980s and early 1990s was a period of deregulation in television. This does not mean that all regulations have been abolished; rather, the television and tele-communications industries have been reregulated. Significantly, the new regulations are considerably less stringent than their predecessors. This has been occasioned by a number of factors:

- the growth of 'new' communication technologies, which has invali-dated the natural monopoly argument since digital technology allows frequencies to be split and alternative delivery systems employed;
- the upholding by court rulings in various countries of the legal rights to communicate and the adoption of diversity as a key public prin-ciple;
- new governmental enthusiasm for the market, including a prefer-ence for the funding of television by commercial means rather than through taxation.

Thus it was the relaxation of television and newspaper ownership rules that allowed Murdoch to launch Fox cable TV in America and to own newspapers and television companies in the UK. Similarly, deregulation has allowed AT&T, the biggest telephone operator in America, to participate in the television market, from which it had previously been excluded by law.

Deregulation and commercial expansion have prompted wide-spread discussion about the emerging shape of the new tele-landscapes. Outside of America, the 'old order' was marked by the subordination of broadcasting to public service goals set in the context of a broadly political process of regulation. Television was of a largely national character and was generally non-commercial in principle. In contrast, the 'new order' in television is marked by:

- the co-existence of public and commercial broadcasting;
- the deregulation of commercial television;

- the increasing emergence of multi-media transnational companies;
- pressure on public service television to operate with a commercial logic.

These are the world-wide trends which underpin the emergence of a global electronic culture.

GLOBAL ELECTRONIC CULTURE

In the context of globalization, culture can be seen to span time and place. In the age of *electronic* reproduction, culture comes to us via the screen, video, radio, etc., rather than requiring us to explore it in the context of ritualized spaces. Cultural artefacts and meanings from different historical periods and geographical places can mix together and be juxtaposed so that, while the values and meanings attached to place remain significant, the networks in which people are involved extend far beyond their physical locations. For some critics this involves mixing, matching and cultural exchange; for others it is a form of cultural domination.

Media imperialism

Schiller (1969, 1985) makes the case that the media fit into the world capitalist system by providing ideological support for capitalism, and transnational corporations in particular. The media are seen as vehicles for corporate marketing, manipulating audiences to deliver them to advertisers. This is allied to the assertion of a general ideological effect by which media messages create and reinforce audience attachment to the status quo.

Concerns about media and **cultural imperialism** have been fuelled by a limited number of studies of the global television trade which have concluded that programming flows are dominated by the USA (Varis, 1974, 1984). Certainly America is the major exporter of television programmes, a position enabled by the economics of the industry, which allow US producers to cover much of their costs in the domestic market leaving exports as profit. However, while in the late 1980s 44 per cent of all imported television hours to Western Europe came from the USA, Sepstrup (1989) argues that of greater relevance is that 73 per cent of the total national supply in all of Western Europe was domestically produced. Further, 'more and more nations are producing an increasing proportion of their own programming', a significant number of which are 'doing over half of their own programming, both in the total broadcast day and during primetime' (Straubhaar, 1997: 293).

Regionalization

While the US can claim 'at least 75% of the world-wide television programme exports' (Hoskins et al., 1995), there has been a distinct move towards *regionalization* of markets on the basis of shared language, culture and historical trade links. During the 1980s, 80 per cent of US overseas distribution was going to seven countries: Australia, Canada, France, Germany, Italy, Japan and the UK (Waterman, 1988). Straubhaar (1997) argues that there are a number of 'geo-cultural' markets emerging, including those based on Western Europe, Latin America, the Francophone world of France and its former colonies, an Arabic world market, a Chinese market and a South Asian market. Further, these markets are not necessarily bounded by geographical space but involve diaspora populations distributed across the world. For example, the Indian film industry serves not only the Indian sub-continent but areas of Africa, Malaysia, Indonesia and Europe.

The US-media imperialism argument does not take on board the contradictory, unpredictable and heterogeneous meanings that active audiences are able to take from television. While television does plays a direct role in the penetration of cultures by meaning systems from elsewhere, rather than obliterating local conceptions, it is better to understand the process as the overlaying of local meanings by alternative definitions, so relativizing both and creating new senses of ambiguity and uncertainty (Ferguson, 1990). What we are seeing is a set of economic and cultural processes dating from different historical periods, with different developmental rhythms, being overlaid upon each other to create global disjunctures as well as new global connections and similarities (Appaduria, 1993; Smith, 1990).

The global and the local

Television can be said to be global in its circulation of similar narrative forms around the world: soap opera, news, sport, quiz shows and music videos can be found in most countries. Soap opera, for example, is a global form in two senses: it is a narrative mode *produced* in a variety of countries across the globe, and it is one of the most exported forms of television *viewed* in a range of cultural contexts. The global attraction of soap opera can be attributed to the apparently universal appeal of particular open-ended narrative forms, the centrality of the personal and kinship relations, and in some circumstances the emergence of an international style embedded in the traditions of Hollywood. However, the success of soap opera also reflects the possibilities offered to audiences of engaging in local or regional issues located in recognizable 'real' places. For example, while South African television screens a good deal of American and Australian soap opera, it is also possible to watch the locally produced *Generations*.

The tensions between the poles of the global and the local are highlighted by, on the one hand, the enormous global popularity of soaps like *Neighbours* and *Dallas*, and, on the other hand, the failure of these very same soaps in particular countries (e.g. *Neighbours* in America, *Dallas* in Japan). As Crofts (1995) has pointed out, the global success, and failures, of soap opera depends on the specificities of soap opera as a televisual form and the particularities of the conditions of reception. While we have witnessed the emergence of an international prime-time soap opera style, including high production values, pleasing visual appearances and fast-paced action-oriented narrative modes, many soaps retain local settings, regional language audiences and slow-paced melodramatic story-telling.

Likewise, news exhibits global similarities as well as local differences. Straubhaar's (1992) cross-cultural study concluded that 'what is news' is 'fairly consistent' from country to country. Data collected by Gurevitch et al. (1991) about the Eurovision News Exchange and the 36 countries which regularly use it suggests that the availability of common news footage and a shared professional culture has led to 'substantial, but not complete' convergence of news stories. This may reflect 'the drift towards an international standardization of basic journalistic discourses' (Dahlgren, 1995: 49) together with the domination of global news agendas by western news agencies. However, the fact that western news agencies tend to supply 'spot news' and visual reports without commentary allows different interpretations of events to be dubbed over the pictures, leading to what Gurevitch et al. (1991) call the 'domestication' of global news. This is regarded as a 'countervailing force to the pull of globalization'.

Beyond specific genres like soap opera and news, the global multiplication of communications technologies has created an increasingly complex **semiotic** environment in which television produces and circulates an explosive display of competing signs and meanings. This creates a flow of images and juxtapositions which fuse news, views, drama and reportage into an electronic **bricolage** (Williams, 1974). Thus, the globalization of television has contributed to the construction of a collage of images from different times and places which has been dubbed postmodern.

Global postmodern culture

Lash (1990) identifies the shift from the 'discursive' to the 'figural' as core to the **postmodern** turn. By this he means that the signifying logics of the modern and postmodern work in different ways. For Lash, the modernist 'regime of **signification**' priorit- izes words over images, promulgates a rationalist world view, explores the meanings of cultural texts and distances the spec- tator from the cultural object. In contrast, the postmodern 'figural' is more visual, draws from everyday life, contests rationalist views of culture and immerses the spectator in his/her desire for the cultural object. We may conclude that the globalization of the essentially *visual* medium of television forms a central part of the postmodern cultural turn.

Hutcheon argues that postmodernism 'takes the form of self- conscious, self-contradictory, self-undermining statement. It is rather like saying something with inverted commas around what is being said' (Hutcheon, 1989: 1). In other words, postmodernism is a form of ironic knowingness, **ironic** because it explores the limitations and conditions of its own knowing. The stylistic markers of the postmodern in television have been seen as:

- aesthetic self-consciousness/self-reflexiveness;
- juxtaposition/montage/bricolage;
- paradox/ambiguity/uncertainty;
- intertextuality and the blurring of genre boundaries;
- irony, parody and pastiche.

Techniques include montage, rapid cutting, non-linear narrative techniques and the de-contextualization of images. Programmes which have commonly been identified with the postmodern decentre the importance of linear narrative in favour of a new look and feel in which image takes preference over story-telling (Kellner, 1992). Self-conscious **intertextuality** involves explicit allusion to particular programmes and oblique references to other genre conventions and styles, for example explicit reference to *Thelma and Louise* and *The Graduate* in *The Simpsons* or to *Twin Peaks* in *Northern Exposure*. This intertextuality is an aspect of enlarged cultural self-consciousness about the history and func- tions of cultural products.

Arguably postmodern is *The Simpsons*, which has made a 'dysfunctional' American family the ironic heroes of a series which is, on the one hand, simply a cartoon and, on the other hand, a set of subtle reflections on American life and culture. It is not coincidental that the centre of the Simpsons' life is the television set and that the programme makes a series of intertextual references to other television programmes and genres. *The Simpsons* requires us to be aware of a range of other television and film genres so that, for example, the ending of one episode is entirely an ironic reworking of the final sequence of *The Graduate*, while *Itchy and Scratchy*, a cartoon watched by the Simpson children, parodies *Tom and Jerry* and mocks the double standard by which we seem to condemn television violence even as we lap it up.

HYPERREALITY AND TV SIMULATIONS

A more apocalyptic view is taken by Baudrillard (1983a, 1983b), for whom television is the heart of a postmodern culture marked by an all-encompassing flow of fascinating simulations and facsimiles, a **hyperreality** in which we are overloaded with images and information. This is a world where a series of modern distinctions – the real and the unreal, the public and the private, art and reality – have broken down, or been sucked into a 'black hole'.

For Baudrillard, 'hyperreality' is produced according to a model. It is not a given but is artificially reproduced as real so that 'hyper' signifies 'more real than real', a real retouched in a 'hallucinatory resemblance' with itself. Baudrillard describes a process leading to the collapse of boundaries, which he calls 'implosion', between the media and the **social**, so that news and entertainment blur into each other and 'TV is the world'. Thus, television simulates real-life situations, not so much to represent the world as to execute its own. For Baudrillard, postmodern television is flat and one-dimensional, its continual flow of images and **simulacra** having no connotational hierarchy. It is both literally and metaphorically 'superficial'.

In contrast, for Kellner (1992), television is meaningful and does not represent 'a black hole where all meaning and messages are absorbed in the whirlpool' (Kellner, 1992: 156). Rather, he argues for the integrating central role of television as **myth** and ritual celebrating dominant values and modes of thought and behaviour. As such, he suggests that television provides models by which people construct their attitudes, values and consequent actions.

Consumer culture

Globalization, consumer culture and postmodernism are closely allied phenomena because of the following:

- Globalization has involved the 'displacement' of the West and its philosophical categories from the centre of the universe; indeed, some have seen the collapse of western classifications as *the* marker of postmodernism.
- The rise in visibility and status of popular culture, hastened by electronic media, has meant that the distinction between high and low culture is no longer viable.
- The blurring of the boundaries between art, culture and commerce, allied to the rising prominence of the postmodern 'figural', has resulted in a general aestheticization of everyday life (Featherstone, 1991, 1995).

The development of global television as a fundamentally commercial form has placed that core activity of consumer culture, visual-based advertising, at the forefront of its activities (Mattelart and Mattelart, 1992). Television is pivotal to the production and reproduction of a *promotional culture* focused on the use of visual imagery to create value-added brands or commodity-signs. Indeed, Wernick argues that cultural phenomena which serve to communicate a promotional message of some type or another have become 'virtually co-extensive with our produced symbolic world' (Wernick, 1991: 184). The phrase 'Coca Cola culture' encapsulates the global reach of this promotional culture and highlights the alleged link between global capitalism, advertising and cultural homogenization. That is, for some critics global processes represent a form of cultural homogenization, particularly in the field of consumer culture where Coca Cola, McDonald's, Nike and Microsoft Windows circulate world-wide.

However, the global circulation of consumer goods should not lead us to assume that their impact is the same the world over. Consumer goods are subject through **glocalization** to a variety of meanings on the level of local consumption which prevents us from equating Coca Cola culture with homogeneous cultural identities. Indeed, it is the juxtaposition of Windows and ox-drawn carts, *The Simpsons* and *Hum Log* (an Indian soap opera), Hollywood and Bollywood, The Prodigy and traditional dance music that suggests the idea of a global postmodern.

Creative consumption

The majority of cultural studies writers have taken a more positive view than Baudrillard of the creative potential inherent in contemporary television and consumer culture. For example, Chambers (1987) and Hebdidge (1988) have discussed the ways in which commodities, including television, form the basis of **multiple**

identity construction. They have emphasized the active and meaning-oriented activity of consumers, who act as bricoleurs selecting and arranging elements of material commodities and meaningful signs.

Likewise, Fiske (1987), who argues that **popular culture** is constituted by the meanings that people make with it rather than those identifiable within the texts. Fiske discusses television in terms of two separate economies: a financial economy of production and a cultural economy of consumption. The former is primarily concerned with money and the exchange value of commodities. The latter is the site of cultural meanings, pleasures and **social identities**. While the financial economy 'needs to be taken into account' in any investigation of the cultural, it does not determine it nor invalidate the power audiences have as producers of meaning at the level of consumption. Indeed, popular culture is seen as a site of semiotic warfare and of popular tactics deployed to evade or resist the meanings produced and inscribed in commodities by producers.

Paul Willis (1990) argues that the processes of **commodification** underpin a 'common culture' in the consuming practices of young people. Rather than meaning being inherent in the commodity, he points to the construction of meaning and value in actual usage. This he calls 'grounded aesthetics'. For Willis, contemporary culture is not meaningless or superficial surface but involves the active creation of meaning by all people as cultural producers. Willis takes the familiar line that audiences (he is talking about young people in particular) are sophisticated readers of images, having learned to play with interpreting television codes.

In this way, the contemporary television world can be read not as a one-dimensional hyperreality but as a democratic and creative culture. The creative play through which such cultural forms are produced and consumed offers democratizing possibilities because, while the production of popular music, film, television and fashion is in the hands of transnational capitalist multi-media corporations, the meanings are produced, altered and managed at the level of consumption by people who are active producers of meaning.

SUMMARY

Television has been a long-standing concern of cultural studies because of its central place in the communicative practices of western societies and its proliferation across the globe. These concerns have become increasingly acute as global television turns away from public service broadcasting towards commercial television dominated by multi-media corporations in search of synergy and convergence.

The globalization of the institutions of television is paralleled by the world-wide circulation of key television narratives and genres, including news, soap opera, music television, sport and game shows, set within an advancing 'promotional' and postmodern culture marked by brico-lage, intertextuality and genre blurring.

Attention was paid to the ideological construction of television pro-grammes, including hegemonic versions of world news which exclude alternative perspectives. However, it was also argued that television programmes are polysemic; they contain many meanings which are commonly contradictory. Thus, audiences can explore a range of poten-tial meanings. Further, evidence was given to suggest that audiences are active producers of meaning and do not simply take on board those textual meanings identified by critics. Hence, global television is better understood as the promotion of bricolage and **hybridity** rather than as cultural imperialism.

The significance of television is not confined to textual meanings for it is situated and sustained within the activities of everyday life. While the political economy and programme flows of television may be global, watching television is situated within the domestic practices of the day to day. In particular, it was argued that the domestic space of the home is a site for the construction and contestation of wider cultural identities, including those of gender.

10

Cultural Space and Urban Place

Since the 1970s there has been a growing interest within social and cultural theory in questions of space and place. Previously, modern theory was more interested in time, seeing this as the dynamic field of social change, with space regarded as dead, fixed and immobile, traversed by the movement of history. As Foucault remarked, 'a whole history remains to be written of spaces – which would at the same time be the history of powers – both these terms in the plural – from the great strategies of geopolitics to the little tactics of the habitat' (Foucault, cited Soja, 1995b: 14).

In this chapter we will consider what is meant by **space** and **place**, including the manner in which they are constituted by social relations of **power**, before taking a look at cities as a specific formation of socio-cultural places. Attention will be paid to:

- the political economy of global cities;
- the symbolic or cultural economies of urban regeneration;
- the emergence of postmodern cites as contested spaces;
- the idea that cities can be read as texts;
- the virtual world of cybercities.

SPACE AND PLACE IN CONTEMPORARY THEORY

As Giddens (1984) argues, understanding the manner in which human activity is distributed in space is fundamental to analysis of **social** life. Human interaction is situated in particular spaces which have a variety of social meanings. For example, a 'home' is divided into different living spaces – front rooms, kitchens, dining rooms, bedrooms, etc. – which are used in diverse ways and in which we carry out a range of activities with different social meanings. Accordingly, bedrooms are intimate spaces into which we would rarely invite strangers, whereas a front room or parlour is deemed the appropriate space for such an encounter.

Giddens (1984) deploys Goffman's (1969) concepts of 'front' and 'back' regions to illustrate a fundamental divergence in social-spatial activity. Front space is constituted by those places in which we put on a public 'on-stage' performance acting out stylized, formal and socially acceptable activities. Back regions are those spaces where we are 'behind the scenes', preparing for public performance or where we can relax into less formal modes of behaviour and speech. The social division of space into front and back regions or into the appropriate uses of kitchens, bedrooms and parlours is of course *cultural*. Distinct cultures design homes in different ways, allocating contrasting meanings or modes of appropriate behaviour.

Time-geography

The socio-cultural world is spatially organized into a range of places in which different kinds of social activity occur – places of work, places of leisure, places of sleep, places to eat, places to shop, and so forth. Given the complexity of contemporary life, it is a requirement on us all to move across and through these spaces and places. Time-geography (Hagerstrand, 1973) has been concerned to map the movements and pathways of persons through physical environments. It traces the variety of social activities which occur and the constraints which material and social factors place on the patterns of our movement.

A simple time-geography might include my catching a train from one town to another, followed by a short walk to my place of work, where I enter through the front doors and move along a corridor to my office, where I stay for an hour. Later I move to a lecture hall, and from there to the canteen and subsequently the library. On my return home I call in at the supermarket to do some shopping before going to the cinema. During the course of these movements I encounter a series of physical limitations – distance, walls, traffic jams – and social expectations – those surrounding the performance of a lecture, for example. As I do so I cross paths with a variety of other people – students, librarians, checkout operatives etc. – each of whom has his or her own daily time-space paths. As Gillian Rose puts it:

> Time-geography traces the routinized paths of individuals in time-space, and is especially interested in the physical, technological, economic and social constraints on such movement. It claims to demonstrate how society as a whole is constituted by the unintended consequences of the repetitive acts of individuals. (Rose, 1993: 75)

The account of space and social relations presented thus far has a good deal to recommend it for it points to the spatial distribution of social activities and to the situated character of all social action.

However, there is a telling grammar in play which situates the social *in* space or *across* space at given moments of time. This implies that space is a flat surface across which history moves, with time and space radically opposed to each other. Physics and social theory have both questioned this assumption.

Time-space

Massey (1994) argues that, following Einstein's theory of relativity, space and time are to be thought of not as separate entities but as inextricably interwoven. Space is not an absolute but is relationally defined, for at least two particles are required for space to occur. Further, time is constituted by the movement of these particles, which simultaneously establishes both time and space. Thus, it is not that time moves across a static space, but that space and time constitute each other, requiring us to speak of time-space. In principle then, time-space is relationally formed through the interrelations of objects. It follows that social space is also relationally constituted out of the simultaneous co-existence of social relations and interactions. From this point, Massey proposes five arguments about space:

- Space is a social construct.
- The social is spatially constructed.
- Social space is not static but dynamic, constituted by changing social relations.
- Space is implicated in questions of power and symbolism, that is, the 'power-geometry' of space.
- Social space implies 'a simultaneous multiplicity of spaces: cross-cutting, intersecting, aligning with one another, or existing in relations of paradox or antagonism' (Massey, 1994: 3).

Space and place

Thus far, I have used the language of space and place as if they were interchangeable terms, whereas it is usually thought necessary to distinguish between them. Giddens (1990) characterizes space and place in terms of absence–presence, where place is marked by face-to-face encounters and space by the relations between absent others. Space refers to an abstract idea, an empty or dead space which is filled with various concrete, specific and human places. Thus, home is a place where I meet my family with regularity, whereas e-mail or letters establish contact between absent persons across space. In a not dissimilar move, Seamon (1979) regards the place called home as the product of physical presence and social rituals. However, the absence–presence distinction, while suggestive, seems a bit stark since, as Harvey (1993) remarks, place has a rather richer range of metaphorical meanings than are encompassed by presence.

We may distinguish between space and place on the grounds that the latter are the focus of human experience, memory, desire and **identity**. That is, places are discursive constructions which are the target of emotional **identification** or investment (Relph, 1976).

> Home . . . is a manifestation of an investment of meaning in space. It is a claim we make about a place. It is constructed through social relations which are both internal and external and constantly shifting in their power relations. (Silverstone, 1994: 28)

The social construction of place

Whatever conceptual distinction between space and place we may settle for, the most significant question to ask (Harvey, 1993) is: by what social processes is place constructed? Two examples will suffice: Massey's (1994) arguments about gendered space, and Nzegwu's (1996) discussion of the city of Lagos.

GENDERED SPACE

Since **gender** is an organizing principle of social life thoroughly saturated with power relations, it follows that the social construction of space will be gendered. As Massey (1994) suggests, gender relations vary over space: spaces are symbolically gendered and some spaces are marked by the physical exclusion of particular sexes. The classical western gendering of space is manifested in the division between 'home' and 'workplace' articulated with the 'private' and the 'public'. Thus, the home is regarded as the domain of the 'private' and the feminine while sites of paid work have been **coded** masculine within the public sphere. Homes have been cast as the unpaid domain of mothers and children, connoting the secondary values of caring, love, tenderness and domesticity. In contrast, places of paid work have been regarded as the domain of men, connoting the primary values of toughness (either physically or mentally), hardness, comradeship and reality. While this crude spatial map has been changing as gender relations are being transformed, much of this cultural coding remains.

Massey argues that: 'The limitation of women's mobility, in terms of both space and identity, has been in some cultural contexts a crucial means of subordination' (Massey, 1994: 179). She notes that as a child she was struck by the way large tracts of the Mersey flood plain had been given over to playing fields for boys. This was a place to which she did not go, and, while she did go to the art gallery, her place within it was quite different from that of men, for whom high culture was a domain in which to gaze at pictures of naked women. Today, cricket, rugby and football remain as primarily (though not solely) male practices in male spaces. More threateningly, certain streets, parks and pubs are not safe for women to enter alone, especially at night. Thus, attempts by some women to 'reclaim the night' are essentially spatial practices.

Masculine modernism

The rise of **modernism** as an aesthetics is deeply associated with the spatial and social organization of the city. For example, modernism's figure of the *flâneur* or stroller is one who walks the anonymous spaces of the modern city, experiencing the complexity, disturbances and confusions of the streets with their shops, displays, images and variety of persons. Massey argues that these city spaces and the modernist experience were deeply gendered. The experience of the *flâneur* and of modernism was one of male-coded public spaces from which women were excluded (e.g. the boulevards and cafés) or entered only as objects for male consumption. Thus:

- The *flâneur* was a male figure who walked spaces from which women were largely excluded.
- The *flâneur*'s gaze was frequently erotic, and women were the object of that gaze.
- The paintings of modernism are often of women and spatially organized in such a way as to privilege a male-coded sense of a 'detached' (but not disinterested) view.

THE MULTIPLE SPACES OF LAGOS

Nzegwu's (1996) study of Lagos, Nigeria, is a multi-levelled analysis which directs our attention to the way that spaces and places, cities and homes, are constructed in terms of **class**, gender, **race**, **ethnicity**, colonialism, modernization, multinational capitalism, urban planning, military power, government intervention and other manifestations of symbolic and material power. Nzegwu sets out to show that cultural desires and symbolic representations are central to the evolution of urban space as sites of contestation and interaction. Thus, an analysis of space reveals the presence of value systems and their transformatory impact.

According to Nzegwu, Lagos is more than a place of residence or domicile, it is *ile* (home), and a recovery of Yoruba ideas of land and *ile* is key to understanding the character of the contemporary city. Central to the notion of *ile* as homespace is the family, and Yoruba architectural style spatially organizes families into interlocking horizontally organized households and compounds which stress an expansive conception of kinship. Land, which is regarded as sacred, is viewed as belonging to an entire lineage and not as a commodity for sale to the highest bidder. Nzegwu argues that the cultural beliefs underpinning Yoruba conceptions of land encouraged a 'freestyle' approach to urban space which, organized as a warren of interconnected sub-houses, courtyards and decorated walls, is different from the regimented grid-iron order of western urban space. Further, given the emphasis on lineage within Yoruba spatial organization, the typical modernist zonal distribution of city spaces into distinct parts for the rich and poor was largely absent from their communities.

Postcolonial city

The annexation of Lagos as a British colony led to the introduction of a land-law system underpinned by a commodity logic and 'modern' western restructuring which guided colonial and **postcolonial** responses to the influx of diverse ethnic groups and the subsequent demand for new housing. The colonial solution to housing needs was revealing of endemic racism in keeping European dwellings apart from Africans and in building houses which in design and location disrupted Yoruba family organization.

The small size of the houses built for 'natives' and the high densities of these homes restricted the extended family, preventing the traditional expansion of courtyards and buildings. In contrast to the Yoruba organization of space into multiple horizontally distributed sites of power for both men and women, the western vertical buildings coded an order of power and gender relations which hierarchically formalized domestic space and privileged men, as reflected in for example the master bedroom and the drawing room, with the the kitchen, in which women's domestic work took place, hidden from view, unlike in Yoruba life.

By 1960, when independence was established for Nigeria, Lagos had been reorganized along modern grid-lines which divided the city into racially segmented areas including low-density European zones, high-density poor-quality African sectors, a Brazilian quarter and a commercial district. Later, as colonial influence declined, the European sectors were taken over by upper-class Nigerian families who maintained the trappings of colonial power.

Also figurative of class ascendancy was the arrival of towering skyscrapers of modernist design in the central and commercial districts, symbolically and materially epitomizing the presence of powerful multinational capitalist corporations and their ethos of investment, trade and commerce. These had been encouraged by the military government as signs of 'development'. Of course, such development has its losers as well as its winners, so that significant spaces between the high-rise buildings were contested and taken over by the poor, market traders and financial hustlers. Indeed, with economic downturn in the 1980s and 1990s, class polarization widened, crime increased and walls grew up around the premises of the wealthy.

CITIES AS PLACES

Space, as Massey and Nzegwu clearly show, is a construction and materialization of social relations revealing cultural assumptions and practices. Our continuing example will be that of cities as places. Western academic explorations of urban life are virtually coterminous with the emergence of modern social science, especially the discipline of sociology. All three of the so-called 'founders' of sociology – Durkheim, Marx and Weber – regarded urbanization as one of the key features of capitalist industrialization, viewing it with a certain ambivalence.

Durkheim hoped that urban life would be a space for creativity, progress and a new moral order but feared it was to be the site of moral decay and anomie. For Weber, urban life was the cradle of modern industrial democracy whilst also engendering instrumental reason and the 'iron cage' of bureaucratic organization. One the one hand, Marx viewed the city as a sign of progress and the great leap of productivity which capitalism bought about, while, on the other hand, he saw it as a site of poverty, indifference and squalor. A more positive modernist view of urban life was held by Simmel, for whom the city was the birthplace of the aesthetic of modernism and the escape from the controls of tradition. In short, the city can be regarded as both product and symbol of **modernity**, and the ambivalence of Durkheim, Weber and Marx is indicative of the Janus-face of modernity itself (Chapter 5).

The Chicago School

The breakthrough in establishing urban studies as a specific field of inquiry came with one of Simmel's students, Robert E. Park,

and fellow members of the 'Chicago School', Ernest Burgess and
Louis Wirth. Although differing in a number of respects, these
writers, Burgess in particular, cast their work in the language of
'science' and sought after the 'underlying laws' of urban life.
Burgess' prime metaphor for the city was that of the organism
struggling for survival and undergoing evolutionary change in the
context of a specific environment. This is a functionalist 'urban
ecology' approach to cities in which concentric urban zones were
territories to be fought over, invaded and altered before the
establishment of a new equilibrium. According to Burgess:

> The typical processes of expansion of the city can best be illustrated,
> perhaps, by a series of concentric circles, which may be numbered to
> designate both the successive zones of urban extension and the types
> of areas differentiated in the process of expansion. (Burgess, 1967: 50)

Burgess' 'ideal-type' construction of the city expands radially
from the Central Business District (CBD), with each subsequent
zone inhabited by a particular type or class of people and activities. As we move outward from the CBD, we pass through:

- a zone of transition;
- a belt of working-class housing;
- a zone of high-class dwellings;
- a commuter belt of satellite towns.

In effect, various social class groups are allocated specific residential zones by income selection. Although originally constructed
from fieldwork in Chicago, Burgess' urban map was taken to be a
general model of city growth and in particular of the 'tendency of
each inner zone to extend its area by invasion of the next outer
zone' (Burgess, 1967: 50). Although using the language of invasion
and succession, along with marking the zone of transition as one
of deterioration and disorganization, Burgess took an essentially
optimistic view of urban life, viewing it as inevitably progressive.

Wirth displays a more cultural than ecological approach to
urban life, being primarily concerned with urbanism as a way of
life and a form of social existence. He was interested in the
cultural and lifestyle diversity of urban living, which, as he saw it,
promoted impersonality and mobility (social and spatial) as people
lost a sense of 'place' and stable social relationships.

According to Wirth, urban living was based on having large
numbers of people living in close proximity without really knowing each other, requiring them to conduct instrumental transactions and passing encounters. This led to superficial, transitory,

competitive relationships and a sense of alienation and power-lessness. However, Wirth also points to the way city dwellers form associations with each other based on lifestyle, **culture** and ethnicity. Indeed, so-called 'community studies' was to argue that cities developed a range of communities or urban villages of tight-knit social relations, for example Italian-Americans in Boston (Gans, 1962) and working-class neighbourhoods in London (Young and Willmott, 1962).

Criticisms of urban studies

There are a number of problems with these early versions of urban studies, namely:

- the functionalism and spurious science;
- the overgeneralization from American cities, and particularly Chicago, to elsewhere;
- the greater variety of urban life than the ecology model acknowl-edged;
- a stress on the idea that *where* you live is the central factor in determining *how* you live, so that space is determinate of culture and economy.

Thus, Gans (1968) argued that the crucial factor shaping lifestyle was not so much the locality where people live but their social class and place in the 'family life cycle'. This argument is closer to the views of those for whom the structures and transformations of **capitalism** are the prime forces which shape city life, for example the contemporary emphasis on **political economy** in the emergence of the global city.

POLITICAL ECONOMY AND THE GLOBAL CITY

The work of Harvey (1973, 1985) and Castells (1977, 1983) stresses the structuring and restructuring of space as a created environment through the spread of industrial capitalism. They argue that the geography of cities is the result not of 'natural forces' but of the power of capitalism in creating markets and controlling the workforce.

Capitalism and the urban environment

The **commodification** and search for new markets which capitalist corporations promote makes them sensitive to questions of location and their relative advantages. Lower labour costs, weaker unionization and tax concessions lead firms to favour some places over others as locations for plants, markets and development. Similarly, the need to find alternative forms of investment, and the particular conditions of markets and state intervention, assists some sectors of the economy (and thus some places) in gaining preference.

For Harvey, the state has played a major role in the reproduction of capitalism and its shaping of the urban environment. For example, the post-war expansion of suburbia was an outcome, at least in part, of tax relief given to home-owners and construction firms, the setting up of lending arrangements by banks/building societies, and the laying down of the transport, telecommunications and welfare infrastructure required for the suburbs to flourish. For Castells, these homes, schools, transport services, leisure facilities and welfare provisions are an aspect of the 'collective consumption' inherent to capitalism and the creation of an urban environment conducive to business.

The city is said to be the site of a class struggle engendered by capitalism and marked by contestation over the control of space and the distribution of resources. This includes the conflicts over the cutting of welfare spending during the restructuring of capitalism in the 1980s and 1990s. Indeed, for Harvey and Castells, the reorganizing of the city is an aspect of the restructuring of capitalism on a global scale, illustrating the place of urban life in the long line of dependency and exploitation constitutive of worldwide capitalism. As King argued:

> All cities today are 'world cities', yet they have not just assumed that role over night. The agenda for urban history which perceives them in this way is clearly vast. Yet such a perspective would enable urban problems, economic, social and physical, to be seen in a much more realistic light. . . . The cosy viewpoint of looking at our cities from within must be replaced by the more uncomfortable view of seeing them from outside. (King, 1983: 15)

According to Harvey (1989), global recession hastened a renewed **globalization** of world economic activity involving the speed-up of production and consumption turnover. Assisted by the use of information and communication technology, a new **post-Fordist** 'regime of accumulation' was established (Chapter 4). The restructuring of capitalism on a global scale is described by Lash and Urry (1987) as a 'disorganized' set of global flows of capital, resources and people. They point to the deconcentration of capital through globalized production, financing and distribution.

At the same time, western economies have experienced a decline in the extractive/manufacturing sectors as economies are de-industrialized. This has led a decrease in the absolute and relative size of the core working class in tandem with the emergence of a service class. Like Harvey, Lash and Urry stress the rise in flexible forms of work organization and a decline in national bargaining procedures.

Global cities

In this context, the restructuring of urban space can be explored in terms of the emergence of global cities and the place of 'culture' in urban regeneration. Underpinning the concept of the **global city** is the sense that the urban world and global economy are dominated by a small number of centres which act as command and control points for an increasingly dispersed set of economic activities. These centres – London, New York, Tokyo, Seoul, Los Angeles, Frankfurt, Paris, Singapore – have significance not because of population size or volume of business but because key personnel and activities are located within them. That is, they are sites for the accumulation, distribution and circulation of capital where information and decision-making functions are more telling than size.

According to Clarke (1996), ten cities host the headquarters of nearly half of the world's largest 500 transnational manufacturing corporations. The top four cities, London, New York, Tokyo and Seoul, account for 156 of these. He suggests three reasons behind the emergence and patterning of global cities:

- growth in the number and range of the institutions of global capital;
- geographical concentration of capital;
- the extension of global reach via telecommunications and transport.

Finance and banking have become the crucial facets of a city's claim to global significance. For example, though the manufacturing sector of the UK is relatively small (in planetary terms), London is a world city because it is the prime centre for and supplier of financial services to global markets. After New York, perhaps the major financial centre, London has the largest stock exchange in the world and all the world's top 100 banks are represented there.

Tokyo's global status was originally based on the research-led, government-protected microelectronics industry and the flexible production methods it pioneered. On the back of this success,

Tokyo developed as a commercial centre through the transnationalization of the capital it had accumulated and subsequently
exported to nearby Asian economies (Korea, Taiwan, etc.) and to
Europe and the USA in the guise of investment in cars and
electronics.

The post-industrial global city

Sassen (1991, 1996) explores the variety of spaces which make up
the urban forms of the contemporary post-industrial global city
symbolized by New York, London and Tokyo. These include the
high-rise CBD, the declining **post-industrial** zones and the spaces
of ethnicity. The contrast between the homogeneity of the high-rise
offices of the CBD and the diversity of the urban forms which mark
immigrant communities reveals how power inscribes itself in the
urban landscape. 'One represents technological advance and cosmopolitan culture, the other economic and cultural backwaters'
(Sassen, 1996: 24). Of course, 'advanced' and 'backward' are relational concepts and representational effects. As Sassen argues,
the so-called 'backwaters' are a vital part of the economic and cultural life of cities and deeply intertwined with the self-nominated
'advanced' sectors.

The increasing globalization of capitalism gives rise to the need
for command, control and co-ordination nodal centres which constitute the core of 'global cities'. This is manifested spatially and
architecturally in the high-rise, high-density office developments
of the downtown districts of New York, London and Tokyo. These
centres, constituted by the offices of large multinational corporations, require servicing by suppliers, sub-contractors and consult-
ancy firms, etc. Thus, around the command posts grow other layers
of economic activity, including the small firms and labour force of
separate ethnic communities whose physical and cultural presence
represents another aspect of globalization. Consequently, the
expansion of global economic activity is premised, in part, on local
informal (i.e. unregulated) economic activity (Sassen, 1991, 1996).

THE SYMBOLIC ECONOMY OF CITIES

While Harvey and Sassen focus on political economy, Zukin
explores the **symbolic** and **representational** aspects of cites.

> To ask 'Whose city?' suggests more than a politics of occupation; it also
> asks who has the right to inhabit the dominant image of the city. This

often relates to real geographical strategies as different social groups battle over access to the center of the city and over symbolic representations in the center. (Zukin, 1996b: 43)

Questions concerning the symbolic economy of cities focus on two fundamental issues:

- The relationship between representations and 'readings' of social groups which mark inclusion and exclusion. For example, particular districts, streets, parks or buildings whose symbolism marks zoning and the materialization of social rules. Thus, the unwritten 'keep out' which the high-rise corporate buildings of the CBD signs to the poor, blacks and Latinos in North American cities.
- Economic redevelopment, including the transformation of wharfs and canals into shopping centres or areas of leisure activity, which signifies the role of symbolic economy in material economic power. This encompasses the role played by representations in the constitution of place whereby a vibrant symbolic economy attracts investment, giving particular cites comparative advantages over rivals. Spaces and places are formed by the synergy of capital investment and cultural meanings, uniting legibility and identity (Zukin, 1996a).

Zukin (1991) argues that the increasing significance of the symbolic economies of cities is rooted in the long-term relative decline of urban areas in comparison with suburbs, the expansion of financial speculation, the growth of cultural consumption, the arrival and visibility of 'ethnic immigration' and the marketing of **identity politics**. This leads her to suggest that we cannot understand cities without considering:

- how cities use culture as an economic base;
- how capitalizing on culture spills over into the privatization and militarization of public space;
- how the power of culture is related to the aesthetics of fear. (Zukin, 1996a: 11)

Cultural economics

Culture plays an economic role in a number of ways:

- It acts as a *branding* for a city, associating it with desirable 'goods': for example, movie representations of the New York skyline; the meeting houses of the American Revolution hosted by Boston; the Bridge, Opera House and harbour of Sydney; the art culture of Florence; the 'mother of parliaments' in London; and the high-tech neon of Tokyo.
- The *culture industries*, including film, television, advertising agencies and the music business lend glamour to cities, bringing direct employment and other economic benefits.

■ The museums, restaurants, shops, theatres, clubs and bars of cities provide convivial *consumption spaces* for business meetings and tourism. For example, Paris is a 'world city' not for its manufacturing or financial clout but because its architectural history and gastronomic reputation attract international conventions and organizational headquarters.

While discussion of urban regeneration and the symbolic economies of cities has centred on North American cities, the place of culture in urban restructuring is also prominent in a European context. For example, the British city of Birmingham has attempted to shift its internal centre of power and public space so as to reposition itself in the symbolic culture and economic order of Europe and the world. The city's hosting of the G8 summit and Eurovision Song Contest in 1998 within its International Convention Centre (ICC) and canal development area was a sign of its success. It was also a part of its strategy as the city plastered itself with the slogan 'Birmingham Welcomes the World'. As Tim Hall (1997) argues, the redevelopment of Birmingham exemplifies the tactics by which 'peripheral' places use cultural strategies to win investment.

For Birmingham this strategy involved the opening up of a series of spectacular 'flagship' spaces based on technical excellence, prestige, modern design and professionalism with a stress on display. This included the ICC, the shops, restaurants and waterside walkways surrounding the canal basin and the cultural symbol of the Symphony Hall associated with the high cultural world of classical music and the spectacle of performance. Thus, 'the city imagined itself within certain cultural spaces, those of high culture, international culture and spectacle' (Hall, 1997). Subsequently, Birmingham attempted to circulate these discourses through the media, linking civic identity to the processes of transformation and the colonization of the future.

Privatizing public space

Zukin's (1996a) prime example of the privatization of public space is the evolution and transformation of the public park. The major cities of the western world have parks and squares, built, usually during the nineteenth century, as places of public access where people could meet, walk, talk and participate in a common culture. Often these collective spaces were created in celebration of civic achievements and as monuments to public figures. Today, it is argued, these spaces are on the decline and the new arenas of public meeting, public culture and the **public sphere** are situated in private commercial spaces – the private park, the shopping mall and the simulated theme world. This is the product of a combination of factors, including:

- the inability or unwillingness of city government to fund and maintain public spaces;
- increased levels of everyday fear surrounding perceptions of rising crime in general and public assault and robbery in particular (often linked to ethnic and racial tensions);
- the rise of the leisure industries and an increased involvement of private security and leisure companies in the management of 'public' space.

Zukin (1996a) gives a number of examples, including Bryant Park, New York, where a once flourishing public space had become a litter-filled danger zone inhabited by drug users, homeless people and other victims of urban poverty. Under the auspices of a privately funded restoration company the park was 'cleaned up' and redesigned. Entertainment was introduced, opening hours restricted and security guard patrols were established to oversee the park. This scheme and others like it have been successful in creating 'safe' public space which is popular and busy during key times of the day. Equally, the consequence has been to turn the park into a visual and spatial representation of middle-class public culture inhabited by mainly white office workers.

The public culture of private elites

Zukin's concern is that public culture – if such can be said to exist – is shaped by private sector elites. This poses three problems:

- Only certain profitable sites will be developed, that is, those with the potential to enhance property prices or retail business.
- Control of access to these 'public' spaces is in the hands of security regimes who explicitly exclude 'undesirable' social groups, that is, the urban poor, in which people of colour are overrepresented.
- There is an attempt to control the total environment through population flow and control of a symbolic culture conducive to commerce, exemplified by shopping malls and theme parks. Accordingly:

  Disneyland and Disney World are two of the most significant public spaces of the late 20th century. They transcend ethnic, class, and regional identities to offer a national public culture based on aestheticizing differences and controlling fear. (Zukin, 1996a: 49)

Disney: fantasy and surveillance

The Disney landscape provides a multi-media experience representing a tourist attraction and a symbolically desirable lifestyle. This is a 'public' culture where civility and social interaction occur in the context of a security regime in which there are no guns, no homeless people and no drugs. Disney's idealized and fantasized 'Main Street USA', which presents to us in symbolic and imaginary form the pleasurable aspects of urban life while removing the fear, is a far cry from the 'real' streets of New York. Disney World, through its private management, spatial control and stimulating/simulated visual culture, is the new model for public space whose principles are echoed in numerous shopping malls. For Zukin, Disney World is important because it confirms and consolidates the significance and power of culture as a form of commerce and social control. It imposes a form of meaning and manages social diversity through a combination of visual imagery and physical spatial control.

Disney World has been defended on the grounds that it is a safe, defensible public space. However, critics influenced by Baudrillard have attacked it for its hyperreality, its collapsing of the real and the fake (and indeed its celebration of the fake). Others have reviled Disney World for being all too real in its total control of space through the use of its own rules, vocabulary, norms, security force and even sanitation workers – most of whom are the relatively low-paid workforce of an ever-increasing service sector (Zukin, 1996a). This arguably marks the postmodernization of contemporary life (Chapter 5).

THE POSTMODERN CITY

According to Edward Soja: '. . . a *postmodern urbanization process* can be defined as a summative depiction of the major changes that have been taking place in cities during the last quarter of the twentieth century' (Soja, 1995a: 60). As Watson and Gibson (1995) remark, every city in the world is to some degree **postmodern**. However, for Soja (1989, 1995a), the 'quintessential' case of postmodern urbanization is Los Angeles, which represents for him an 'extraordinary intensity' of urban restructuring and a 'comprehensive vividness' of change. Although too much has been made of LA as 'the future', it stands in the literature as the city that 'must be discussed'.

Postmodern urbanization

For Soja, postmodern urbanization does not imply total transformation of the urban landscape into something wholly new, for
the postmodern city has continuities with its past. On the other
hand, the concept of the postmodern does suggest 'something
more than piecemeal reform'. Soja argues that we can see in Los
Angeles six intertwined processes and relationships that together
produce a composite postmodern urban geography. These are as
follows:

- *Fordist to post-Fordist urbanization*: The move from Fordism to post-
  Fordism (Chapter 4) involves a move from mass production and consumption of standardized goods to small batch production through
  flexible specialization for niche markets. For Soja, it involves processes of deindustrialization and reindustrialization which constitute
  a dramatic change in the foundations of the urban economy. The
  reindustrialization of Los Angeles is constituted by the development
  of high-technology industries, including aerospace and electronics
  (situated outside of the old industrial zones), and by the growth of
  low-skill, labour-intensive, design-sensitive industries which, though
  once clustered in Downtown, are increasingly dispersed across the
  urban landscape. In addition, the growth of the finance, insurance
  and real-estate business is a marker of LA's postmodern restructuring. Together, these developments have reorganized not only the
  economic base of LA but the residential areas, including the emptying out of the centre and the urbanization of suburbia.
- *Globalization and the formation of world cities*: Los Angeles is an
  especially vivid example of the world city as a finance/trade centre
  and is marked by global, but particularly Japanese, inward investment. It is also the location of 'the most culturally heterogeneous
  population ever agglomerated in any city in the world' (Soja, 1995a:
  130). A city which was once 80 per cent Anglo is now at least one-third
  foreign-born, many of whom are the backbone of a cheap and weakly
  organized labour force essential to the growth of the LA economy.
- *A combination of decentralization and recentralization*: The urban
  form of the postmodern city is said by Soja to be significantly different from its predecessors. He argues that it no longer conforms to the
  concentric rings of the Chicago School or even the late modern
  'disjointed metropolis' constituted by a Central Business District, an
  inner city poor zone and a series of sprawling suburbs. Rather, while
  these areas continue to exist, the postmodern city has juggled them
  around. The 'inner city' poor zone is not necessarily located within
  the physical inner city, while the residential suburbs are increasingly the site of new forms of industrial development. This is the
  outcome of a restructuring and redistribution of jobs, affordable
  housing, transport systems and lines of racial/ethnic divide.

■ *New patterns of social fragmentation, segregation and polarization*: Post-Fordism, deindustrialization, globalization and the reconfiguration of the spatial geography of the city are bound up with the changing social structure of urban life, including new patterns of fragmentation, segregation and polarization. For Soja this involves increasing social, economic and cultural inequality. A complex new social kaleidoscope leads to creative cross-cultural mixing in the arts, business and politics but also to even greater depths of despair, impoverishment, crime and violence. In particular, the social landscape is now marked by an enlarging managerial technocracy, a shrinking middle class and a growing base of the homeless, welfare dependants and cheap labour.

■ *The increasingly 'carceral' city*: The postmodern kaleidoscopic city has become increasingly ungovernable, leading to walled-in estates, armed guards, patrolled shopping centres, surveillance cameras and wire fences, all aimed at keeping the threatening spectre of crime, violence and ethnic difference at bay. LA is marked by turf wars of gangs and police, the latter armed with the latest technology of control. However, Soja also points to an increasing **politics** of place, including greater neighbourhood participation in local municipal issues.

■ *A new mode or regulation involving the rise of hyperreality and simulacra*: The most obviously postmodern aspect of Soja's argument refers to the emergence of a new form of social control, or mode of regulation, constituted by a transformed 'urban imaginary'. This is a new **epistemology** in which the relationship between image and reality is blurred or even deconstructed. The most visible example is the growing significance of the hyperreal or **simulacrum**. What is new, Soja argues, is not the production of hyperreal Hollywood or Disneyland but the proliferation and dissemination of the hyperreal into ordinary everyday life evidenced by the vocabulary of spin doctors, virtual reality, cyberspace, sound-bites and pop culture.

Urban change: suburbs and edge cities

Soja attempts to map the postmodern city from the elevated heights of the metaphorical mountain-top. He works with the language of globalization and macro-economic restructuring. However, patterns of change can also be understood through the more localized language of urban studies with its vocabulary of the inner city, suburbs, gentrification and edge cities.

The 'modern' Anglo-American city has commonly been discussed in terms of a poor, non-white inner city zone of decay paralleled by the growth of suburbs populated by a predominantly middle class. Typically, this involved a degree of 'white flight' from the city to the suburbs and the emptying out of the inner city so that, at its most extreme, a city like Detroit (USA) has a poor black inner zone with whole sections not supplied with basic services like electricity and water. In the popular imagination these are dangerous places of gang wars, drug abuse and crime.

Soja's argument is that residential suburbs have become the site of industrial activity while so-called 'inner city' poverty is increasingly located across the urban landscape. Further, some parts of the inner city, especially those areas which have suffered most from deindustrialization, have been taken over by middle-class groups who have benefited from the regeneration of dockland areas or taken to 'loft living' (Zukin, 1988), that is, *gentrification*. This has involved an increase in house prices and the generation of cultural activities based on the lifestyles of a 'college-educated generation', with the consequential displacement of lower income groups.

Edge cities are urban places of residence and work which have grown up on the outer rims of established cities. Usually of middle-class suburban character, edge cities have emerged in spaces which often have no designated name or immediate local government structures. By resisting being incorporated into established places, these edge cities in the USA have allowed the middle classes to achieve, or at least lobby for, lower rates and reduced public administration, including the privatization of local government. That edge cities are not just suburbs but places of work and economic activity is significant for, according to Zukin, edge city development in America indicates

> a major reversal of meaning between the city and its suburbs. Until quite recently we thought of cities as the economic heartland whose vast wealth nourished a surrounding, and clearly subordinate, regional culture. The city had sleek office towers; the suburbs had poky commuter trains. The city had theaters and concert halls for original performances; the suburbs had mass culture's derivative shopping centers and drive-in movies. This socio-spatial differentiation repeated the pattern of form following function, with 'suburbanization' considered a form of consumption derived from the city's productive functions. More critical, however, is the fact that the city has always financed the suburbs. Investment by the city's banks builds highways and shopping centers. Employment in the city's offices pays mortgages on the suburban homes. And the concentration of 'social problems' in the city fuels the exodus outward into the suburbs of all those people who can afford to move away. Even in the glossiest cultural representations, it was never imagined that the suburbs would compete with the city as a source of productive wealth, a landscape of economic power. (Zukin, 1991: 135–6)

Urban unrest

The kind of urban change typically seen in the USA, and to some extent the UK and Australia, is argued by its critics to be driven by the agenda of the professional and managerial middle class and large corporate business. This has increased and intensified social polarization, manifested by the abandonment of an 'underclass' to mass unemployment, drug trafficking, poverty and homelessness. Here are the conditions for the urban rioting witnessed in the UK during the 1980s (Toxteth, Handsworth, Brixton, Tottenham) and of course in LA in 1992.

While the popular image is of black or Latino urban rioters located in the inner city, McGuigan (1996a) notes that significant numbers of the people involved are white and from working-class estates on the edges of urban areas. In either case, cities must be considered as contested areas so that, in parallel to urban unrest, there has been an increase in techniques of **surveillance** and control. Again, the paradigm case is Los Angeles, described vividly by Mike Davis (1990) in his book *City of Quartz*, where he offers an apocalyptic vision of Los Angeles marked by the following features:

- a city built on the myth of sunshine and the good life;
- property and land prices as the central dynamic and social value;
- rapid population increase and surburbanization;
- the decay of infrastructure and the development of pollution and other environmental problems;
- an indifferent, selfish middle class bent on tax reductions and reduced public expenditure;
- a corrupt political establishment which, though divided along ethnic lines and increasingly fragmented, still holds enormous power;
- the growing influence of LA as a global city in the sway of Japanese capital;
- growing social and economic polarization, poverty, low pay and urban unrest;
- gangland crime and high-tech policing;
- commuter belts and urban wastelands;
- severe racial divisions and discriminatory practices;
- a racist police force committed to an ongoing, because inherently flawed, 'war on drugs' which has virtually curfewed non-Anglo youth.

Fortress LA

These factors represent the conditions for riots and underpin the construction of the city as Fortress LA. Davis argues that, in post-liberal Los Angeles, the defense of luxury lifestyles is translated into a proliferation of new repressions in space and movement, undergirded by the ubiquitous 'armed response'. This obsession with physical security systems, and, collaterally, with the architectural policing of social boundaries, has become a zeitgeist of urban restructuring, a master narrative in the emerging built environment of the 1990s. (Davis, 1990: 223)

For Davis, LA merges urban design, architecture and police apparatus into a comprehensive security endeavour in which fear becomes a function of the security mobilization itself. He cites the redesign and rebuilding of the Downtown area in which street frontage is denuded, pedestrians carefully channelled, 'undesirable' sectors cut off from access and certain 'types of people' (notably people of colour and the poor) 'discouraged' and excluded. Parallel with this 'cleansing' of Downtown there has, he argues, been a deliberate strategy of 'containment' of the poor into designated spaces where they can be policed and harassed. This has included banning cardboard shelters and even avoiding the erection of public toilets in designated areas.

The concern for security has been elevated to the point where it structures the design of buildings from the 'fortified' public library to ever greater numbers of gated and guarded residential facilities. Increasingly, contemporary residential security in Los Angeles depends on private security services and an implicit division of labour between private police and the public LAPD, with the later concentrating on high-tech surveillance and information gathering, leaving much of the 'leg work' to commercial organizations.

The excitement of the city

Davis' account is a useful, informative and frightening antidote to unreflective celebrations of cities as places of unrestricted cultural mixing and merging. At the same time, a pessimistic stance oriented by political economy pointing only to the problems of urban life misses the specifically cultural aspects of cities and the pleasures they offer. For those in a position to enjoy them, cities offer unrivalled opportunities for work and leisure, for mixing and meeting with a range of different kinds of people and cultures, for excitement, uncertainty and the surprise encounter. In big cities, as nowhere else, one can eat, listen to music, go to the movies, dress up, set off on travels and play with identities.

CYBERSPACE AND THE CITY

The heterogeneous pleasures and representations of contemporary urban life are increasingly derived from a growing electronic culture, which includes film, television, virtual reality games, electronic arcades, PCs and the Internet. This is a heavily 'mediatized' (Thompson, 1995) culture in which the spaces of social and cultural interaction are separated from specific social and geographical places. While the potential exists for electronic culture to offer more flexibility and scope in the construction of **identity projects**, electronic technologies are also the means for increased surveillance and control.

The concept of cyberspace, commonly attributed to novelist William Gibson (1984), suggests the 'nowhere' space where e-mails pass, electronic money transfer takes place, digital messages move and world-wide web sites are accessed. 'A conceptual "spaceless place" where words, human relationships, data, wealth status and power are made manifest by people using computer-mediated communications technology' (Ogden, 1994: 715).

The main technologies of electronic culture are computers, cable systems, satellites, television, video and virtual reality technology. These technologies form the domain of 'telematics', that is, services and infrastructures which link computers and digital technologies over telecommunication links. The central features of these technologies are:

- electronics;
- abundance;
- speed;
- convergence;
- plurality;
- interactivity.

Electronic technology provides more information and services at increased speed across greater distances to more people. Some services are interactive, though at present this is at a relatively low level. The idea of PC-TV or the 'information superhighway' highlights the issue of technological **convergence**, that is, technologies which had been produced and used separately merge into one. Technological convergence is enabled by digital technology which enables information to be electronically organized into bytes, or discrete bundles of information, which can be compressed during transmission and decompressed on arrival. This allows a good deal more information to travel at greater speed over larger distances.

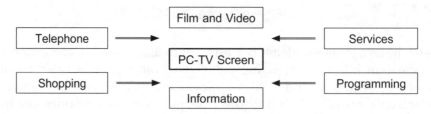

Figure 10.1   *Television as the visual terminal of the information superhighway*

The information superhighway

The current model of electronic development is the Internet. Originally set up by the US military, the Internet is a communications infrastructure of linked but decentred computer terminals with no central regulatory authority. The Internet has a number of different levels of use: e-mail, newsgroups, world-wide web sites and on-line services, with the last two the most rapidly expanding areas. It has been estimated that there are around 5 million Internet host computers with probably 25–30 million users.

To date, the Internet has largely involved free access. However, this is changing as multinational corporations develop subscription services and web sites or explore the possibilities of setting up their own 'information superhighways' in which one could order and pay for shopping, transfer e-money, keep an eye on one's bank account, call up a selection of films, videos and programmes and search the world-wide web for information. Both Microsoft and News Corporation have ambitions to develop their own information superhighway in which the television would be the visual terminal for a whole range of services and activities (Figure 10.1). Indeed, the component parts of this picture are already being put in place in the USA, where 34 per cent of the population have PCs and 40 per cent of these have modems (required to access the Internet).

Electronic urban networks

According to Graham and Marvin, there are three key areas of analysis for exploring the relationship between telecommunications and cities, namely:

- the functional and material tensions between the fixity of urban places and the mobility supported by telecommunications and electronic spaces;

- the social struggles which develop over the shaping of urban places and electronic spaces;
- the issues surrounding social representation, identity and perception in cites and telecommunications. (Graham and Marvin, 1996: 113)

Traditionally, cities have been regarded as relatively fixed places whose great strength lay in their overcoming of the 'frictional distance of space'. That is, cities brought together the elements of industrialization, work and leisure. Cities reduced the need to transport people and goods over long distances. However, since electronic technology is able to overcome distance in an instant, it creates new networks and new senses of time and space.

> The idea of telecommunications as 'distance-shrinking' makes it analogous to other transport and communication improvements. However, in doing so the idea fails to capture the essential essence of advanced communications, which is not to reduce the 'friction of distance' but to render it entirely meaningless. When the time taken to communicate over 10,000 miles is indistinguishable from the time taken to communicate over 1 mile, then 'time-space' convergence has taken place at a fairly profound scale. (Gillespie and Williams, 1988: 1317)

As Castells (1989) argues, the new geometry of production, consumption and information flows denies the meaning of place outside of its position in a network. Specifically, cities are the electronic hubs of a global information economy with urban areas as the nodal points of social, technological, cultural and economic networks. Further, the growth of telematics as integral to cities is an aspect of the deindustrialization and restructuring of global economies in which information is the key commodity of post-industrial 'information cities' (Chapter 4). Telematics supports the dispersal of economic activity across the 'megalopolis' and indeed the planet.

The informational city

For Castells (1989, 1994), we are witnessing epochal changes driven by the agenda of a professional and managerial class. This is constituted by:

- the technological revolution of computers and information transfer;
- the emergence of an 'information society' with economic, social, military and cultural capabilities being information-based;
- the emergence of a global economy operating in real time on a planetary scale;
- the significance of cities as command centres of the global economy, including competition for relative advantage;

- increased social polarization between regions of the world (North–South) and within cities divided by race and class (the dual city).

Telematics challenges the fixity of cities while increasing social polarization and conflictual struggles over the meaning of technologies and city spaces. On the horizon lies an increasing distance between the information-rich and the information-poor. Electronic technology is also at the heart of social control and surveillance through the increase used of CCTV cameras in urban centres, security systems surrounding houses, police helicopters using infra-red cameras, and the use of electronic shopping cards which record information for store management of consumer spending patterns and promotional activities.

> The computerized credit card, the home computer, and the sophisticated television system that permits home banking, shopping, opinion polls, and so on also allows corporations to collect massive amounts of information on users. One analyst estimates that within five years 40 million so-called smart cards for automatic banking, shopping and other services will be in circulation in the United States alone. How much money you have, what you like to buy, your views on capital punishment, your preference for president or laundry detergent – the new technology is used to draw detailed marketing profiles of individual households for what is called . . . precise targeting of potential buyers. (Mosca, 1988: 6)

In short, the development of electronic technologies which are intrinsic to contemporary cities is bound up with issues of social power and conflict. Cities are terrains of contestation in which various ethnic, class, gender and organizational agents struggle to shape the social and built environment. This is manifested in disputes over the redevelopment of inner cities, docklands or downtown areas and debates about whether the Internet will remain a free dispersed network of computers accessible in principle by all or a commercially dominated pay-per-view complex.

Electronic homes in global space

One of the urban places that electronic technologies threaten to change is the home. As Castells suggests:

> homes . . . are becoming equipped with a self-sufficient world of images, sounds, news, and information exchanges. . . . Homes could become disassociated from neighbourhoods and cities and still not be lonely, isolated places. They would be populated by voices, by images, by sounds, by ideas, by games, by colors, by news. (Castells, 1985: 34)

For some writers, we are heading towards a new home-centred society based on home-working, interactive home tele-services and the 'smart' home. That is, the home becomes a terminal in a range of electronic flows emanating from, for the most part, transnational corporations.

The home is one of the major locations of electronic culture by which we can become armchair travellers. Electronic culture spans time and place, coming to us via the screen, video, radio, etc. Cultural artefacts and meanings from different historical periods and geographical places can mix together and be juxtaposed so that, while the values and meanings attached to place remain significant, the networks in which people are involved extend far beyond their physical locations (Chapters 4 and 9).

This is the postmodern culture of visual **bricolage**, **intertextuality**, aesthetic self-consciousness, paradox, ambiguity, **irony**, parody, pastiche, montage, rapid cutting, non-linear narrative techniques and the de-contextualization of images (Chapter 9). It includes the blurring of the boundaries between art, culture and commerce, allied to the rising prominence of the postmodern 'figural', resulting in a general aestheticization of everyday life (Featherstone, 1991, 1995).

THE CITY AS TEXT

Most of the approaches to the city that we have explored fail to register the problematic notion of representation which underpins them. They tend to assume that they are offering us an accurate picture of the city over and against ideological distortions. However, representing the city involves the techniques of writing – metaphor, metonym and other rhetorical devices – rather than a simple transparency from the 'real' city to the 'represented' city. For example, we have seen the city described in the languages of:

- plant life and ecology (the Chicago School);
- economic development, restructuring and investment (Harvey);
- power and surveillance (Davis);
- symbolic culture, suburbanization and gentrification (Zukin);
- postmodernism (Soja);
- information technology (Castells).

In the context of the 'crisis of representation' (Chapter 3), accounts of the city have increasingly been recast in the language of **poststructuralism** and its problematization of representation so that the city is read as **text**. According to Shields,

While we may happily speak of the 'reality' of the city as a thing or form, they are the result of a cultural act of classification. We classify an environment as a city, and then 'reify' that city as a thing. The notion of 'the city', *the city itself, is a representation*. It is a gloss on an environment which designates by fiat, resting only on the assertion of the self-evidence that a given environment is 'a city'. (Shields, 1996: 227)

There is no unmediated access to 'the real'. What counts as true and as real is the outcome of discursive constructions which bring the objects of knowledge into view through the processes of classi-fication. Representations of cities – maps, statistics, photographs, films, documents, etc. – make the city available to us. However, we then discuss these representations as if the city was a thing, a clear-cut object external to human cultural representation. Shields argues that representations summarize the complexity of the city and displace the physical level of the city onto **signs** – simulacra which present themselves as 'reality'. These representations, which give meaning to places, are political because they are linked to normative notions, that is, to what is appropriate social behaviour.

Classified spaces

Representations of the spatial divisions of cities are symbolic fault lines of social relations by which people come to think about the world through the built environment. That is, the cultural rep-resentation and classification of city zones as, say, black or white, working class or middle class, safe or dangerous, business or resi-dential, glamorous or squalid are concrete cultural abstractions through which the world is lived. These are *poetic* representations with definite consequences raising questions about what is hidden and what is shown. A politics of representation needs to ask about the operations of power which are brought to bear to classify environments. By revealing only some aspects of the city, rep-resentations have the power to limit courses of action or frame 'problems' in certain ways.

Shields suggests that there is a tendency to represent the city in terms of public spaces rather than domestic ones. Thus, much of the world of women and children is rendered invisible for the easily visible city is the old male public sphere. Likewise, rep-resentations of 'dangerous places' which play on fear (commonly associated with people of colour) fail to acknowledge that so-called 'dangerous places' are so only to certain people or at certain times. This poststructuralist-informed account of representation and the city tends to analysis in which:

- the social and the spatial are indivisible;
- the city is constituted and lived through representation;
- a decentred account of the social is offered, that is, there are a series of available sites in which the urban is produced so that 'the city is *many* cities' (Westwood and Williams, 1997: 6).

The city which is not one

Shields (1996) argues that we should view the city as a complex surface of activities and interactions which can be explored through a multidimensional analysis and dialogic representation which does not seek to synthesize or overcome contradictions but juxtaposes and celebrates a diversity of opposing voices. The languages used to describe the city are, it is argued (Tagg, 1996), also languages of the city, languages of social science which emerged from the modern city and which as discursive formations produce the city, having no common prior object. The discursivity of the city is multiple and heterogeneous. This is the city which, in Tagg's (1996) phrase, with its echoes of Irigaray, 'is not one'.

SUMMARY

This chapter has explored the growing concern in cultural studies with questions of space and with cities in particular. It was argued that space and place are social and cultural constructions, with the latter marked by human emotional investment and identification. Space and place are always matters of the social relations of class, gender, ethnicity, etc., that is, places of power marked by contestation over their meanings. The city is never one thing but rather is manifested and read as a series of contested spaces and representations – cities rather than the city.

From the perspective of political economy we noted the emergence of global cites as command points of the world economy. It was argued that the restructuring of cities is an aspect of the reorganization of the global economy. We also explored the symbolic economies of cities as playing a role in their restructuring and regeneration. Thus, urban places sought comparative advantage through the acquisition of symbolic capital.

We discussed the trends of postmodern urbanization towards fragmentation, polarization, surveillance, control, conflict and simulacra. These, together with the development of suburban edge cites, the privatization of public space in the context of reduced public spending and growing urban unrest, mark the direction and growth of cities as we approach the turn of the century. However, we also noted that the city is a place of excitement, fun, strange encounters and the mixing and matching of playful identities.

11

Youth, Style and Resistance

A significant marker of the post-war western world has been the emergence and proliferation of distinct musical forms, fashion styles, leisure activities, dances and languages associated with youth. The question of youth cultures has a significant place in cultural studies, not least because the first wave of postgraduates at the Centre for Contemporary Cultural studies (CCCS) Birmingham, UK – Hebdige, Clarke, Cohen, McRobbie, Willis, Grossberg, etc. – were themselves part of the babyboomer rock generation. Youth culture was 'their' culture, and taking it seriously formed part of the validation of popular culture in the face of high cultural disdain (Chapter 2).

The Birmingham group's analysis of youth subcultures, *Resistance through Rituals* (Hall and Jefferson, 1976), was a landmark publication in cultural studies whose network remains one populated by students and lecturers who have personal and professional engagements with popular music, style and fashion. Further, the study of youth cultures raises a number of significant concerns and themes which echo down and across the pathways of cultural studies, namely:

- the cultural classification of persons into social categories (youth);
- the demarcations of class, race and gender;
- the questions of space, style, taste, media and meaning (i.e. questions of culture);
- the place of consumption within capitalist consumer societies;
- the vexed question of 'resistance'.

These themes will structure our exploration of youth cultures. However, we should note that cultural studies has tended to explore the more spectacular youth cultures, the visible, loud, different, avant-garde youth styles which have stood out and demanded attention. This has been to the detriment of sociological explorations of what the majority of young people do with their time. This chapter is no exception to that general rule.

THE EMERGENCE OF YOUTH

Common sense tells us that youth is a natural and inevitable marker of a biologically determined age, an organically founded classification of persons who as a consequence of their age hold specific social positions. However, as documented by sociologists like Talcott Parsons, youth is not a universal category of biology but a changing **social** construct which appeared at a particular moment of time under definitive conditions.

Youth as moratorium

For Parsons (1942, 1963), youth or adolescence is a social category which emerged with the changing family roles generated by the development of **capitalism**. In pre-capitalist societies, he argues, the family fulfilled all the major biological, economic and cultural functions of social reproduction. The transition from childhood to adulthood was marked by rites of passage and was not an extended period of youth or adolescence. With the emergence of specialized, universalized and rationalized occupational and adult roles in capitalist society there was a discontinuity between the family and the wider society which needed to be filled by a period of transition and training for young people. This marked not only the category of youth but a moratorium of 'structured irresponsibility' between childhood and adulthood which allowed youth culture to emerge and whose functions were essentially socializing.

The specificity of youth as a social position between childhood dependence and adult responsibility can be seen in the institutions of the family, education and work. For example, youth is regarded as undergoing preparation for the inevitability of leaving home and joining the adult world. Youths are granted some greater responsibilities than children but are still subject to adult control. This view leads to a set of significant assumptions and classifications of youth by agencies of social control – politicians, policy makers and youth professionals. These include the following:

1 Youth is a unitary category, with certain psychological characteristics and social needs common to an age group.
2 Youth is an especially formative stage of development, where attitudes and values become anchored to ideologies and remain fixed in this mould for life.
3 The transition from childhood dependence to adult autonomy normally involves a rebellious phase, which is itself part of a cultural tradition transmitted from one generation to the next.

4   Young people in modern societies experience difficulty in making
    successful transitions and require professional help. advice and
    support to do so. (Cohen, 1997: 182)

Youth as cultural classification

Cultural studies writers would agree that the concept of youth has
no universal meaning to it. However, the 'biological age' deployed
by Parsons is itself part of a cultural classificatory system and not
a fixed point upon which social expectations are hung. Youth as
an age has no unified characteristics, nor is it a secure transitional stage. This much is apparent if we ask:

- When does youth start and end biologically?
- Are all 16-year-olds biologically and culturally the same?
- What do all 25-year-olds have in common?
- Why is it that young people seem to be different in New York,
  Bombay and Rio de Janeiro?
- How can it be that a section of the adult population over 40 strives to
  be youthful?
- How is it possible that the period of 'youth' seems to be getting longer
  in western societies?

Youth is not so much a biological category overlaid with social
consequences as a complex set of shifting cultural classifications
marked by **difference** and diversity. As a cultural construct, the
meaning of youth alters across time and space according to who is
being addressed by whom. Youth is a discursive construct. It is
formed by the organized and structured way we talk about and
bring into being youth as category of persons. Of particular significance are **discourses** of style, image, difference and **identity**.

The ambiguity of youth

However we seek to define it, youth remains an ambiguous concept. Even legal definitions are uneven. In the UK, for example, the
ages at which a person can buy alcohol, consent to heterosexual
intercourse, engage in homosexual practices and vote for governments are different. Physical age is thus being deployed impre-
cisely and differentially as a marker to define, control and order
social activity (James, 1986). As Sibley argues, youth remains a
contested ambivalent classification wedged between the boundaries of childhood and adulthood:

The limits of the category child vary between cultures and have changed considerably through history within western, capitalist societies. The boundary separating child and adult is a decidedly fuzzy one. Adolescence is an ambiguous zone within which the child/ adult boundary can be variously located according to who is doing the categorizing. Thus, adolescents are denied access to the adult world, but they attempt to distance themselves from the world of the child. At the same time they retain some links with childhood. Adolescents may appear threatening to adults because they transgress the adult/child boundary and appear discrepant in 'adult' spaces. . . . [T]he act of drawing the line in the construction of discrete categories interrupts what is naturally continuous. It is by definition an arbitrary act. (Sibley, 1995: 34–5)

For Grossberg (1992), what matters is the way that the ambiguous category of youth is **articulated** with other discourses of, for example, music, style, **power**, responsibility, hope, the future, Americanness, etc. As he argues, 'The issue is not whether the various discourses about youth are referentially accurate, but that they are themselves part of the context in which youth is organized' (Grossberg, 1992: 199).

Trouble and fun

While adults may view youth as merely a state of transition, young people have invested in it as a privileged site in which to foreground their own sense of **difference**. This includes a refusal to identify with the perceived boredom of routinized everyday life. Youth has became an ideological signifier charged with utopian images of the future even as it is feared by others as a potential threat to existing norms and regulations. Thus is youth 'ambivalently valued' (Grossberg, 1992).

Hebdige (1988) remarks that youth has been constructed within and across the discourses of 'trouble' (youth-as-trouble: youth-in-trouble) and/or 'fun'. For example, through the figures of football hooligans, motorbike boys and street corner gangs youth has been associated with crime, violence and delinquency. Alternatively, youths have been represented as playful consumers of fashion, style and a range of leisure activities. This is figured by the party-goer, the fashion stylist and, above all, by the consuming 'teenager'. According to Hebdige, the teenager drives a wedge between childhood and adulthood. It represents the **commodification** of youth, the creation of the youth consumer market forged on the back of the surplus cash which working-class youth was thought to have at its disposal.

YOUTH SUBCULTURES

Though the concept of the teenager has framed much popular discourse on youth, cultural studies was drawn instead to the analytic concept of subculture. The concept of **subculture** is a mobile one constitutive of its object of study. It is a classificatory term which attempts to map the social world in an act of **representation** (Thornton, 1997). Subcultures do not exist as authentic objects but have been brought into being by subculture theorists (Redhead, 1990). Thus, we might ask not so much what a subculture is as how the term has been used.

For cultural studies, the **culture** in subculture has referred to a 'whole way of life' or 'maps of meaning' which make the world intelligible to its members. The 'sub' has connoted notions of distinctiveness and difference from the dominant or mainstream society. Hence, the notion of an authentic subculture depends on its binary opposite, the idea of an inauthentic mass-produced mainstream or dominant culture.

> The defining attribute of 'subcultures', then, lies with the way the accent is put on the distinction between a particular cultural/social group and the larger culture/society. The emphasis is on variance from a larger collectivity who are invariably, but not unproblematically, positioned as normal, average and dominant. Subcultures, in other words, are condemned to and/or enjoy a consciousness of 'otherness' or difference. (Thornton, 1997: 5)

Subterranean values

As Thornton argues, another significant resonance of the prefix 'sub' is that of subaltern or subterranean. Subcultures have been seen as spaces for deviant cultures to renegotiate their position or to win space for themselves. Hence, in much subcultural **theory** the question of 'resistance' to the dominant culture comes to the fore. This was initially conceived of within cultural studies through the category of **class** but later expanded to include questions of gender, race, sexuality, etc.

The resonances of subterranean values, of deviance and of class, were absorbed into cultural studies through an engagement with the American sociology of 'delinquency'. In particular, the Chicago School explored 'juvenile delinquency' as a collective set of behaviours organized in and through subcultural class values. Young people's publicly troublesome behaviour was understood not as individual pathology, or as the outcome of an undifferentiated 'youth', but as a collective practical solution to the structurally imposed problems of class. In this context, various scenarios were advanced regarding the character of 'delinquency', namely that it was:

- a rejection and inversion of the middle-class values of work, success and money enacted by working-class young people in order to cope with their perceived deficiencies in those terms (Cohen, 1955);
- the enactment and emphasis on subterranean working-class values, especially those of leisure, which were deviant only from the perspective of middle-class social controllers (Matza and Sykes, 1961; Miller, 1958);
- the attempt by working-class young people to enact the values of success, wealth and power (Merton, 1938) and/or of leisure and hedonism (Cloward and Olin, 1960) via alternative routes given that the socially approved ones were blocked off by the structures of class.

Magical solutions

Cultural studies theorists agreed that conceptualizing 'youth' as a homogeneous group was to be rejected in favour of the differences of class and their articulation with the values of the dominant or mainstream culture. Subcultures were seen as magical or **symbolic** solutions to the **structural** problems of class. Or, as Brake was later to express it,

> subcultures arise as attempts to resolve collectively experienced problems resulting from contradictions in the social structure . . . they generate a form of collective identity from which an individual identity can be achieved outside that ascribed by class, education and occupation. (Brake, 1985: ix)

Brake goes on to consider five functions that subcultures may play for their participants:

- providing magical solutions to socio-economic structural problems;
- offering a form of collective identity different from that of school and work;
- winning space for alternative experiences and scripts of social reality;
- supplying sets of meaningful leisure activities in contrast to school and work;
- furnishing solutions to the existential dilemmas of identity.

In this context, the concept of homology was applied by Willis (1978) to describe the 'fit' between a structural position in the social order, the social values of subcultural participants and the cultural symbols and styles by which they expressed themselves.

Homologies

The concept of **homology** connects a located lived culture as a set of 'constitutive relationships' to 'the objects, artefacts, institutions and systematic practices of others which surround it' (Willis, 1978: 189). Homological analysis, which is synchronic, records snapshots of social structures and cultural symbols. It involves two levels of related analysis: the examination of the social group and the examination of their preferred cultural item.

> Essentially it is concerned with how far, in their structure and content, particular items parallel and reflect the structure, style, typical concerns, attitudes and feelings of the social group. Where homologies are found they are actually best understood in terms of structure. It is the continuous play between the group and a particular item which produces specific styles, meanings, contents and forms of consciousness. (Willis, 1978: 191)

Subcultural participants are not held to understand homologies in the way the cultural theorist does. Nevertheless, the creativity and cultural responses of groups are not random but expressive of social contradictions. 'They "understand" in the logic of cultural action something of their own conditions of existence' (Willis, 1978: 170). Sacred objects which lie at the heart of a profane culture provide the **coded** value-systems of a coherent subculture.

MOTORBIKE BOYS

Willis holds that 'the ensemble of the bike, noise, rider *on the move*' expressed the motorbikeboys' culture, values and identities. 'The solidity, responsiveness, inevitableness, the *strength* of the motorcycle matched the concrete, secure nature of the bikeboys' world' (Willis, 1978: 53). The motorcycle underwrites the boys commitment to tangible things, to roughness and power, so that 'the surprise of its fierce acceleration, the aggressive thumping of the unbaffled exhaust, matches and symbolizes the masculine assertiveness, the rough camaraderie, the muscularity of language, of their style of social interaction' (Willis, 1978: 53).

According to Willis, subcultures live out important criticisms and insights into contemporary capitalism and its culture. For example, hippies subvert and reorganize industrial capitalism's linear, ordered and disciplinary sense of time. Motorbike boys' 'taming of a fierce technology for a symbolic human purpose' shows us the 'terror of gigantic technologies' of capitalism. It expresses alienation and a profound loss of human scale. Consequently, the creative, expressive and symbolic work of subcultures can be read as forms of **resistance**.

Resistance through ritual

As Hebdige (1979) argues, the concept of homology, crossed with that of **bricolage**, was to play a significant part in CCCS's seminal book on youth cultures, *Resistance Through Rituals* (Hall and Jefferson, 1976). Bricolage describes 'the re-ordering and re-contextualization of objects to communicate fresh meanings' (Clarke, 1976: 177). That is, objects which already carried sedimented symbolic meanings are re-signified in relation to other artefacts in a new context. Clarke (1976) points to the construction of the Teddy Boy style through a combination of the otherwise unrelated Edwardian upper-class look, the bootlace tie and brothel-creepers. Likewise, the boots, braces, cropped hair, stay-prest shirts and Ska music of Skinheads were a stylistic symbolic bricolage which communicated a 'hardness, masculinity and working classness' (Clarke et al., 1976). This theme is said to resonate with the group's situated social relations in a homological unity.

THE DOUBLE ARTICULATION OF YOUTH

In this analysis youth subcultures are explored as stylized forms of resistance to **hegemonic** culture. Youth is constituted through a 'double articulation' to parent working-class culture and to the dominant culture. The parent working-class culture is said to develop its own distinctive ways of being and modes of meaning in relation and in opposition to hegemonic culture. Thus,

> In relation to the hegemony of a ruling class, the working class is, by definition, a subordinate social and cultural formation. . . . Of course, at times, hegemony is strong and cohesive, and the subordinate class is weak, vulnerable and exposed. But it cannot, by definition, disappear. It remains as a subordinate structure, often separate and impermeable, yet still contained by the overall rule and domination of the ruling class. The subordinate class has developed its own corporate culture, its own forms of social relationships, its characteristic institutions, values, modes of life. (Clarke et al., 1976: 41)

Though working-class resistance is subject to historical ebb and flow, it never entirely disappears for it is placed in a position of structural defence and resistance to the hegemonic culture. Youth cultures are said to 'share the same basic problematic' in relation to the dominant culture as the parent working-class culture, while simultaneously differentiating themselves from it. Subcultures involve the expression of difference from and **identification** with the parent culture. Youth has a specific generational consciousness and lives the class problematic in sets of institutions and experiences which are distinct from the parent culture.

Youth subcultures are marked, it is argued, by the development of particular **styles**. That is, the active organization of objects with activities and attitudes through the modes of dress, music, ritual and argot. This a process of re-signification through bricolage by which commodities, which are also cultural signs, are organized into new codes of meaning. Youth subcultures are said to 'win space' for themselves from the parent and dominant cultures through symbolic resolutions of the class contradictions they face.

TEDS, MODS AND SKINS

It is suggested in *Resistance Through Rituals* that Teddy Boy expropriation of upper-class style 'covers the gap' between manual working-class experience and the 'all-dressed-up-and-nowhere-to-go' Saturday night experience. Similarly, the fetishization of style and consumption by Mods 'covers the gap' between the never-ending weekend and the resumption of boring Monday morning dead-end work.

It was further argued that, in reaction to the decline of traditional British working-class values and spaces, itself coterminous with the disappearance of jobs and the redevelopment of established housing communities marking the dawn of a **post-industrial society**, certain youth subcultures sought to reinvent through stylization the lost community and values of the working class. Skinheads were held to be enacting an imaginary recapturing of working-class male 'hardness' through their cropped hair, boots, jeans and braces. Their style stressed the resources of working-class collectivism and territoriality through the coherence and loyalty of 'the gang' of mates. Thus, a stylistic ensemble is a form of symbolic resistance forged on the terrain of hegemonic and counter-hegemonic struggle. However, there is no subcultural solution to low pay, boring routine work and miseducation, so that youth subcultural 'resolutions' remain at the level of the symbolic ritual.

SIGNS OF STYLE

One of the problems with the concept of homology as deployed by Clarke et al. (1976) is that it threatens to become a form of **reductionism** explaining youthful style in terms of class structures. That is, style is derived from and explained through class. In contrast, Hebdige (1979) not only brought the question of **race** into play, but also interrogated style on the level of the autonomous play of **signifiers**. In doing so, he asserts the specificity of the **semiotic** and cultural while retaining the concepts of bricolage and resistance.

For Hebdige, style is a **signifying practice** which, in the case of spectacular subcultures, is an obviously fabricated display of codes of meaning. Through the **signification** of difference, style constitutes a group identity. This is largely achieved through the transformation of the signs of commodities through the process of bricolage and acts as a form of semiotic resistance to the dominant order.

> Subcultures represent 'noise' (as opposed to sound): interference in the orderly sequence which leads from real events and phenomena to their representation in the media. We should therefore not underestimate the signifying power of the spectacular subculture not only as a metaphor for potential anarchy 'out there' but as an actual mechanism for semantic disorder; a kind of temporary blockage in the system of representation. (Hebdige, 1979: 90)

British Punk was Hebdige's favoured exemplar. He argued that Punk was not simply responding to the crisis of British decline manifested in joblessness, poverty and changing moral standards but *dramatized* it. Punk appropriated the media language of crisis, recycling it in corporeal and visual terms. Punk style was an expression of anger and frustration cast in a language generally available but now re-signified as symptomatic of a cluster of contemporary problems.

Punk style was an especially dislocated, self-aware and **ironic** mode of signification. It 'reproduced the entire sartorial history of post-war working class youth cultures in "cut up" form, combining elements which had originally belonged to completely different epochs . . . punk style contained distorted reflections of all the major postwar subcultures' (Hebdige, 1979: 26). As bricolage signifying noise and chaos at every level, Punk style was, for Hebdige, ordered and meaningful. Punk was a 'revolting style' which created an ensemble of the perverse and abnormal: safety-pins, bin liners, dyed hair, painted faces, graffitied shirts and the iconography of sexual fetishism (leather bondage gear, fishnet stockings, etc.). Through disordered dancing, cacophonous sound, desecrating lyrics, offensive language and anarchic graphics Punk 'did more than upset the wardrobe. It undermined every relevant discourse' (Hebdige, 1979: 108).

CRITIQUES OF SUBCULTURAL THEORY

In response to the work of Hall, Hebdige, Willis and others, Cohen (1980) argued that 'youth' in the hands of cultural studies theorists was always something more than itself. He comments that it is not possible to be a 'mere' delinquent anymore as a result of CCCS's overstretched concept of resistance. Style, he suggests, is over-inflated as resistance while resistance is reduced to questions of style. Style is robbed of its elements of fun and flattened down to become only a political question. Similarly, Laing (1985) argued that Punk was primarily a musical **genre** which Hebdige reduces to a signifying practice in the name of contestable political purposes and assumed political destiny.

Cohen expresses a fundamental problem with the work of Hall et al. (1976) and Hebdige (1979) (but less so Willis) when he suggests that 'The nagging sense here is that these lives, selves and identities do not always coincide with what they are supposed to stand for' (Cohen, 1980: xviii). The problem is one of relating the analysts' structural interpretation to the meanings held by knowing subjects. He suggests that not only are the interpretations offered by Hebidge and others disputable, but that young people are made to 'carry too much'. At heart, the criticism is that CCCS failed to engage with members' accounts of subcultural involvement (Widdicombe and Wooffitt, 1995).

The substantive criticism of CCCS subcultural theory from within cultural studies concerned its framing of youth subcultures as mainly white, male and working class. It was argued that CCCS celebrated spectacular youth cultures while handily glossing over strands of racism and sexism. This is held to be an aspect of subcultural theorists over commitment to subcultures, to an emphasis on the spectacular at the expense of the routine and to questions of meaning and style over those of pleasure and fantasy. In the end, whatever we take youth to be, it is divided by class, race and gender as much as it is united by age, attitudes or style.

YOUTHFUL DIFFERENCE: CLASS, GENDER, RACE
The self-damnation of the working class

One of the most widely read and enduring texts in cultural studies is Paul Willis' *Learning to Labour*, in which he seeks, via ethnographic study, to explore the question of 'how working-class kids get working-class jobs [and] why they let themselves' (Willis, 1977: 1). Willis follows a group of working-class boys, 'the lads', as they resist the discipline and promises of schooling through messing-up, evasion and a refusal to behave according to the expectations of the school authorities. These boys are contrasted with the 'ear'oles' (as nominated by the lads), who, with expectations of long-term gains, work co-operatively with teachers.

'The lads' understandings and actions involved what Willis calls 'penetrations' and 'limitations'. In Willis' view, the lads called the bluff on the 'teaching paradigm', which promises personal growth and social advancement in return for compliance and docility. They grasped the unpleasant fact that education is a pathway to 'success' for a limited few which only rarely includes working-class boys like them. Consequently, they see no point in 'playing the game'. Rather, they 'have a laugh' at the expense of teachers and the 'ear'oles' as they pursue the pleasures of leisure and sexuality.

However, the lads' perspective is also tragically limited and constitutes a form of 'self-damnation'. In recursive fashion, the structures of class (which are implicated in the lads' consciousness) are reproduced and enacted through the boys' own actions. Their positive valuation of manual labour and the perceived uselessness of mental labour lead to a refusal to engage with school work, with the result that the lads deliver themselves to working-class jobs.

Gendered youth

The great strength of Willis' study is the articulation of 'youth' with and through class. However, this is also a limitation in so far as the working class in question is held to be exclusively white and male. McRobbie and Garber argued that:

> Very little seems to have been written about the role of girls in youth cultural groupings. They are absent from the classic subcultural ethnographic studies, the pop histories, the personal accounts and the journalistic surveys of the field. When girls do appear, it is either in ways which uncritically reinforce the stereotypical image of women . . . or they are fleeting and marginally presented. (McRobbie and Garber, 1991: 1)

McRobbie and Garber are not dismissing the value of subcultural studies, for they explicitly retain the stress on class, school, leisure, and subculture. However, they are raising the profile of **gender** issues by suggesting the following:

- Girls have been ignored by male researchers.
- Girls have been marginalized and subordinated in male subcultures.
- Girls' youth cultures are structurally located in a different place from those of boys.

McRobbie and Garber criticize Willis' (1978) exploration of motorbike culture as dismissive of girls, who, it is claimed, are evaluated only in terms of their relationships to men. McRobbie also argues that the language of 'the lads' in *Learning to Labour* is 'unambiguously degrading to women' (McRobbie, 1991a: 23). She suggests that Willis fails to confront this and side-steps the way in which working-class male resistance to oppressive class structures is constructed in and through violence to women. 'A fully sexed notion of working-class culture would have to consider such features more centrally' (McRobbie, 1991a: 22). She further argues that Hebdige's exploration of youth culture (see below) involves a 'usage of "style" [which] structurally excludes women' (McRobbie, 1991a: 25).

ANOTHER SPACE FOR GIRLS

McRobbie and Garber argued that if women are marginal to spectacular subcultures it is because they are marginal to the male world of work and discouraged from 'loitering on street corners'. Instead, they suggest, women are central to the family and to an alternative female youth culture of magazines, pop music, posters and bedrooms. In her early work, McRobbie is still suspicious of the consumer culture from which this 'girl-culture' stems. For example, the magazine *Jackie* (McRobbie, 1991b) is held to operate through the codes of romance, domesticity, beauty and fashion, thereby defining the world of the personal sphere as the prime domain of girls. *Jackie*, argues McRobbie, presents 'romantic individualism' as the ethos *par excellence* of the teenage girl (McRobbie, 1991b: 131). In her account of working-class girls, McRobbie (1991c) explores the way in which this culture of femininity is used by girls to create their own space while at the same time securing them for boyfriends, marriage, the family and children.

Later, in conjunction with the general shift in cultural studies from a concern with text to a focus on consumption, McRobbie (1991d) critiques her own reliance on the analysis of documents. She suggests that girls are more active and creative in relation to girls' magazines and other forms of consumer culture than she had given them credit for. She points to the productive, validating and inventive bricolage of fashion style that women originate and to the dynamic character of shopping as an enabling activity (McRobbie, 1989).

McRobbie argues that the active and changing character of femininity is marked by the transformation of girls' magazines in response to the 'sophisticated and discerning young consumer'

(McRobbie, 1991d). This involved a shift of attention from romance to pop, fashion and more a self-confident sexuality. McRobbie underscores the productive role of fantasy in marking the transition from pre-pubertal femininity to adolescent femininity, including its capacity to leave gaps and spaces open for individual interjection. She sees youth magazines marketed for girls as a space for the **politics** of **feminism** and exhorts students to look for jobs within them. No doubt in doing so it would help to be white, like the assumed audience for most British girls' magazines of the time.

Racialized youth

According to Hebdige, 'We can watch, played out on the loaded surfaces of British working-class youth cultures, a phantom history of race relations since the war' (Hebdige, 1979: 45). That is, British youth cultures can be read as 'a succession of differential responses to the black immigrant presence in Britain' (Hebdige, 1979: 29). For example:

- Teddy Boys juxtaposed black rhythm and blues with aristocratic Edwardian style while being implicated in attacks on West Indians.
- Mods sought to emulate the 'cool' style of West Indians as they adopted soul music.
- Skinheads appropriated dress items, argot and music from West Indians while gaining a reputation for racism.
- Punk found resonances in black youths' rejection of Britishness and authority. Reggae was embraced by Punk at the same time as it produced musical forms which were black music's antithesis.

Hebdige sees in Reggae, sound systems and the signs of Rastafarianism resources for resistance to white culture and racial subordination. Reggae, which encompasses the transgressive features of black speech and African rhythms, is understood as a living record of black–white relations from slavery through to the present. Rastafarianism involves a 'profound subversion of the white man's religion' through appropriation and reversal of the Bible. Together, Reggae and Rasta 'proclaimed unequivocally the alienation felt by many young black Britons' (Hebdige. 1979: 36).

Although there are numerous aspects of black culture that have been articulated with youth, Mercer's (1994) discussion of black hair as 'style politics' is of particular interest for its resonances with Hebdige's (1979) exploration of white British working-class youth culture through the concept of style.

THE ARTIFICE OF BLACK HAIR

Hair, Mercer remarks, is never a straightforward fact of nature but a symbolic artifice of culture. Hair is cut, groomed and shaped, making it the instrument of declarations about the self and society. In particular, hair is a key **ethnic** signifier second only to skin. Through hair, racist discourses have cast 'black' on the side of nature, wildness and ugliness with 'white' positioned on the side of culture, civilization and beauty. Strategies for revalorizing the ethnic signifier of black hair have taken two fundamental forms, argues Mercer: one emphasizing *natural* looks and the other *artifice*.

Set against the claim that black hair can only be beautiful if cultivated to imitate white hair through straightening and other techniques, the Afro and Dreadlock styles asserted themselves as natural. In valorizing the materiality of the texture of black hair, they reconstructed a link with Africa, resonating anti-colonial, **postcolonial** and anti-racist struggles. However, it is a romanticized and imaginary Africa that the Afro brings into play. Mercer argues that there was nothing particularly African about the Afro. Indeed, he suggests the Afro was dependent on European conceptions of Africa and nature. Consequently, the tactical reversal involved in the claim that black is naturally beautiful depends on the same association of Africa with nature as do racist and imperial discourses. Further, once commodified as a style, the Afro was neutralized as a signifier of opposition.

Rather than condemn straightened black hairstyles as imitative of white culture, however, Mercer sees them as indicative of black innovation. **Diasporian** black hair involves the creolizing and radical transformation of western forms. Black hairstyles within the West refract elements from white and black cultures through processes of exchange, appropriation, imitation and incorporation. Black style is a manifestation of shared experience and an encoded refusal of passivity by way of active inflection and recoding of hegemonic conventions. The Conk, for example, did not copy anything, but, while suggesting resemblance with white people's hair, emphasized difference through artifice. For Mercer, black style encoded a set of subversive messages to those in the know. The diversity of black hairstyles testifies to an inventive, improvisational aesthetic and to the value of cultural plurality.

SPACE: A GLOBAL YOUTH CULTURE?

Youth is a cultural category differentially articulated with (constructed in relation to) class, gender and race. In addition, youth is understood as a spatial matter, that is, youth may be produced differently in divergent **spaces** and **places**. Youth is enacted in clubs, pubs, schools and parks, which give rise to a range of meanings and behaviours.

The street and the shopping mall have become significantly charged and contested zones for they are amongst the few quasi-autonomous spaces that young people can create for themselves. However, they are also areas in which adults may contest a youthful presence as being a threat to order. At home, questions of privacy and personal boundaries manifested through issues of noise, door locks, tidiness and the hour of comings and goings are the stuff of generational family politics. There has also been a growing interest in **globalization** and the apparently transnational space of 'youth culture'. For some critics the emergence of brands like Nike, Levi, Playstation, Coca Cola and MTV alongside international pop stars represents the commodification and subsequent homogenization of youth culture. For others, global cultural developments, including those connected to youth, are more chaotic and syncretic in character, representing creative **hybrid** cultures (Chapter 4).

Rapping and raving around the globe

Rap, argues Gilroy, is

> a hybrid form rooted in the syncretic social relations of the South Bronx where Jamaican sound-system culture, transplanted during the 1970s, put down new roots and, in conjunction with specific technological innovations, set in train a process that was to transform black America's sense of itself and a large portion of the popular music industry as well. (Gilroy, 1987: 144)

In addition, Rap can trace its routes along pathways which include the influence of West African music and the impact of slavery. As American, Jamaican, West African, South African, British, Indian, German and Icelandic (amongst others), Rap cannot be said to have any obvious point of origin or authenticity. Rap is always already a cultural hybridization marked by rhizomorphic cultural flows.

In Britain, Asian youths have produced their own hybrid forms of Ragga–Banghra–Reggae–Rap cross-overs. Indeed, African-American and black British fashion, music and dance styles are appropriated by Asian youths into their lifestyles (Gillespie, 1995). For Mercer, these 'emerging cultures of hybridity, forged among the overlapping African, Asian and Caribbean diaspora'

(Mercer, 1994: 3), are a challenge to white western authority as well as being ways of living with and in 'conditions of crisis and transition'.

Communications technologies have constructed commodities, meanings and identifications of youth culture which cut across the boundaries of races or nation-states: global Rap, global Rave and global Salsa. Champion (1997) recounts the expansion of Rave culture in the unlikely setting of the conservative and rock-dominated American Midwest. Raving, which she describes as America's new outlaw culture, adapts to local environments, having travelled to Wisconsin via Chicago, Detroit, Ibiza, London, Manchester and the UK dance scene. 'Dance culture is a virus which mutates as it spreads, and in the Midwest they have taken "rave" and made it their own' (Champion, 1997: 114). In a Wisconsin context, cars take on a prominent role (absent in the British scene) in a pastiche of *American Graffiti*. Young people dance the night away not so much in warehouses (Britain) or bunkers (Germany) but on ski slopes and in cowsheds.

Syncretic global youth

Massey (1998) highlights some of the issues raised by the emergence of a global youth culture. She recounts how, after interviewing a group of Mayan women in the Yucatán (Mexico), she turned away from this picture of apparently authentic and indigenous culture to be confronted by a dozen young people playing computer games and listening to western music. 'Electronic noises, American slang and bits of Western music floated off into the night-time jungle' (Massey, 1998: 121). She argues that while this youth culture of Yucatán Maya is not a closed 'local' culture, it is not an undifferentiatedly global (or American) one either. It is a product of interaction in which the terms 'local' and 'global' are themselves in dispute. In each particular youth culture the mix of the global and the local will be different. Indeed, what is or is not a global status symbol for youth will vary by location.

What is at stake is not just an understanding of youth but the place of culture. Culture is less a matter of locations with roots than of hybrid and creolized cultural routes in global space. Youth cultures are not pure, authentic and locally bounded; rather, they are syncretic and hybridized products of interactions across space. They are 'constellations of temporary coherence (and amongst such constellations we can identify local cultures) set within a social space which is the product of relations and interconnections from the very local to the intercontinental' (Massey, 1998: 125).

Global interconnections are always imbued with power and the terms of cultural mixing are uneven. It is American popular culture that is valued by Mayan youth as the symbol of international status. Equally, the traffic is not all one-way. The Afro-Caribbean-originated 'Red, Green and Gold' of Rastafarianism became a diasporian sign of resistance and solidarity, while some First World young people have been politically engaged in issues of global inequity (e.g. Live Aid).

International youth culture puts a particular twist on Clifford's (1992) notion of 'travelling cultures', where culture is conceptualized in terms of peoples and cultures which travel and places/cultures as sites of criss-crossing travellers. For example, 'checking out the planet' (Desforges, 1998) in a search for authenticity is a growing strand of youth culture. Here, travel is framed as the experience of a series of differences which form the basis of a narrative of self-development, accruing cultural capital upon return. However, as Culler (1981) argues, no place is an untouched authentic site for the traveller to discover. All places are always already marked out and signed as to their significance. Travelling is a branch of tourism (not in itself an inauthentic practice) and not a different category.

Redhead (1990) extends the challenge to the authenticity of youth culture. He suggests that any clear-cut distinction between the media, the culture industries and an oppositional and authentic youth subculture is problematic for the latter is 'heavily influenced and shaped by the global leisure industry, of which pop is now structurally so much an integral part (Redhead, 1990: 54). The 'death of youth culture' is marked by the end of the relevance of the concept of an authentic subculture which played such a prominent part in cultural studies' understanding of youth.

AFTER SUBCULTURES

Sarah Thornton (1995) articulates a set of criticisms of subcultural theory. She argues the following:

- Youth cultural difference is not necessarily resistance.
- Differences are classifications of power and distinctions of taste.
- Subcultural theory relies on unsustainable binaries, namely mainstream–subculture, resistance–submission, dominant–subordinate.
- Youth cultures are not formed outside and opposed to the media.
- Youth cultures are formed within and through the media.
- Youth cultures are not unified but marked by internal differences.
- Youth cultures mark not the politicization of youth but aestheticization of politics.

These criticisms stand not just as indicators of the blind-spots of subcultural theory but as markers of the new analytic attitude towards the leisure activities of young people (with dance cultures as the most common object of inquiry). Redhead suggests that the concept of subculture is 'no longer appropriate – if, indeed, it ever was – to conceptual apparatuses' need to explain pop music culture's developments since the publication of Hebdige's major book in 1979' (Redhead, 1997a: x). The 'end of subcultures' is announced not because distinctive cultures of youth do not occur, but because (a) they are increasingly fragmented and (b) the idea of a grass-roots media-free authentic subculture cannot be sustained.

Media spotlights

The deviancy theory from which CCCS's subcultural work drew inspiration accords the mass media a role of considerable significance. Through the concepts of 'moral panics' and 'deviant amplification', writers like Cohen and Young (Cohen, 1972; Young, 1971) attribute to media coverage a central role in the creation and sustaining of youth subcultural deviancy. The media are said to latch onto a particular group of young people and label their behaviour as deviant, troublesome and likely to reoccur. That is, youth are labelled as contemporary 'folk devils'. The public response is a moral panic which seeks to track down and punish deviant youth culture. Young people respond with increased deviancy, so that a cycle of labelling, amplification and deviancy is set in motion. Many of these themes are echoed in the work of CCCS subcultural theorists where Mods, Punks and Skins are the media 'folk devils' of the day.

In this model it is assumed that the media work on previously existing subcultural activities which are held to exist in authentic distinct and pristine form prior to media intervention. Subculture theory perceived youth culture to be 'outside' of the media and opposed to it. In contrast, contemporary theorists suggest that youth cultures are always 'inside' the media, being dependent on it even as they wish to deny this.

> Cultural studies and sociologies of 'moral panic' tend to position youth cultures as innocent victims of negative stigmatization. But mass media 'misunderstanding' is often an objective of certain sub-cultural industries, rather than an accident of youth's cultural pursuits. 'Moral panic' can therefore be seen as a form of hype orchestrated by culture industries that target the youth market. (Thornton, 1995: 136)

Media devils and subcultural hero(in)es

Thornton argues that the idea of an authentic culture formed outside of the media is a resilient but misguided one for 'the distinctions of youth subcultures are, in many cases, phenomena of the media' (Thornton, 1995: 116). Media, she says, are integral to the formation of subcultures and to young people's formulations of their own activities. For example, the notion of the 'underground' is defined against the mass media and delights in 'negative' media coverage. There is nothing more likely to kill the pleasures of subculture membership than mass media approval. Indeed, radio or TV bans and /or ironic mocking performances are the highlights of subcultural lifestyles. A devil in the media will be a hero(ine) in the subculture. Indeed, Punk and House were marketed by subcultural entrepreneurs and record companies in and through moral panics or distinctions of 'hipness' which they helped to foster.

It is not that the media, and the tabloid press in particular, do not engage in the production of moral panics. Headlines like 'Acid House Horror', 'Ban This Killer Music' and 'Drug-Crazed Acid House Fans' (Redhead, 1997b) attest that they do. Coverage frames and disseminates subcultures as events worthy of attention, which record companies exploit for marketing purposes. Subculture studies, argues Thornton, have tended to suggest that youth subcultures are subversive until the moment they are represented by the media. In contrast, she argues that in the perpetual search for significance, subcultures 'become politically relevant only when framed as such. Derogatory media coverage is not the verdict but the essence of their resistance' (Thornton, 1995: 137).

Postmodernism: the end of authenticity

If youth cultures are thoroughly embroiled in **surveillance**, the mass media and the cultural industries, then claims to **authenticity** by members and subculture theorists look dubious. This is a problem for a concept of style which, as the active enactment of resistance, relied on a moment of originality, purity and authenticity. Bricolage, in the hands of Clarke and Hebdige, was dynamic and creative, in contrast to the passive consumption of cultural industry commodities.

Previous theorists of postwar popular music, youth culture and deviance (whether Cultural Studies or Radical, or New Deviancy, or

Deviancy Theory traditions) have tended to look beneath or behind the surfaces of the shimmering mediascape in order to discover the 'real', authentic subculture, apparently always distorted by the manufactured press and television image, which in turn becomes 'real' as more and more participants act out the media stereotypes. This 'depth model' is no longer appropriate – if it ever was – for analysing the surfaces of the (post)modern world, a culture characterized by shallowness, flatness and hyperreality. (Redhead, 1993: 5)

Style, it is now argued, involves bricolage without reference to the meanings of originals. Style has no underlying message or ironic transformation. It is the look and only the look. Merely another mode of fashion. Pastiche rather than parody (Muggleton, 1997). For Jameson (1984), this cannibalization of styles from the past and present represents a loss of artistic depth in favour of a superficial pastiche. This Baudrillardian version of **postmodernism** suggests that 'Contemporary popular culture is merely a seductive sign-play that has arrived at the final referent: the black hole of meaninglessness' (Chambers, 1987: 5).

However, the birth of youth fashion and style in the media does not reduce style to meaninglessness. The end of authenticity is not the death of meaning. Postmodern bricolage, including the eclectic ransacking of history for items of dress (McRobbie, 1989), involves the creative recombination of existing items to forge new meanings. Here, 'post-subculturalists' can 'revel in the availability of subcultural choice' (Muggleton, 1997: 198).

Postmodern bricoleurs

In this context, Chambers (1987, 1990) and Hebdige (1988) discuss ways in which commodities form the basis of **multiple identity** construction. They emphasize the meaning-oriented activity of consumers, who act as bricoleurs selecting and arranging elements of material commodities and meaningful **signs**.

> . . . postmodernism, whatever form its own intellectualizing might take, has been fundamentally anticipated in the metropolitan cultures of the last twenty years: among the electronic signifiers of cinema, television and video, in recording studios and record players, in fashion and youth styles, in all those sounds, images and diverse histories that are daily mixed, recycled and 'scratched' together on that giant screen which is the contemporary city. (Chambers, 1987: 7)

This creativity takes place 'inside the whale' of postmodern consumer capitalism, where the binary divisions of inside–outside and authentic–manufactured collapse. Style is on the surface, culture is industry, subcultures are mainstream, high culture is a subculture, the avant-garde is commercial pop art, fashion is retro. Thus postmodern culture is marked by 'ironic knowingness' (Caughie, 1990), deconstruction of authenticity and fixity (Kaplan, 1987), the creative juxtaposing of second-hand clothes styles (McRobbie, 1989) and/or radicalized strategies of re-articulation (Collins, 1992).

Claims to authenticity

The deconstruction of authenticity at the level of theory does not prevent participants in youth subcultures from laying claim to it. Indeed, empirical research suggests that claims to authenticity are at the heart of contemporary youth subcultures and club cultures. In Widdicombe and Wooffitt's (1995) interviews with a range of subcultural 'members', participation is explained by reference to the emergence and maintenance of a 'true' inner self. Members' own 'deepness' and 'authenticity' is constructed in relation to the claimed inauthenticity and shallowness of others. Authenticity, then, is an accumulated social achievement.

Distinctions of taste

Rock has always made declarations of artistic authenticity on the basis of live performance, disparaging dance music and disco in particular. By contrast, dance music, through a long process of enculturalization, has authenticated the record and the DJ over live performance (Thornton, 1995). Subsequently, club cultures are marked by a whole series of internal authenticity claims and distinctions.

> Club cultures are *taste cultures* . . . club cultures embrace their own hierarchies of what is authentic and legitimate popular culture . . . club cultures are riddled with cultural hierarchies . . . which can be briefly designated as: the authentic versus the phoney, the 'hip' versus the 'mainstream', and the 'underground' versus 'the media'. (Thornton, 1995: 3–4)

Thornton follows Bourdieu (1984) in claiming that distinctions are never simply statements of equal difference; they entail claims to authority, authenticity and the presumed inferiority of others. This argument is based on the concept of *cultural capital* or accumulated knowledge that confers power and status. For example, education and/or the ability to talk knowledgeably about high culture has traditionally been a form of upper-middle-class cultural capital. Cultural capital is distinguished from *economic capital* (wealth) and *social capital* (whom you know). In the context of club cultures, where young people's codes predominate, Thornton suggests that it makes sense to talk of *subcultural capital* to designate the way that clothes, records, haircuts, dance styles and knowledges confer status and power on young people.

Subcultural capital involves distinctions between 'us' (alternative, cool, independent, authentic, minority) and 'them' (mainstream, straight, commercial, false, majority). It also involves distinctions *within* club culture: knowing the latest releases and dances, wearing the most fashionable clothes, seeing the coolest DJs, attending the right clubs. So fast moving is contemporary club culture as it undergoes metamorphosis after metamorphosis that maintaining subcultural capital is a highly skilled task. Consumption is a creative and productive process.

CREATIVE CONSUMPTION

A review of the German dance scene argues that 'In the equal, loving space of the rave, young people are creating a potential blueprint for the whole of society to follow' (Richard and Kruger, 1998: 173). Despite Rave being 'a very commercialized form of youth culture', the authors consider the Techno scene to be women-friendly while offering a utopian critique of contemporary society. However, Reynolds (1997) considers that the Rave dream of transracial, cross-class unity has fallen foul of Rave music's fixation with its own sensations. Not only are these authors opposed in their assessments of Rave culture, but they do not supply any empirical evidence with which to substantiate their arguments. By contrast, during the 1980s and 1990s a critical mass of consumption studies built up which argued that **textual** analysis (in its very broadest sense) could not tell us which meanings are brought into play by actual readers/audiences/consumers.

It was argued that audiences are active creators of meaning, bringing previously acquired cultural competencies to bear on cultural texts. Audiences are not thought to be cultural dopes but are active producers of meaning from within their own cultural contexts. Fiske (1987), in particular, argued that popular culture is constituted not by texts but by the meanings that people produce with them. While **political economy** and textual analysis form part of any investigation of the power of the culture industries, they do not determine cultural significance nor invalidate the power **active audiences** have as producers of meaning.

Common culture

One of the more wide-ranging studies of the consuming practices of young people is Paul Willis' (1990) *Common Culture*. Willis argues that young people have an active, creative and symbolically productive relation to the commodities that are constitutive of youth culture. Meaning, he suggests, is not inherent in the commodity but is produced through actual usage. This he calls 'grounded aesthetics':

> . . . the specifically creative and dynamic moments of a whole process of cultural life, of cultural birth and rebirth. . . . This is a making specific of the ways in which the received natural and social world is made human *to them* and made, to however small a degree (even if finally symbolic), controllable by them. (Willis, 1990: 22)

For Willis, contemporary culture is not meaningless or superficial surface but involves the active creation of meaning by all people as cultural producers. 'The symbolic creativity of the young is based in their everyday informal life and infuses with meaning the entirety of the world as they see it' (Willis, 1990: 98). Through a series of interviews with young people it is proposed that they:

- have an active and creative relation to television;
- are sophisticated and inventive viewers of advertising;
- assert their personal competencies through dancing and the customization of fashion;
- transform and recode the meanings of everyday objects.

Willis argues that it is, ironically, capitalism and the expansion of consumerism that have provided the increased supply of symbolic resources for young people's creative work. Capitalism (in the world of work) may be that from which escape is sought, but it also provides the means and medium (in the domain of consumption) by which to do so. Consumerism is an active not a passive process.

In response, McGuigan (1992) argues that Willis represents an uncritical embracing of the pleasures of consumer sovereignty in the marketplace. According to McGuigan, Willis has lost his conviction that there are grounds for criticizing the current order or for providing alternative visions. Others (Silverstone, 1994) have suggested that audiences/consumers are *always* active but that this does not guarantee a challenge to the hegemonic order.

Whether activity produces a challenge or acquiescence is ultimately a case-by-case empirical question. The evidence that young consumers are active creators of meaning is overwhelming and irrefutable. Nevertheless, **agency** and activity do not have to imply resistance; they can also signify active appropriation of hegemonic values. Activity may be *required* to take up **ideology**. Indeed, it is unclear what 'resistance' means in a postmodern, post-authentic world.

RESISTANCE REVISITED

Stuart Hall writes that:

> There are many different kinds of metaphors in which our thinking about cultural change takes place. These metaphors themselves change. Those which grip our imagination, and, for a time, govern our thinking about scenarios and possibilities of cultural transformation, give way to new metaphors, which make us think about these difficult questions in new terms. (Hall, 1996e: 287)

Metaphors of change are tools rather than analytic categories of **truth** and falsity. Hall (1996e) suggests that metaphors of change do two things: they allow us to imagine what it would be like if the prevailing cultural hierarchies were transformed; and they help us to 'think' the relationship between the social and the symbolic. The question of 'resistance' is a matter of utility and value rather than truth or falsity.

Resistance is conjunctural

Hall (1996e) argues that the strength of *Resistance Through Rituals* (whatever its other limitations) lay in its conception of resistance not as a fixed quality or act but relationally and **conjuncturally**. That is, resistance is not thought of in the singular and universal, an act which defines itself for all time; rather, it is constituted by repertoires whose meanings are specific to particular times, places and social relationships. If we are to consider youth culture as 'resistance', we need to ask some basic questions:

- What or who is youth culture resisting?
- Under what circumstances is resistance taking place?
- In what form is resistance manifested?
- Where is resistance sited?

Resistance as defence

For Bennett, 'Resistance is an essentially defensive relationship to cultural power that is adapted by subordinate social forces in circumstances where the forms of cultural power in question arise from a source that is clearly experienced as external and other' (Bennett, 1998: 171). That is, resistance issues from relationships of power and subordination where a dominating culture is seeking to impose itself on subordinate cultures from without. Consequently, resources of resistance are to be located in some measure outside of the dominating culture. Bennett argues that the merit of *Resistance Through Rituals* was that it saw spectacular youth cultures as essentially defensive reactions to a new aggressive phase of capitalist expansion. Resistance was rooted in the conditions of working-class culture, which stands as a distinct space opposed to ruling-class culture.

For Bennett, this is a productive characterization of resistance because it is clear about the who, where and when of resistance in a bipolar construction of the field of power (the ruling class and the working class; hegemony and subordination). This is contrasted to those formulations of resistance which, Bennett argues, are unspecific and romantic about its character, seeing virtually any response to power as resistance (his target is de Certeau, see below).

Inside the whale

However, we might see the bipolarity of Bennett's reading of resistance as less a strength than a problem. Capitalism is the stated target for resistance yet our discussion of youth culture has suggested that none of young people's cultural texts, symbols and artefacts are outside of capitalism. As bricoleurs of commodities, young people are immersed in, not separated from, consumer capitalism and the mass media. If resistance is taking place, it is happening inside the whale. Youth cultures are not authentic alternative spaces of resistance but places of *negotiation* where the positions of resistance are strategic and themselves enabled by the structures of power (Best, 1997).

For Hall, the strength of *Resistance Through Rituals* lay in its conception of resistance 'as challenges to and negotiations of the dominant order which could not be assimilated to the traditional categories of revolutionary class struggle' (Hall, 1996e: 294). Hall is making the case that resistance is not best understood as a simple reversal of the order of high and low, of power and its absence. Contemporary cultural theory, Hall (1996e) argues, has given up on the idea of pure transcendence.

Instead, ambivalence and ambiguity occupy the space of resistance as exemplified by the transgressive character of the 'carnivalesque'. The carnivalesque is a temporary reversal of the order of power through the rituals, games, mockeries and profanities by which the polite is overthrown by the vulgar and the king by the fool. However, the power of the 'carnivalesque' for Hall lies not in a simple reversal of distinctions but in the invasion of the high by the low, creating 'grotesque' hybrid forms. The challenge is not to the high by low but to the very act of cultural classification by power.

This is a challenge Hall also attributes to the concept of the 'popular', which transgresses the boundaries of cultural power (for it is of value though classified as low), exposing the arbitrary character of cultural classification. In this way, aspects of youth culture can be seen as transgressive **popular culture** and/or carnivalesque subversions of the order of power.

Hiding in the light

Hebdige (1988) applies Foucauldian ideas regarding the micro-relations of power to the construction of youth as trouble and fun. He records how a nineteenth-century fear of the crowd as illegible and ungovernable led social reformers to document through systematic monitoring 'uncivilized' working-class street cultures. This impulse to control, penetrate and supervise has been carried over into the production of youth. Youth subcultures respond to surveillance by making a 'spectacle' of themselves for the admiring glances of strangers (and the media in particular). Hebdige goes on to offer three propositions regarding youth cultures.

- Youth is only present when its presence is regarded as a problem. When young people go 'out of bounds', they get noticed and become visible. This allows them to 'play with the only power at their disposal – the power to discomfort, to pose . . . a threat'.
- New forms of power produce new forms of powerlessness and new types of resistance. Consequently, the politics of youth and the micropolitics of pleasure cannot be collapsed into old/existing organized political activity.
- The politics of youth culture is a politics of gesture, symbol and metaphor which deals in the currency of signs. As such, it is ambiguous and there can be no authoritative interpretation of it for it is underneath authorized discourses. Thus,

> Subculture forms at the interface between surveillance and the evasion of surveillance. It translates the fact of being under scrutiny to the pleasure of being watched, and the elaboration of surfaces which takes place within it reveals a darker will to opacity, a drive against classification and control, a desire to exceed. (Hebdige, 1988: 54)

Hebdige argues that subculture is neither an affirmation nor a refusal. It is a declaration of independence and of alien intent. It is at one and the same time an insubordination of and conformation to powerlessness. It is a play for attention and a refusal to be read transparently.

Tactics and strategies

An alternative account of resistance with considerable currency within cultural studies is that of Michel de Certeau (1984), which has been popularized through the work of Fiske (1987, 1989a, 1989b, 1989c). De Certeau's work has the merits of conceptualizing the resistive practices of everyday life as always already in the space of power. For de Certeau, as with Foucault (1980), there are no 'margins' outside of power from which to lay an assault on it or from which to claim authenticity. Rather, the poetic and illegible practices of the popular are forms of resistance which make creative and adaptive play inside power.

De Certeau makes the distinction between the strategies of power and the tactics of resistance. A *strategy* is the means by which power marks out a space for itself distinct from its environs through which it can operate as a subject of will. Thus, the power of an enterprise involves the creation of its own space and the means by which to act separately from its competitors, adversaries, clients, etc. By contrast:

> a *tactic* is a calculated action determined by the absence of a proper locus. No delimitation of an exteriority, then, provides it with the condition necessary for autonomy. The space of a tactic is the space of the other. Thus it must play on and within a terrain imposed on it and organized by the law of a foreign power. . . . It does not, therefore, have the options of planning a general strategy and viewing the adversary as a whole within a distinct visible, and objectifiable, space. It operates in isolated actions, blow by blow. It takes advantages of 'opportunities' and depends on them, being without any base where it could stockpile its winnings, build up its own position, and plan raids. (de Certeau, 1984: 36–7)

Tactics are the plays of the poacher, the ruses and deceptions of everyday life using the resources of 'the other' which seek to make space habitable. These include the devious productions of consumption, which 'insinuates itself everywhere, silently and almost invisibly, because it does not manifest itself through its own products, but rather through its ways of using the products imposed by a dominant economic order' (de Certeau, 1984: xii–

xiii). For example, youth cultures take the commodities of record companies, clothes manufacturers and magazines and, in the spaces of clubs, pubs and streets, make them their own, investing them with their own meanings, negotiating their own place.

Banality in cultural studies

De Certeau's conception of resistance has the merit of displacing the idea of a monolithic and impenetrable culture industry which imposes its meanings on a passive set of consumers. This is a position also advanced in the work of Chambers, Willis and Fiske. However, for its critics, this line of argument runs the risk of turning almost every piece of pop culture and youth style into resistance. According to Morris (1996), it leads to a 'banality in cultural studies' by which an endless series of writers find resistance in popular culture at every turn. She parodies this as a formulation in which 'people in modern mediatized societies are complex and contradictory, mass cultural texts are complex and contradictory, therefore people using them produce complex and contradictory culture' (Morris, 1996: 161).

For Morris, what is missing is a balance sheet of gains and losses, of hope and despair. What is required, she suggests, is a critical edge which can articulate the notion that 'they always fuck us over' while constructing a space in which we can posit the utopian. Likewise for Bennett (1998), resistance in the work of Fiske and de Certeau does not distinguish sufficiently between types of resistance under sociologically and historically specific circumstances. It is not sufficiently conjunctural.

Resistance: the normative stance of cultural critics

At this stage we might usefully ask two questions of the concept of resistance:

- Is resistance constituted by *any* acts contrary to power, or must they be in the service of particular goals or *values*? Is it enough to make subcultural noises, or must those noises, in order to constitute resistance, be in pursuit of values (e.g. of equality or diversity)?
- Must resistance be a matter of consciousness and intentionality? Can resistance be identified by critics and analysts even though actions might not be conceived of in this way by subcultural participants?

Resistance could be understood in terms of one force meeting another where both are forces and resistances, that is, it could be descriptive of the balance of forces (a use sometimes encountered in Foucault). We may have no interest in the outcome of resistive forces. However, in the context of cultural studies, to describe and act as resistance is a matter not of truth or falsity but of utility and value. Given cultural studies' commitment to a **cultural politics** of insubordination and the politics of difference, resistance is *a normative* concept with success measured strategically against normative criteria. That is, resistance has to be in pursuit of named values.

For example, Skinheads were conceived as resisting middle-class power in the name of the values of working-class solidarity or masculinity. Punks were resisting the normal semantic order in the name of difference and diversity. Of course, it is another matter to claim success for resistance: what did Punks achieve against what criteria? The merit of the values defined as resistance is also a matter of contention. While cultural studies critics might value 'working class', they are unlikely to value the 'masculinity' of Skinheads. Thus, resistance is doubly a matter of value; the identification of the values which resistance upholds, and our identification with those values.

Resistance is not a quality of an act but a category of judgement about acts. Consequently, it is possible and legitimate for critics to identify resistance when participants do not understand it in this way. Resistance is a distinction of value which classifies the classifier (to paraphrase Bourdieu, 1984). It is a judgement that reveals the values of the cultural studies critic just as youth culture is an analytic category of adults.

SUMMARY

Although less widely discussed in cultural studies than the eternal triumvirate of class, gender and race, age is a significant marker of social classification and stratification. The descriptors child, youth, adolescence, adult, elderly, pensioner, etc., are identity categories that carry connotations regarding capabilities and responsibilities. Youth is a cultural classification of an elastic age band which has been ambiguously coded by adults to indicate 'trouble' and 'fun'. Youth carries adult hopes for the future but also incites fear and concern.

The early work of British cultural studies concerned itself with the idea of spectacular youth subcultures as the manifestation of symbolic resistance to the class hegemonic order. Subcultures as distinct domains of subterranean values were argued to offer magical solutions to the structural problems of class. Three main analytic tools were foregrounded: (a) the concept of homology, by which subcultural symbolic objects were held to be expressions of the underlying concerns and structural positions of youth groups; (b) bricolage, by which previously unconnected symbols are juxtaposed to create new meanings; and (c) style, a bricolage of symbols constituting a coherent and meaningful expression of subcultural values.

Contemporary commentators on the youth scene, particularly those focused on dance culture, now question the usefulness of the concept of subculture. They argue that youth culture is increasingly fragmented and 'incoherent', with the notion of an authentic subculture no longer viable. It is not that distinct clusterings of fashion, dance, music and other manifestations of youth cultural style cannot be found; rather, it is that they are 'inside' not 'outside' of mass-mediated consumer capitalism. They are best understood as marked by internal distinctions of taste (and claims to authenticity) rather than as coherent expressions of resistance or opposition.

This argument does not lead youth into the black hole of insignificance. Rather, the creative usage of commodities to achieve a postmodern 'cut 'n' mix' by active, productive consumers represents a set of meaningful activities. Indeed, the production of hybrid youth cultures is an increasingly global phenomenon which challenges any conception that culture has a secure place in the world. Whether this can be regarded as 'resistance' is a moot point. It depends on who is said to be resisting what by whom under particular circumstances. Resistance is relational, conjunctural and normative.

12

Cultural Politics and Cultural Policy

This chapter is concerned with the related issues of cultural politics and cultural policy. We begin by exploring 'cultural politics' in the context of the cultural studies 'tradition' since its formation as an institutionalized mode of study and research. This involves consideration of the way concepts drawn from Gramsci have informed cultural studies, including their modification in the light of poststructuralism. In particular, we will consider the 'politics of difference' and the 'politics of representation' in relation to ethnicity, citizenship and the public sphere.

The discussion of cultural politics will be followed by debates critical of cultural studies regarding:

- the relationship of textual cultural studies to political economy;
- the need to develop cultural policy.

We will review arguments put by critics that cultural studies has been insufficiently centred on cultural policy and has, as a consequence, become a marginalized academic concern. We will consider the relation between cultural criticism, essentially a textual practice, and the pragmatic politics of policy formation and implementation.

CULTURAL STUDIES AND CULTURAL POLITICS

Cultural studies is a multi-disciplinary or even post-disciplinary field of inquiry which blurs the boundaries between itself and other disciplines. However, since cultural studies does not wish to be thought of as 'anything' (Hall, 1992a), it has sought to differentiate itself through its politics. Cultural studies consistently claims to be centred on issues of power, **politics** and the need for social change. Indeed, cultural studies has aspirations to form links with political movements outside of the academy. Thus, cultural studies is a body of **theory** and a set of political stances, including the production of theory as a political practice (indeed, its pre-eminent practice). For cultural studies, knowledge is never a neutral or objective phenomenon, but a matter of **positionality**, what Gray describes as 'Who can know what about whom, by what means and to what purposes' (Gray, 1997: 94).

Naming as cultural politics

In broad terms we may consider **cultural politics** to be about:

- the power to name;
- the power to represent common sense;
- the power to create 'official versions';
- the power to represent the legitimate social world. (Jordan and Weedon, 1995: 13)

One of the central arguments of cultural studies is that its object of study, **culture**, is a zone of contestation in which competing meanings and versions of the world have fought for ascendancy and the pragmatic claim to truth. In particular, meaning and truth in the domain of culture are constituted within patterns of **power**. It is in this sense that the 'power to name' and to make particular descriptions stick is a form of cultural politics.

Issues of cultural **representation** are 'political' because they are intrinsically bound up with questions of power. Power, as social regulation which is productive of the self, enables some kinds of knowledge and identities to exist while denying it to others. It matters whether we are black or white, male or female, African or American, rich or poor, because of the differential cultural resources by which we will have been constituted and to which we will have access.

For example, to describe women as full human beings and citizens with equal social rights and obligations is quite a different matter from regarding them as sub-human domestic workers with bodies designed to please men. To use the language of citizenship to describe women is a different representation of common sense and official ideology from one in which they are described as whores, tarts and servants. The language of citizenship legitimates the place of women in business and politics while the language of sexual and domestic servitude denies this place, seeking to confine women to the traditional spheres of domesticity and as objects of the male gaze.

CULTURAL POLITICS: THE INFLUENCE OF GRAMSCI

Discussion about cultural politics during the 1970s and 1980s was framed within a vocabulary drawn from Antonio Gramsci (1968, 1971) (see also Chapter 2). The most significant concept within

Gramscian cultural studies is **hegemony**. Here, an 'historical bloc' of ruling-class factions is said to exercise 'social authority' and 'leadership' over subordinate classes through the winning of consent. Hegemony involves those processes of meaning-making by which a dominant or authoritative set of representations and practices is produced and maintained.

Winning hegemony

It is central to Gramscian analysis that hegemony involves education and the winning of consent rather than the use of brute force and coercion alone. Though the state is not conceived as a crude arm of the ruling class, it is nevertheless implicated in class hegemony. Gramsci makes a distinction between the 'night-watchman state' as a repressive apparatus reliant on the army, the police and the judicial system, and the 'ethical state', which plays an educative and formative role in the creation of citizens and the winning of consent. Though force remains an option for social control, during times of relative stability it takes a back seat to the unifying role of **ideology**.

After Gramsci, cultural studies adopted the view that ideology, understood in terms of maps of meaning which support the power of particular social groups, is rooted in the day-to-day conditions of popular life. For Gramsci, ideologies provide people with rules of practical conduct and moral behaviour. Ideologies are both lived experience and a body of systematic ideas whose role is to organize and bind together a bloc of diverse social elements in the formation of hegemonic and counter-hegemonic blocs. Ideological hegemony is the process by which certain ways of understanding the world become so self-evident or naturalized as to render alternatives nonsensical or unthinkable.

For Gramsci, the common sense and **popular culture** through which people organize their lives and experience becomes the crucial site of ideological contestation. This is the place where hegemony, understood as a fluid and *temporary* series of alliances, needs to be constantly rewon and renegotiated. The creation and dissolution of cultural hegemony is an ongoing process and culture a terrain of continuous struggle over meanings.

The deployment of Gramscian concepts proved to be of long-lasting significance because of the central importance given to popular culture as a site of ideological struggle. Further, while the concept of hegemony was originally utilized in relation to social **class**, its scope become broader as it encompassed the power relations of **sex**, **gender**, **race**, ethnicity, age and **national**

identity. Notions of ideology and hegemony became pertinent to feminism, **postcolonial** theory, the politics of race, queer theory, etc., in the ongoing cultural 'war of position' within civil society.

The role of intellectuals

Gramscian thinking places cultural analysis and ideological struggle at the heart of western politics and by implication elevates cultural studies to a place of pre-eminence for those concerned with social change. Indeed, it places a special premium on the work of intellectuals and their relations with other participants in social struggle. Here Gramsci's distinction between 'traditional' and 'organic' intellectuals was of significance.

Traditional intellectuals are those persons who fill the scientific, literary, philosophical and religious positions in society, including in universities, schools, churches, the media, medical institutions, publishers and law firms. Though traditional intellectuals may be drawn from different class backgrounds, their status, position and functions lead them to view themselves as independent of any class allegiances or ideological role. However, for Gramsci they produce, maintain and circulate those ideologies constitutive of hegemony which become embedded and naturalized in common sense. For example, numerous analyses of contemporary media output (Chapter 9) have argued for the ideological role of journalists, television producers and other media intellectuals.

By contrast, organic intellectuals are said to be a constitutive part of working-class (and later feminist, postcolonial, African-American, etc.) struggle; they are to be the thinking and organizing elements of the counter-hegemonic class and its allies. As Gramsci puts it, as a new class develops, it creates 'organically . . . one or more strata of intellectuals which give it homogeneity and an awareness of its own function, not only economic but also in the social and political fields' (Gramsci, 1971: 5). Given that Gramsci has an expansive notion of the organic intellectual, this role is not to be played only by those situated within the educational world, but by trade unionists, writers, campaigners, community organizers, teachers, and so forth.

Cultural studies as a political project

As cultural studies developed, many of its adherents adopted the model of organic intellectuals. For many of its leading figures, cultural studies was conceived of as an intellectual project aimed at providing wider social and political forces with intellectual resources in the ideological struggle. Here cultural studies sought to play a 'de-mystifying role' by pointing to the constructed character of cultural texts. It aimed to highlight the myths and ideologies embedded in texts in the hope of producing subject positions which, and real subjects who, are enabled to oppose subordination. Indeed, as a political theory, cultural studies has hoped to organize disparate oppositional groups into an alliance of cultural politics.

Given that the emergence of cultural studies as an institutionally located enterprise did not coincide with an upsurge of class struggle, it has been the 'new' social and political movements of identity politics which have, more often than not, provided cultural studies with its alleged constituency. Even then, it is open to doubt whether cultural studies has been connected with these movements in any 'organic' way. Rather, as Hall (1992a) has commented, cultural studies intellectuals acted 'as if' they were organic intellectuals or in the hope that one day they could be. Others, notably Bennett (1992), have been more sanguine in questioning whether cultural studies has ever been conceivable in terms of organic intellectuals.

Gramscian texts

One of the seminal texts of cultural studies, *Resistance Through Rituals* (Hall and Jefferson, 1976), encapsulates the Gramscian thrust of cultural studies in its title. Here, youth subcultures are explored as stylized forms of **resistance** to hegemonic culture. It was argued that, in reaction to the decline of traditional working-class values, spaces and places, youth subcultures sought to reinvent through stylization the lost community and values of the working class. Skinheads were held to be recapturing in an imaginary way the tradition of working-class male 'hardness' through their cropped hair, boots, jeans and braces. This was combined with a stress on the resource of working-class collectivism and territoriality through the coherence and loyalty of 'the gang' of mates.

Style is read as a form of **symbolic** resistance forged on the terrain of hegemonic and counter-hegemonic struggle. However, it is a limited form of resistance because symbolic resources cannot overcome the structural position of the working class. They cannot abolish unemployment, educational disadvantage, low pay or urban regeneration. This would require a more fully articulated and organized anti-capitalist politics of resistance and insurrection.

Gramscian themes of ideology, hegemony, resistance and containment are also apparent in *Policing the Crisis* (Hall et al., 1978), which explores the 1970s moral panic in the British press surrounding street robbery. The authors explore the articulation of 'mugging' with race and the alleged black threat to law, order and the British way of life. Specifically, the text set out to:

- dispute the association of mugging with an alien black presence and to offer alternative explanations;
- give an account of the political, economic, ideological and racial crisis of Britain which formed the context of the moral panic;
- demonstrate the ideological work done by the media in constructing mugging and connecting it with concerns about racial disorder;
- illustrate the popularization of dominant ideology through the professional working practices of the media;
- explicate the argument that the moral panic around mugging facilitated the move into the 'exceptional state' of an authoritarian 'law and order' society.

These core arguments are expanded by Hall (1988) in his Gramscian exploration of the success of Thatcherism in Britain. Thatcherism represented the most right-wing government Britain had seen in the post-war period, yet also one of its most popular. Hall describes this as an 'authoritarian populism' whose great strength was its ability to sustain popular support for an authoritarian and moralistic state bent on rolling back the boundaries of welfare provision and trade unionism. Hall imputes this success to an ideological struggle which transformed common sense so that it embraced the virtues of 'possessive individualism'. Thatcherism exploited a very real popular sense of the intrusion of the state into personal life, the inefficiency of welfare provision, increased personal choice engendered by consumer **capitalism** and the changing class structure of New Times (Hall and Jacques, 1989; see Chapter 4).

The Gramscian influence in cultural studies can also be seen in a series of textual analyses related to ideology in news and current affairs (Brunsdon and Morley, 1978), soap opera (Dyer et al., 1981), advertising (Williamson, 1978) and popular film (Bennett et al., 1986). It also framed the turn to audience research through Hall's (1981) essay on encoding–decoding and Morley's research (1980) into the *Nationwide* audience (Chapter 9). However, the whole terrain of cultural studies and cultural politics was to shift considerably under the influence of poststructuralism, postmodernism and the politics of difference.

THE CULTURAL POLITICS OF DIFFERENCE

The central arguments of **poststructuralism** and **postmodern-ism** are discussed elsewhere in the text, notably Chapters 2 (language), 4 (postmodernity) and 6 (identity). Consequently, I shall not repeat them at length here. However, I do wish to draw attention to those facets of poststructuralist and postmodern arguments which have been absorbed into cultural studies, prompting a revision of Gramscian modes of thinking. These would include:

- the constitutive place of language and **discourse** within culture;
- the discursive construction of **identity** and social life;
- the **anti-essentialist** character of all social categories;
- the 'no-necessary' correspondence between discursive elements;
- the dispersed character of power which is central to all social relationships;
- the decline of grand **narratives** (notably of Marxism) and totalizing fields of inquiry;
- a stress on micro-fields of political power and resistance;
- the significance given to **New Social Movements** and identity **politics**;
- the instability of meaning in language (*différance*);
- a stress on the politics of **difference**.

New languages of cultural politics

Through assimilation of poststructuralist thinking, cultural studies' understanding of 'politics' has come to centre on the power of discourse to describe and regulate **cultural identities** and social action. Cultural politics now involves the struggle over 'naming' and the power to redescribe ourselves in what Rorty (1989) calls 'new languages'. These questions of cultural power translate into the practical purposes of identity politics when African-Americans challenge the invisibility of black people on television or their representation as marginal and criminalized; when women redescribe themselves as citizens of equal standing with men; when the 'gray panthers' voice the discontents of forgotten and excluded older people; and when gays and lesbians stage 'Pride'.

Social change becomes possible through rethinking and redescribing the social order and the possibilities for the future. Since there is no such thing as a private language, then redescription is a social and political activity. Rethinking ourselves, which emerges through social practice and more often than not through social contradiction and conflict, brings new political subjects and practices into being. For example, in relation to Rastafarians in Jamaica, Hall has argued that:

> Rasta was a funny language, borrowed from a text – the Bible – that did not belong to them; they had to turn the text upside-down, to get a meaning which fitted their experience. But in turning the text upside-down they remade themselves; they positioned themselves differently as new political subjects; they reconstructed themselves as blacks in the new world: they *became* what they are. And, positioning themselves in that way, they learned to speak a new language. And they spoke it with a vengeance. . . . [T]hey only constitute a political force, that is, they *become* a historical force in so far as they are constituted as new political subjects. (Hall, 1996b: 143–4)

The theorization of the 'new' cultural politics of difference has come from a number of directions, though the work of Laclau and Mouffe (1985) and Hall (1988, 1990, 1992a, 1996a) has been of particular significance. Each retains the concept of hegemony but reworks it into a form of **post-Marxism** which draws on post-structuralist theory. Post-Marxism is said to selectively retain that which is held to be valuable in Marxism but to have super-seded it. Thus, Marxism is no longer held to be the primary grand narrative of our time as it once was for cultural studies.

The politics of articulation

Following Derrida, Laclau and Mouffe take meaning to be inher-ently unstable, that is, *différance* – 'difference and deferral' – whereby the production of meaning is continually deferred and added to (or supplemented) by the meanings of other words (Chapter 2). For example, if you look up a word in a dictionary you will be referred to other words in an infinite process. The con-tinual supplementarity of meaning, the continual substitution and adding of meanings through the play of signifiers, challenges the identity of words with fixed meanings. This includes 'women', 'class', 'society', 'identities', 'interests', etc., which are no longer conceived of as single unitary objects with fixed meanings or single underlying **structures** and determinations.

Consequently, for Laclau and Mouffe, the '**social**' is constituted through a series of discursive differences involving multiple points of power and antagonism which does not cohere (as in Marxism and Gramscian theory) around class and the mode of production. The social is not an object but a field of contestation in which multiple descriptions of self and others compete for ascendancy. It is to be thought of not as a totality but as a set of contingently related aggregates of difference articulated or sutured together.

Articulation (Chapter 3) refers to the temporary juxtaposition or unity of discursive elements which do not have to 'go together'. Articulation is the form of the connection that *can* make a unity of two different elements under certain conditions.

For example, we commonly speak of the nation as 'a society', yet not only can a country's people never meet, but they are fundamentally *different* in terms of class, gender, sexuality, race, age, political persuasion, morality, etc. Here, the nation is a discursive device for unifying difference through **identification** with, for example, 'England' or 'Australia'. For Laclau and Mouffe, it is the role of ideology and of hegemonic practices to try to fix difference, to put closure around the unstable meanings of signifiers in the discursive field; that is, to stabilize what, for example, masculinity or American identity means.

No class-belonging

Points of closure or temporarily stabilized meaning are plural, leading Laclau and Mouffe to put aside the final determination of class and the economic. For them, economic relations do not determine cultural meanings (which can be articulated together in a variety of ways). From this it follows that Laclau and Mouffe regard the Gramscian concept of hegemony as mistakenly centred on class for they stress that history has no prime agents of social change nor one central point of antagonism. For Laclau and Mouffe, ideology has no 'class-belonging' (Barrett, 1991) and the social no single originatory point or underlying principle of determination fixing the field of differences. Instead, hegemonic and counter-hegemonic blocs are formed through temporary and strategic alliances of a range of discursively constructed subjects and groups of interest.

The prime agents of social change, it is argued, are not so much classes (though they play a part) as movements which have developed from a proliferation of new social antagonisms centred less in the workplace and more in the spaces of consumption, welfare and habitat. In this context, the ideology of liberal democracy is reworked to stress a broader sphere of 'social rights'. In pursuit of those rights a new political axis is sought around the struggles of 'urban, ecological, anti-authoritarian, anti-institutional, feminist, anti-racist, ethnic, regional or . . . sexual minorities' (Laclau and Mouffe, 1985: 159).

The 'cut' in language

Consistent with this line of democratic anti-essentialist thinking, Hall (1993) has argued that because discourse is a potentially endless and infinite semiois of meaning, any sense of self, of identity or of communities of identification (nations, ethnicities, sexualities, classes, etc.) and the politics that flow from them are fictions marking a temporary, partial and arbitrary closure of meaning. It is possible, given the instability of language, to go on redescribing what it means to be a 'woman' for ever in an endless process of supplementarity. However, in order to say anything (to mark significance), and in order to take action, a temporary closure of meaning is required.

Thus, feminist politics need at least momentary agreement about what constitutes a woman and what is in women's interests under particular circumstances. For Hall, there has to be a full stop, albeit provisionally, a cut in the flow of meaning, so that while identities and identification are fictions, they are necessary ones.

> All the social movements which have tried to transform society and have required the constitution of new subjectivities, have had to accept the necessarily fictional, but also the fictional necessity, of the arbitrary closure which is not the end, but which makes both politics and identity possible. [This is] a politics of difference, the politics of self-reflexivity, a politics of that is open to contingency but still able to act . . . there has to be a politics of articulation – politics of hegemonic project. (Hall, 1993: 136–7)

According to West (1993), the 'new cultural politics of difference' proceeds by way of the following:

- *Deconstruction*: A reading of texts which challenges the tropes, metaphors and binaries of rhetorical textual operations. For example, the binaries of male/female and white/black, in which the former term is privileged as 'the good', are first overturned and subsequently put into a productive tension. In short, **deconstruction** (Chapter 1) helps us to see the political assumptions of texts.
- *Demythologization*: Highlighting the social construction of metaphors that regulate descriptions of the world and their possible consequences for classifying the social. That is, mapping the metaphors by which we live and their link with politics, values, purposes, interests and prejudices. De-mythologization shows why we must speak not of History but histories, not of Reason but historically contingent forms of rationality.
- *Demystification*: Describing and analysing the complexity of institutional and other power structures in order to disclose options for

transformative praxis. For West, such 'prophetic criticism' requires social analysis which is explicit and partisan in its moral and political aims. Further, the development of critical positions and new theory must be linked with communities, groups, organizations and networks of people who are actively involved in social and cultural change.

DIFFERENCE, ETHNICITY AND THE POLITICS OF REPRESENTATION

Emblematic of the 'politics of difference' is work on 'new ethnicities' (Chapter 7) in which **ethnicity**:

- defines new spaces for identities;
- constitutes new hybrid identities;
- insists on the specificity and positionality of all knowledge and identities.

Formed and enunciated in an unstable language, ethnic identity is a discursive construction rather than a reflection of an essential, fixed, natural, state of being (Hall, 1990, 1992a, 1996a). For Hall, a reworking of the concept of ethnicity helps us to explore cultural practices within specific historical and political **conjunctures** so that we are all ethnically located (Hall, 1996d). As such, an exploration of ethnicity must concern itself with the relations between groups which define each other in the context of power. Ethnicity is concerned with relations and representations of centrality and marginality in the context of changing historical forms and circumstances.

Invisibility and namelessness

According to West (1993), the central cultural problematic for the black **Diaspora** is one of 'invisibility and namelessness', that is, a relative lack of power to represent themselves as complex human beings and to contest the negative stereotypes that abound. Responses to this problem have involved the adoption of a number of strategies which we might call:

- the demand for positive images;
- the search for multiculturalism;
- the adoption of anti-racism;
- the politics of representation.

POSITIVE IMAGES

The demand for positive images can be understood as the need to show that black people are 'really as good as' or 'as human as' white people in the context of negative stereotypes and the assimilationist expectations of white society. However, this strategy entails a number of problems:

- Assimilation requires that people of colour adopt the 'way of life' of Anglo culture, thereby losing their own cultural and social specificity in a bid to gain white acceptance.
- This response promotes a homogenization of black people which tends to obliterate differences of class, gender, region, sexuality, etc.
- It rests on a reflectionist or **realist** conception of representation by which it is thought possible to bring representation closer to 'real' black people. This is an impossibility since representations of race are always already constructions (Chapters 2 and 7).
- Given that representations are always matters of contestation, it is difficult to know what an unambiguously positive image would be.

MULTICULTURALISM AND ANTI-RACISM

The multiculturalist strategy also demands positive images but gives up the requirement for assimilation. Instead, ethnic groups are held to be of equal status, having the right to preserve their cultural heritage. Multiculturalism aims to celebrate difference. For example, the teaching of multi-faith religious education, the performance of rituals and the promotion of ethnic food become facets of educational policy.

While this strategy has much to commend it, the process of relativizing cultures can, in the context of institutionally racist social orders, overlook the dimension of power. The day-to-day experiences of racism in relation to housing, employment and physical violence may slip from view. In contrast, the anti-racist argument highlights the operations of power, challenging the ideological and structural practices which constituted racist societies. This includes contesting racist language in school books and the overrepresentation of black pupils in school exclusions and suspensions.

THE POLITICS OF REPRESENTATION

Though multiculturalism and anti-racism have their merits, they rest on essentialist versions of black identity, homogenizing experience to the signifier 'black'. As Hall (1996d) has commented, black identity is not an essentialist category but one that had to be learned. Consequently, he has looked towards a 'politics of representation' which registers the arbitrariness of **signification** and seeks the willingness to live with difference. Rather than demand positive images alone, a politics of representation explores representations which themselves inquire into power relations and deconstruct the very terms of a black–white binary. Hall (1996d, 1997c) has seen such a politics in Kureishi's film *My Beautiful Laundrette*, the photography of Robert Mapplethorpe, the work of film maker Isaac Julien and the emergence of **hybrid** identities.

A politics of representation is double-**coded**. On the one hand, it concerns questions of discourse, images, language, reality and meaning. On the other hand, questions of representation are part of the discourse of democracy, **citizenship** and the public sphere. Indeed, the concept of citizenship is a mechanism for linking the micro-politics of representation/identity with the official macro-politics of institutional and cultural rights. Thus, Mercer argues that 'The concept of citizenship is crucial because it operates in the hinge that articulates civil society and the state in an open-ended and indeterminate relationship' (Mercer, 1994: 284). From within the British Asian context, Parekh highlights what a stress on citizenship and cultural rights might mean for the politics of 'new ethnicities'.

> First, cultural diversity should be given public status and dignity. . . . Second, minorities can hardly expect to be taken seriously unless they accept the full obligations of British citizenship. . . . Third, the minority communities must be allowed to develop at their own pace and in a direction of their own choosing. . . . Fourth, like individuals, communities can only flourish under propitious conditions. . . . Fifth, the distinct character of ethnic communities needs to be recognized by our legal system. (Parekh, 1991: 194–5, cited McGuigan, 1996a: 152)

DIFFERENCE, CITIZENSHIP AND THE PUBLIC SPHERE

According to Dahlgren (1995), citizenship is a form of identity. It is one aspect of our multiple selves whereby a civic 'identity of citizenship' holds together a diversity of values and lifeworlds within a democratic framework. The identity of citizenship may be the only thing we have in common, but a commitment by diverse groups to the procedures of democracy and to intersubjectively recognized rights and duties of citizenship in the social, civil and political domains advances democracy and provides the conditions for particularistic identity projects. This involves the 'hegemony of democratic values' developed in the public sphere.

Habermas and the public sphere

For Habermas (1989), the **public sphere** is a realm which emerged in a specific phase of 'bourgeois society'. It is a space which mediates between civil society and the state, where the public organizes itself and in which 'public opinion' is formed. Within this sphere individuals are able to develop themselves and engage in debate about the direction of society. Habermas goes on to document what he sees as the decline of the public sphere in the face of the development of capitalism towards monopoly and the strengthening of the state. Nevertheless, he attempts to ground its renewal in the notion of an 'ideal speech situation' where competing truth claims are subject to rational debate and argument. Thus the public sphere is conceived as a space for debate based on conversational equality.

However, as Fraser (1995b) has argued, no such conditions exist in practice. Rather, social inequality means that citizens are denied equal access to the public sphere. Subordinate groups do not have participatory parity and the space to articulate their own languages, needs and demands. According to Fraser, Habermas' modern conception of the public sphere requires interlocutors to bracket status differences, to confine discussion to questions of the public good (barring private concerns), and to create only one, because common, public sphere.

Given that social inequality cannot be bracketed, that many private issues are public (e.g. domestic violence), and that there are competing versions of the public good, she argues that a postmodern conception of the public sphere should accept the desirability of multiple publics and multiple public spheres while at the same time working to reduce social inequality. She argues that feminism represents such a 'counter-public sphere' of debate and political activity.

The democratic tradition

The concept of the public sphere does not require Habermas' attempt to construct universal and transcendental rational justification for it. The defence of the public sphere is *normative* and pragmatic rather than epistemological for it can be warranted through the values associated with cultural human rights and cultural pluralism. One supports a democratic public sphere because one believes it to be good rather than true or the destiny of the species.

Principles which the democratic tradition regards as good include the values of *justice*, *diversity*, *liberty* and *solidarity*. The concepts of *justice* and *diversity* suggest the need for cultural pluralism and the representation of the full range of public opinions, cultural practices and social and geographical conditions. *Liberty* and *solidarity* suggest forms of sharing and co-operation which are genuine and not enforced, that is, they imply supportive liberality and togetherness rather than control.

Radical democracy

The values of justice, tolerance, solidarity and difference, formed on the historically contingent grounds of a western democratic political tradition, are also those which drive Laclau and Mouffe's vision of 'radical democracy', whose aim is: 'A society where everyone, whatever his/her sex, race, economic position, sexual orientation, will be in an effective situation of equality and participation, where no basis of discrimination will remain and where self-management will exist in all fields' (Mouffe, 1984: 143). The achievement of this vision demands the articulation of 'chains of equivalence' under what Mouffe (1992) calls the 'hegemony of democratic values'. By this is meant that the 'democratic revolution' proposes the idea of equality and difference. Divergent manifestations of inequality and disparate forms of oppression are by a logic of comparison put on the same footing. That is, inequalities of gender, of class, of race, of nation, etc., are given equal priority and require to be linked up in the formation of counter-hegemonic practices.

QUESTIONING CULTURAL STUDIES

The cultural politics of difference as constituted by a politics of representation has been subject to the criticism that it overlooks material inequalities and relations of power. It is said to lack a **political economy** of housing, labour markets and educational achievement (McGuigan, 1996b). Critics claim that because cultural studies fails to grasp the material circumstances and power relations that pertain between people, it lacks the means to bring about change. An overly textual and populist cultural studies is said to be unable to engage in cultural policy. The most common targets of such criticism have been:

- **textual** deconstruction;
- **active audience** research which celebrates the 'productive' capacities of readers.

The critique of cultural populism

Although cultural studies has many 'external' critics (Ferguson and Golding, 1997), we shall concern ourselves only with those broadly sympathetic to the overall project. For example Jim McGuigan's (1992, 1996a, 1996b) critiques of 'cultural populism'. McGuigan's argument is that cultural studies rightly took issue with the 'mass culture' arguments of the Frankfurt School and the 'cultural elitism' of Leavisism (Chapter 2) which denigrated popular culture as unworthy of either participation or study. This critique took two fundamental forms: first, the philosophical attack on high–low cultural boundaries; second the marking of the moment of consumption as itself a moment of meaningful production.

However, McGuigan argues that the increased 'postmodernization' of culture has itself collapsed the high–low division, while the celebration of the productive and resistive capacities of audiences has gone too far, becoming complicit with the ideology of consumer sovereignty. Cultural studies, it is argued, is unable to critique the products of consumer culture because it has lost sight of any profound conception of cultural value from which to critique texts. Further, it over-endows audiences with the cultural competencies to deconstruct ideology, failing to note the uneven distribution of such competencies across the divisions of class, gender, ethnicity, ages, etc. Consequently, cultural studies is unable to offer, at the level of either analysis or policy, any transformative alternative to the market as it stands.

McGuigan's central target is John Fiske (1987, 1989a, 1989b), who had argued that popular culture is constituted by the meanings that people make rather than those identifiable within texts. For Fiske, popular culture is a site of **semiotic** warfare and of popular tactics deployed to evade or resist the meanings produced and inscribed in commodities by producers. McGuigan accuses Fiske of a retreat from critical thinking and an abandonment of any form of political economy, leading to the acceptance of the free market and consumer capitalism. Ang has countered that recognition of the plural meanings that audiences produce is not an abandonment of the need to explore media institutions or texts but the sign of a new problematic, namely the need to inquire about 'the way in which cultural contradiction, inconsistency and incoherence pervade contemporary, postmodern culture' (Ang, 1996: 11).

A multiperspectival approach

McGuigan asks cultural studies to engage more thoroughly with the political economy of culture, that is, with questions of ownership, institutions, control and power, exploring the ways in which the moment of production inscribes itself in the range and meanings of cultural products. He argues for a multiperspectival approach which interrogates the relationships between political economy, representations, texts and audiences alongside an engagement with cultural policy. Also supportive of a multiperspectival approach, Kellner (1997) recommends political economy to textual cultural studies as able to:

- show how cultural production takes place within specific historical, political and economic relations which structure textual meanings;
- highlight the way capitalist societies are organized according to a dominant mode of production centred on **commodification** and the pursuit of profit;
- call attention to the fact that culture is produced within vectors of domination and subordination;
- illuminate the limits and range of political and ideological discourses and texts possible at specific historical conjunctures.

Thus, a textual analysis of Madonna (see Chapter 8) concentrating on her sign value and audience responses while engaging with questions of ideology and resistance would need to take account of the fact that she has 'deployed some of the most proficient production and marketing teams in the history of popular music' (Kellner, 1997: 118). Since this argument does not in itself displace the analysis of Madonna as a **sign**, Kellner suggests that the divide between cultural studies (as textual studies) and political economy is a false one.

The circuit of culture

While the call to political economy may be a timely reminder of its uses (and abuses), the case is overstated, for political economy has never really disappeared from cultural studies. A series of recent cultural studies texts involving Stuart Hall have put the notion of a multiperspectival approach based on the 'circuit of culture' at their core. The argument is that each of the moments of the circuit – representation, regulation, consumption, production and identity – is articulated together and productive of meanings which are necessary for the continuation of the circuit but insufficient to determine the form and content of other instances.

The challenge is to grasp just how the moment of production inscribes itself in representation in each case without assuming that it can be 'read-off' from economic relations. We would also be interested in the reverse case, namely how culture or representation is implicated in the forms and modes of organization that production takes, that is, how the economic is cultural. Since this model is a development of Hall's earlier encoding–decoding model published in 1981, and has been operative within cultural studies for a long time, much of the cultural studies versus political economy debate appears overstated.

If the debate about textual politics and political economy is a contemporary version of an old debate, which is what I take it to be, then the call for a turn to cultural policy is a more radical and recent event for cultural studies. Cultural studies has not taken cultural policy or the possibility of working with state or commercial organizations very seriously. Indeed it has often seemed contemptuous of such an idea. Cultural studies has held cultural politics to be constituted by the long-haul building of anti-hegemonic coalitions outside of mainstream institutions (which have been regarded as somewhat corrupting). However, during the 1980s and 1990s a significant discussion about **cultural policy** was prompted by the work of Tony Bennett (1998).

THE CULTURAL POLICY DEBATE

Bennett (1992) argues that the textual politics with which cultural studies has been engaged ignores the institutional dimensions of cultural power. He urges cultural studies to adopt a more pragmatic approach, to work with cultural producers and to 'put policy into cultural studies'. For Bennett, cultural politics centres on *policy* formulation and enactment within the institutions which produce and administer the form and content of cultural products. This would include organizations like the Arts Council in the UK, museums, government departments of education/arts/culture/media/sport, etc., schools, institutions of higher education, theatre administration, television organizations (public and commercial), record companies and advertising agencies.

Redirecting the cultural studies project

Bennett is critical of cultural studies for displacing its politics onto the level of signification and text. This, he argues, has been at the expense of a material politics of the institutions and organizations which produce and distribute cultural texts. For Bennett, cultural studies has been too much concerned with consciousness and the ideological struggle as conceived through Gramsci and not enough with the material technologies of power and of cultural policy. He argues that cultural studies needs to:

- understand itself as located in the higher education system as an arm of government;
- conceptualize culture as constituting 'a particular field of government' and social regulation;
- identify the different 'regions' of culture and their managerial operations;
- study the different technologies of power and forms of politics associated with different domains of cultural practice;
- accord cultural policy a more central place in its cosmology;
- work with other 'governmental' organizations of culture to develop policy and modes of strategic intervention, since 'we are not discussing the relations between two separate realms (critique and the state) but, rather, the articulations between two branches of government, each of which is deeply involved in the management of culture' (Bennett, 1998: 6).

Governmentality

Bennett's arguments depend on a specific notion of culture and **governmentality** drawn from an interpretation (for some, contentious) of Foucault.

By this word [governmentality] I mean three things:

1 The ensemble formed by the institutions, procedures, analyses and reflections, the calculations and tactics that allow the exercise of this very specific albeit complex form of power, which has as its target population, as its principal form of knowledge political economy, and as its essential technical means apparatuses of security.
2 The tendency which, over a long period and throughout the West, has steadily led towards the pre-eminence over all other forms (sovereignty, discipline, etc.) of this type of power which may be termed government, resulting, on the one hand, in the formation of a whole series of specific governmental apparatuses, and, on the other, in the development of a whole complex of *savoirs*.
3 The process, or rather the result of the process, through which the state of justice of the Middle Ages, transformed into the administrative state during the fifteenth and sixteenth centuries, gradually becomes 'governmentalized'. (Foucault, 1991: 102–3)

While governmentality is associated with the state, it is better understood in the broader sense of regulation throughout the social order, or, to put it in Foucault's preferred manner, the 'policing' of societies by which a population becomes subject to bureaucratic regimes and modes of discipline. Governmentality is a growing aspect of the micro-capillary character of power, the multiplicity of force relations which are not centralized but dispersed. This includes modes of regulation which operate through medicine, education, social reform, demography and criminology by which a population can be categorized and ordered into manageable groups. The state is held to be a more or less contingent collection of sometimes conflicting institutions and apparatuses with the 'bureau' an autonomous 'technology for living' organized around its own faculties and possessing its own modes of conducts of life.

Culture and power

The concept of governmentality stresses that processes of social regulation do not so much stand over and against the individual but are constitutive of self-reflective modes of conduct, ethical competencies and social movements. Culture in this reading is understandable in terms of governmentality since

> the relations of culture and power which most typically characterize modern societies are best understood in the light of the respects in which the field of culture is now increasingly governmentally organized and constructed. (Bennett, 1998: 61)

For Bennett, culture is caught up in, and functions as a part of, cultural technologies which organize and shape social life and human conduct. A cultural technology is part of the 'machinery' of institutional and organizational structures that produce particular configurations of **power/knowledge**. Culture is a matter not just of representations and consciousness but of institutional practices, administrative routines and spatial arrangements.

The domains of culture and governmentality to which Bennett most often refers are education and museums. For example, he argues that cultural studies must be understood as a part of the expansion of higher education and the provision of a curriculum addressing students who entered it without the traditional resources of 'high culture'. This widening of the curriculum was, argues Bennett, already well underway in schools long before cultural studies emerged. Thus, cultural studies is an arm of reforming and regulatory government.

Museums are explored for their self-conscious deployment of culture's alleged 'civilizing effects' to regulate working-class subjectivities and modes of behaviour. In particular, museums have aimed to produce self-regulating persons (notably men) who were to become better citizens through the formation and policing of 'new' subjectivities. In this sense, culture is 'a reformer's science'.

Foucault or Gramsci?

Bennett compares his Foucauldian conceptualization of culture focused on governmentality with a Gramscian version of cultural studies centred on the concepts of ideology, consciousness and the winning of consent (i.e. a version of culture centred on meaning and representations). Revisionist Gramscian cultural studies, 'the politics of articulation', is, argues Bennett, overtly and overly discursive, with struggle operating primarily at the level of language and ideology. In contrast, for Bennett's Foucault, the order of relations between practices (which are contingently established) must be charted through a dense materialism.

In Gramscian theory, argues Bennett, the conceptualization of descending flows of ideology (hegemony) leads to the attempt to organize generalized struggles of the subordinate against a single source of power, that is, counter-hegemonic struggles. By contrast, for Foucault, there is no single originatory source of power. Rather, power is held to be dispersed and conflict is specific to a 'region' of culture and the particular technologies pertaining to it.

For Bennett, the Gramscian tradition has accorded little attention to the specificities of cultural institutions, technologies and apparatuses, concentrating instead on textual analysis and the personal rewards of a certain 'ethical style' which unduly celebrates notions of marginality. By contrast, in Bennett's reading, Foucault demands a 'politics of detail' in order to be effective in relation to governmental technologies, cultural policy and cultural technologies.

Gramscian cultural studies hankers after the 'organic intellectual' with his/her pivotal role in the intellectual armoury and political co-ordination of social movements into a historic counter-hegemonic bloc. For Bennett, such a vision is an impossibility. The primary location of cultural studies in the higher education system means that intellectuals within its domain are an arm of governmentality. Thus, they are not able to function as organic intellectuals whose knowledge is required to have grown directly out of and in conjunction with specific communities and movements. At best, cultural studies can provide 'the development of forms of work – of cultural analysis and pedagogy – that could contribute to the development of the political and policy agendas associated with the work of organic intellectuals' (Bennett, 1998: 33).

For Bennett, the concept of governmentality leads intellectuals to focus on the specifics of cultural practices and technologies. Although he concedes that such work points in many directions, the privileged route for Bennett is 'towards the bureau', for it is within the machinery of government, he argues, that the work of organic intellectuals is carried out. Rather than bypass existing forms of social administration, cultural studies is urged to answer the bureaucrat's question, 'What can you do for us?' Cultural studies might usefully envisage its role as the 'training of cultural technicians' who are less committed to cultural critique and alterations in consciousness and more inclined to 'modifying the functions of culture by means of technical adjustments to its governmental deployment' (Bennett, 1992: 406).

Policy and the problem of values

Bennett's work offers a *prima facie* case for taking the pragmatic politics of cultural organizations seriously. However, even if we are convinced by the need for an engagement with cultural policy, questions remain unanswered, namely:

- What political and social values will guide our policy work?
- What as a consequence are the 'targets' we are trying to achieve?

Bennett might argue that the latter is context- and technology-specific, that is, what is aimed for depends on the particular kind of cultural technology and organization under consideration. Nevertheless, when **truth** is a pragmatic question of what is taken to 'count as truth' (as Bennett says it is), then truths and actions are formed within and through social *values*. The problem is that Bennett does not make clear what values his cultural policy would pursue. Is he committed to the values of equality, justice, liberty, solidarity, etc.? Is he adopting a liberal democratic strategy or is he, like Hall, Laclau and Mouffe, committed to the politics of difference and 'radical democracy'?

Shifting the command metaphors of cultural studies

Another exponent of the cultural policy approach, Stuart Cunningham (1992a, 1992b, 1993), has been more forthright about his commitment to social democracy and the values of liberty, equality and solidarity as the motor of a new reformism. He advances a 'social democratic view of citizenship and the trainings necessary to activate and motivate it' (Cunningham,

1993: 134). This would involve a shift in the 'command metaphors' of cultural studies

> away from the rhetorics of resistance, oppositionalism and anti-commercialism on the one hand, and populism on the other, towards those of access, equity, empowerment and the divination of opportunities to exercise appropriate cultural leadership. (Cunningham, 1993: 137–8)

Cunningham (1992b) argues that an increased policy sensitivity in cultural studies would lead to:

- greater attention being paid to the modes of interaction between cultural politics and *institutional* politics, for example to feminist social reform initiated within government agencies and bureaucracies;
- a reconstructed *textual* analysis which could engage with the important policy issues of 'quality', 'excellence', 'diversity', etc., which form a significant aspect of the broadcasting debate in particular;
- *reception* work, which, rather than seeking cultural **authenticity**, would be committed to charting audience tastes with a view to cultural maintenance and a renewed sense of citizenship.

The horizon of the thinkable

Cunningham's work has the merits of being clear about the necessity of cultural studies being normative and in particular his commitment to social democratic citizenship. Nevertheless, one might wish to take issue with the specific values or policy proposals he advances. For example, Cunningham argues that as a matter of cultural policy we should take seriously national content regulations in television advertising in order to boost (Australian) national identity. He speaks as if Australian national identity were a fixed phenomenon which would be boosted by Australian content. However, since there is no essential Australian national identity (Chapter 6), we need to ask about the kind of national identity (if any) we find desirable and what kind of exclusions are enacted by all forms of identity and policy regulation. While we might think it desirable to advance citizenship, this ought not to be on the exclusionary grounds of nationality and ethnicity.

The point is not to dispute Cunningham's concern for policy or the significance of television as an object of policy. Rather, it is to raise again the question of *values* in relation to policy by querying his specific analysis of television and national identity. As Morris (1992) argues in another context, Cunningham makes assumptions about what progressive ends are instead of opening them up

for debate. Under changing socio-cultural contexts we need to
keep reconsidering the values that make a policy orientation
worthwhile. This is the continuing importance of cultural theory
and criticism.

O'Regan (1992a, 1992b) makes a similar point in describing
Bennett and Cunningham's work as 'a pragmatic politics as the
horizon of the thinkable'. For O'Regan, their policy initiative
remains bound within current ways of thinking rather than
letting us challenge and expand our purposes through inventing
'new languages' (Rorty, 1989) or what he calls 'agenda setting
social research'. In short, O'Regan is advocating the role of critical
intellectuals in formulating the value goals of policy, so that, for
example, research on social class may inform and secure policy
aimed at equality and equal opportunity. As he argues:

> Cultural criticism and policy certainly are different, but they are both
> part of the policy process. Rather than berating cultural criticism, it is
> more productive to locate the particular form, direction and nature of
> the criticism and analyse its contribution to policy. The social power of
> the cultural critic may be difficult to mobilize; but such figures may
> shape the public agenda in ways that provide policy with valuable
> resources and arguments. (O'Regan, 1992b: 530–1)

Criticism and policy

Morris (1992) argues that for feminists involved in the academy,
bureaucracies and policy initiatives (praised by Cunningham),
there is always a 'critical outside' of feminism, an unregulated site
from which the actions of professional feminists can be scrutinized
and criticized. This means, she argues, that feminism rarely falls
for the binary logic of criticism *or* policy that has marked the
policy debate.

There is no necessary reason why cultural studies cannot attend
to the important pragmatic calls of policy without relinquishing
the role that 'critical cultural theory' has to play. Similarly, if it
takes politics rather than posturing seriously, then cultural
criticism does need to engage with cultural policy. To this end, I
want to briefly explore a strand of thought which may have a
useful part to play in the debate, that is, the American tradition
of pragmatist philosophy and its current revival in the hands of
Richard Rorty. Since pragmatism is a stream of thought which has
not been strongly represented within cultural studies, though its
influence is growing, readers may take this to be the expression of
a personal predilection.

NEO-PRAGMATISM AND CULTURAL STUDIES

There are many versions of pragmatist philosophy which can be traced through the work of Peirce, James, Dewey and others. West regards the following as the best definition of pragmatism:

Pragmatism could be characterized as the doctrine that all problems are at bottom problems of conduct, that all judgements are, implicitly, judgements of value, and that, as there can be ultimately no valid distinction of theoretical and practical, so there can be no final separation of questions of truth of any kind from questions of the justifiable ends of action. (C.I. Lewis, cited West, 1993: 109)

Pragmatism and cultural studies

Pragmatism shares with the poststructuralist strand of a cultural studies an anti-foundationalist, anti-representationlist, anti-realist view of truth. However, this is combined with a commitment to pragmatic social reform. Pragmatism suggests that the struggle for social change is a question of language/text *and* of material practice/policy action.

Like cultural studies, pragmatism attempts to render contingent that which appears 'natural', seeking after a 'better' world. However, unlike the revolutionary rhetoric of the 'cultural left', pragmatism weds itself to the need for practical political change within the current socio-economic system. Unlike much of the cultural left, but in common with cultural policy arguments, pragmatism regards liberal democracies as the best kind of system the world has yet come up with, requiring us to work within them even as they are urged to do better. In this sense, pragmatism has a 'tragic' view of life for it does not share the utopian push of Marxism. In contrast, it favours a trial-and-error experimentalism which seeks after new ways of doing things which we can describe as 'better' measured against our values.

As with postmodern cultural studies, pragmatism is against 'grand theory', agreeing with Lyotard's 'incredulity towards meta-narratives'. Pragmatists have a radically contingent view of the world where truth ends with social practice. However, this does not mean that all theory is to be jettisoned; rather, local theory becomes a way of redescribing the world in normative ways. In other words, it envisages possible new and better ways of doing things.

Since pragmatism sees the universe as always 'in the making', so the future has ethical significance. We can, it is argued, make a difference and create new better futures. In this sense, pragmatism insists on the irreducibility of human **agency** even as it recognizes the causal stories of the past. Agency is to be understood as the socially constructed capacity to act and is not to be confused with a self-originating transcendental subject. We are not constituted by an inner core which possess attitudes, beliefs and the capacity to act. We *are* a network of attitudes, beliefs, etc., which does act. Pragmatism shares with poststructuralist post-Marxist cultural studies the idea that social and cultural change is a matter of 'politics without guarantees'. Without Marxism's 'laws of history', politics is centred on ethical commitment and practical action.

Richard Rorty: politics without foundations

Rorty (1980, 1989, 1991a, 1991b) has consistently spelled out a philosophy which combines an anti-representationalist view of language with an anti-foundational politics.

ANTI-REPRESENTATIONALISM

Anti-representationalism means that the relationship between language and the rest of the material universe is one of causality not of adequacy of representation or expression. That is, we can usefully try to explain how human organisms come to act or speak in particular ways but we cannot usefully see language as representing the world in ways which more or less correspond to the material world. For Rorty, 'no linguistic items represent *any* non-linguistic items' (Rorty, 1991a: 2). That is, no chunks of language line up with or correspond to chunks of reality. Above all, there is no Archimedean vantage point from which one could verify the 'truth' of any correspondence between the world and language.

ANTI-FOUNDATIONALISM

Anti-foundationalism means that we cannot found or justify our actions or beliefs in any universal truths. We can describe this or that discourse, chunk of language, as being more or less useful and as having more or less desirable consequences. However, we cannot claim it to be true in the sense of correspondence with an independent reality. Further, human history has no *telos*, or inevitable historical point to which it is unfolding. Rather, human 'development' is the outcome of numerous acts of chance and environmental adaptation which make the 'direction' of human evolution contingent. 'Progress' or 'purpose' can only be given meaning as a *retrospectively* told story.

CONTINGENCY, IRONY, SOLIDARITY

Rorty argues that we do not require universal foundations to pursue a pragmatic improvement of the human condition on the basis of the values of our own tradition. Indeed, we cannot escape values any more than we can ground them in metaphysics, so that an historically and culturally specific value-based politics is an inevitable and inescapable condition of human existence.

For Rorty (1989), the contingency of language and the **irony** which follows from this (irony here means holding to beliefs and attitudes which one knows are contingent and could be otherwise, i.e. they have no universal foundations) lead us to ask about what kind of human being we want to be (for no transcendental truth and no transcendental God can answer this question for us). This includes questions about us as individuals – who we want to be – and questions about our relations to fellow human beings – how shall we treat others? For Rorty, these are pragmatic questions requiring political-value responses. They are not metaphysical or epistemological issues.

TRUTH AS SOCIAL COMMENDATION

Rorty argues that most of the beliefs that we hold to be 'true' are indeed 'true'. However, truth is not an **epistemological** statement about correspondence between language and reality but a consensual term referring to degrees of agreement and co-ordination of habits of action. To say that something is not necessarily true is to suggest that someone has come up with a better way of describing things, where 'better' refers to a value judgement about the consequences of describing the world in this way (including its predictive power).

It follows that since truth, knowledge and understanding can only be from within particular **language-games**, then all truth is the consequence of particular kinds of **acculturalization**. Or, to paraphrase William James, 'Truth is what it is good for us to believe.' This is best understood not as a narrow loyalty to a particular socio-political culture but as an inescapable cultural condition. As Rorty puts it:

> no description of how things are from a God's-eye-view, no skyhook provided by some contemporary or yet-to-be developed science, is going to free us from the contingency of having been acculturated as we were. Our acculturation is what makes certain options live, or momentous, or forced, while leaving others dead, or trivial, or optional. We can only hope to transcend our acculturation if our culture contains (or, thanks to disruptions from outside or internal revolt, comes to contain) splits

which supply toeholds for new initiatives. . . . So our best chance for transcending our acculturation is to be brought up in a culture which prides itself on not being monolithic-on its tolerance for a plurality of subcultures and its willingness to listen to neighbouring cultures. (Rorty, 1991a: 13–14)

I take Rorty to be arguing that it is desirable to open ourselves up to as many possible descriptions and redescriptions of the world as possible. Knowledge is a matter not of getting a true or objective picture of reality but of learning how best to cope with the world. We produce various descriptions of the world and use those which seem best suited to our purposes. We have a multiplicity of vocabularies because we have a multiplicity of purposes. In this view, continued redescription of our world and the playing off of discourses against each other is a pragmatically desirable thing to do because of the following:

- It offers the possibility of an enlargement of the self and the improvement of the human condition through comparison between different actual practices.
- '[O]ur minds gradually [grow] larger and stronger and more interesting by the addition of new options – new candidates for belief and desire, phrased in new vocabularies' (Rorty, 1991a: 14).
- We are encouraged to listen to the voices of others who may be suffering, where the avoidance of suffering is taken to be the paramount political virtue.

FORGING NEW LANGUAGES

Acceptance of the legitimacy of a range of truth claims entails a commitment to the politics of democratic cultural pluralism. Individual **identity projects** and the cultural politics of collectivities require us to forge new languages, new ways of describing ourselves, which recast our place in the world. The struggle to have new languages accepted in the wider society is the realm of cultural politics. For example, Rorty argues that feminism represents the redescription of women as subjects. The critical point of his argument is that

injustices may not be perceived as injustices, even by those who suffer them, until somebody invents a previously unplayed role. Only if somebody has a dream, a voice, and a voice to describe the dream, does what looked liked nature begin to look like culture, what looked liked fate begin to look like a moral abomination. For until then only the language of the oppressor is available, and most oppressors have had the wit to teach the oppressed a language in which the oppressed will sound crazy – *even to themselves* – if they describe themselves as oppressed. (Rorty, 1995: 126)

Thus, the language of feminism brings oppression 'into view' and expands the logical space for moral and political deliberation. In this sense, feminism (and all forms of identity politics) does not need essentialism or foundationalism. What is required are 'new languages' in which the claims of women do not sound crazy but come to be accepted as 'true' (in the sense of a social commendation). Feminism does not involve less distorted perception, but is a language with consequences which serve particular purposes and values. The emergence of such a language is not the discovery of universal truth in opposition to ideology but is part of an evolutionary struggle which has no pre-determined destiny.

PROPHETIC PRAGMATISM

Rorty regards feminism as fashioning 'women's experience' by creating a language rather than finding what it is to be a woman or 'unmasking' truth and injustice. As such, feminism is a form of *prophetic pragmatism* which imagines, and seeks to bring into being, an alternative form of community. Feminism forges a moral identity for women as women by gaining semantic authority over themselves and not by assuming that there is a universal essential identity for women waiting to be found. In this sense, Rorty, along with Foucault, breaks with a notion of ideology which is contrasted with truth.

Fraser (1995a) concurs with Rorty's pragmatism but argues that he locates the redescriptions involved exclusively in individual women. In contrast, she suggests that such redescriptions are to be seen as a part of a *collective* feminist politics. Such a politics must involve argument and contestation about which new descriptions will count and which women will be empowered. Fraser links feminism with the best of the democratic tradition and to the creation of a 'feminist counter-sphere' of collective debate and practice.

West (1993), like Fraser a cultural critic sympathetic to pragmatism, worries about Rorty's failure to analyse *power* and to deploy sociological kinds of explanations to identify the realistic and pragmatic collective routes for social change. This is perhaps the major criticism of Rortian pragmatism with West locating his analysis at the level of de-mythologization rather than de-mystification. Foucauldians will share this concern with the place of power in social life.

PRIVATE IDENTITIES AND PUBLIC POLITICS

The distinction between the 'public' and the 'private' is a culturally contingent one. Nevertheless, if one accepts that there are benefits from maintaining this distinction for practical purposes, then one may argue for the kind of society which will 'make it easy as possible for people to achieve their wildly different private ends without hurting each other' (Rorty, 1991b: 196).

Since private projects are set within larger social and historical narratives which give coherence to individual lives, it is consistent to forge social institutions which best allow for different and diverse private identity projects to prosper. While cultural politics must accept that we all have our private and contingent projects to pursue (that we have a right to 'make ourselves' as we see fit and to pursue our own 'originality'), these projects depend on the development of a *collective* cultural space and politics since, as Bauman argues, 'Survival in the world of contingency and diversity is possible only if each difference recognizes another difference as the necessary condition of the preservation of its own' (Bauman, 1991: 256). This suggests the need for dialogue and underpins the procedural arguments for a diverse and plural public sphere of citizens, where citizenship as a form of identity provides the grounds for a shared polity. That is, our best chance of pursuing a private identity project may be to live in a culture which prides itself on being heterogeneous.

Rorty advocates both a politics of 'new languages' and political action on the level of institutions and policy. The 'Left', Rorty argues, is, or should be, 'the party of hope' (Rorty, 1998: 14) in the struggle for social justice. However, 'In so far as the Left becomes spectorial and retrospective, it ceases to be a Left' (Rorty, 1998: 14). It is Rorty's contention that to a major extent the cultural left has become a spectator left. That it is more interested in theorizing than in the practical politics of material change. The cultural left, he suggests, prefers knowledge to hope. It imagines that it can somehow 'get it right' on the level of theory and has given up on the practical task of making democratic institutions once again serve social justice. This is not to discount the fact that:

> This cultural Left has extraordinary success. In addition to being centers of genuinely original scholarship, the new academic programs have done what they were, semi-consciously, designed to do: they have decreased the amount of sadism in our country. (Rorty, 1998: 80–1)

Consequently, while there has been little legislative change for social justice, 'the change in the way we treat one another has been enormous' (Rorty, 1998: 81). For example, 'It is still easy to be humiliated for being a women in America, but such humiliation is not so frequent as it was thirty years ago' (Rorty, 1998: 81–2). However, the contemporary left remains more interested in cultural power than economic, social and political power. Further, it has given up on practical reform in favour of an abstract and wholly theoretical revolutionary desire to overturn the 'system'.

Rorty concurs with the anti-representionalism of Nietzsche, Foucault and Derrida, the most influential philosophers within cultural studies. He also concurs with their criticisms of enlightenment rationalism. However, for Rorty, these criticisms are compatible with reformism and pragmatic social experimentalism. Further, while Derrida's declarations of impossibility, undecidability, unrepresentability, are illuminating philosophical insights (Rorty has said Derrida is the most interesting living philosopher writing today) which are of use to us in our private quests, in the public sphere, 'the infinite and the unrepresentable are merely nuisances . . . a stumbling-block to effective political organization' (Rorty, 1998: 96–7).

This has much in common with Hall's (1993) argument, referred to earlier in this chapter, that in order to take practical action a temporary closure of meaning is required. For example, feminist politics needs at least momentary agreement about what constitutes a woman and what is in women's interests under particular circumstances.

Anti-representationalism, anti-foundationalism and pragmatism do not of necessity suppport any *particular* political projects, values or strategies. We may thus disagree with some of Rorty's programmatic suggestions. Nevertheless, his pragmatism combines a commitment to the cultural *politics of difference*, that is, language-based redescriptions of the world which expand the realm of democratic cultures, with the need for the public *policy* necessary to maintain it. A cultural politics of representation and a cultural policy orientation need not, within liberal-democratic states, be opposed.

In order to combine policy and cultural politics we may require a kind of 'utopian realism' (Giddens, 1990). Utopian, because it is in the nature of the contemporary human mind to contemplate questions of love, death, life, happiness, and to project possible improved futures. 'Realism', because moral convictions pursued without reference to the sociologically grounded and politically possible may not only fail to achieve positive results by may also be counter-productive.

SUMMARY

In this chapter we have explored a number of different ways in which cultural studies has conceived of cultural politics inside and outside of the academy. Cultural politics was defined as the power to name and represent the world, where language is constitutive of the world and a guide to action. Cultural politics can be conceived of as a series of collective social struggles organized around class, gender, race, sexuality, age, etc., which seeks to redescribe the social in terms of specific values and hoped-for-consequences.

In the course of the chapter we encountered a number of conceptualizations of cultural politics operating within the broad frame of the struggle over and within meaning. For example, we noted the influential 'Gramscian moment' in cultural studies and its revision by Laclau, Mouffe and Hall towards a politics of difference. This involved a move away from class as the central axis of politics, an acceptance of the contingent anti-essential character of social classifications and political alliances, along with a move towards the 'politics of articulation' and 'the politics of representation'.

We noted a number of challenges to the cultural politics of difference, concentrating for the most part on Bennett's call for cultural studies to engage more productively in cultural policy formation and implementation. This argument was based on an interpretation of Foucault's concept of 'governmentality' whereby culture is an arm of government and a 'reformer's science'. At the same time, we noted a sense in which the cultural policy call seemed to downplay the question of values and the need for critical intellectual inquiry. Finally, we briefly explored pragmatism as a philosophy which may offer a route for uniting the politics of difference and representation with cultural policy.

Glossary

The Language-Game of Cultural Studies

Acculturalization: A set of social processes by which we learn how to 'go on' in a culture, including the acquisition of language, values and norms.

Active audience: The capability of audiences to be dynamic creators and producers of meaning rather than being passive receptors of those generated by texts.

Agency: The socially determined capability to act and make a difference.

Anti-essentialism: Words are not held to have referents with essential or universal qualities. Rather, being discursive constructions, categories change their meanings according to time, place and usage. For example, since words do not refer to essences, identity is not a fixed universal 'thing' but a description in language.

Articulation: A temporary unity of discursive elements which do not have to 'go together'. An articulation is the form of the connection that *can* make a unity of two different elements under certain conditions. Articulation suggests expressing/representing and a joining together so that, for example, questions of gender may connect with race but in context-specific and contingent ways.

Authenticity (claims): A claim that a category is genuine, natural, true and pure. For example, that the culture of a place is authentic because uncontaminated by tourism or that a youth culture is pure and uncorrupted by consumer capitalism. Closely related to the notion of essentialism in that authenticity implies immaculate origins.

Bricolage: The rearrangement and juxtaposition of previously unconnected signifying objects to produce new meanings in fresh contexts. A process of re-signification by which cultural signs with established meanings are reorganized into new codes of meaning.

Capitalism: A dynamic and globalizing system of industrial production and exchange based on private property and the pursuit of profit. For Marxism, capitalism is an exploitative order giving rise to social relations of class conflict.

Citizenship: A form of identity by which individuals are granted social rights and obligations within political communities.

Class: A classification of persons into groups based on shared socio-economic conditions. Class is a relational set of inequalities with economic, social, political and ideological dimensions. Marxism has defined class as a relationship to the means of production. Post-Marxists have seen class as a discursively formed collective subject position.

Codes (cultural): A system of representation by which signs and their meanings are arranged by cultural convention to temporarily stabilize significances in particular ways. Traffic light signs are coded in a sequence red (stop), amber (pause) green (go). Objects are commonly gender-coded: washing machine (female), drill (male), cooker (female), car (male).

Commodification: The process associated with capitalism by which objects, qualities and signs are turned into commodities, where a commodity is something whose prime purpose is sale in the marketplace.

Conjunctural (analysis): Analysis which is historically and contextually specific. An exploration of the assemblage, coming together or articulation of particular forces, determinations or logics at specific times and places.

Convergence: Breaking down barriers between technologies and industrial sectors, for example the information superhighway.

Cultural identity: A snapshot of unfolding meanings relating to self-nomination or ascription by others. Cultural identity relates to the nodal points of cultural meaning, most notably class, gender, race, ethnicity, nation and age.

Cultural imperialism: Said to involve the domination of one culture by another. Usually conceived of in terms of the ascendancy of specific nations and/or global consumer capitalism.

Cultural materialism: Concerned to explore how and why meanings are inscribed at the moment of production. Exploration of signification in the context of the means and conditions of production. The connections between cultural practices and political economy.

Cultural policy: Procedures, strategies and tactics which seek to regulate and administer the production and distribution of cultural products and practices. An engagement with the institutions, organizations and management of cultural power.

Cultural politics: Concerned with issues of power in the acts of naming and representation which constitute our cultural maps of meaning. Contestation over the meanings and resources of culture. The writing of new languages by which to describe ourselves in the belief that they will have desirable social consequences.

Cultural studies: An interdisciplinary or post-disciplinary field of inquiry which explores the production and inculcation of maps of meaning. A discursive formation, or regulated way of speaking, concerned with issues of power in the signifying practices of human formations.

Culture: Overlapping maps of criss-crossing discursive meaning which form zones of temporary coherence as shared but always contested significance in a social space. The production and exchange of meanings, or signifying practices, which form that which is distinctive about a way of life.

Deconstruction: To take apart, to undo, in order to seek out and display the assumptions, rhetorical strategies and blind-spots of texts. The dismantling of hierarchical binary oppositions such as reality/appearance, nature/culture, reason/madness, in order to show: (a) that one part of the binary is devalued as inferior; (b) that the binary serves to guarantee truth; and (c) that each part of the binary is implicated in the other.

Diasporas: Dispersed networks of ethnically and culturally related peoples. Concerned with ideas of travel, migration, scattering, displacement, homes and borders. Commonly, but not always, connotes aliens, displaced persons, wanderers, forced and reluctant flight.

Différance: After Derrida, 'difference and deferral'. Meaning is unstable and never complete since the production of meaning is continually deferred and added to by the meanings of other words. The continual supplementarity of meaning, the substitution and adding of meanings through the play of signifiers.

Difference: Non-identical, dissimilar, distinction, division, otherness, variance. Difference as the mechanism for the generation of meaning. Difference is not an essence or attribute of an object but a position or perspective of signification.

Discourse: Language and practice, regulated ways of speaking which define, construct and produce objects of knowledge.

Discursive formation: A pattern of discursive events which refer to, or bring into being, a common object across a number of sites.

Epistemology: Concerned with the source and status of knowledge. The question of truth is an epistemological issue.

Essentialism: Essentialism assumes that words have stable referents. For example, social categories would reflect an essential underlying identity. By this token there would be stable truths to be found and an essence of, for example, femininity. Words refer to fixed essences and thus identities are regarded as a fixed entities.

Ethnicity: A cultural term for boundary formation between groups of people who have been discursively constructed as sharing values, norms, practices, symbols and artefacts and are seen as such by themselves and others. Closely connected to the concept of race.

Ethnography: An empirical and theoretical approach which seeks detailed holistic description and analysis of cultures based on intensive participative fieldwork. Qualitative small-scale and detailed exploration of the norms, values and artefacts of culture as they are connected to the wider social processes of a 'whole way of life'.

Feminism: (a) diverse body of theoretical work; (b) social and political movement. Feminism aims to examine the position of women in society and to further their interests.

Foundationalism: The attempt to give absolute universal grounds or justifications for the truth of knowledge and values.

Gender: The cultural assumptions and practices which govern the social construction of men, women and their social relations. Femininity and masculinity are culturally regulated forms of behaviour regarded as socially appropriate to a given sex. Gender is always a matter of how men and women are represented.

Genealogy: Concerned with derivation and lineage. A Foucauldian usage in cultural studies examines power and the historical continuities and discontinuities of discourses as they are brought into play under specific and irreducible historical conditions.

Genre: A regulated narrative process producing coherence and credibility through patterns of similarity and difference.

Global city: Urban conglomerations acting as command and control points for dispersed sets of economic activities. They are sites of accumulation, distribution and circulation of capital as well as nodal points of information exchange and decision-making processes.

Globalization: Increasing multi-directional economic, social, cultural and political global connections across the world and our awareness of them. The global production of the local and the localization of the global. Associated with the institutions of modernity and time-space compression or the shrinking world.

Glocalization: A term used to express the global production of the local and the localization of the global. The way in which the global is already in the local. The production of the local, that is, what counts as local is a global discourse.

Governmentality: A form of regulation throughout the social order by which a population becomes subject to bureaucratic regimes and modes of discipline. The institutions, procedures, analyses and calculations which form specific governmental apparatuses and forms of knowledge which are constitutive of self-reflective conduct and ethical competencies.

Hegemony: A temporary closure of meaning supportive of the powerful. The process of making, maintaining and reproducing the governing sets of meanings of a given culture. For Gramsci, hegemony implies a situation where an 'historical bloc' of ruling-class factions exercise social authority and leadership over the subordinate classes through a combination of force and, more importantly, consent.

Homology: Synchronic relationship by which social structures, social values and cultural symbols are said to 'fit' together.

Hybridity: The mixing together of different cultural elements to create new meanings and identities. Hybrids destabilize and blur established cultural boundaries in a process of fusion or creolization.

Hyperreality: A reality effect by which the real is produced according to a model. More real than the real. The distinction between the real and a representation collapses or implodes. A simulation or artificial production of real life which executes its own world to constitute reality.

Identification: Contingent and temporary points of attachment or emotional investment which, through fantasy, partially suture or stitch together discourses and psychic forces.

Identity: A temporary stabilization of meaning, a becoming rather than a fixed entity. The suturing or stitching together of the discursive 'outside' with the 'internal' processes of subjectivity. Points of temporary attachment to the subject positions which discursive practices construct for us.

Identity politics: Forging 'new languages' of identity and acting to change social practices, usually through the formation of coalitions where at least some values are shared.

Identity project: The ongoing creation of narratives of self-identity relating to our perceptions of the past, present and hoped-for future.

Ideology: The attempt to fix meanings and world views in support of the powerful. Maps of meaning which, while they purport to be universal truths, are historically specific under-standings which obscure and maintain the power of social groups (e.g. class, gender, race).

Intertextuality: The accumulation and generation of meaning across texts, where all meanings depend on other meanings. The self-conscious citation of one text within another as an expression of enlarged cultural self-consciousness.

Irony: A reflexive understanding of the contingency or lack of foundations of one's own values and culture. Said to be a feature of the postmodern condition. The self-knowledge that what is being said or done has been said and done before. The doubleness of a self-undermining statement by which the already known is spoken in inverted commas.

Language-game: By which the meaning of words are located in their usage in a complex network of relationships between words and not from some essential characteristic or referent. Meaning is contextual and relational. It depends on the relationships between words which have family resemblances and on specific utterances in the context of pragmatic narratives.

Marxism: A body of thought derived from the work of Karl Marx which stresses the determining role of the material conditions of existence and the historical specificity of human affairs. Marxism, which has focused on the development and dynamics of capitalism and class conflict, makes claims to be an emancipatory philosophy of equality.

Modernism: (a) The cultural experience of modernity marked by change, ambiguity, doubt, risk, uncertainty and fragmentation; (b) artistic style marked by aesthetic self-consciousness, montage and the rejection of realism; (c) philosophical position by which certain knowledge is sought after, even though it is recognized as subject to continual and chronic revision.

Modernity: A post-traditional historical period marked by industrialism, capitalism, the nation-state and forms of surveillance.

Multi-media corporations: Media corporations operating across the range of media outlets.

Multiple identities: The assumption of different and potentially contradictory identities at different times and places which do not form a unified coherent self.

Myth: Story or fable which acts as a symbolic guide or map of meaning and significance in the cosmos. After Barthes, the naturalization of the connotative level of meaning.

Narrative: An ordered sequential account or record of events. The form, pattern or structure by which stories are constructed and told.

National identity: A form of imaginative identification with the nation-state as expressed through symbols and discourses. Thus, nations are not only political formations but systems of cultural representation, so that national identity is continually reproduced through discursive action.

New Social Movements: Provisional symbolic and political collectives which stress democratic participation and ethics-based action located outside of the workplace and distinct from class. Encompasses the feminist movement, ecology politics, peace movements, youth movements and the politics of cultural identities.

News values: The values which structure the selection of news items and their presentation.

Patriarchy: The recurrent and systematic domination of men over subordinated women across a range of social institutions and practices. Connotations of the male-headed family, mastery and superiority.

Performativity: Discursive practice which enacts or produces that which it names through citation and reiteration of the norms or conventions of the 'law'. Thus, the discursive production of identities through repetition and recitation of regulated ways of speaking about identity categories (e.g. masculinity).

Phallocentrism: Male-centred discourse. From the perspective of masculinity. The Phallus as symbolic transcendental universal signifier of source, self-origination and unified agency.

Place: Socially constructed site or location in space marked by identification or emotional investment. Bounded manifestations of the production of meaning in space.

Political economy: Concerned with power and the distribution of economic resources. Political economy explores the questions of who owns and controls the institutions of economy, society and culture.

Politics: Concerned with the numerous manifestations and relations of power at all levels of human interaction. Cultural studies has been particularly concerned with the 'politics of representation': the way that power is implicated in the construction, regulation and contestation of cultural classifications through the temporary stabilization of meaning.

Polysemic: Signs carry many potential meanings. Signs do not have transparent and authoritative meaning by dint of reference to an independent object world but depend on actual usage within a dialogic relationship between speaker and listener. The 'multi-accentuality' of signs is the site of attempts by social convention and social struggles to fix meaning.

Popular culture: Widespread and common public texts. The meanings and practices produced by popular audiences. As a political category, the popular is a site of power and the struggle over meaning. The popular transgresses the boundaries of cultural power and exposes the arbitrary character of cultural classification through challenging notions of high/low.

Positionality: Indicating that knowledge and 'voice' are always located in time, space and social power. The who, where, when and why of speaking, judgement and comprehension.

Postcolonialism: Critical theory which explores the discursive condition of post-coloniality, that is, colonial relations and their aftermath. Postcolonial theory explores postcolonial discourses and their subject positions in relation to themes of race, nation, subjectivity, power, subalterns, hybridity and creolization.

Post-Fordism: From mass production of standardized goods for an aggregated market (Fordism) to small-scale customized production for niche markets marked by flexibility of labour and the individualization of consumption patterns. From a production- to consumption-oriented society.

Post-industrial society: A concept suggesting that industrialized societies are witnessing a shift of locus from industrial manufacturing to service industries centred on information technology. Information production and exchange along with the displacement of significance from production to consumption are said to be markers of the post-industrial society.

Post-Marxism: After Marxism, by which Marxism is no longer held to be the primary explanatory narrative of our time. The superseding of Marxism in cultural studies through the selective retention of that which is held to be valuable in it.

Postmodernism: (a) Cultural style marked by intertextuality, irony, pastiche, genre blurring and bricolage; (b) philosophical movement which rejects 'grand narratives' (i.e. universal explanations of human history and activity) in favour of irony and local knowledges.

Post-modernity: (a) An historical period after modernity marked by the centrality of consumption in a post-industrial context; (b) a cultural sensibility which rejects 'grand narratives' in favour of local truths within specific language-games.

Poststructuralism: 'After structuralism' involving both critique and absorption. Poststructuralism absorbs structuralisms, stress on the relational character of language and the production of significance through difference. Poststructuralism rejects the idea of a stable structure of binary pairs; rather, meaning is always deferred, in process and intertextual. Poststructuralism rejects the search for origins, stable meaning, universal truth and the 'direction' of history.

Power: Commonly thought of in terms of a force by which individuals or groups are able to achieve their aims or interests against the will of others. Power here is constraining (power over) and a zero-sum model (you have it or you do not) organized into binary power blocs. Cultural studies has, after Foucault, stressed that power is also productive and enabling (power to), that power circulates through all levels of society and all social relationships.

Power/Knowledge: After Foucault, knowledge is not neutral but always implicated in questions of social power. Power and knowledge are mutually constitutive.

Psychoanalysis: Body of thought and therapeutic practice developed from the work of Freud which argues that the human subject is divided into the ego, superego and unconscious. Psychoanalysis within cultural studies has been deployed to explore the construction and formation of sexed subjectivity.

Public sphere: A space for democratic public debate and argument which mediates between civil society and the state, in which the public organizes itself, and in which 'public opinion' is formed.

Race: A signifier indicating categories of people based on alleged biological characteristics, including skin pigmentation. A 'racialized group' would be one identified and subordinated on the grounds of race as a discursive construct.

Realism: An epistemological claim that the truth is identifiable as that which corresponds to or pictures the real. A set of aesthetic conventions by which texts create 'reality effects' and purport to represent the real.

Reductionism: By which one category or phenomenon is likened to and explained solely in terms of another category or phenomenon. In particular, cultural studies has argued against economic reductionism, by which cultural texts are accounted for in terms of political economy.

Reflexivity: Self-monitoring and the use of knowledge about social life as a constitutive element of it. Discourse about experience and revision of social activity in the light of new knowledge.

Representation: By which signifying practices appear to stand for or depict another object or practice in the 'real' world. Better described as a 'representational effect' since signs do not stand for or reflect objects in a direct 'mirroring' mode. Representations are constitutive of culture, meaning and knowledge.

Resistance: A category of normative judgement about acts. Resistance issues from relationships of power and subordination in the form of challenges to and negotiations of the ascendant order. Resistance is relational and conjunctural.

Self-identity: The way we think about ourselves and construct unifying narratives of the self.

Semiotics: The study (or 'science') of signs and signification.

Sex: Sex has been taken to refer to the biology of the body, while gender concerns the cultural assumptions and practices which govern the social construction of men and women. Butler holds that sex and gender can both be taken to be discursive-performative social constructions.

Signification: The processes of generating meaning through a system of signs (signifying system).

Signifieds: Concepts, ideas, sense, significance, meaning.

Signifiers: The form or medium of signs, for example a sound, an image, the marks that form a word on the page.

Signifying practices: Meaning-producing activities. The production and exchange of signs generating significance, that is, meaning, sense and importance.

Signs: Marks and noises which generate or carry meaning through their relationship with other signs. Signs stand in for or represent concepts.

Simulacrum: Imitation or copy without an original or referent. The simulation becomes more real than the real, the reality of simulation is the measure of the real.

Social: Of or in society, where society is held to be the organization of human association and relationships through rule-governed interactions. Here, the social is held to be an autonomous sphere of activity. However, many cultural studies theorists hold the 'social' to have no proper object of reference, being a sign constituted through a series of discursive differences. For them, the social is not an object but a field of contestation in which multiple descriptions of self and others compete for ascendancy.

Social formation: The social is conceived of as a concrete historically produced complex assemblage composed of different practices (ideological, political, economic). Levels of practice, each of which has its own specificity, are articulated together in particular conjunctures which have no necessary or automatic correspondence or relationship to each other.

Social identity: Social expectations, normative rights and obligations ascribed to individuals. The notion of what it is to be an individual is social in character and identity is formed from social and cultural resources, notably language.

Space: Space is defined by the relationship between at least two particles. Social space is a dynamic, multitudinous and changing social construction constituted in and through social relations of power.

Stereotype: Vivid but simple representations which reduce persons to a set of exaggerated, usually negative, character traits. A form of representation which essentializes others through the operation of power.

Strategic essentialism: Acting 'as if' identities were stable for specific political reasons, for example, accepting the category of 'woman' to be a stable unity for the purposes of mobilising women in feminist political action.

Structuralism: Body of thought (derived from the study of language) concerned with the structures of language which allow linguistic performance to be possible. A structuralist understanding of culture is concerned with 'systems of relations' of an underlying structure forming the grammar which makes meaning possible (rather than actual performance in its infinite variations).

Structure: Regularities or stable patterns. The rules and conventions which organize language (*langue*). Recurrent organization and patterned arrangements of human relationships (social structure).

Style: A signifying practice involving the organization of objects in conjunction with activities and attitudes through active bricolage to signify difference and identity. Associated with youth subcultures and the display of codes of meaning through the transformation of commodities as cultural signs.

Subculture: Groups of persons so labelled who share distinct values and norms which are held to be at variance with dominant or mainstream society. Subcultures offer maps of meaning which make the world intelligible to its members.

Subjectivity: The condition and processes of being a person or self. For cultural studies, subjectivity is often regarded, after Foucault, as an 'effect' of discourse because subjectivity is constituted by the subject positions which discourse obliges us to take up. The characteristics of agency and identity which discursive subject positions enable for a speaking subject.

Subject positions: Empty spaces or functions in discourse from which the world makes sense. The speaking subject is dependent on the prior existence of discursive positions. Discourse constitutes the 'I' through the processes of signification.

Surveillance: The monitoring and collection of information about subject populations with an eye to the supervision and regulation of activities.

Symbolic: Where one item stands in for or represents another. The symbolic order is regulated and patterned forms of significance or meaning constituted by the relations of difference between signs.

Synergy: The bringing together of previously separate activities or moments in the processes of production and exchange to produce higher profits. Manifested in the formation of multinational multi-media corporations.

Text: Everyday usage of the term refers to writing in its various forms so that books and magazines are texts. However, it is an axiom of cultural studies that a text is anything that generates meaning through signifying practices. Hence, dress, television programmes, images, sporting events, pop stars, etc. can all be read as texts.

Theory: Narratives which seek to distinguish and account for the general features which describe, define and explain persistently perceived occurrences. A tool, instrument or logic for intervening in the world through the mechanisms of description, definition, prediction and control. Theory construction is a self-reflexive discursive endeavour which seeks to interpret and intervene in the world.

Truth: Common sense, and realist epistemology, understands truth to be that which corresponds to or pictures the real in an objective way. Constructionism, of which cultural studies is a manifestation, argues that truth is a social creation. Cultural studies speaks of 'regimes of truth', a Foucauldian term meaning that which comes to count as truth through the operation of power. For Rortian pragmatism, truth is a social commendation suggesting a consensual term of approval inseparable from values.

Under erasure: Derridean term which forms part of the vocabulary of deconstructionism. To place a word under erasure is to indicate that a word is inaccurate or mistaken but remains one which we cannot escape using. This suggests the undecidablity of metaphysical binary oppositions.

References

Abercrombie, N., Hill, S. and Turner, B. (1980) *The Dominant Ideology Thesis*. London: Allen & Unwin.

Abercrombie, N., Lash, S. and Longhurst, B. (1992) 'Popular Representation: Recasting Realism' in S. Lash and J. Friedman (eds) *Modernity and Identity*. Oxford: Blackwell.

Adorno, T. (1941) 'On Popular Music', *Studies in Philosophy and Social Science*, IX (1).

Adorno, T. (1977) 'Commitment' in E. Bloch (ed.) *Aesthetics and Politics*. London; New Left Books.

Aglietta, M. (1979) *A Theory of Capitalist Regulation: The US Experience*. London: Verso.

Alasuutari, P. (1995) *Researching Culture: Qualitative Method and Cultural Studies*. London: Sage.

Alcoff, L. (1989) 'Cultural Feminism versus Post-Structuralism: The Identity Crisis in Feminist Theory' in M. Malson, J. O'Barr, S. Westphal-Wihl and M. Wyer (eds) *Feminist Theory in Practice and Process*. Chicago: University of Chicago Press.

Allen, J. (1992) 'Post-Industrialism and Post-Fordism' in S. Hall, D. Held and T. McGrew (eds) *Modernity and its Futures*. Cambridge: Polity Press.

Allen, R. (1985) *Speaking of Soap Operas*. Chapel Hill, NC: University of North Carolina Press.

Allen, R. (ed.) (1995) *To Be Continued . . . Soap Opera around the World*. London and New York: Routledge.

Althusser, L. (1969) *For Marx*. London: Allen Lane.

Althusser, L. (1971) *Lenin and Philosophy and Other Essays*. London: New Left Books.

Anderson, B. (1983) *Imagined Communities: Reflections on the Origins and Spread of Nationalism*. London: Verso.

Ang, I. (1985) *Watching Dallas: Soap Opera and the Melodramatic Imagination*. London: Metheun.

Ang, I. (1996) *Living Room Wars*. London and New York: Routledge.

Ang, I. and Stratton, J. (1996) 'On the Impossibility of a Global Cultural Studies: "British" Cultural Studies in an International Frame' in D. Morley and D.-K. Chen (eds) *Stuart Hall*. London: Routledge.

Appadurai, A. (1993) 'Disjuncture and Difference in the Global Cultural Economy' in P. Williams and L. Chrisman (eds) *Colonial Discourse and Post-Colonial Theory*. Hemel Hempstead: Harvester Wheatsheaf.

Appiah, K. (1995) 'African Identity' in L. Nicholson and S. Seidman (eds) *Social Postmodernism*. Cambridge: Cambridge University Press.

Arnold, M. (1960) *Culture and Anarchy*. Cambridge: Cambridge University Press.

Ashcroft, B., Griffiths, G. and Tiffin, H. (1989) *The Empire Writes Back*. London and New York: Routledge.

Bahia, K. (1997) 'An Analysis of the Representation of Femininity in Popular Hindi Film of the 1980s and 1990s'. Unpublished dissertation, University of Wolverhampton.

Bakhtin, M. (1984) *Rabelais and his World*. Bloomington, IN: University of Indiana Press.

Ballard, R. (ed.) (1994) *Desh Pardesh: The South Asian Presence in Britain*. London: Hurst & Co.

Barker, C. (1997a) *Global Television: An Introduction*. Oxford: Blackwell.

Barker, C. (1997b) 'Television and the Reflexive Project of the Self: Soaps, Teenage Talk and Hybrid Identities', *British Journal of Sociology*, 44 (4).

Barker, C. (1998) '"Cindy's a Slut": Moral Identities and Moral Responsibility in the "Soap Talk" of British Asian Girls', *Sociology*, 32 (1).

Barker, C. (1999) *Television, Globalization and Cultural Identities*. Milton Keynes: Open University Press.

Barker, C. and Andre, J. (1996) 'Did You See? Soaps, Teenage Talk and Gendered Identity', *Young: Nordic Journal of Youth Research*, 4 (4).

Barker, M. (1982) *The New Racism*. London: Junction Books.

Barrett, M. (1991) *The Politics of Truth: From Marx to Foucault*. Stanford, CA: Stanford University Press.

Barth, F. (1969) *Ethnic Groups and Boundaries*. London: Allen & Unwin.

Barthes, R. (1967) *The Elements of Semiology*. London: Cape.

Barthes, R. (1972) *Mythologies*. London: Cape.

Barthes, R. (1977) *Image, Music, Text*. Glasgow: Fontana.

Baudelaire, C. (1964) *The Painter of Modern Life and Other Essays*. Oxford: Phaidon Press.

Baudrillard, J. (1983a) *Simulations*. New York: Semiotext(e).

Baudrillard, J. (1983b) *In the Shadow of the Silent Majorities*. New York: Semiotext(e).

Baudrillard, J. (1988) *America*. London: Verso.

Bauman, Z. (1991) *Modernity and Ambivalence*. Cambridge: Polity Press.

Beck, U., Giddens, A. and Lash, S. (1995) *Reflexive Modernization*. Cambridge: Polity Press.

Bell, D. (1973) *The Coming of the Post-Industrial Society*. New York: Basic Books.

Bennett, R. (1990) *Decentralization, Local Governments and Markets*. Oxford: Clarendon Press.

Bennett, T. (1992) 'Putting Policy into Cultural Studies' in L. Grossberg, C. Nelson and P. Treichler (eds) *Cultural Studies*. London and New York: Routledge.

Bennett, T. (1998) *Culture: A Reformer's Science*. St Leonards, NSW: Allen & Unwin.

Bennett, T., Martin, G., Mercer, C. and Woollacott, J. (eds) (1981) *Popular Television and Film*. London: British Film Institute.

Bennett, T., Mercer, C. and Woollacott, J. (eds) (1986) *Popular Culture and Social Relations*. Milton Keynes: Open University Press.

Benson, S. (1997) 'The Body, Health and Eating Disorders' in K. Woodward (ed.) *Identity and Difference*. London and Thousand Oaks, CA: Sage.

Berger, J. (1972) *Ways of Seeing*. Harmondsworth: Penguin.

Berman, M. (1982) *All That Is Solid Melts into Air*. New York: Simon & Schuster.

Best, B. (1997) 'Over-the-Counter-Culture: Retheorizing Resistance in Popular Culture' in S. Redhead with D. Wynne and J. O'Connor (eds) *The Clubcultures Reader: Readings in Popular Cultural Studies*. Oxford: Blackwell.

Best, S. and Kellner, D (1991) *Postmodern Theory: Critical Interrogations*. Basingstoke and London: Macmillan.

Bhabha, H. (ed.) (1990) *Nation and Narration*. London and New York: Routledge.

Bhabha, H. (1994) *The Location of Culture*. London and New York: Routledge.

Blumler, J. (1986) *Television in the United States: Funding Sources and Programming Consequences*. Leeds: University of Leeds.

Bogle, D. (1973) *Toms, Coons, Mulattoes, Mammies and Bucks: An Interpretative History of Blacks in American Films*. New York: Viking Press.

Bordo, S. (1993) *Unbearable Weight: Feminism, Western Culture and the Body*. Berkeley: University of California Press.

Bourdieu, P. (1984) *Distinction: A Social Critique of the Judgement of Taste*. Cambridge, MA: Harvard University Press.

Brah, A. (1996) *Cartographies of Diaspora*. London: Routledge.

Brake, M. (1985) *Comparative Youth Culture: The Sociology of Youth Culture and Youth Subcultures in America, Britain and Canada*. London: Routledge & Kegan Paul.

Bramlett-Solomon, S. and Farwell, T. (1996) 'Sex on Soaps: An Analysis of Black, White and Interracial Couple Intimacy' in V. Berry and C. Manning-Miller (eds) *Mediated Messages and African American Culture*. London and Thousand Oaks, CA: Sage.

Braverman, H. (1974) *Labor and Monopoly Capitalism*. New York: Monthly Review Press.

Brecht, B. (1964) 'A Short Organum for the Theatre' in J. Willett (ed.) *Brecht on the Theatre: The Development of an Aesthetic*. London: Eyre Methuen.

Brecht, B. (1977) 'Against George Lukács' in E. Bloch (ed.) *Aesthetics and Politics*. London: New Left Books.

Brunsdon, C. (1990) 'Problems with Quality', *Screen*, 31 (1).

Brunsdon, C. and Morley, D. (1978) *Everyday Television: 'Nationwide'*. London: British Film Institute.

Buckingham, D. (1987) *Public Secrets: EastEnders and Its Audience*. London: British Film Institute.

Burgess, E. (1967) 'The Growth of the City: An Introduction into a Research Project' in R. Park and E. Burgess (eds) *The City*. London: University of Chicago Press

Burnham, J. (1941) *The Managerial Revolution*. New York: Doubleday.

Butler, J. (1990) *Gender Trouble*. New York and London: Routledge.

Butler, J. (1991) 'Imitation and Gender Subordination' in D. Fuss (ed.) *Inside/Out: Lesbian Theories, Gay Theories*. London: Routledge.

Butler, J. (1993) *Bodies That Matter*. London and New York: Routledge.

Campbell, C. (1995) *Race, Myth and the News*. London and Thousand Oaks, CA: Sage.

Cantor, M. (1991) 'The American Family on Television: From Molly Goldberg to Bill Cosby', *Journal of Comparative Family Studies*, 22 (2).

Cantor, M. and Cantor J. (1992) *Prime Time Television: Content and Control*. London and Newbury Park, CA: Sage.

Carby, H. (1984) 'White Woman Listen' in Centre for Contemporary Cultural Studies (ed.) *The Empire Strikes Back*. London: Hutchinson.

Castells, M. (1977) 'The Class Struggle and Urban Contradictions: The Emergence of Urban Protest Movements in Advanced Industrial Societies' in J. Cowley, A Kaye, M. Mayo and A. Thompson (eds) *Community or Class Struggle?* London: Stage 1.

Castells, M. (1983) *The City and the Grasssroots*. London: Edward Arnold.

Castells, M. (1985) 'High Technology, Economic Restructuring and the Urban–Regional Process in the United States', in M. Castells (ed.) *High Technology, Space and Society*. London and Newbury Park, CA: Sage.

Castells, M. (1989) *The Informational City: Information Technology, Economic Restructuring and the Urban–Regional Process*. Oxford: Blackwell.

Castells, M. (1994) 'European Cities, the Informational Society, and the Global Economy', *New Left Review*, 204.

Caughie, J. (1990) 'Playing at Being American', in P. Mellencamp (ed.) *Logics of Television: Essays in Cultural Criticism*. London: British Film Institute.

Chambers, I. (1986) *Popular Culture: The Metropolitan Experience*. London: Methuen.

Chambers, I. (1987) 'Maps for the Metropolis: A Possible Guide to the Present', *Cultural Studies*, I (1).

Chambers, I. (1990) 'Popular Music and Mass Culture' in J. Downing, A. Mohammadi and A. Sreberny-Mohammadi (eds) *Questioning the Media*. London: Sage.

Champion, S. (1997) 'Fear and Loathing in Wisconsin' in S. Redhead with D. Wynne and J. O'Connor (eds) *The Clubcultures Reader: Readings in Popular Cultural Studies*. Oxford: Blackwell.

Chodorow, N. (1978) *The Reproduction of Motherhood*. Berkeley: University of California Press.

Chodorow, N. (1989) *Feminism and Psychoanalytic Theory*. Cambridge: Polity Press.

Clarke, D. (1996) *Urban World/Global City*. London: Routledge.

Clarke, J. (1976) 'Style' in S. Hall and T. Jefferson (eds) *Resistance Through Rituals: Youth Subcultures in Post-War Britain*. London: Hutchinson.

Clarke, J., Hall, S., Jefferson, T. and Roberts, B. (1976) 'Subcultures, Cultures and Class' in S. Hall and T. Jefferson (eds) *Resistance Through Rituals: Youth Subcultures in Post-War Britain*. London: Hutchinson.

Clifford, J. (1988) *The Predicament of Culture: Twentieth Century Ethnography, Literature, and Art*. Cambridge, MA: Harvard University Press.

Clifford, J. (1992) 'Traveling Cultures' in L. Grossberg, C. Nelson and P. Treichler (eds) *Cultural Studies*. London and New York: Routledge.

Clifford, J. and Marcus, G. (eds) (1986) *Writing Culture*. Berkeley: University of California Press.

Cloward, R. and Ohlin, L.E. (1960) *Delinquency and Opportunity*. New York: Free Press of Glencoe.

Cohen, A.K. (1955) *Delinquent Boys: The Subculture of the Gang*. London: Collier Macmillan.

Cohen, P. (1997) *Rethinking the Youth Question: Education, Labour and Cultural Studies*. London: Macmillan.

Cohen, S. (1972) *Folk Devils and Moral Panics: The Creation of the Mods and Rockers*. London: MacGibbon & Kee.

Cohen, S. (1980) 'Symbols of Trouble: An Introduction to the New Edition' in S. Cohen, *Folk Devils and Moral Panics: The Creation of the Mods and Rockers*. London: Martin Robertson.

Collard, A. with Contrucci, J. (1988) *Rape of the Wild*. London: Women's Press.

Collins, J. (1989) *Uncommon Cultures*. London and New York: Routledge.

Collins, J. (1992) 'Postmodernism and Television' in R. Allen (ed.) *Channels of Discourse, Reassembled*. London and New York: Routledge.

Collins, R. (1990) *Culture, Communication and National Identity*. University of Toronto Press.

Commission for Racial Equality (1984) *Report into Ethnic Minorities on Television*. London: Commission for Racial Equality.

Connell, R.W. (1995) *Masculinities*. Cambridge: Polity Press.

Connell, R W., Ashendon, D J., Kessler, S. and Dowsett, G.W. (1982) *Making the Difference: Schools, Families and Social Division*. Sydney: Allen & Unwin.

Cowie, E. (1978) 'Women as Sign', *M/F*, 1.

Crimp, D. (1992) 'Portraits of People with AIDS' in L. Grossberg, C. Nelson and P. Treichler (eds) *Cultural Studies*. London and New York: Routledge.

Crofts, S. (1995) 'Global *Neighbours*?' in R. Allen (ed.) *To Be Continued . . .: Soap Opera around the World*. London and New York: Routledge.

Crook, S., Pakulski, J. and Waters, M. (1992) *Postmodernization*. London and Thousand Oaks, CA: Sage.

Culler, J. (1976) *Saussure*. London: Fontana.

Culler, J (1981) 'Semiotics of Tourism', *American Journal of Semiotics*, 1.

Cunningham, S. (1992a) *Framing Culture*. Sydney: Allen & Unwin.

Cunningham, S. (1992b) 'The Cultural Policy Debate Revisited', *Meanjin*, 51 (3).

Cunningham, S. (1993) 'Cultural Studies from the Viewpoint of Cultural Policy' in A. Gray and J. McGuigan (eds) *Studying Culture*. London: Arnold.

Curran, J. (1991) 'Rethinking the Media and the Public Sphere' in P. Dahlgren and C. Sparks (eds) *Communication and Citizenship*. London and New York: Routledge.

Dahlgren, P. (1995) *Television and the Public Sphere*. London and Newbury Park, CA: Sage.

Daly, M. (1987) *Gyn/Ecology*. London: Women's Press.

Dandeker, C. (1990) *Surveillance, Power and Modernity*. Cambridge: Polity Press.

Daniels, T. and Gerson, J. (eds) (1989) *The Colour Black*. London: British Film Institute.

Dasgupta, D. and Hedge, R. (1988) 'The Eternal Receptacle: A Study of the Mistreatment of Women in Hindi Film' in R. Ghanially (ed.) *Women in Indian Society*. London and Newbury Park, CA: Sage.

Davidson, D. (1980) 'Mental Events', in D. Davidson (ed.) *Essays on Actions and Events*. Oxford: Clarendon Press.

Davidson, D. (1984) *Inquiries into Truth and Interpretation*. Oxford: Clarendon Press.

Davis, M. (1990) *City of Quartz: Excavating the Future of Los Angeles*. London: Verso.

de Certeau, M. (1984) *The Practice of Everyday Life*. Berkeley: University of California Press.

Deleuze, G. and Guattari, F. (1988) *A Thousand Plateaus*. Minneapolis: University of Minneapolis Press.

Derrida, J. (1976) *Of Grammatology*. Baltimore: Johns Hopkins University Press.

Derrida, J. (1980) *Le Carte Postal*. Chicago: University of Chicago Press.

Desforges, L. (1998) '"Checking Out the Planet": Global Representations/Local Identities and Youth Travel' in T. Skelton and G. Valentine (eds) *Cool Places: Geographies of Youth Cultures*. London and New York: Routledge.

Du Gay, P., Hall, S., Janes, L., Mackay, H. and Negus, K. (1997) *Doing Cultural Studies*. London and Thousand Oaks, CA: Sage

Durkheim, E. (1952) *Suicide: A study in Sociology*. London: Routledge & Kegan Paul.

Durkheim, E. (1982) *The Rules of Sociological Method*. London: Macmillan.

Dyer, R. (1977) *Gays and Film*. London: British Film Institute.

Dyer, R. (1997) 'Seeing White', *Times Higher Education Supplement*, 27 June.

Dyer, R., Geraghty, C., Jordan, M., Lovell, T., Paterson, R. and Stewart, J. (1981) *Coronation Street*. London: British Film Institute.

Dyson, K. and Humphries, J. (eds) (1990) *Political Economy of Communications*. London and New York: Routledge.

Eagleton, T. (1984) *The Function of Criticism*. London: Verso.

Eco, U. (1986) *Travels in Hyperreality*. London: Picador.

Eisenstein, S. (1951) *Film Form*. London: Dobson.

Entman, R. (1990) 'Modern Racism and the Images of Blacks in Local Television News', *Critical Studies in Mass Communication*, 7 (4).

Evans, M. (1997) *Introducing Contemporary Feminist Thought*. Cambridge: Polity Press.

Featherstone, M. (1991) *Consumer Culture and Postmodernism*. London and Newbury Park, CA: Sage.

Featherstone, M. (1995) *Undoing Culture: Globalization, Postmodernism and Identity*. London and Newbury Park, CA: Sage.

Ferguson, M. (1990) 'Electronic Media and the Redefining of Time and Space' in M. Ferguson (ed.) *Public Communication: The New Imperatives*. London and Newbury Park, CA: Sage.

Ferguson, M. and Golding, P. (eds) (1997) *Cultural Studies in Question*. London and Newbury Park, CA: Sage.

Fiske, J. (1987) *Television Culture*. London: Methuen.

Fiske, J. (1989a) *Understanding Popular Culture*. London: Unwin Hyman.

Fiske, J. (1989b) *Reading the Popular*. London: Unwin Hyman.

Fiske, J. (1989c) 'Everyday Quizzes, Everyday Life' in J. Tulloch and G. Turner (eds) *Australian Television: Programs, Pleasures and Politics*. London and Sydney: Allen & Unwin.

Fiske, J. (1992) 'British Cultural Studies' in R. Allen (ed.) *Channels of Discourse, Reassembled*. London and New York: Routledge.

Foucault, M. (1972) *The Archaeology of Knowledge*. New York: Pantheon.

Foucault, M. (1973) *The Birth of the Clinic*. London: Tavistock.

Foucault, M. (1977) *Discipline and Punish*. London: Allen Lane.

Foucault, M. (1979) *The History of Sexuality, Vol. 1: The Will to Truth*. London: Penguin Lane.

Foucault, M. (1980) *Power/Knowledge*. New York: Pantheon.

Foucault, M. (1984a) 'Nietzsche, Genealogy, History' in P. Rabinow (ed.) *The Foucault Reader*. New York: Pantheon.

Foucault, M. (1984b) 'On the Genealogy of Ethics: An Overview of Work in Progress' in P. Rabinow (ed.) *The Foucault Reader*. New York: Pantheon.

Foucault, M. (1984c) 'What is the Enlightenment?' in P. Rabinow (ed.) *The Foucault Reader*. New York: Pantheon.

Foucault, M. (1984d) *The Foucault Reader*, ed. P. Rabinow. New York: Pantheon.

Foucault, M. (1985) *The Uses of Pleasure: The History of Sexuality, Vol. 2*. Harmondsworth: Penguin.

Foucault, M. (1986) *The Care of the Self: The History of Sexuality Vol. 3*. London: Penguin.

Foucault, M. (1991) 'Governmentality' in G. Burchill, C. Gordon and P. Miller (eds) *The Foucault Effect: Studies in Governmentality*. Hemel Hempstead: Harvester Wheatsheaf.

Frank, A.-G. (1967) *Capitalism and Underdevelopment in Latin America*. London and New York: Monthly Review Press.

Franklin, S., Lury, C. and Stacey, J. (1991) *Off-Centre: Feminism and Cultural Studies*. London: HarperCollins.

Fraser, N. (1995a) 'From Irony to Prophecy to Politics: A Reply to Richard Rorty' in R.S. Goodman (ed.) *Pragmatism*. New York: Routledge.

Fraser, N. (1995b) 'Politics, Culture and the Public Sphere: Towards a Postmodern Conception' in L. Nicholson and S. Seidman (eds) *Social Postmodernism*. Cambridge: Cambridge University Press.

Freud, S. (1977) *Three Essays on Sexuality. The Pelican Freud Library, Vol. 7*. Harmondsworth: Penguin.

Fukuyama, F. (1989) 'The End of History?' *The National Interest*, 16.

Fukuyama, F. (1992) *The End of History and the Last Man*. Harmondsworth: Penguin.

Gadamer, H.-G. (1976) *Philosophical Hermeneutics*. Berkeley: University of California Press.

Gallagher, M. (1983) *The Portrayal and Participation of Women in the Media*. Paris: UNESCO.

Galtung, J. and Ruge, M. (1973) 'Structuring and Selecting News' in S. Cohen and J. Young (eds) *The Manufacture of News*. London: Constable.

Gans, H. (1962) *The Urban Villagers*. Glencoe, IL: Free Press.

Gans, H. (1968) 'Urbanism and Suburbanism as Ways of Life' in R.E. Pahl (ed.) *Readings in Urban Sociology*. Oxford: Pergamon Press.

Gardner, K. and Shukur, A. (1994) 'I'm Bengali, I'm Asian, and I'm Living Here' in R. Ballard (ed.) *Desh Pardesh: The South Asian Presence in Britain*. London: Hurst & Company

Garfinkel, H. (1967) *Studies in Ethnomethodology*. Englewood Cliffs, NJ: Prentice Hall.

Geertz, C. (1973) *The Interpretation of Cultures*. New York: Basic Books.

Geraghty, C. (1991) *Women in Soap*. Cambridge: Polity Press.

Gergen, K. (1994) *Realities and Relationships*. Cambridge, MA and London: Harvard University Press.

Gibson, W. (1984) *Neuromancer*. London: HarperCollins.

Giddens, A. (1979) *Central Problems in Social Theory*. London: Macmillan.

Giddens, A. (1984) *The Constitution of Society*. Cambridge: Polity Press.

Giddens, A. (1985) *The Nation-State and Violence*. Cambridge: Polity Press.

Giddens, A. (1989) *Sociology*. Cambridge: Polity Press.

Giddens, A. (1990) *The Consequences of Modernity*. Cambridge: Polity Press.

Giddens, A. (1991) *Modernity and Self-Identity*. Cambridge: Polity Press.

Giddens, A. (1992) *The Transformation of Intimacy*. Cambridge: Polity Press.

Giddens, A. (1994) 'Living in a Post-Traditional Society' in U. Beck, A. Giddens and C. Lash (eds) *Reflexive Modernization*. Cambridge: Polity Press.

Gillespie, A. and Williams, H. (1988) 'Telecommunications and the Reconstruction of Regional Comparative Advantage', *Environment and Plannning*, A20.

Gillespie, M. (1995) *Television, Ethnicity and Cultural Change*. London and New York: Routledge.

Gilligan, C. (1982) *In a Different Voice*. Cambridge, MA: Harvard University Press.

Gilpin, R. (1987) *The Political Economy of International Relations*. Princeton: Princeton University Press.

Gilroy, P. (1987) *There Ain't No Black in the Union Jack*. London: Unwin Hyman.

Gilroy, P. (1993) *The Black Atlantic*. London: Verso.

Gilroy, P. (1997) 'Diaspora and the Detours of Identity' in K. Woodwood (ed.) *Identity and Difference*. London and Thousand Oaks, CA: Sage.

Goffman, E. (1969) *The Presentation of Self in Everyday Life*. Harmondsworth: Penguin.

Goldthorpe, J. (1982) 'On the Service Class, its Formation and Future' in A. Giddens and G. Mackenzie (eds) *Social Class and the Division of Labour*. Cambridge: Cambridge University Press.

Goldthorpe, J. and Lockwood, D. (1968) *The Affluent Worker*. Cambridge: Cambridge University Press.

Gorden, D. (1988) 'The Global Economy: New Edifice or Crumbling Foundations?' *New Left Review*, 168.

Gorz, A. (1982) *Farewell to the Working Class*. London: Pluto Press.

Graham, S. and Marvin, S. (1996) *Telecommunications and the City: Electronic Spaces, Urban Places*. London: Routledge.

Gramsci, A. (1968) *Prison Notebooks*. London: Lawrence & Wishart.

Gramsci, A. (1971) *Selections from the Prison Notebooks*, eds Q. Hoare and G. Nowell-Smith. London: Lawrence & Wishart.

Gray, A. (1992) *Video Playtime: The Gendering of a Leisure Technology*. London: Routledge.

Gray, A. (1997) 'Learning from Experience: Cultural Studies and Feminism' in J. McGuigan (ed.) *Cultural Methodologies*. London and Thousand Oaks, CA: Sage.

Gray, H. (1996) 'Television, Black Americans, and the American Dream' in V. Berry and C. Manning-Miller (eds) *Mediated Messages and African American Culture*. London and Thousand Oaks, CA: Sage.

Grossberg, L. (1987) 'The In-difference of Television', *Journal of Communication Enquiry*, 10 (2).

Grossberg, L. (1992) *We Gotta Get Out of This Place: Popular Conservatism and Postmodern Culture*. London and New York: Routledge.

Grossberg, L., Nelson, C. and Treichler, P. (1992) 'Cultural Studies: An Introduction' in L. Grossberg, C. Nelson and P. Treichler (eds) *Cultural Studies*. London and New York: Routledge.

Gurevitch, M., Levy, M. and Roeh, I. (1991) 'The Global Newsroom: Convergence and Diversities in the Globalization of Television News' in P. Dahlgren and C. Sparks (eds) *Communication and Citizenship*. London and New York: Routledge.

Habermas, J. (1972) *Knowledge and Human Interests*. London: Heinemann.

Habermas, J. (1987) *The Philosophical Discourse of Modernity*. Cambridge: Polity Press.

Habermas, J. (1989) *The Structural Transformation of the Public Sphere*. Cambridge, MA: MIT Press.

Hagerstrand, T. (1973) 'The Domain of Human Geography' in R.J. Chorley (ed.) *Directions in Geography*. London: Methuen.

Hall, S. (1972) *On Ideology: Cultural Studies 10*. Birmingham: Centre for Contempoary Cultural Studies.

Hall, S. (1977) 'Culture, the Media and the Ideological Effect' in J. Curran, M.

Gurevitch and J. Woollacott (eds) *Mass Communications and Society*. London: Edward Arnold.

Hall, S. (1981) 'Encoding/Decoding' in S. Hall, D. Hobson, A. Lowe and P. Willis (eds) *Culture, Media, Language*. London: Hutchinson.

Hall, S. (1988) *The Hard Road to Renewal*. London: Verso.

Hall, S. (1989) 'The Meaning of New Times' in S. Hall and M. Jacques (eds) *New Times: The Changing Face of Politics in the 1990s*. London: Lawrence & Wishart.

Hall, S. (1990) 'Cultural Identity and Diaspora' in J. Rutherford (ed.) *Identity: Community, Culture, Difference*. London: Lawrence & Wishart.

Hall, S. (1992a) 'Cultural Studies and its Theoretical Legacies' in L. Grossberg, C. Nelson and P. Treichler (eds) *Cultural Studies*. London and New York: Routledge.

Hall, S. (1992b) 'The Question of Cultural Identity' in S. Hall, D. Held and T. McGrew (eds) *Modernity and Its Futures*. Cambridge: Polity Press.

Hall, S. (1993) 'Minimal Selves' in A. Gray and J. McGuigan (eds) *Studying Culture*. London: Edward Arnold.

Hall, S. (1995) 'Fantasy, Identity, Politics' in E. Carter, J. Donald and J. Squites (eds) *Cultural Remix: Theories of Politics and the Popular*. London: Lawrence & Wishart.

Hall, S. (1996a) 'Who Needs Identity?' in S. Hall and P. Du Gay (eds) *Questions of Cultural Identity*. London: Sage

Hall, S. (1996b) 'On Postmodernism and Articulation: An Interview with Stuart Hall' in D. Morley and D-K. Chen (eds) *Stuart Hall*. London: Routledge.

Hall, S. (1996c) 'Gramsci's Relevance for the Study of Race and Ethnicity' in D. Morley and D.-K. Chen (eds) *Stuart Hall*. London: Routledge.

Hall, S. (1996d) 'New Ethnicities' in D. Morley and D.-K. Chen (eds) *Stuart Hall*. London: Routledge.

Hall, S. (1996e) 'For Allon White: Metaphors of Transformation' in D. Morley and D.-K. Chen (eds) *Stuart Hall*. London: Routledge.

Hall, S. (1997a) 'The Work of Representation' in S. Hall (ed.) *Representations*. London and Thousand Oaks, CA: Sage.

Hall, S. (1997b) 'The Centrality of Culture: Notes on the Cultural Revolutions of Our Time' in K. Thompson (ed.) *Media and Cultural Regulation*. London: Sage.

Hall, S. (ed.) (1997c) 'The Spectacle of the Other' in S. Hall (ed.) *Representations*. London and Thousand Oaks, CA: Sage.

Hall, S. (ed.) (1997d) 'Race, Culture and Communications' in J. Storey (ed.) *What is Cultural Studies?* London: Routledge.

Hall, S. and Jacques, M. (eds) (1989) *New Times: The Changing Face of Politics in the 1990s*. London: Lawrence & Wishart.

Hall, S. and Jefferson, T. (eds) (1976) *Resistance Through Rituals: Youth Subcultures in Post-War Britain*. London: Hutchinson.

Hall, S., Critcher, C., Jefferson, T. Clarke, J. and Roberts, B. (1978) *Policing the Crisis: Mugging, the State and Law and Order*. London: Macmillan.

Hall, S., Hobson, D., Lowe, A. and Willis, P. (eds) (1981) *Culture, Media, Language*. London: Hutchinson.

Hall, S., Held, D. and McGrew, T. (eds) (1992) *Modernity and its Futures*. Cambridge: Polity Press.

Hall, T. (1997) '(Re)placing the City: Cultural Relocation and the City as Centre' in S. Westwood and J. Williams (eds) *Imagining Cities*. London: Routledge.

Halpern, D. (1992) *Sex Differences in Cognitive Abilities*. London: Lawrence Erlbaum Associates.

Hamelink, C. (1983) *Cultural Autonomy in Global Communications*. New York: Longman.

Hammersley, M. and Atkinson, P. (1983) *Ethnography: Principles and Practice*. London: Tavistock Books.

Hartley, J. (1982) *Understanding News*. London: Methuen.

Harvey, D. (1973) *Social Justice and the City*. London: Edward Arnold.

Harvey, D. (1985) *The Urbanization of Capital*. Oxford: Blackwell.

Harvey, D. (1989) *The Condition of Postmodernity*. Oxford: Blackwell.

Harvey, D. (1993) 'From Place to Space and Back Again: Reflections on the Condition of Postmodernity' in J. Bird, B. Curtis, T. Putnam, G. Roberston and L. Tickner (eds) *Mapping the Futures: Local Cultures, Global Change*. London and New York: Routledge.

Hebdige, D. (1979) *Subculture: The Meaning of Style*. London and New York: Routledge.

Hebdige, D. (1988) *Hiding in the Light*. London: Comedia.

Hebdige, D. (1990) 'Fax to the Future', *Marxism Today*, January.

Held, D. (1991) 'Democracy, the Nation-State and the Global System' in D. Held (ed.) *Politcal Theory Today*. Cambridge: Polity Press.

Held, D. (1992) 'Liberalism, Marxism and Democracy' in S. Hall, D. Held and T. McGrew (eds) *Modernity and Its Futures*. Cambridge: Polity Press.

Henriques, J., Hollway, W., Urwin, C., Venn, C. and Walkerdine, V. (1984) *Changing the Subject: Psychology, Social Regulation and Subjectivity*. London: Metheun.

Hertz, J. (1957) 'The Rise and Demise of the Territorial Nation-State', *World Politics*, ix.

Hetherington, K. (1998) 'Vanloads of Uproarious Humanity: New Age Travellers and the Utopics of the Countryside' in T. Skelton and G. Valentine (eds) *Cool Places: Geographies of Youth Cultures*. London and New York: Routledge.

Hobsbawm, E.J. (1969) *Industry and Empire*. Harmondsworth: Penguin.

Hobson, D. (1982) *Crossroads: Drama of a Soap Opera*. London: Methuen.

Hoggart, R. (1957) *The Uses of Literacy*. Harmondsworth: Penguin.

Honneth, A. (1985) 'An Aversion Against the Universal', *Theory, Culture & Society*, 2 (3).

hooks, b. (1990) *Yearning: Race, Gender and Cultural Politics*. Boston, MA: South End Press.

hooks, b. (1992) *Black Looks: Race and Representation*. Boston, MA: South End Press.

hooks, b. (1986) *Ain't I a Woman? Black Women and Feminism*. London: Pluto Press.

Horkheimer, M. and Adorno, T.W. (1979) *Dialectic of Enlightenment*. London: Verso.

Hoskins, C., McFadyen, S., Finn, A. and Jackel, A. (1995) 'Film and Television Co-productions: Evidence from Canadian–European Experience', *European Journal of Communication*, 10 (2).

Hoyenga, K. and Hoyenga, K.T. (1993) *Gender-Related Differences*. New York: Allyn & Bacon.

Hutcheon, L. (1989) *The Politics of Postmodernism*. London and New York: Routledge.

Irigaray, L. (1985a) *Speculum of the Other Woman*. Ithaca, NY: Cornell University Press.

Irigaray, L. (1985b) *This Sex Which Is Not One*. Ithaca, NY: Cornell University Press.

Iser, W. (1987) *The Act of Reading: A Theory of Aesthetic Responses*. London and New York: Routledge & Kegan Paul.

James, A. (1986) 'Learning to Belong: The Boundaries of Adolescence' in A.P. Cohen (ed.) *Symbolizing Boundaries: Identity and Diversity in British Cultures*. Manchester: Manchester University Press.

Jameson, F. (1984) 'Postmodernsim or the Cultural Logic of Late Capitalism', *New Left Review*, 46.

Jencks, C. (1986) *What is Post-Modernism?* New York: Academy/St Martins Press.

Jhally, S. and Lewis, J. (1992) *Enlightened Racism: The Cosby Show, Audiences, and the Myth of the American Dream*. Boulder, CO: Westview Press.

Jones, J. (1996) 'The New Ghetto Aesthetic' in V. Berry and C. Manning-Miller (eds) *Mediated Messages and African American Culture*. London and Thousand Oaks, CA: Sage.

Jordan, G. and Weedon, C. (1995) *Cultural Politics: Class, Gender, Race and the Postmodern World*. Oxford: Blackwell.

Kaplan, E. (1987) *Rocking Around the Clock: Music Televison, Postmodernism and Consumer Culture*. Boulder, CO: Westview Press.

Kaplan, E. (1992) 'Feminist Criticism and Television' in R. Allen (ed.) *Channels of Discourse, Reassembled*. London and New York: Routledge.

Kaplan, E. (1997) *Looking for the Other: Feminism, Film and the Imperial Gaze*. London and New York: Routledge.

Kellner, D. (1992) 'Popular Culture and the Construction of Postmodern Identities' in S. Lash and J. Friedman (eds) *Modernity and Identity*. Oxford: Blackwell.

Kellner, D. (1995) *Media Culture: Cultural Studies, Identity and Politics between the Modern and the Postmodern*. London and New York: Routledge.

Kellner, D. (1997) 'Overcoming the Divide: Cultural Studies and Political Economy' in M.Ferguson and P. Golding (eds) *Cultural Studies in Question*. London and Newbury Park, CA: Sage.

Kerner Commission (1968) *Report of the National Advisory Committee on Civil Disorders*. New York: E.P. Dutton.

Kerr, C., Dunlop, K., Harbison, F. and Mayers, C. (1973) *Industrialism and Industrial Man*. Harmondsworth: Penguin.

King, A.D. (1983) 'The World Economy in Everywhere: Urban History and the World System' in *The 1983 World History Yearbook*. Leicester: Leicester University Press.

Krishnan, P. and Dighe, A. (1990) *Affirmation and Denial: The Construction of Femininity on Indian Television*. London and Newbury Park, CA: Sage.

Kristeva, J. (1986a) 'Revolution in Poetic Language' in T. Moi (ed.) *The Kristeva Reader*. Oxford: Blackwell.

Kristeva, J. (1986b) 'Women's Time' in T. Moi (ed.) *The Kristeva Reader*. Oxford: Blackwell.

Kristeva, J. (1986c), T. Moi (ed.) *The Kristeva Reader*. Oxford: Blackwell.

Kuhn, T.S. (1962) *The Structures of Scientific Revolutions*. Chicago and London: University of Chicago Press.

Kundera, M. (1984) *The Unbearable Lightness of Being*. London and Boston: Faber & Faber.

Lacan, J. (1977) *Écrits: A Selection*. London: Tavistock.

Laclau, E. (1977) *Politics and Ideology in Marxist Theory*. London: New left Books.

Laclau, E. and Mouffe, C. (1985) *Hegemony and Socialist Strategy: Toward a Radical Democratic Politics*. London: Verso.

Laing, D. (1985) *One Chord Wonders: Power and Meaning in Punk Rock*. Milton Keynes: Open University Press.

Lash, S. (1990) *Sociology of Postmodernism*. London and New York: Routledge.

Lash, S. and Urry, J. (1987) *Disorganized Capitalism*. Cambridge: Polity Press.

Leab, D. (1976) *From Sambo to Superspade*. New York: Houghton Mifflin.

Leach, E. (1974) *Lévi-Strauss*. Glasgow: Collins.

Leavis, F.R. and Thompson, D. (1933) *Culture and the Environment*. London: Chatto & Windus.

Liebes, T. and Katz, E. (1991) *The Export of Meaning*. Oxford: Oxford University Press.

Lopez, A. (1995) 'Our Welcomed Guests: Telenovelas in Latin America' in R. Allen (ed.) *To Be Continued . . .: Soap Opera around the World*. London and New York: Routledge.

Lovell, T. (1978) 'Jane Austen and the Gentry: A Study of Literature and Ideology' in D. Laurenson (ed.) *The Sociology of Literature: Applied Studies*. Keele: Sociological Review Monograph 26.

Lukács, G. (1972) 'Ideology of Modernism' in D. Lodge (ed.) *Twentieth-Century Literary Criticism*. London: Longman.

Lukács, G. (1977) 'Realism in the Balance' in E. Bloch (ed.) *Aesthetics and Politics*. London: New Left Books.

Lull, J. (1991) *China Turned On: Television, Reform and Resistance*. London: Routledge.

Lull, J. (1997) 'China Turned On (Revisited): Television, Reform and Resistance' in A. Sreberny-Mohammadi, D. Winseck, J. McKenna and O. Boyd-Barrett (eds) *Media in a Global Context*. London: Edward Arnold.

Lyotard, J.-F. (1984) *The Postmodern Condition*. Minneapolis: University of Minnesota Press.

McAnany, E. and La Pastina, A. (1994) 'Telenovela Audiences', *Communication Research*, 21 (6).

MacCabe, C. (1981) 'Realism and the Cinema: Notes on Some Brechtian Themes', *Screen*, 5 (2).

McGrath, J. (1972) 'TV Drama: The Case Against Naturalism', *Sight & Sound*, Spring.

McGrew, A. (1992) 'A Global Society?' in S. Hall, D. Held and T. McGrew (eds) *Modernity and its Futures*. Cambridge: Polity Press.

McGuigan, J. (1992) *Cultural Populism*. London: Routledge.

McGuigan, J. (1996a) *Culture and the Public Sphere*. London: Routledge.

McGuigan, J. (1996b) 'Cultural Populism Revisited' in M. Ferguson and P. Golding (eds) *Cultural Studies in Question*. London and Newbury Park, CA: Sage.

McGuigan, J. (1997a) 'Introduction' in J. McGuigan (ed.) *Cultural Methodologies*. London: Sage.

McGuigan, J. (ed.) (1997b) *Cultural Methodologies*. London: Sage.

Mackinnon, C. (1987) *Feminism Unmodified*. Cambridge, MA and London: Harvard University Press.

Mackinnon, C. (1991) 'Difference and Domination' in K. Bartlett and R. Kennedy (eds) *Feminist Legal Theory*. Boulder, CO and London: Westview Press.

McLean, C., Carey, M. and White, C. (eds) (1996) *Men's Ways of Being*. Boulder, CO: Westview Press.

McLuskie, K. (1982) 'Feminist Deconstruction: The Example of Shakespeare's *Taming of the Shrew*', *Red Letters*, 12.

McNay, L. (1992) *Foucault and Feminism*. Cambridge: Polity Press.

McQuail, D., De Mateo, R. and Tapper, H. (1992) 'A Framework for Analysis of Media Change in Europe in the 1990s' in K. Siune and W. Truetzschler (eds) *Dynamics of Media Politics: Broadcasting and Electronic Media in Western Europe*. London and Newbury Park, CA: Sage.

McRobbie, A. (1989) *Zoot Suits and Second-Hand Dresses*. London: Macmillan.

McRobbie, A. (1991a) 'Settling Accounts with Subcultures' in A. McRobbie, *Feminism and Youth Culture*. London: Macmillan.

McRobbie, A. (1991b) '*Jackie*: Romantic Individualism and the Teenage Girl' in A. McRobbie, *Feminism and Youth Culture*. London: Macmillan.

McRobbie, A. (1991c) 'Working-Class Girls and the Culture of Femininity' in A. McRobbie, *Feminism and Youth Culture*. London: Macmillan.

McRobbie, A. (1991d) '*Jackie* and *Just Seventeen* in the 1980s' in A. McRobbie, *Feminism and Youth Culture*. London: Macmillan.

McRobbie, A. (1992) 'Post-Marxism and Cultural Studies: A Post-Script' in L. Grossberg, C. Nelson and P. Treichler (eds) *Cultural Studies*. London and New York: Routledge.

McRobbie, A. and Garber, J. (1991) 'Girls and Subcultures' in A. McRobbie, *Feminism and Youth Culture*. London: Macmillan.

Martindale, C. (1986) *The White Press in Black America*. Westport, CT: Greenwood Press.

Marx, K. (1961) *Karl Marx: Selected Writings in Sociology and Social Philosophy*, eds T. Bottomore and M. Rubel. London: Pelican.

Marx, K. and Engels, F. (1967) *The Communist Manifesto*. London: Penguin.

Marx, K. and Engels, F. (1970) *The German Ideology*. London: Lawrence & Wishart.

Massey, D. (1994) *Space, Place and Gender*. Cambridge: Polity Press.

Massey, D. (1998) 'The Spatial Construction of Youth Cultures' in T. Skelton and G. Valentine (eds) *Cool Places: Geographies of Youth Cultures*. London and New York: Routledge.

Mattelart, M. and Mattelart, A. (1992) *The Carnival of Images*. New York: Bergin & Garvey.

Matza, D. and Sykes, G. (1961) 'Juvenile Delinquency and Subterranean Values', *American Sociological Review*, 26.

Medhurst, A. (1989) 'Laughing Matters: Introduction' in T. Daniels and J. Gerson (eds) *The Colour Black*. London: British Film Institute.

Meehan, D. (1983) *Ladies of the Evening: Women Characters of Prime-Time Television*. Metuchen, NJ: Scarecrow Press.

Melucci, A. (1980) 'The New Social Movements: A Theoretical Approach', *Social Science Information*, 19 (2).

Melucci, A. (1981) 'Ten Hypotheses for the Analysis of New Movements' in D. Pinto (ed.) *Contemporary Italian Sociology*. Cambridge: Cambridge University Press.

Mercer, K. (1994) *Welcome to the Jungle: New Postions in Black Cultural Studies*. London and New York: Routledge.

Merton, R.K. (1938) 'Social Structure and Anomie', *American Sociological Review*, 3.

Meyrowitz, J. (1986) *No Sense of Place*. Oxford: Oxford University Press.

Miller, D. (1995) 'The Consumption of Soap Opera: *The Young and the Restless* and Mass Consumption in Trinidad' in R. Allen (ed.) *To Be Continued . . .: Soap Opera around the World*. London and New York: Routledge.

Miller, W.B. (1958) 'Lower Class Culture as a Generating Milieu of Gang Delinquency', *Journal of Social Issues*, 14.

Mishra, V. (1985) 'Toward a Theoretical Critique of Bombay Cinema', *Screen*, 26.

Mitchell, J. (1974) *Psychoanalysis and Feminism*. London: Allen Lane.

Modleski, T. (1982) *Loving with a Vengeance*. London: Methuen.

Moi, T. (1985) *Sexual/Textual Politics: Feminist Literary Theory*. London and New York: Routledge.

Moir, A. and Moir, B. (1998) *Why Men Don't Iron: The Real Science of Gender Studies*. London: HarperCollins Publishers.

Morley, D. (1980) *The Nationwide Audience*. London: British Film Institute.

Morley, D. (1986) *Family Television: Cultural Power and Domestic Leisure*. London: Comedia.

Morley, D. (1992) *Television, Audiences and Cultural Studies*. London and New York: Routledge.

Morley, D. and Robins, K. (1995) *Spaces of Identity: Global Media, Electronic Landscapes and Cultural Boundaries*. London and New York: Routledge.

Morris, M. (1992) 'A Gadfly Bites Back', *Meanjin*, 51 (3).

Morris, M. (1996) 'Banality in Cultural Studies' in J. Storey (ed.) *What is Cultural Studies? A Reader*. London and New York: Edward Arnold.

Morrison, D. (1992) *Television and the Gulf War*. London: John Libbey.

Mort, F. (1989) 'The Politics of Consumption' in S. Hall and M. Jacques (eds) *New Times: The Changing Face of Politics in the 1990s*. London: Lawrence & Wishart.

Mosca, V. (1988) 'Introduction: Information in the Pay Society' in V. Mosca and J. Wasko (eds) *The Political Economy of Information*. Madison: University of Wisconsin Press.

Mouffe, C. (1992) 'Democratic Citizenship and the Political Community' in C. Mouffe (ed.) *Dimensions of Radical Democracy*. London: Verso.

Mouffe, C. (1984) 'Towards a Theoretical Interpretation of "New Social Movements"' in S. Hanninen and L. Palden (eds) *Rethinking Marx*. New York & Bagnolet: International General/IMMRC.

Mowlana, H., Gerbner, G. and Schiller, H. (eds) (1992) *Triumph of the Image: The Media's War in the Persian Gulf*. Boulder, CO: Westview Press.

Muggleton, D. (1997) 'The Post-Subculturalist' in S. Redhead (ed.) *Subcultures to Clubcultures: An Introduction to Popular Cultural Studies*. Oxford: Blackwell.

Murdock, G. (1990) 'Redrawing the Map of the Communications Industries: Concentration and Ownership in the Era of Privatisation' in M. Ferguson (ed.) *Public Communication: The New Imperatives*. London and Newbury Park, CA: Sage.

Murdock, G. and Golding, P. (1977) 'Capitalism, Communications and Class Relations' in J. Curran, M. Gurevitch and J. Woollacott (eds) *Mass Communications and Society*. London: Edward Arnold.

Murray, R. (1989a) 'Fordism and Post-Fordism' in S. Hall and M. Jacques (eds) *New Times: The Changing Face of Politics in the 1990s*. London: Lawrence & Wishart.

Murray, R. (1989b) 'Benetton Britain' in S. Hall and M. Jacques (eds) *New Times: The Changing Face of Politics in the 1990s*. London: Lawrence & Wishart.

Musa, M. (1990) 'News Agencies, Transnationalization and the New Order', *Media, Culture and Society*, 12.

Neale, S. (1980) *Genre*. London: British Film Institute.

Newcombe, H. (1988) 'One Night of Prime Time' in J. Carey (ed.) *Media, Myth, Narrative*. London and Newbury Park, CA: Sage.

Nicholson, L. (ed.) (1990) *Feminism/Postmodernism*. London and New York: Routledge.

Nicholson, L. (1995) 'Interpreting Gender' in L. Nicholson and S. Seidman (eds) *Social Postmodernism*. Cambridge: Cambridge University Press.

Nietzsche, F. (1967) *The Will to Power*. New York: Random House.

Nixon, S. (1997) 'Exhibiting Masculinity' in S. Hall (ed.) *Representations*. London and Thousand Oaks, CA: Sage.

Norris, C. (1987) *Derrida*. Cambridge, MA: Harvard University Press.

Nzegwu, N. (1996) 'Bypasssing New York in Re-presenting Eko: Production of Space in a Nigerian City' in A.D. King (ed.) *Re-presenting the City*. London: Macmillan.

Oakley, A. (1974) *Housewife*. London: Allen Lane.

Ogden, M. (1994) 'Politics in a Parallel Universe: Is There a Future for Cyber-democracy?', *Futures*, 26 (7).

O'Regan, T. (1992a) '(Mis)taking Policy: Notes on the Cultural Policy Debate', *Cultural Studies*, 6 (3).

O'Regan, T. (1992b) 'Some Reflections on the "Policy Moment"', *Meanjin*, 51 (3).

Parekh, B. (1991) 'British Citizenship and Cultural Difference' in G. Andrews (ed.) *Citizenship*. London: Lawrence & Wishart.

Parsons, T. (1942) 'Age and Sex in the Social Structure of the United States', *American Sociological Review*, 7.

Parsons, T. (1963) 'Youth in the Context of American Society', *American Sociological Review*, 27.

Pendakur, M. (1991) 'A Political Economy of Television: State, Class and Corporate Influence in India' in G. Sussman and J. Lent (eds) *Transnational Communications*. Newbury Park, CA: Sage.

Pieterse, J. (1995) 'Globalization as Hybridization' in M. Featherstone, S. Lash and R. Robertson (eds) *Global Modernities*. London and Newbury Park, CA: Sage.

Popper, K. (1959) *The Logic of Scientific Discovery*. London: Hutchinson.

Porter, V. (1989) 'The Re-regulation of Television: Pluralism, Constitutionality and the Free Market in the USA, West Germany, France and the UK', *Media, Culture and Society*, 11.

Poulantza, N. (1976) *Political Power and Social Classes*. London: New Left Books.

Propp, V. (1970) *Morphology of the Folktale*. Austin: University of Texas Press.

Rabinow, P. (ed.) (1984) *The Foucault Reader*. New York: Pantheon.

Rajagopal, A. (1993) 'The Rise of National Programming: The Case of Indian Television', *Media, Culture and Society*, 15.

Rajan, S.R. (1991) *Ideal and Imagined Women*. London: Routledge.

Redhead, S. (1990) *The End-of-the-Century Party: Youth and Pop Towards 2000*. Manchester: Manchester University Press.

Redhead, S. (1993) *Rave Off: Politics and Deviance in Contemporary Youth Culture*. Aldershot: Avebury.

Redhead, S. (1997a) 'Introduction: Reading Pop(ular) Cult(ural) Stud(ie)s' in S. Redhead with D. Wynne and J. O'Connor (eds) *The Clubcultures Reader: Readings in Popular Cultural Studies*. Oxford: Blackwell.

Redhead, S. (1997b) 'PopTime, Acid House' in S. Redhead (ed.) *Subcultures to Clubcultures: An Introduction to Popular Cultural Studies*. Oxford: Blackwell.

Real, T. (1998) *I Don't Want to Talk About It: Men and Depression*. Dublin: Newleaf.

Relph, E. (1976) *Place and Placelessness*. London: Pion.

Reynolds, S. (1997) 'Rave Culture: Living Dream or Living Death' in S. Redhead (ed.) *Subcultures to Clubcultures: An Introduction to Popular Cultural Studies*. Oxford: Blackwell.

Rich, A. (1986) *Of Woman Born*. London: Virago Press.

Richard, B. and Kruger, H.H. (1998) 'Ravers Paradise? German Youth Cultures in the 1990s' in T. Skelton and G. Valentine (eds) *Cool Places: Geographies of Youth Cultures*. London and New York: Routledge.

Robertson, R. (1992) *Globalization*. London and Newbury Park, CA: Sage.

Robertson, R. (1995) 'Glocalization: Time–Space and Homogeneity–Hetrogeneity' in M. Featherstone, S. Lash and R. Robertson (eds) *Global Modernities*. London and Newbury Park, CA: Sage.

Robins, K. (1991) 'Tradition and Translation: National Culture in its Global Context' in J. Corner and S. Harvey (eds) *Enterprise and Heritage: Crosscurrents of National Culture*. London: Routledge.

Rogers, E. and Antola, L. (1985) 'Telenovelas: A Latin American Success Story', *Journal of Communication*, 35.

Rorty, R. (1980) *Philosophy and the Mirror of Nature*. Cambridge: Cambridge University Press.

Rorty, R. (1989) *Contingency, Irony and Solidarity*. Cambridge: Cambridge University Press.

Rorty, R. (1991a) *Objectivity, Relativism, and Truth: Philosophical Papers, Volume 1*. Cambridge: Cambridge University Press.

Rorty, R. (1991b) *Essays on Heidegger and Others: Philosophical Papers, Volume 2*. Cambridge: Cambridge University Press.

Rorty, R. (1995) 'Feminism and Pragmatism', in R.S. Goodman (ed.) *Pragmatism*. New York: Routledge.

Rorty, R. (1998) *Achieving Our Country*. Cambridge, MA: Harvard University Press.

Rose, G. (1993) *Feminism and Geography*. Cambridge: Polity Press.

Rose, J. (1997) *Sexuality in the Field of Vision*. London: Verso.

Rose, N. (1996) 'Identity, Genealogy, History' in S. Hall and P. Du Gay (eds) *Questions of Cultural Identity*. London and Newbury Park, CA: Sage.

Rowbotham, S. (1981) 'The Trouble with Patriarchy' in R. Samuel (ed.) *People's History and Socialist Theory*. London: Routledge.

Rowe, D. (1988) *Choosing Not Losing*. London: Fontana.

Rowe, D. (1997) *Depression*. London: Routledge.

Said, E. (1978) *Orientalism*. London: Routledge.

Said, E. (1981) *Covering Islam*. London and New York: Routledge.

Sainath, P (1992) 'The New World Odour: The Indian Experience' in H. Mowlana, G. Gerbner and H. Schiller (eds) *Triumph of the Image: The Media's War in the Persian Gulf*. Boulder, CO: Westview Press.

Sassen, S. (1991) *The Global City: New York, London, Tokyo*. Princeton: Princeton Univerity Press.

Sassen, S. (1996) 'Rebuilding the Global City: Economy, Ethnicity and Space' in A.D. King (ed.) *Re-presenting the City*. London: Macmillan.

Saussure, F. de (1960) *Course in General Linguistics*. London: Peter Owen.

Scannell, P. (1988) 'Radio Times: The Temporal Arrangements of Broadcasting in the Modern World' in P. Drummond and R. Paterson (eds) *Television and its Audiences*. London: British Film Institute.

Schiller, H. (1976) *Communication and Cultural Domination*. New York: M.E. Sharpe.

Schiller, H. (1969) *Mass Communications and the American Empire*. New York: Augustus M. Kelly.

Schiller, H. (1985) 'Electronic Information Flows: New Basis for Global Domination?' in P. Drummond and R. Patterson (eds) *Television in Transition*. London: British Film Institute.

Schlesinger, P. (1978) *Putting Reality Together*. London: Constable.

Scott, J. (1990) 'Deconstructing Equality vs Difference' in M. Hirsch and E. Fox Keller (eds) *Conflicts in Feminism*. London and New York: Routledge.

Seidler, V. (1989) *Rediscovering Masculinity: Reason, Langauge and Sexuality*. London: Routledge.

Seamon, D. (1979) *A Geography of the Life World*. London: Croom Helm.

Seiter, E. (1989) 'Don't Treat Us Like We're Stupid' in E. Seiter, H. Borchers, G. Kreutzner and E.-M. Warth (eds) *Remote Control*. London and New York: Routledge.

Sepstrup, P. (1989) 'Research into International Television Flows: A Methodological Contribution', *European Journal of Communication*, 4.

Shaw, M. (1991) *Post-Military Society*. Cambridge: Polity Press.

Shields, R. (1996) 'A Guide to Urban Representation and What to Do About It: Alternative Traditions in Urban Theory' in A.D. King (ed) *Re-presenting the City*. London: Macmillan.

Shotter, J. (1993) *Conversational Realities*. London and Newbury Park, CA: Sage.

Sibley, D. (1995) *Geographies of Exclusion*. London: Routledge.

Silverstone, R. (1994) *Television and Everyday Life*. London and New York: Routledge.

Simmel, G. (1978) *The Philosophy of Money*. London: Routledge & Kegan Paul.

Smith, A.D. (1990) 'Towards a Global Culture?' in M. Featherstone (ed.) *Global Culture*. London and Newbury Park, CA: Sage.

Smith, K. (1996) 'Advertising Discourse and the Marketing of *I'll Fly Away*' in V. Berry and C. Manning-Miller (eds) *Mediated Messages and African American Culture*. London and Thousand Oaks, CA: Sage.

Soja, E. (1989) *Postmodern Geographies*. London: Verso.

Soja, E. (1995a) 'Postmodern Urbanisation: The Six Restructurings of Los Angeles' in S. Watson and K. Gibson (eds) *Postmodern Cities and Spaces*. Oxford: Blackwell.

Soja, E. (1995b) 'Heterotopologies: A Rememberance of Other Spaces in the Citadel-LA' in S. Watson and K. Gibson (eds) *Postmodern Cities and Spaces*. Oxford: Blackwell.

Spivak, G. (1976) 'Translator's Introduction' in J. Derrida, *Of Grammatology*. Baltimore: Johns Hopkins University Press.

Spivak, G. (1993) 'Can the Subaltern Speak?' in P. Williams and L. Chrisman (eds) *Colonial Discourse and Post-Colonial Theory*. Hemel Hempstead: Harvester Wheatsheaf.

Storey, J. (1993) *Cultural Theory and Popular Culture*. Edinburgh: Edinburgh University Press.

Straubhaar, J. (1992) 'What Makes News? Western, Socialist, and Third World Television Newscasts Compared in Eight Countries' in F. Korzenny and S. Ting Toomey (eds) *Mass Media Effects across Cultures*. London and Newbury Park, CA: Sage.

Straubhaar, J. (1997) 'Distinguishing the Global, Regional and National Levels of World Television' in A. Sreberny-Mohammadi, D. Winseck, J. McKenna and O. Boyd-Burnett (eds) *Media in a Global Context*. London: Edward Arnold.

Tagg, J. (1996) 'The City Which is Not One' in A.D. King (ed.) *Re-presenting the City*. London: Macmillan.

Taylor, F. (1911) *Principles of Scientific Management*. New York: Harper.

Thompson, E. (1963) *The Making of the English Working Class*. New York: Vintage.

Thompson, J. (1995) *The Media and Modernity*. Cambridge: Polity Press.

Thompson, P. and McHugh, D. (1990) *Work Organization: A Critical Introduction*. London: Macmillian.

Thornton, S. (1995) *Club Cultures: Music, Media and Subcultural Capital*. Cambridge: Polity Press.

Todorov, T. (1977) *The Poetics of Prose*. Ithaca, NY: Cornell University Press.

Tomlinson, J. (1991) *Cultural Imperialism*. London: Pinter Press.

Touraine, A. (1971) *The Post-Industrial Society*. New York: Random House.

Touraine, A. (1981) *The Voice and the Eye: An Analysis of Social Movements*. Cambridge: Cambridge University Press.

Touraine, A. (1985) 'An Introduction to the Study of New Social Movements', *Social Research*, 52 (4).

Tuchman, G., Daniels, C. and Benet, J. (eds) (1978) *Hearth and Home: Images of Women in the Mass Media*. New York: Oxford University Press.

Turner, G. (1990) *British Cultural Studies: An Introduction*. London: Unwin Hyman.

Turner, G. (1992) 'It Works for Me: British Cultural Studies, Australian Cultural Studies, Australian Film' in L. Grossberg, C. Nelson and P. Treichler (eds) *Cultural Studies*. London and New York: Routledge.

Varis, T. (1974) 'Global Traffic in Television', *Journal of Communication*, 24 (1).

Varis, T. (1984) 'International Flow of Television Programmes', *Journal of Communication*, 34 (1).

Vink, N. (1988) *The Telenovela and Emancipation*. Amsterdam: Royal Tropical Institute.

Volosinov, V.N. (1973) *Marxism and the Philosophy of Language*. London: Seminar Press.

Wallace, M. (1979) *Black Macho*. London: Calder.

Wallerstein, I. (1974) *The Modern World System*. New York: Academic Press.

Waterman, D. (1988) 'World Television Trade: The Economic Effects of Privatization and New Technology', *Telecommunications Policy*, June.

Waters, M. (1995) *Globalization*. London: Routledge.

Watson, J. (ed.) (1977) *Between Two Cultures*. Oxford: Blackwell.

Watson, S. and Gibson, K. (1995) 'Introduction' to S. Watson and K. Gibson (eds) *Postmodern Cities and Spaces*. Oxford: Blackwell.

Weber, M. (1948) *From Max Weber*. London: Routledge & Kegan Paul.

Weber, M. (1978) *Economy and Society: An Outline of Interpretative Sociology*. Berkeley: University of California Press.

Weedon, C. (1997) *Feminist Practice and Poststructuralist Theory*. Oxford: Blackwell.

Weedon, C., Tolson, A. and Mort, F. (1980) 'Introduction to Language Studies at the Centre' in S. Hall, D. Hobson, A. Lowe and P. Willis (eds) *Culture, Media, Language*. London: Hutchinson.

Weeks, J. (1990) 'The Value of Difference' in J. Rutherford (ed.) *Identity: Community, Culture, Difference*. London: Lawrence & Wishart.

Wernick, A. (1991) *Promo Culture*. London and Newbury Park, CA: Sage.

West, C. (1992) 'The Postmodern Crisis of the Black Intellectuals' in L. Grossberg, C. Nelson and P. Treichler (eds) *Cultural Studies*. London and New York: Routledge.

West, C. (1993) *Keeping Faith*. London and New York: Routledge.

Westwood, S. and Williams, J. (1997) 'Imagining Cities' in S. Westwood and J. Williams (eds) *Imagining Cities*. London: Routledge.

Widdicombe, S. and Wooffitt, R. (1995) *The Language of Youth Subcultures*. Hemel Hempstead: Harvester Wheatsheaf.

Williams, P. and Chrisman, L. (eds) (1993) *Colonial Discourse and Post-Colonial Theory*. Hemel Hempstead: Harvester Wheatsheaf.

Williams, R. (1965) *The Long Revolution*. London: Penguin.

Williams, R. (1973) 'Base and Superstructure in Marxist Cultural Theory', *New Left Review*, 82.

Williams, R. (1974) *Television: Technology and Cultural Form*. London: Fontana.

Williams, R. (1979) *Politics and Letters: Interviews with New Left Review*. London: New Left Books.

Williams, R. (1981) *Culture*. London: Fontana.

Williams, R. (1983) *Keywords*. London: Fontana.

Williams, R. (1989) *Resources of Hope*. London: Verso.

Williamson, J. (1978) *Decoding Advertisements*. London: Marion Boyars.

Willis, P. (1977) *Learning to Labour*. Farnborough: Saxon House.

Willis, P. (1978) *Profane Culture*. London: Routledge & Kegan Paul.

Willis, P (1980) 'Notes on Method' in S. Hall, D. Hobson, A. Lowe and P. Willis (eds) *Culture, Media, Language*. London: Hutchinson.

Willis, P. (1990) *Common Culture*. Milton: Keynes: Open University Press.

Wilson, T. (1993) *Watching Television: Hermeneutics, Reception and Popular Culture*. Cambridge: Polity Press.

Winship, J (1981) 'Sexuality for Sale' in S. Hall, D. Hobson, A. Lowe and P. Willis (eds) *Culture, Media, Language*. London: Hutchinson.

Wittgenstein, L. (1953) *Philosophical Investigations*. Oxford: Blackwell.

Wolff, J. (1980) *The Social Production of Art*. London: Macmillan.

Women's Study Group, Centre for Contemporary Cultural Studies (1978) *Women Take Issue*. London: Hutchinson.

Woodward, K. (1997) 'Motherhood: Identities, Meanings and Myths' in K. Woodward (ed.) *Identity and Difference*. London and Thousand Oaks, CA: Sage.

Worsley, P. (1990) 'Models of the Modern World System' in M. Featherstone (ed.) *Global Culture*. London and Newbury Park, CA: Sage.

Wright, H. (1996) 'Dare We De-centre Birmingham?' Conference paper. 'Crossroads in Cultural Studies', University of Tampere, Finland. July.

Young, J. (1971) *The Drugtakers: The Social Meaning of Drug Use*. London: Paladin.

Young, M. and Willmott, P. (1962) *Family and Kinship in East London*. Harmondsworth: Penguin.

Zukin, S. (1988) *Loft Living: Culture and Capital in Urban Change*. London: Century Hutchinson.

Zukin, S. (1991) *Landscapes of Power: From Detroit to Disneyworld*. Berkeley: University of California Press.

Zukin, S. (1996a) *The Culture of Cities*. Oxford: Blackwell.

Zukin, S. (1996b) 'Space and Symbols in an Age of Decline' in A.D. King (ed.) *Representing the City*. London: Macmillan.

Index

abjection, 246
acculturalization, 92, 165, 167, 169, 375–6, 381
addiction, male, 230
Adorno, T., 44–5, 139, 140, 142, 143
advertising, 61–2, 100, 110, 262, 287
  gender and, 10, 252–3
aestheticization of everyday life, 154, 155, 287, 315
aesthetics, 41–8
age, 206, 222, 347
agency, 81, 179–84, 190–1, 192, 238, 239, 342, 374, 381
agenda setting, 263
Aglietta, M., 103
AIDS, 254–5
Alcoff, L., 234–5
alcoholism, 228
alienation, 13–14
Allen, R., 41, 266
Althusser, L., 51–2, 56–8, 63, 171
Amos 'n' Andy, 212
Anderson, B., 198–9
Ang, I., 4, 114, 118, 236, 257, 266, 267, 272–3, 364
anthropology, 37–8
anti-essentialism, 11, 20–1, 25, 77, 166, 173, 176–7, 186–90, 191, 192, 195, 227, 355, 381
anti-foundationalism, 374, 379
anti-racism, 360
anti-representationalism, 90–3, 374, 379
Appadurai, A., 114, 117, 283
Appiah, K., 191
archeology, of Foucault, 144–5, 146
Arnold, M., 36
art, 42, 154
  as aesthetic quality, 42
  modernism in, 137–40
  representation of women in, 251–2
articulation, 9–10, 82–3, 356–7, 369, 380, 381
  and the circuit of culture, 53–4, 110
  of identities, 177–8
Ashcroft, B., 118, 219–20
Asians, British, 203–7, 333
assimilation, racial, 214, 360
AT&T, 281
attitudes, 166
audiences, 32–3
  active, 11, 45, 154, 256–7, 268–73, 283, 289, 340–2, 381
  and cultural identity, 273–8
Austen, J., 252

authenticity, 381
  of identities, 256
  and youth cultures, 335, 337–8, 339
autonomy, of the state, 122–3

Bacon, F., 131
Bakhtin, M., 72
Ballard, R., 203, 204
Barker, C., 202, 206, 273, 274
Barthes, R., 18, 68–71, 72
Baudelaire, C., 135
Baudrillard, J., 108, 110, 131, 157–8
Bauman, Z., 131, 149, 378
beauty, 41, 42
Bell, D., 104, 105
Benetton, 102–3
Bennett, T., 7, 34, 61, 342–3, 346, 353, 354, 366–70, 380
Benson, S., 254, 255
Berman, M., 134, 222
Best, S., 143–4
Bhabha, H., 133, 200, 203, 221
biochemistry, 231–2
biological determinism, 231–2, 235
biological reductionism, 231
biology, as discourse, 186–7
Birmingham, England, 303
black feminism, 25, 226, 227
black identity, 176, 201–2, 207, 360
black people, 194, 207, 208–23, 262–3, 332–3, 354, 359–60
  criminalization of, 210, 262–3, 354
  positive images of, 217–19, 360
  stereotyping of, 208–10, 212
body
  discursive construction of the, 237–8, 244
  the slender, 253
Bogle, D., 209
Bourdieu, P., 44, 339
Brah, A., 196, 200–1, 204
Brake, M., 323
Brecht, B., 139, 140
bricolage, 154, 155, 284, 289, 315, 325, 337–8, 348, 381–2
British Asians, 203–7
bureaucracy, 132, 136
Burgess, E., 297
Butler, J., 94, 186, 244–6, 247, 248

Cable News Network (CNN), 260, 263, 264
cable and satellite technology, 280–1, 311
Campbell, C., 213, 214
Cantor, M., 43